# The Suffragette Derby

# THE
# SUFFRAGETTE
# DERBY

## MICHAEL TANNER

The Robson Press

First published in Great Britain in 2013 by
The Robson Press (an imprint of Biteback Publishing Ltd)
Westminster Tower
3 Albert Embankment
London SE1 7SP
Copyright © Michael Tanner 2013

ISBN 978-1-84954-518-1

10 9 8 7 6 5 4 3 2 1

A CIP catalogue record for this book is available from the British Library.

Set in Caslon and Bodoni

# Contents

# Prologue

The skies above London on the morning of Wednesday 4 June 1913 hang heavy with cloud, suggesting the forecast of bright sunshine and temperatures in the high 60s to have been misleading. The sun will eventually prevail, however, good news indeed for a quartet of men who are keener than most to inspect the heavens for signs of rain. Their business is horse racing and they desire perfect conditions for a horse race – the most famous horse race in the world. Perfect conditions to run the Blue Riband of the Turf: the Derby.

To the woman walking down Kingsway, on the other hand, the weather is of no consequence. It may rain or shine as far as she is concerned. The weather won't make a scrap of difference to her plans for this afternoon. She has made an early start from her lodgings at 133 Clapham Road in order to call in at the headquarters of the Women's Social and Political Union and purchase two flags en route to Victoria station where she intends boarding a race-day 'special' to Epsom Downs. This race-goer has no interest in who might win the Derby. She's setting out for Epsom to strike a blow for her cause, the suffragette cause dedicated to obtaining 'Votes for Women'. She means to leave Epsom having written her name into the history books. But she has to be back in Kensington by early evening. She's due to help out at the Suffragette Summer Festival in the Empress Rooms. Her name is Emily Wilding Davison.

Tall and slender, with unusually long arms that lend her an

awkwardness, she's wearing a dark blue skirt and matching blouse with a short black jacket edged with silk braid. A light grey felt hat is jammed down on her head, obscuring the mop of thick reddish-brown hair swept up into a fashionable chignon, yet it can't hide the fact that she's no longer in the first flush of youth. Handsome rather than pretty would best describe her looks, even as a teenager. Her face is small and rather square, featuring a strong brow and an equally strong nose separating green eyes described variously as elusive and whimsical. Her mouth is straight, wide and thin, rather severe in repose but frequently caught in a half-smile that one acquaintance compares to the mocking expression of the *Mona Lisa*. She appears a bit of a battleaxe. Those of a more charitable disposition might settle for frumpy, old-before-her-time, gone to seed, an impression reinforced by a braying 'haw-haw' accent even her friends find grating. Those friends are women. She doesn't court male company. She prefers the companionship of her own sex. She equates men with the Establishment, the boot with its heel on the neck of womankind. She sees her sex denied entry to almost every profession; the inclusion of 'obey' in the marriage vows means precisely that – wives surrender personal wealth to husbands whose conjugal rights also run to sex and child-bearing on demand. Under exclusively man-made laws women have been reduced to the condition of legal slavery. But she sees herself as one of the 'New Women', a class of well-educated women intent on gaining their personal liberty.

Now she sits in a third-class carriage of a race-day special run by the London, Brighton and South Coast Railway, the hubbub swirling around her head which, as ever, tilts to one side as if locked in jaunty contemplation of life's absurdities. Little wonder she looks worn out. The forty-year-old boasts a charge sheet few hardened criminals can match, because there's no one more committed to the campaign for women's suffrage than she. She's served seven terms of imprisonment in the past four years, a grand total of eight months' incarceration during which she embarked on seven hunger strikes and endured no fewer than forty-nine instances of forcible feeding. Her militancy has graduated from stone-throwing to firing pillar boxes, an escalating fanaticism that worries the suffragette leadership. It has labelled her 'a self-dramatising individualist, insufficiently capable of acting in the confines of official instructions, clever but headstrong … she tends to walk alone'.

Thus Davison is more than a rebel with a cause. She is a rebel within her cause; the worst kind of rebel – a loose cannon. As a child she didn't play 'dolls': she played 'soldiers'. Now she sees herself as a 'soldier' of God fighting for women's rights, a Bible never far from her hand. She's fearless, but also wilful and impulsive, traits that frequently breed misjudgements under pressure and occasion an intimacy with self-destruction; she is a maverick marginalised by her movement as surely as her sexuality edges her toward the fringes of mainstream society. Such slights only serve to make her opposition to the established order all the more zealous and its expression all the more reckless. Indeed, many racehorse owners are becoming alarmed at the prospect of suffragettes like Davison targeting their valuable livestock following numerous arson attacks on deserted racecourse buildings. *The Sporting Life* spoke up for them, demanding 'Suffragette liability in the event of any measure of the mad women proving successful. There have been so many rash acts attempted and carried out that the threats cannot be lightly dismissed.'

Davison's turmoil mirrored that of the country. Britain was far from a nation at ease with itself. The suffragette's leader, Mrs Emmeline Pankhurst, has incited her membership to 'rebellion!' yet their growing violence can't compare with the explosive forces unleashed by the march of trade unionism, stoked by the yawning gap between the affluent minority and the working-class majority. Recent disputes in the coalfields and the docks have sparked mass demonstrations and rioting. The government's deployment of troops to maintain order resulted in the shooting of three strikers in South Wales. Two warships were even sent up the Mersey. By 1913 industrial disputes are running at 150 a month and Britain's 'Great Unrest' enables Leon Trotsky to crow 'the dim spectre of revolution [is] hanging over Britain'. Across the Irish Sea more rebellion festers, as Irish Nationalism and religious strife drive the country to the brink of civil war: 'I see terrible times ahead, bitter fighting and rivers of blood,' confides one Irish leader. Farther afield the Balkans are already a-fire with just the kind of bloody conflict that many Britons dread will engulf the entire European continent. If this constant round of grim headlines in its daily newspapers isn't sufficiently depressing, the nation is obliged to come to terms with the loss of the *Titanic* and one of its most heroic sons, Scott of the Antarctic. The various struggles of this tempestuous period are coming to a head; the protagonists know there can be no victory without a blood 'sacrifice'. The Irish rebels know it; the suffragettes know it. But on this quintessential English morning all that may be forgotten. For today is Derby Day.

Davison is joining a cross section of Britons that has flocked to Epsom Downs in celebration of this unique occasion every year since 1780. This is the one day Belgravia rubs shoulders with Bermondsey. In a vast crowd consisting of, according to Disraeli, 'all the ruffiansim that London and every racecourse in the kingdom can produce', she finds viscounts mingling with villains; gypsies haggling with generals; housewives and housebreakers enjoying a well-earned day off. They have been massing since six in the morning for, albeit not the national jamboree of the Victorian era when even parliamentary business is suspended, Derby Day is still the nearest the country comes to the traditional embodiment of 'Merrie Englande'. Epsom Downs is transformed into the Edwardian equivalent of old St Bartholomew's Fair, brimming with entertainment and original sin. So many revellers will cram this makeshift arena by three o'clock, possibly as many as a quarter of a million, that the only visible blades of grass will be those comprising the one-and-a-half-mile horseshoe that is the Derby course itself.

Browned by a week of pleasant summer sunshine, this strip of turf awaits the arrival of the fifteen thoroughbreds who constitute the cream of the current three-year-old equine generation.

It is Craganour who occupies the minds of the four men scanning the London skies. The colt is the best of his generation and the worthy favourite for the 134th renewal of the Derby Stakes.

Although separated by seven years, two of the men appear cast from the same bronze, in both appearance (soft-faced; bristling waxed moustache; centre-parted macassar-oiled dark hair) and wealthy background. They might even pass for brothers. But though the mould is similar the metal is not.

The first of them surveying the skies from his town house in Mount Street is a 46-year-old, rather stiff, unemotional and painfully shy Old Etonian, a corner-stone of the Turf, elected to the Jockey Club in 1906 and appointed Steward six years later. He is an abstemious member of a family that accepted a baronetcy in 1887 and represents 'old money'; a former cavalry officer who never saw action; a man who has owned one Derby winner, Spearmint, and bred Craganour – but sold him before he set foot on a racecourse. As a sportsman he's honoured and respected; as a man he's known to very few, being as confirmed a bachelor as Emily Davison is a spinster, the temptations of the flesh seemingly either distasteful or a total mystery. He's a man at one with the concept of hierarchy and his place in it; one who values protocol, puts logic before feelings when he speaks and expects people to listen to his words – and then act upon them. Those few hold it a privilege to regard him, and to be regarded by him, as a friend. He is unquestionably a member of the smart set. His name is listed in *Who's Who:* it is Eustace Loder.

The younger man assessing the weather from his residence on the other side of Berkeley Square in Bruton Street is a handsome Old Harrovian of thirty-nine years for whom the term 'gentleman of leisure' might have been coined; a man who harbours no ambitions to impose his will on the Turf. He embodies Oscar Wilde's axiom that pleasure is 'the only thing one should live for', he is a man-of-the-Shires with an eye for the ladies who comes from a line that rejected the offer of a baronetcy in 1897 and instead represents 'new money' – the ship-owning family tarred by its intimate association with the *Titanic* disaster. He's a volunteer trooper who braved gunfire in the Boer War; a big-game hunter; and a progressively heavy investor in the bloodstock market. He now owns Craganour and hopes to lead in a Derby winner. The fast set rather than the smart set would be more his milieu. His name does not merit a listing in *Who's Who*. It is Charles Bower Ismay.

He and Eustace Loder ought to have enjoyed each other's company. After all, they had much in common beside their appearance and love of all things equestrian. Both entered the world with silver spoons clamped in their mouths. Both came from close-knit and rather puritanical families. Both enjoyed the intimate relationship provided by a twin. And as younger sons both were free of responsibilities, never obliged to do a proper day's work in their lives.

Yet, close study of their portraits drawn for the society magazines of the day betrays telling differences. In *Mayfair*, Ismay is portrayed legs splayed, wearing a bow tie, casual brown suit with jacket unbuttoned and fashionable spats, staring at the artist while holding a lit cigarette between the fingers of one hand and thrusting the other hand inside a trouser pocket. In *Vanity Fair*, Loder is bowler-hatted, stiff-collared, feet rooted at nine-o-clock and grey suit tightly buttoned, his right arm angled and gloved fist arrowed into the hip in proud acknowledgement to the cavalryman, left hand leaning on his walking stick of authority. He's pictured as a man used to telling rather than being told, the binoculars slung round his waist a covert warning to all that he has his eyes on them. Had any artist dared to depict Loder with hand in pocket he'd likely have been sued for defamation of character.

London neighbours they may have been but Loder and Ismay did not clink glasses. On the Turf they were polar opposites. As a member and, more importantly, a Steward of the Jockey Club, Loder represented those forces of the Establishment intent on continuity: the significance of his acceptance into this elite underlined by his being one of the few Jockey Club members without a title. Ismay amounted to a mere Johnny-come-lately, content to wave his cheque-book around, buying bloodstock instead of breeding his own like a true gentleman. Ismay was clearly intent on taking more from the sport than he was prepared to give back, even to the extent of playing fast and loose with the very Rules of Racing that Loder, as a Steward, was honour-bound to enforce. Earlier in the year one of Ismay's trainers had his licence withdrawn after two Ismay horses demonstrated abnormal improvement to secure surprise victories. Ismay was guilty by association. Then Loder was forced to stand by as Ismay sacked his own jockey protégé, Billy Saxby, in the wake of the 2000 Guineas, the first of the season's five Classics. Craganour ought to have won that race. Saxby had ridden him as if he had; many observers believed he had. The judge didn't. He awarded the race to Louvois. Friends assured Ismay the Stewards were bound to hold an enquiry into the decision with a view to revers-ing the result. But they didn't. Those Stewards included Eustace Loder. Although Bower Ismay swallowed his disappointment, he sacked his jockey.

Loder's distaste for Ismay cuts far deeper than suspicions of foul play on the Turf. It's acutely personal. Quite possibly, in another era they'd have settled their differences with pistols at dawn. Ismay has been brazenly conducting an affair with Loder's sister-in-law, an affront to his own moral code and a slight on his family honour. If that alone were insufficient to label Ismay a bounder, there's his connection with the *Titanic* disaster. Loder lost friends when the Ismay family's White Star Line vessel sank the previous April with the loss of 1,500 lives – though not that of Bower Ismay's brother Bruce, the president of the company, who managed to secure one of the precious seats in a lifeboat, an act of self-preservation that did not rest well with the public.

The circles frequented by Loder still expected a 'gentleman' to do the 'right thing'. Once again, Bower Ismay was smeared by association.

Edwardian society was a powerful body, built on great families bound together by generations of inter-marriage and a code of conduct. It was inclined to repel boarders with black balls or white feathers. In Loder's estimation, Bower Ismay was a philanderer and thoroughly 'bad egg' who needed taking down a peg or two. And he had the connections – and the power – to do so.

Loder motored to Epsom with a trying day in prospect. It would be naïve to believe anything else. Almost instant success as a breeder and owner of racehorses earned him the soubriquet of 'Lucky' Loder but he isn't feeling so lucky any more. First of all, his horses haven't been running so well this year. Secondly, he's brooding over recent accusations from another stud owner that threaten to destroy his good name as a breeder. Nor is he feeling himself: the disease that will kill him within fourteen months is beginning to take hold. Yet these issues must be set aside, for he is the Senior Steward on duty this coming afternoon, the man charged with the responsibility of ensuring the Rules of Racing are followed, without 'fear or favour'. However, one nagging voice he can't silence is that telling him he will have to be elsewhere if Craganour is led in as winner of the Derby. The successful breeder doesn't relish having to look the successful owner in the face.

The remaining two men eager to assess the accuracy of the weather forecast will act as the instruments of these two adversaries on the track. They are jockeys. The shorter of the two boasts a baby-face belying his twenty-eight years. He's an American who came to Europe in 1899 at the age of fourteen, feted as 'a child wonder on the pigskin,' only to be hounded out of English racing three years later for 'pulling' horses at the behest of high-rolling American gamblers labelled a cancer to the English Turf by Establishment figures like Eustace Loder. No longer the impressionable youngster, it is he, Johnny Reiff, his talents matured to perfection by a dozen seasons riding in France and Germany, who has the responsibility of riding Craganour this afternoon. The pressure will not ruffle him. It's just another horse race to Reiff. He's just grateful to be alive to ride in one – as the metal plate in his head testifies. And he has already won two Derbies. Today he's been gifted the opportunity to make it three because he has, as *The Sportsman* puts it, 'dropped in for another fortunate mount'.

Craganour is his only mount of the day. Highly selected raids have been Johnny Reiff's calling card since slinking away from the English scene. With luck, it would amount to another smash-and-grab to match that of the 2000 Guineas when he and Louvois had benefitted from the judge's error. Like his fellow Americans, Reiff doesn't suffer from any shortage of confidence. He knows he will need to call on all that confidence in today's Derby. He's riding the favourite but fourteen other jockeys are desperate to beat him, some of them pathologically so. The reason is simple: envy. The mount on Craganour will be only his second ride in England this year, following Louvois in the Guineas. It is all about figures. The Guineas was worth £6,800 to the winner; the Derby £6,450. Two rides; two wins; two fat presents. While the home jockeys dragged themselves round the provincial gaff tracks scratching around for any kind of ride in the big-money races, Reiff sat at home in Maisons Laffitte waiting for the telegram like a hired gun, the mercenary brought into town to fulfil the contract and then depart, handsomely paid. Yet Reiff was merely responding to market forces.

'The dearth of English riders is a serious matter,' commented *The Times*.

There was never a period when the average skill was so low. It is beyond question that innumerable races have been lost during the last season in consequence of defective riding. No one has been able to suggest any reason why native jockeys have thus lost their art. Of the last twelve Derbies, only three have been won by riders of British birth.

Americans had claimed seven, for the sons of Uncle Sam plying their trade in Europe had 'growd like Topsy'. English owners could call on a dozen or more crack American riders in addition to the likes of Danny Maher and 'Skeets' Martin who were based in England. And then there were French-based Englishmen like George Bellhouse and the perennial French champion jockey George Stern.

Thus, Reiff's presence on the favourite's back aroused much resentment among the home jockeys who were fed-up with losing lucrative rides in the major races to the Yanks who'd lorded it over them for the best part of twenty years. 'Rivalry between the English riders and the Yanks borrowed from France is becoming a serious problem,' noted the racing correspondent of the *Daily Express*. There was no telling how this bad feeling might manifest itself during the customary hurly-burly of the Derby.

The second jockey is the disaffected English rider who partnered Craganour in the 1913 Guineas and thinks he should be aboard him today. Billy Saxby was a journeyman jockey until Ismay began patronising him and Craganour brought gigantic pay-days in the summer of 1912. He's smarting at what he sees as an injustice, an unfair dismissal that has inevitably dissuaded other owners and trainers from putting him up on their horses. His confidence knocked, he started making rash decisions, incurring the wrath of the Stewards. He began feeling sorry for himself and piled on weight, every pound spelling fewer opportunities; inactivity spawned additional weight. Saxby was trapped in a spiral of decline that only a big win could arrest. It hurts that he won't be on Craganour this afternoon. Victory in the Derby brought more than money: it bestowed immortality. He's determined to win the race with his new mount, Louvois, or, at the very least, do everything in his power to stop Reiff stealing the prize that ought to have been his. Loder might sympathise: he views this son of a Sergeant-Major in his former regiment like his own and considers himself his Turf guardian. He feels convinced Ismay's initial patronage and ultimate treatment of Saxby was nothing less than another calculated dig at him.

☞

King George V and Queen Mary will be witnesses to this most sensational of Derbies. In marked contrast to his father King Edward VII, who'd revelled in the raffish atmosphere of the Turf and won the Derby three times, the new King's sport of choice is sailing; and rather than collect mistresses in the manner of 'Edward the Caresser', the 'Sailor King' accumulates stamps. In deference to this legacy, twelve months ago he'd fielded a runner in the Derby to finish fourth, but the chances of Pintadeau's full brother achieving likewise in today's renewal are slim. Anmer sports fine looks but lacks matching ability. In the dismissive words of *The Sportsman*, he was one of those participants 'far better in their stables than possibly interfering with some of the others'. One could excuse his jockey, Herbert Jones, for concurring: like every other occupant of the weighing room he has heard the rumours suggesting some suffragette outrage could be in the offing and that, as the King's jockey, he might be singled out. He might even be shot at.

The race their Majesties will watch takes just two minutes 37.6 seconds to run. Yet in this short space of time the intervention of Emily Davison at Tattenham Corner results in the fall of Anmer; the later charge for the winning post involving half-a-dozen horses is described by one of the combatant jockeys as 'a bull fight'. Both events are recorded for posterity by the new-fangled contraption that is the newsreel camera. However, what the cameras couldn't record was a third set of events, of equal sensation, that transpired in the Epsom Stewards' Room during the thirty minutes immediately after the 6/4 favourite Craganour passes the post a head in front of the 100/1 shot Aboyeur. The outcome of this clandestine Stewards enquiry is the single instance of a Derby winner being disqualified on the grounds of foul riding. This enquiry is launched by Eustace Loder; he acts not only as prosecutor but also judge and jury, and he calls upon Saxby as a key witness.

This entire sequence of events – two public and one private – was shot through with acrimony of the sourest kind. It's hard not to conclude that a cocktail of toxic ingredients was stirred that June afternoon. Davison's estrangement from the suffragette leadership made her a loose cannon capable of any outrage. The rough-house denouement of the race was an inevitable consequence of the ill-feeling simmering between the home jockeys and the foreigners. Rancour corroded the judgement of Eustace Loder, a man in the clutches of a terminal disease.

The key to unlocking the mystery at the heart of the 'Suffragette Derby' lies embedded in the psyche of Loder and Davison, two middle-aged egocentrics: the one a pillar of the Establishment whose very stability the other was actively undermining. Trapped in an emotional insularity of their own manufacture, the pair embraced their personality flaws like a suit of armour until, unable to take it off, they were dragged down by the weight of it. Both were assertive individuals, prepared, if necessary, to be the centre of attention. What divided them was the wherewithal. Loder could exploit a position of power and make capital out of the 'Rules', whereas Davison had no option but to make up her own 'Rules' as she went along.

Nothing became Davison more than the apparently heroic exploit that led to her death. It caused her to be sanctified by colleagues eager to validate their crusade with a 'blood sacrifice'; and mythologised by feminist writers whenever an example of peerless and principled womanhood was called from central casting. However, Davison's 'outrage' has been grossly misrepresented. It involved nothing gloriously sacrificial. It resulted from a chain of miscalculations and irrational impulses, the like of which punctuated her entire suffragette career. What else apart from self-delusion could account for an intelligent woman thinking she could walk among galloping racehorses weighing half a ton apiece, emerge unscathed and depart scot-free to fulfil her social obligations that evening? Davison was blessed with great intellect and courage but scant common sense and self-control. Therein lies the truth of the outrage that sullied the 1913 Derby.

If Davison's Achilles heel was self-delusion, Loder's seems to have been the inflexibility born of a life governed by manuals and rule books. Such codes come only in black-and-white. There's no palette with the colours of compromise, no scope for turning a blind eye, little room for extenuating circumstances or hope of forgiveness. Living his life in a moral strait-jacket rendered Loder's Derby objection automatic, albeit not necessarily well-intentioned.

The suspicion lingers, however, that Loder's cardinal sin lay unexposed. The truth of his 'objection' to Craganour's – and Ismay's – victory hinges on a question he was never obliged to answer: would he have shown the same eagerness to orchestrate an enquiry hell-bent on disqualification had the roles of Anmer and Craganour been reversed and the owner at risk of forfeiting the Derby been his King instead of Bower Ismay?

The notion Loder might risk raining on his sovereign's parade is laughable. Spoiling Bower Ismay's party, on the other hand, was evidently pardonable – which demands the distinction be subjected to forensic analysis. And therein lies buried the truth of the objection and disqualification that marred the 1913 Derby.

For so long as this Derby is recounted and reviewed, the names of Davison and Anmer, Loder and Ismay, Reiff and Saxby, Craganour and Aboyeur will be linked inextricably and their roles debated. What is beyond dispute is that the one day of the year when Epsom basked in the national consciousness ended with it under intense scrutiny for all the wrong reasons – a view not lost on the town's own newspaper, the *Epsom Advertiser*:

The Epsom Derby of 1913 will long be remembered by everybody – whether of sporting instinct or otherwise – as one of the most sensational on record. The event is looked upon by a large number of visitors as a day's outing, and many of the parties picnicking on the Hill or other places cared little about the actual racing.

They were out for a day's enjoyment, and it mattered little to them whether the favourite or the biggest outsider carried off the Blue Riband of the Turf.

Disaster followed upon disaster, and people went away from the Downs hardly knowing whether they stood on their head or their heels. On top of the favourite being disqualified after just snatching the race by a narrow margin came the mad act on the part of a suffragette which might have resulted in the loss of more than one life.

The paper was correct: the events of that Derby have never been forgotten; disaster did follow upon disaster. Some may assert Emily Davison's Derby outrage to have been nothing more than a sideshow to the unique Derby objection that followed. Yet the 134th running of the Derby isn't written into history as the 'Suffragette Derby' without reason. Her actions heaped ignominy on a day of national celebration; she was the first to disrupt a sporting occasion in the name of political activism and be filmed so doing. Without Davison, this renewal of the Derby would be forgotten by all bar Turf scholars.

But, where has truth given way to myth?

# ONE

# The Favourite

The heartbeat of a Derby comes from the horses. Not just any horses. The cream of one thoroughbred generation racing at three years old. Colts and fillies only. No geldings: only animals whose blood could further the breed were allowed to run. In any one generation that meant some 1,500 animals might start their lives theoretically holding Derby aspirations. That number was quickly whittled down as owners were obliged to make costly entries, in this instance by 18 July 1911, before their horses had appeared on the racecourse let alone displayed any ability commensurate with a Derby contender. From a total of 344 horses entered for the 1913 renewal just fifteen would go to post.

There had been racing on Epsom Downs of some sort since the reign of James I. The area's additional attributes of spring waters, proximity to London and opportunities for hawking, hunting, boxing and cockfighting combined to make Epsom a fashionable spa to the wealthy. Samuel Pepys refers to racing here in May 1663 though at this date there was no thought given to any form of race approximating to the Derby. By the middle of the eighteenth century English racing began to shift emphasis away from mature older horses (five-year-olds and up) and races over extreme distances (two miles or more, run off in heats) toward shorter distances and younger racehorses. It was this school of thought that had initiated the Oaks, a sweepstakes (the entry fee of all the entrants going to the winner) for three-year-old fillies over one-and-a-half miles, in 1779. Its success spawned the

Derby the following year for three-year-old colts (though fillies might still compete) to be contested over a mile. The distance of the race was only increased to one mile four furlongs in 1783 (plus 29 yards up to 1921) and the route of 1913 was not followed until 1872. The Derby had now outstripped its northern rival, the St Leger, founded in 1776 to become the primary target of every three-year-old colt. The final pair of races ultimately referred to as 'Classics' were the 2000 and 1000 Guineas (fillies only), run at Newmarket over a mile, and instituted in 1809 and 1814 respectively, but they weren't regarded on a par with the other trio until the 1850s. Alongside the term 'Classic' soon appeared the term 'Triple Crown' denoting victory in the three colts' events, or a fillies' equivalent involving Guineas, Oaks and St Leger.

The status of the Derby exceeded crude financial measurement. The 1913 renewal wasn't the most valuable race in the country – or even the most valuable Classic of the year. Its prize of £6,450 lagged a little behind the £6,800 of the 2000 Guineas (the 1000 Guineas was worth £6,400; the Oaks £4,950 and the St Leger £6,450), and all five Classics were overshadowed by the Jockey Club Stakes at £7,440 and the Eclipse at £8,735. But in terms of prestige the Derby looked down on every Classic and every race both domestic and foreign. In 1913 it was quite simply the most important horse race in the world: the very furtherance of the breed depended upon it. The Italian breeder Federico Tesio put its significance most eloquently:

> The thoroughbred exists because its selection has depended, not on experts, technicians, or zoologists, but on a piece of wood: the winning post of the Epsom Derby. If you base your criteria on anything else, you will get something else, not the thoroughbred.

Horses who had passed that 'piece of wood' victorious became barometers of excellence in the history of the thoroughbred: the likes of Voltigeur and Gladiateur; Ormonde and Persimmon;

and latterly Ard Patrick and Sunstar. In 1913 Craganour was a worthy favourite to join this list.

Craganour had proved himself to be head and shoulders above the rest of his generation. He had, at one time or another, met and beaten six of his opponents. Reproduction of his superiority over the Derby distance equated to a bare minimum of a three-length advantage over his nearest challenger. His Foxhill stable in Wiltshire became a fortress and his trainer, Jack Robinson, received letters, purporting to be from the Women's Social and Political Union (WSPU), threatening to burn it down and harm the Derby favourite. The horse, meanwhile, continued to do everything asked of him on the gallops. On the eve of the Derby, Robinson assured reporters that Craganour could 'scarcely fail except by some stroke of bad luck impossible to foresee'. But he also confided to a friend: 'This is always an unlucky race for me.'

William Thomas Robinson was invariably called 'Jack'. So he ought to be: 'Jack' suited him. There's a snap and a crackle about it – as there was about Robinson, who had a reputation for blowing hot and cold. Alert, and occasionally too quick-tempered for his own welfare, he gave the impression that any man who wished to get the better of him would have to be up very early of a morning; and then, likely as not, still fail. The slender frame of his days as a jockey had given way to that of a sturdy red-cheeked bantam with an air of shiny-shoed prosperity and a beady disinclination to allow any of his charges, equine or human, to entertain any thought of slothfulness. He loved the country squire lifestyle his hard work had brought him and entertained his owners and many stable visitors right royally. They included actress Lillie Langtry and the renowned Italian tenor Enrico Caruso – who was once found after a champagne luncheon leaning against a wall, singing at the top of his voice. Robinson liked nothing better than a practical joke and to this end would have a goat led round his dining room if he sensed any of his guests were bored or being boring.

Robinson had been a successful jockey, though never in

contention for the championship owing to a tendency to put on flesh, but before training beckoned he can be said to have left his mark. Within three years of riding his first winner in 1884 he secured the St Leger on Kilwarlin and the Cesarewitch on Humewood, both of which advertised his mettle. The bad-tempered Kilwarlin repeatedly did his utmost to throw Robinson out of the saddle on the way to the start and when the flag fell stood rooted to the spot until the rest of the field had galloped a hundred yards. Robinson still managed to bridge the gap and just pip the Derby winner Merry Hampton. To ride Humewood, the young jockey needed to pare himself down to 7st 6lb. On the morning before the race Robinson was ordered by connections to walk from Newmarket to Cambridge and then back again, a round trip of twenty-six miles or more; the walk was to be broken with a breakfast of a pork chop and a pint of champagne. While Robinson watched, doubtless drooling from hunger and thirst, the chop was trimmed and half the champagne drunk by his escort. His ordeal was rewarded, for Humewood landed hefty bets.

The following season of 1888 was Robinson's most successful, his seventy-five winners including Seabreeze in the Oaks and St Leger. This high point coincided with the end of his apprentice-ship and also the start of his losing battle with the scales: his last four seasonal totals combined failed to reach his 1888 figure.

Thus Robinson retired in 1892 at the age of twenty-four with ample time to forge a reputation for himself as a trainer. He soon established himself at Foxhill, 600 feet up on the Wiltshire Downs close to Swindon, overlooking Wanborough Plain where he laid out eleven gallops and a tan track half a mile in circumfer-ence. Robinson planted 500,000 trees and miles of hedgerow to create a location made for keeping secrets. Only tinkling sheep bells and cawing rooks disturbed the silence.

Robinson set about engineering many a coup. He targeted the opening weeks of the season when he showed a wonderful knack of having his string fit to run for their lives: even his yearlings were tried before Christmas and then trained as hard as their seniors as Lincoln and Liverpool approached in the spring. It's no accident that he landed the fiercely competitive Lincolnshire Handicap during the first week of the season on no fewer than four occasions. The success of 1898 came courtesy of Winkfield's Pride. Deemed a doubtful participant the weekend prior to the race, odds of 100/1 were freely available; within forty-eight hours the price suddenly plummeted to 5/1 and, aided by Robinson's brother Nat, Winkfield's Pride won in a canter. The stampede of Foxhill's heavy bettors to get 'on' the horse at the eleventh hour was so frantic that no one thought to advise the horse's owner. He had to be privately accommodated before he allowed his horse to run.

Handicap successes followed thick and fast. No greater daylight robbery was committed by Foxhill than for the Chester Cup of 1904 when Robinson was abetted by a new confederate in Robert Sievier, punter and rascal extraordinaire. They had three runners engaged in the race, two of whom had good recent form in the book but it was the third, Sandboy, beaten in sellers and carrying just 6st 2lb, who was backed in to 9/2 second favourite and prevailed by three lengths.

It was inevitable that two schemers like Robinson and Sievier would fall out when gambles went astray. 'Robinson's chief failing is a lack of frankness,' wrote Sievier in *The Winning Post* after their split,

> even towards those with whom he is in closest contact. If he has, or thinks he has, a grievance, he is apt to nurse it, instead of openly stating it and clearing the air. Thus his success has been clouded and chequered with quarrels and misunderstandings, and he has missed the respect and popularity which have been freely accorded to less gifted men.

It's safe to say this indictment of Robinson hinted at one Iago not being alerted to the schemes of the other.

Thus it can be said with absolute certainty: Jack Robinson knew the time of day and he was not above recognising a juvenile with class and Classic potential. He won the Gimcrack Stakes four times in five years for Colonel William Hall Walker, for example, and by the spring of 1913 he had won four Classics, three of them in 1905 courtesy of Vedas in the 2000 Guineas and Cherry Lass in the 1000 Guineas and Oaks – which contributed to Robinson finishing the season as leading trainer with fifty-two races and stakes won of £34,466. Two years later Witch Elm added another Oaks.

Robinson may have had his differences with a hands-on gambling owner such as Bob Sievier but he would experience no such problems with a non-punter like Bower Ismay. Only the positive qualities conceded by Sievier would be of any interest to Ismay. 'As a trainer we have always maintained, in spite of our grievances, he is second to none,' wrote Sievier.

> There is no finer judge of a horse's condition; there is no one more successful in getting a horse to the top-notch of condition, and at the same time keeping him in fine heart. He is one of the hardest-working men in his profession and whether the animal is a Classic candidate or the commonest selling plater, Robinson can be trusted to leave no stone unturned to make it produce the utmost of which it is capable.

The partnership between the irascible trainer and the sanguine owner had started slowly, but at the Doncaster September Sales of 1910 Ismay began to dig deeper into his resources: 'Having embarked on a relatively successful career as an owner,' asserts his grandson Michael Manser, 'Bower would not have been Bower had he not wanted to be more successful.' Ismay wrote out a cheque for 1,900 guineas to secure the top lot of the fifteen-strong consignment of yearlings sent up from the Sledmere Stud of Sir Tatton Sykes. This brown colt by Desmond out of Altesse was given the name Hall Cross. Thanks largely to

Hall Cross, who won the British Dominion Plate and the Great Lancashire Breeders Produce Stakes, Ismay won more money on the Flat during the 1911 season than he had during the rest of his Flat-race career to date.

Suitably enthused by the success of Hall Cross, Ismay and Robinson returned to the Doncaster Sales in September 1911 and examined the Sledmere consignment with much anticipation. The progeny of Desmond naturally drew their attention, none more so than a washy bay colt with splashes of brown about him out of a mare called Veneration II. He sported a distinctive white blob on his forehead; more significantly, the colt held a nomination for the Derby. Moreover, although raised at Sledmere he'd been bred elsewhere and purchased privately along with his dam. His actual breeder was Eustace Loder.

The colt destined to race under the name Craganour was foaled at Loder's Eyrefield Lodge on the last day of February 1910 when Veneration II was ten. She had a poor record as a racehorse, her sole success coming as a juvenile at Sandown Park and her performances as a three-year-old did not merit keeping her in training for a further year. Veneration II's potential lay in the paddocks, for she was by Laveno out of Admiration and, thus, a half-sister to no less than Loder's great racemare Pretty Polly. Much to Loder's disappointment, Veneration II failed to redeem herself at stud. None of her first four foals won a race of any description. Furthermore, she didn't share the kudos of being a daughter of champion sire Gallinule, like Pretty Polly: she was an obvious candidate to be culled.

It so happened that in 1910 some new mares were required by Sir Tatton Sykes's Sledmere Stud, from whom Loder had acquired his future Derby winner Spearmint at the knock-down price of 300 guineas in 1904. The 5th Baronet was a more reclusive figure than his father (also named Tatton who was revered as the most popular living Yorkshireman toward the end of his ninety-three-year life) and not a little eccentric. His first act as custodian of his inheritance was to plough up its gardens and lawns. He thought flowers an unnecessary adornment and decapitated with his walking stick any examples he discovered around the estate, advising one tenant: 'If you wish to grow flowers, grow cauliflowers!' He distrusted front doors, always entering Sledmere via the back door, and took great joy in planting false front doors on his properties. Churches he loved restoring but gravestones he loathed and would not permit. His personal habits were no less whimsical. He believed it was important to maintain the body at a constant temperature and employed a collection of colour-coded overcoats fitting one over the other that he might discard whenever and wherever conditions dictated: the children on the estate were paid one shilling for picking them up and returning them to the house. Two pairs of trousers were utilised similarly; socks and shoes might also be removed and feet stuck out of a window if he felt too hot. Sir Tatton's stomach was equally sensitive, causing him to swear by a diet of milk pudding. This odd lifestyle did not endear itself to a wife some thirty years his junior who much preferred drinking, gambling and playing the stock exchange. After 'Lady Satin Tights', as she became known in London circles, squandered £500,000 of his money Sykes used the columns of *The Times* to announce he would no longer be responsible for her debts. In due course he was sued by a moneylender but stated in court he would rather dishonour his wife than honour her debts – and won the case.

Sykes had periodically refreshed Sledmere's band of broodmares since inheriting the East Riding stud in 1863, a strategy vindicated by the breeding of three other Classic winners besides Spearmint, including another Derby winner in Doncaster. Now aged eighty-four, he'd relinquished the day-to-day running of the stud to his nephew, Henry Cholmondeley, who enquired of Loder whether he might have the offer of some of his mares. Loder replied he might have the choice of the entire stud – bar Pretty Polly and two others. Cholmondeley selected Startling (a half-sister to a good horse in Star Shoot) and Veneration II.

He paid 1,800 guineas for Startling and 1,700 for Veneration. Both had foals at foot by Desmond and were in foal to him once more. In keeping with Sledmere's commercial policy, the two Desmond yearlings were sent to the Doncaster Sales of 1911 and went through the ring on Thursday 14 September. The Startling filly fetched 1,550 guineas; named Favilla, she never won a race. Robinson, bidding on Ismay's behalf, had to beat off a strong rival in Lord Lonsdale before the hammer fell at 3,200 guineas for Veneration's colt, making him the most expensive purchase of the week. Ismay's decision to pay that sum for what amounted to a reject from one of the most successful studs in the land was interpreted by some as a deliberate poke in the eye to Eyrefield's owner, Eustace Loder. Bower Ismay said nothing to disabuse them of that notion. He named his new acquisition Craganour after a mountain on his Scottish shoot at Dalnaspidal.

Yet it's inconceivable for Ismay to have spent all that money just for the sake of irritating Eustace Loder. The colt's sire may have appealed. Desmond was a black horse who was a decent two-year-old in 1898, winning the Coventry and July Stakes, but by the time he ran unplaced in the Derby he was already losing his zest for racing. However, as a son of champion sire St Simon and the Oaks winner L'Abbesse de Jouarre, he appeared to have a future as a stallion. His career at the Fort Union Stud of his owner Lord Dunraven in County Limerick had begun inauspiciously, with his initial crop selling for an average of only 48 guineas. Desmond's standing rose when he produced a son easily his superior in The White Knight, whose string of victories included the Coronation Cup-Ascot Gold Cup double two years in succession (1907–08), the Goodwood Cup and the Ascot Gold Vase.

Like his father St Simon, Desmond was apt to transmit a degree of 'hot' temperament to his progeny, and gave ample to Craganour. Steve Donoghue never rode Craganour, but in his autobiography he recalled seeing plenty of him at Foxhill while riding out for Robinson:

Often after he had been out at exercise on the Downs and had been sent a good half-speed gallop, he would be so wrought up with his mighty speed, that it was impossible on getting back to stables to let him go straight into his box; he might have jumped through the roof! So he used to be walked round to cool off in the little railed-off enclosure in the middle of the big stable-yard, and in about ten minutes he would be as quiet as an old sheep, and could be taken in, and Jack Robinson's little daughter, who was about ten-years-old, would go into the box and give him a handful of grass or lucerne.

Craganour wasn't to be one of Robinson's early juveniles. He didn't make his debut until June. The venue was significant. It was Royal Ascot, and the chosen event was the New Stakes over five furlongs: at £1,962 to the winner, the richest juvenile event of the season thus far. Clearly, connections thought a lot of him, and he was sent off 3/1 second favourite in a field of fifteen that included Shogun (the 7/4 favourite, unbeaten in three starts, including the Coventry Stakes on the opening day of the meeting) and two other winners. He proceeded to advertise his inexperience by playing up at the starting gate, but once the tapes rose he showed he'd been well schooled, racing away from his draw on the stands rail to make every yard of the running. The nearest Shogun got to him was the three lengths separating them at the line.

Craganour's subsequent campaign centred on the calendar's other great Turf festival meetings. He went from Royal Ascot to the Newmarket July Meeting for the Exeter Stakes over six furlongs a fortnight later. Only three took him on. Showing how much he had learned from his Ascot debut, he was much better behaved throughout the preliminaries and was never out of a canter, sauntering home by three lengths at odds of 9/2 on. Next stop was 'Glorious' Goodwood, for the six-furlong Molecomb Stakes on 4 August. Starting at 9/4 on he was beaten a head in a muddling race by an American-bred colt named Rock Flint ridden by the American Danny Maher. Ismay's 'journeyman' jockey Billy Saxby, it was said, had been outfoxed by a champion jockey. A top horse, the know-alls told Ismay, demanded a top jockey.

This surprising reverse, and the presence in the field of Shogun's allegedly superior stablemate Fairy King, caused Craganour to start at the more conservative odds of 6/4 for the Prince of Wales's Plate at the York Ebor Meeting. Fairy King was another son of Desmond and he had won his debut race at Goodwood. Craganour gave him 10lb and a three-length beating. Craganour got away slowly (he was held at the gate by one of Robinson's staff) and then found himself almost put through the rail when Fairy King veered into the path of two other runners. According to sound judges, Craganour still had plenty in reserve.

The premier event for two-year-olds at the Doncaster St Leger Meeting was – and remains – the Champagne Stakes. Shogun had won both his races since Ascot and was fancied to reverse New Stakes running at level weights. The market made him 5/4 against with Craganour at 15/8. The presence of a huge crowd again had the effect of upsetting Craganour but once into his stride he proved to the press that he 'must be judged the speediest two-year-old seen out at present', leaving Shogun three lengths adrift once more.

The two rivals were to clash a third time. The championship race for two-year-old colts was the six-furlong Middle Park Plate worth £3,275 to the winner at Newmarket on 18 October. Any colt with proven ability and Classic aspirations for 1913 had to line up. Four others took them on, including Rock Flint, who'd won his race at Doncaster since Goodwood. An unknown threat existed in the form of Louvois, a colt by the Triple Crown winner Isinglass out of a mare called St Louvaine, which made him a half-brother to Louviers whom many believed had won the 1909 Derby for Walter Raphael (a member of a Dutch family of Jewish financiers) rather than being pipped by King Edward VII's Minoru. Raphael's hope had run four times: he'd recorded a hat-trick of wins at Newmarket and been beaten just the once, finishing last of four to another of today's runners, Day Comet, at Goodwood. The remaining two contestants were J. B. Joel's Radiant, a full brother to Derby winner Sunstar, who'd earned his place in the Middle Park line-up by winning the Imperial Produce Plate at Kempton Park from Lord Rosebery's Sanquhar, and H. P. Whitney's American-bred Harmonicon, who had just completed a quartet of successes by winning the Mersey Stakes at Liverpool. The race was over as a contest after just a hundred yards. Craganour (11/8 favourite) drew clear and made every yard of the running to beat Shogun by the customary three lengths; Louvois was the same distance back in third.

Both Craganour and Shogun were then put away for the winter. The only horse to have beaten the latter in eight outings was Craganour; and on his final start of the season Louvois franked the worth of the Middle Park – and the generation's pecking order – by beating Sanquhar a head for the Dewhurst Plate, followed home by Rock Flint, Day Comet, Radiant and Harmonicon. Bower Ismay could entertain realistic hopes of a first Classic success. As could Billy Saxby who'd ridden him on each of his six starts. *The Times*, however, sounded a warning: 'Craganour is a colt of character, good tempered, but requiring firm treatment and disinclined to allow liberties to be taken.'

Craganour's five victories and one second had helped Bower Ismay break into the list of top ten leading owners with a total of £12,072 – almost double Eustace Loder's winnings. Ismay donated half his winnings to the fund raised on behalf of those who had suffered as a result of the *Titanic* disaster.

Craganour was a foregone conclusion to head the Free Handicap. He received 9st 4lb, a decisive 7lb more than Shogun. In the wake of the two leading lights were Rock Flint (8st 10lb); Louvois (8st 8lb); Lord Derby's quadruple winner Sanquhar (8st 5lb); Day Comet and Radiant (8st 3lb). Lord Rosebery's filly Prue (winner of two of her three races including the National Breeders Produce Stakes and second to Shogun in the Woodcote Stakes after starting sluggishly) received 8st 1lb; and Fairy King 8st.

Languishing on 7st 9lb, some 23lb below Craganour, was another son of Desmond by the name of Aboyeur. During the winter of 1912–13 no one gave him a second thought as a possible Derby contender.

# TWO

# Lucky Loder

Selling a colt who developed into the Derby favourite signalled a distinct change of luck for Eustace Loder because he had frequently ascribed his success as one of the most successful owner-breeders on the Turf to more than a fair share of this elusive and priceless commodity. 'You may put all the brains you have into racing,' he was fond of saying, 'but you will be nowhere unless you have luck.' As Edward Moorhouse observed quaintly in an issue of the *Pall Mall Magazine*: 'During the brief period in which he has wooed Fortune on the Turf, the fickle dame has treated him as one of her favourites.' On the Turf as in life Eustace Loder could count himself a very lucky man indeed.

One of Dame Fortune's greatest gifts to Eustace Loder was the birth in late March 1901 of a dark chestnut filly destined to be feted as the most illustrious of her sex to grace the English Turf. Within just four years of purchasing the Eyrefield Lodge Stud it was Eustace Loder's great fortune to breed and own Pretty Polly.

For contemporary writers to talk of 'Peerless Pretty Polly' barely two years after singing the praises of another superb filly in Sceptre, the only horse to win four Classics, declares just how exceptional the daughter of Gallinule and Admiration must have been. In 1902 only the Derby eluded Sceptre, and she might well have secured that too, with a more judicious ride. So might Pretty Polly have won all five in 1904 had Eustace Loder entered her for the two Classics she didn't contest, the 2000 Guineas and Derby. Loder had reasoned that a certain Oaks success might be forfeited by a hard race in the Derby against colts. As it was, Pretty Polly met the Derby and 2000 Guineas victor, St Amant, on five occasions and thrashed him each time, to the tune of an aggregate distance exceeding twenty-two lengths.

Loder's 'luck' came with Pretty Polly's conception, for her dam had done precious little on the racecourse to warrant her retention and possessed no pedigree to speak of. It was necessary to go back sixty years to arrive at a mare in the bottom line with credentials anything other than mediocre. Yet the long-backed chestnut with 'drooping quarters, wide hips and the most magnificent shoulder' had captured the heart of Loder's stud manager, Noble Johnson, and he couldn't bear to part with her. 'I often rode Admiration out as a hack with the horses,' he wrote, 'and a more delightful ride no one could wish for. She was a nice tempered mare, and would stand about or do anything, and had the most perfect mouth and manners; a child could have ridden her.'

Loder paid just 510 guineas for Admiration as a yearling in 1893. Put in training, she lived up to her meagre price tag at two and three, prior to being transferred to Conyngham Lodge in the summer of 1895. Her subsequent record doesn't read exceptionally on paper – handicap successes on the Flat at Baldoyle and Leopardstown – but Johnson wouldn't have her disparaged. 'I have heard it said that she was no good as a racehorse. This is not quite correct. I don't think it is fair to say she had no racing merit. Up to a mile she could hold her own in fair class company, and was very honest.' Admiration's final appearance came in the Irish Grand Military Steeplechase at Punchestown, in the hands of Loder's friend and fellow cavalryman Arthur Hughes-Onslow. She was sent off favourite and finished third after striking into herself landing over one of the big drop fences. Loder and Johnson earmarked her for their new stud, Eyrefield Lodge. She would repay Johnson's faith by producing thirteen consecutive foals, nine of whom won a total of forty-two races worth over £52,000. The second of those, by Laveno, only won a single contest: her name was Veneration II and she was to go down in the history of the Turf as the dam of Craganour. Her third foal, by Gallinule, was named Pretty Polly and she would re-write Turf history.

Loder's retention of Admiration suggested his luck was running strong and her union with the sire Gallinule franked the point. Gallinule was a fine-looking specimen who'd shown smart form as a juvenile but never won thereafter in thirteen attempts. He retired with the dubious reputation of being both a 'roarer' and a 'bleeder' but this failed to deter Captain Henry Greer from speculating £900 and standing him at his Brownstown Stud not far from Eyrefield. 'Who's the mug?' Gallinule's profligate and hard-drinking owner, George 'The Squire' Baird, was alleged to have asked. 'I hope he's got the money.' To begin with things didn't go well as Gallinule's infirmities discouraged breeders. Greer was reduced to offering a free service in order to gain any custom. Once he even put Gallinule up for sale at £300 but received no takers. Fortunately, in 1895, Portmarnock became the first of a string of Gallinule offspring to land the Irish Derby (six of the next seven renewals). By the time of his death in 1912, Gallinule had sired the winners of six Classics in England and been champion sire twice.

Noble Johnson had always shared Greer's faith in Gallinule as a potentially successful stallion and, thanks to their friendship, nominations were always found for Eyrefield mares at Brownstown, even after the stallion's services became highly sought. Gallinaria, Game Chick and Hammerkop were outstanding Eyrefield fillies by Gallinule but the union between the stallion and Admiration seemed blessed in heaven. In six visits, Admiration threw five winners. More to the point, the result of their first mating was Pretty Polly.

Sceptre was still in training when Pretty Polly, trained at Newmarket by Peter Purcell Gilpin, made her debut in the British Dominion Plate at Sandown Park on 27 June 1903 and her exalted status was thus a constant benchmark against which

Pretty Polly might be measured. Yet once Polly won her first race by an official margin of ten lengths (actually closer to twenty; the photograph of the finish struggled to accommodate the placed horses) and completed her juvenile season unbeaten in nine races, the cognoscenti recognised they were chronicling the career of a second very special animal, who might conceivably even overshadow Sceptre. Facile juvenile victories in the Champagne, Cheveley Park and Middle Park Stakes saw them state, 'she appears to be practically invincible' (*Illustrated Sporting and Dramatic News*); her 1000 Guineas, Oaks and St Leger Triple Crown the following season drew comments like 'she is nothing short of a wonder' (*The Strand*); and her brace of Coronation Cups as a four- and five-year-old (in the first setting a track record for Epsom's one-and-a-half miles that stood for twenty-three years) had them drooling 'she must have come near to flying' (*Illustrated Sporting and Dramatic News*). The *Daily Telegraph* did not equivocate: 'Possibly the best filly of this or any other generation.' Two defeats failed to dim her greatness and there were extenuating circumstances for each. She lost in France following a long and gruelling Channel crossing and railway journey; and she lost her final start in the Ascot Gold Cup when showing signs of sickness. 'I would rather forfeit £40,000 than see her beaten,' said Loder on the eve of her journey to France but, as a true racing man, he wanted to see his horse prove her worth against all-comers.

Raking the embers of Pretty Polly's racing career in this way is of some relevance to the story of her owner-breeder. Loder's marvellous mare raced for four seasons and the public took her to their hearts. When she won the St Leger the racecourse sold 15,000 postcards of her. Her image could also be found on button badges and even sticks of rock: in the words of the *Daily Telegraph*, 'Quite a halo of sentiment had begun to hang around Pretty Polly.' Indeed, the Bishop of Sheffield referred to her qualities from the pulpit and wondered whether her fame would cause a spate of 'Pollys' to be christened. Like any female aristocrat, 'Her Ladyship', as she was known in Gilpin's yard, enjoyed a female companion, in her case a cob called Little Missus who accompanied her to the races and was to be found waiting for her in the winner's enclosure ready to nuzzle noses and share the sugar lumps proffered by the titled ladies and other willing acolytes. She received birthday cards in the mail and love poems in the press:

> Of all the mares that are so smart
> There's none like Pretty Polly
> The darling of the tipster's heart
> She makes the racing jolly.
> There is no grand dame in the land
> So sweet as Pretty Polly
> And if she's beat below the stand
> What price our melancholy.

Pretty Polly's fame reflected on Eustace Loder. Her legion of supporters sported scarves and neckties in his dark blue, yellow and black colours. From being merely an anonymous 'Toff' who bred and owned a few racehorses, Eustace Loder was suddenly transformed into the guardian angel of a public heroine. He wasn't only able to bask in her glory but also in the affection for her. Loder had gained a public profile, an image – a positive image. His name was even adopted as rhyming slang for 'soda' – as in 'Large whisky and Major Loder!'

If the gift of Pretty Polly alone wasn't sufficient evidence of Dame Fortune's munificence, she'd also presented Loder with a Derby winner. 'There are people who will tell you that there is no such thing as luck,' said Edward Moorhouse. 'They are wrong; at any rate, every man who has anything to do with racing will tell you they are wrong. Luck has no doubt played a big part in fashioning his career. But it was not luck pure and simple that placed Spearmint in Major Loder's possession.'

Indeed it wasn't. Nine yearlings were sent up from Sir Tatton

Sykes's Sledmere Stud to the Doncaster Sales of 1904. Loder and
Noble Johnson had visited Sledmere to inspect the yearlings
and took an instant fancy to the bay colt by Carbine out of Maid
of the Mint on pedigree, attracted by the appearance of the influential broodmare Pocahontas who also featured in Pretty Polly's
pedigree. Carbine had been imported from Australia to stand at
stud in England by the Duke of Portland: back home he was the
winner of thirty-three races including the 1890 Melbourne Cup
from a record field of thirty-eight others in record time under
10st 5lb. Sykes paid 2,000 guineas for Maid of the Mint as she
was waiting to be covered by Carbine; the colt she foaled was to
be known as Spearmint. As Carbine's stock wasn't popular, the
colt attracted one other bidder who could go no higher than 280
guineas. At 300 guineas, Loder had got his horse for the price of
a selling plater.

Moorhouse declared in the *Pall Mall Magazine*:

> That was where good fortune came to his aid, but it was sound
> judgment that enabled him to single out a horse which other
> men, commanding unlimited capital, and prepared to invest
> thousands of pounds in fashionably-bred stock, would not look
> at for a second time.

At first Loder's famous 'luck' appeared to have deserted him.
As soon as trainer Peter Purcell Gilpin got Spearmint back to
Newmarket the colt fell ill: he developed a cough which ailed
him for five months. That Gilpin persevered with such a cheap
yearling is testimony to the hopes be entertained for him. Gilpin
was not to be disappointed, even though Spearmint only ever
saw a racecourse five times in his life. Spearmint scraped home
by a head on his debut and was beaten on his two other starts
as a two-year-old. His two races at three sealed his reputation.
His first target was to be the Grand Prix de Paris rather than
the Derby because Gilpin's yard also housed Pretty Polly's well-
regarded half-brother Admiral Crichton and the filly Flair, who

won the 1000 Guineas so easily she was made favourite for the Derby. Flair broke down – opening the door for Spearmint to be re-routed to Epsom. Loder's 'luck' seemed to be running – and appeared even more so when Spearmint worked upsides Pretty Polly on the Limekilns. News of an impending 'trial' had, needless to say, found its way to the ears of the Newmarket touts. Gilpin wasn't about to share information. He evaded the gang lurking outside the main gates of the yard by taking down part of the railing at the back of the stables and sending Spearmint and Pretty Polly through Lord Derby's private ground to the gallops. When the party returned through the front gates, past the astonished touts camped there since dawn, he had all the jockeys who had ridden in the trial locked up until the stable commissions had been safely invested. Gilpin was wise to have taken every precaution. According to gossip, at almost weight-for-age, Spearmint gave Polly a half-length beating. Either the mare was becoming sluggish on the gallops, or Spearmint was a stone-cold certainty for the Derby.

Spearmint duly won the Derby in record time and eleven days later travelled to Paris to fulfil his original programme in the Grand Prix. After the desperate journey experienced by Pretty Polly two years earlier, Loder took no chances with Spearmint's travelling arrangements: he went by special train and special boat accompanied by a stablemate for company, his own blacksmith, stable-lad and Gilpin's head-man in addition to an interpreter just in case any misunderstandings might need smoothing out on the far side of the Channel. Spearmint became the first English horse to win the Grand Prix for twenty years, fighting off persistent challenges from the home contingent. That night the victorious party retired to the Jardin de Paris where one of Loder's young nephews reputedly danced the can-can with a mature member of the chorus who outranked him by a good thirty years and at least nine stone. There's no mention of how Eustace Loder celebrated.

Loder's luck had just held: Spearmint's bad forelegs prevented him from ever seeing a racecourse again. Perhaps one shouldn't be surprised. The accident of birth had given Loder a head start.

☞

He was one of twin sons born to Robert and Maria Loder on 16 May 1867. He and Sydney followed six other boys; two sisters completed the family. The Loders were a Dorset family from Haselbury Bryan, where they appear in parish registers going back to the sixteenth century. Thanks to a combination of business acumen and inspired marriages, the family prospered. In 1816 Eustace Loder's grandfather Giles, a 'Merchant Adventurer', married the daughter of a St Petersburg trader with Imperial connections and went on to accumulate a fortune, leaving £2.5 million (the equivalent of £200 million nowadays) to his son, Robert, when he died in 1871. Robert hardly needed the money, having made a lucrative marriage of his own to yet another rich heiress in the shape of Maria Busk whose family prosperity stemmed from the Swedish wool trade. Robert Loder spent some of his money on coursing greyhounds, but most of it went toward acquiring real estate. Besides properties in Sweden and Russia, he owned three estates in Northamptonshire (Whittlebury, Maidwell and Floore) and one – High Beeches – in Sussex. 'He belonged,' wrote Sir Alfred Pease,

> to a class of English country gentleman, not of rare type in the reign of Victoria, but a particularly good example of it … a good administrator exacting good conduct and regular habits from those over whom he was placed … serving his country where opportunity was given, by personal service and liberal benevolence.

Loder served as a Justice of the Peace in both counties and was Sheriff of Northamptonshire and Deputy-Lieutenant for Sussex; between 1880 and 1885 he sat as Conservative MP for Shoreham – which earned him a baronetcy in Queen Victoria's Golden Jubilee Honours list of 1887.

Eustace and his twin brother grew up at High Beeches, near Crawley, with its wonderful views toward the distant Downs and the Devil's Dyke. Their upbringing was supervised by their mother, Maria, a tall, thin woman who was a slave to religious ritual: no games were allowed on Sundays when church attendance was compulsory and the children took turns in saying 'Grace' at meals – in French. According to Pease, Robert Loder 'did not give a great deal of attention to his children unless they were ill, until one after another they earned his notice by some achievement or exploit'. One such attainment was to slide down the precipitous banister outside the nursery which frequently resulted in a flying dismount, a collision with their father's study door and subsequent acquaintance with his slipper. All the boys were said to be imbued with the 'Loder vitality', being especially adept with rifle and gun. Edmund was an exceptionally gifted sprinter and long-jumper; Alfred excelled over the hurdles; Reginald shone at football, cricket and athletics. The young Eustace's sporting proclivities are not deemed worthy of mention – though Sydney's prowess with a rifle is lauded by reference to him killing 1,173 stags during thirty-one seasons of stalking the Scottish Highlands. The twins trod the familiar family path to Eton, though not in complete tandem. Sydney entered the school in January 1881, a term before his twin and stayed only until Christmas of the following year, eventually going on to Magdalene College, Cambridge. Eustace, however, spent five years at Eton, leaving in July 1886 a month after his acceptance by Trinity College, Cambridge. His Eton career is characterised by anonymity: he won no school prizes nor represented any school teams; the solitary contribution made to his house was election to the debating society in Michaelmas term 1883. Nor did he stand out at Cambridge. He was admitted to Trinity as a pensioner (fee-paying student) and didn't graduate; it's possible he didn't go up to Trinity with the intention of taking a degree at all – like a quarter of all university students of the day. He did, however, join the boat club.

On Robert Loder's death in 1888, Whittlebury, and his title, passed to eldest son Edmund; Maidwell to Reginald; Floore to Sydney; and High Beeches to Wilfred. For Eustace, however, there was no estate. Even so, various legacies and monies to the tune of £300,000 (£24 million) ensured he would never have to lift a finger for the rest of his life. 'There is always more brass than brains in the aristocracy,' says Wilde. In 1888 rich young bachelors with no responsibilities went into the Army and Eustace secured a commission in the 12th Lancers. The regiment's official history paints a vivid portrait of the calibre of recruit it sought:

> No man under the size of 5' 7 ½" high without their shoes: they must be light and straight made (by no means gummy) broad shoulders, long thighs, a good face, and every way well made. No man who has the least defect. In particular, care must be taken that all recruits are examined by a knowing surgeon … for any man who is troubled with fits or has the appearance of rupture, broken bones, sore legs, scold head or ulcers on any part of his body will not be approved.

As a young subaltern Loder was taught to ride afresh, attend stables, learn foot-drill, the lance exercise and made to box. He was also expected to pay for his uniform, his barrack-room furniture and his saddlery. He had to provide himself with two chargers, the first a chestnut, which he was only allowed to ride on parade and hacking, and a second which he was allowed to hunt with one day a week – if approved by his commanding officer. This basic outlay involved a good £1,000. In addition, he should stable at least one polo pony, with all the necessary accoutrements: polo had become the peacetime equivalent of the charge for every cavalry regiment in the British Army and had generated inter-regimental rivalry of matching ferocity. Then there were monthly subscriptions to the mess, the coach, the band and numerous charitable funds. All for 6s 8d per day

– which rose to 7s 6d (37.5p) on his promotion to lieutenant in 1890. Private income was critical.

Above all, Eustace Loder needed a thick skin. His wealthy background was immaterial to his brother officers who were apt to pretend all juniors scarcely existed in the mess. Any presumption this boorish behaviour was some sort of inducement to marry would be mistaken, for any married officer saw his mess fee doubled. Loder didn't marry. His chosen partner was his regiment.

Such was the figure that the young Eustace Loder cut. A clean-limbed upstanding specimen from the upper classes who knew precisely where he stood in both the military hierarchy comprising officers and other ranks, and in the social hierarchy hinged around landed gentry and their inferiors. He expected others to know likewise. His lifestyle exploited his class but, equally, was restricted by it. His class didn't mix with outsiders. Moreover, his was a man's world: the closed world of the common room, the mess and the club. There appears to have been no room in it for a woman: no reported dalliances; no sowing of wild oats. He was not given to frivolities and his inherent timidity was cloaked by a brusqueness that often led him to be mistaken for something of a cold fish – which the melancholy captured in his portraits does nothing to subvert. But the man of few words became a man of his word. A man of honour. Men such as Eustace Loder made loyal friends and, as likely, equally devout enemies.

Loder joined the 12th Lancers on its return from India with the Empire at peace. The military year thus found itself divided into a seven-month summer season of training and a five-month winter season of leave with each officer receiving a block of two-and-a-half months uninterrupted repose. Loder faced a succession of tedious postings – Manchester, Birmingham, Preston – with little to commend them other than occasional hunting or polo. 'It would probably be not very wrong to assert that at that time,' observed the regimental history tartly, 'the principal objective of most officers was to get away from Preston as soon, as often, and as quickly as possible.' By comparison, the two years stationed in Edinburgh (1893–95) were exceedingly pleasant for him. Aside from the honour of escorting the future King George V and Queen Mary on their honeymoon visit to the city, official duties were light and social obligations many and varied. If he so chose Loder could dance five nights a week; hunt with Lord Eglinton's or the Duke of Buccleuch's hounds; fly-fish on Loch Leven; stalk deer or shoot pheasant and grouse; enjoy polo, tennis, cricket and swimming. Sport, especially equestrian sport, was in the regiment's blood. One of Loder's comrades summed it up thus:

> Though duty was rigidly supposed to be first, yet sport I fear was uppermost in the minds of every young officer. It was everyone's ambition not only to have his name on the regimental, subalterns or point-to-point trophies, but also to put up a really good exhibition of riding for the credit of the regiment. To complete the course in spite of mischances or falls was a point of honour.

Loder threw himself enthusiastically into this new life, adding his name to the list of Subaltern Cup winners and partnering his bay mare Jenny in polo competitions at Hurlingham. In 1890 he usurped his father's colours, never used, of 'yellow, dark blue sleeves and black cap' and wore them to success in a Maiden Hunters' Chase at that year's Grand Military Meeting at Sandown aboard his steeplechaser Field Marshal. Loder was already demonstrating a knack for gravitating toward the premier practitioners of the day. Field Marshal was prepared under the supervision of the pre-eminent Victorian trainer of jumpers, Arthur Yates. Though Yates acted as mentor to many aspiring gentleman riders, Loder knew his limitations. When Field Marshal returned to Sandown to win the Grand Military Gold Cup in 1895, Loder's fellow Etonian and 12th Lancer, Eustace Crawley, was in the saddle. A naturally gifted sportsman who also excelled at cricket, polo and rackets, Crawley embodied the Corinthian spirit of the regiment.

It was typical of his nerveless character that when he could not be found to weigh out for the Grand Military he was eventually located in the lunch tent consuming strawberries and cream. Eight years later Loder would win the race again with Marpessa ridden by the equally talented amateur Arthur 'Junks' Hughes-Onslow of the 10th Hussars. Loder's best chaser, however, was Covert Hack, who won the Conyngham Cup at Punchestown four times in five years. Covert Hack fell at the first in the 1900 Grand National, but then made a name for himself by galloping on riderless and bringing down the favourite on the second circuit, thereby paving the way for his stablemate Ambush II to give the Prince of Wales his only victory in the race. Loder was fond of laughing at the jibe of deliberate sabotage.

To begin with, Loder's colours were far less conspicuous on the Flat. Between 1892 and 1900 he won only eight races in England, four of those in 1892 – the most noteworthy courtesy of the four-year-old filly Billow, who won the Ascot Stakes.

By the time Marpessa and Covert Hack came to carry his colours, Loder had received a posting that changed the course of his life. In May 1895 he was promoted captain and made adjutant when the 12th Lancers were sent to Ireland. This elevation speaks loudly of those attributes that made him of value to the military, for the post of regimental adjutant was a significant one that required him to assist his commanding officer in matters of organisation, administration and discipline. En route from Dublin to Ballincollig, its new base in County Cork, the Lancers stopped briefly on the Curragh, home to Irish thoroughbred racing for over 200 years. Eustace Crawley seized this opportunity to visit the stables run by his friend Tommy Lushington at Conyngham Lodge. He asked Loder along and Loder jumped at the invitation. Lushington was a top amateur rider, more than a match for most professionals, and ran the stables with Noble Johnson. They complemented each other's attributes perfectly for Johnson's area of expertise was bloodstock; his eye for conformation was sharpness itself and his knowledge of the stud-book encyclopaedic. Loder and Johnson established an instant rapport. That winter Johnson frequently hunted with the 12th Lancers' pack and it was on one such meet that Loder asked him if he would go over to England and inspect his stock with a view to weeding out the useless. The only remaining question to resolve was what to do with those Johnson thought worth retaining.

The answer presented itself on the death in March 1897 of champion trainer Henry Linde, a legend on the Irish Turf. During a career lasting three decades, the tall and severe-looking master of Eyrefield Lodge gave the Irish training profession a giant push toward the modern era, through a combination of character, talent and integrity. He sent out the winners of two Grand Nationals, three Irish Grand Nationals and two of the Grand Steeplechase de Paris, as well as an Irish Derby. Linde had no heirs and Eyrefield Lodge was put up for sale.

Lushington and Johnson knew the place intimately, considering it the most desirable stud farm and stable in Ireland. They thought it would be ideal for Eustace Loder's purposes. They told him they didn't think it would fetch much more than £5,000. In view of the 12th Lancers' imminent return to Aldershot, Loder's regimental duties as adjutant prevented him from leaving Ballincollig to inspect the property in person, but he authorised Johnson to buy it on his behalf at the forthcoming auction. The task of bidding was delegated to Johnson's lawyer but he was soon knocked out and it appeared as if Loder had lost the property. However, Lushington, in Johnson's words, 'started bidding away as if he had the Bank of England behind him instead of an overdraft', and made the successful bid at £8,000. Johnson wired Loder the outcome, fearing that he and Lushington, having far exceeded their brief, were going to be left holding the baby. Loder replied:

I am delighted we have secured the place, of course it was a pity we had to pay so much, but we must make up for it by working all the harder to make it a paying concern. I am sure we should have

both been very sorry if we had let it slip. I hope having to pay so
high for the place will not stop your buying anything useful. I
enclose you balance of deposit.

Loder's purchase comprised a Queen Anne house, a set of stables
and a well-maintained stretch of typical Curragh horse land.
Loder also inherited Linde's priceless staff, led by Dan McNally,
dubbed 'Eyrefield Dan' by the locals. McNally soon made his
value known to his new employer. One day in 1898 he was found
in the tack room nursing a sickly foal which he'd placed on a bed
of horse blankets before the fire; protecting the vulnerable creature from the elements was a human wall of staff whose fatigue
and boredom McNally was relieving with a stream of anecdotes.
The foal pulled through. Named Star Shoot, the colt went on to
win in 1900 three of the most valuable races for two-year-olds
in the English calendar: the British Dominion Plate, National
Breeders' Produce Stakes and Hurst Park Foal Plate. After being
exported to the USA, Star Shoot topped the stallions' list on five
occasions and sired Sir Barton, the first American Triple Crown
winner. The notion of 'Lucky' Loder was born.

Loder acted on the old cavalry maxim 'horses first, men
second, officers last' to assemble a crack team for his new operation. Noble Johnson managed the stud side and Lushington
managed the racehorses, riding most of them. Nonetheless,
Loder's contribution should not be undervalued. 'To breed
race-horses with continual success requires not only a great
knowledge of the animal,' wrote Sir Alfred Pease in tribute, 'but
also of men to whom a stud is confided, the trainers who are
to prepare horses for their career and the jockeys to ride them.
Nothing must be left to chance which intelligence can direct
or control.' Loder ensured just that. Eyrefield's racing operation
achieved instant success with a hat-trick of notable victories in
England and Ireland during 1900. The Grand National fell to
the Prince of Wales' Ambush II and the Irish Derby and Oaks
to Loder's two fillies Gallinaria and May Race.

By this time the Boer War was raging in South Africa. However, Loder, a major since August 1900, didn't accompany the 12th Lancers and, in September 1902, once the war concluded, he handed in his papers. This was done not without some regrets. 'I had no luck in soldiering,' he admitted with a rueful nod toward his contrasting fortunes on the Turf. 'I've never been under fire nor on foreign service.' Nonetheless, the regiment had done its job. It had given Loder a template for life. Service life was structured. Loder knew his place within that structure, coped with its restrictions and orders, thrived on the sense of duty it demanded of him and the clarity of purpose to deliver it. In short, it gifted him a personality where once there was none.

Loder threw himself into the reorganisation of Eyrefield Lodge. Racing stock retained in Ireland was transferred to Conyngham Lodge under Lushington's supervision while the more promising youngsters, like Pretty Polly and Spearmint, were sent to Newmarket to be trained by Kildare-raised Peter Purcell Gilpin, who had taken over their supervision from John Huggins on the American's repatriation in 1902. Eyrefield Lodge was designated solely for stud purposes. Astrology (the dam of Star Shoot), Sibola (dam of St Leger second Baltinglass) and Concussion comprised, with Admiration, the initial quartet of Eyrefield broodmares. Concussion repaid her purchase price of £500 by producing an Irish Oaks winner in Dabchick; Llangibby, winner of the Eclipse of 1906; and the tough staying mare Hammerkop who won a Cesarewitch and Ascot's Alexandra Plate twice. By the start of the 1913 season, these and other home-breds had won Loder 110 races for £122,505 in prize-money (over £6 million).

However, the picture wasn't quite as bright as it seems. Returns hadn't been so lofty since the halcyon days of Pretty Polly and Spearmint. The seasons 1907–13 saw Loder's fortunes as an owner gradually dip: scores of 10, 2, 7, 6, 4 and 9 for a grand total of thirty-eight races won didn't stand comparison with the total for the preceding six seasons of sixty-one in terms of quantity, let alone quality. Successes in the top flight, once commonplace,

were restricted to Galvani (1907 Champion Stakes); Admiral
Hawke (1909 Coventry Stakes); Knockfeerna (1911 Coronation
Stakes); Mountain Mint (1911 National Breeders' Produce Stakes);
and Lance Chest (1912 Princess of Wales's Stakes). These were
successes of which many an owner-breeder would justifiably be
proud, yet by Loder's standards, slim pickings.

To some degree Loder had become increasingly identified
with his role as a racecourse Steward and Turf administrator.
These unpaid positions were less prestigious than they might
appear. The feeling persisted that anyone acting as a local
Steward or being elected to the Jockey Club at the turn of the
nineteenth century must either be moronic or dishonest. Eton
and the Cavalry were frequently deemed the sole attributes
for the former, irrespective of age or infirmity, because, as the
doggerel ran, 'the Stewards lunch till half-past three/when they
commence to have their tea'. Another barb suggested the solitary
requirement was to go racing with a collar and tie. To become
a member of the Jockey Club, it was said with equal feeling,
one had to be a relation of God – and a close one at that. It was
an institution described as the purest example of the eighteenth
century still surviving: self-elected; autocratic; oligarchic. Not
even an Establishment journalist such as Sidney Galtey of the
*Daily Telegraph* could muster much enthusiasm for the calibre of
the average Jockey Club member:

> Most of the members were of considerable age and probably
> too tired to bother about the obligations of stewardship. With
> few exceptions they were not men who had been, or were,
> conspicuous in Parliamentary or local government or industry.
> Entry to membership was jealously guarded. Families were well
> represented as if membership was regarded by them as a form
> of heirloom. Youth, which in later years in our great institutions
> was to hammer at the door and force entry and recognition, was
> only noticed with obvious reluctance. One felt that the honour
> of election to the Jockey Club must not necessarily be given

to individuals whose brains in finance or industry had enabled them to invest vast sums in the breeding and the racing of the thoroughbred.

If the Jockey Club did possess a template for its ideal member at this time it's fair to say Loder was a snug fit and he was duly elected to the Irish Turf Club in 1898 (serving as a Steward between 1902–04) and the Jockey Club eight years later. At least his years as regimental adjutant spoke of the necessary attention to detail, order and discipline ideally required of the role. His principles dictated he adopt a tough stance on the doping issue and rough riding, both of which cancers had infiltrated the English Turf thanks to the influx of American trainers, jockeys – and gamblers.

Beyond the Turf his interests were still those of his class: hunting, shooting, polo – a life of pleasure paid for by public service. He was a Justice of the Peace for Kildare and in 1912 acted as High Sheriff. Still there was no woman in his life, no hint of romance, no marriage prospect, or even the suggestion that Loder believed 'marriage ruins a man … it's as demoralising as cigarettes and far more expensive'. Neither was there any semblance of male relationships that were anything other than transparently platonic. Loder did advertise several of the stereotypical traits attributed to the old-fashioned, so called 'snob queers' of the era. His photographs show him self-evidently narcissistic; he was sensitive to criticism, be it justified or unjustified; he was aloof to the point of superciliousness. Yet he seems to have been completely asexual. Unlike the South African character bearing his name in Morley Roberts's 1900 political pot-boiler *Lord Linlithgow* – 'a very dangerous man not to be trusted' – no whiff of scandal hung around his name. 'He is a man who can carry weight,' added the novelist. 'He wants responsibility – the very heaviest.' That sounded more like Eustace Loder.

Loder appeared wedded to his regiment and his horses. He held a life-long interest in the fortunes of the regimental polo team and demonstrated his love for the 12th Lancers by organising the Old Comrades Dinner and seeing to it that as many veterans as possible might be put in touch with each other to share reminiscences of former glories. In 1911 he was instrumental in setting up the Regimental Association. Its aim was to maintain and promote

> Fellowship among past and present members of the regiment … the welfare of discharged soldiers by helping them to establish themselves respectfully in civilian life … to assist those who, through no fault of their own, are unable to earn their own livelihood … and the wives and families of members who are in distressed circumstances.

Former Lancers such as Troop Sergeant-Major William Saxby, for example, reduced to supporting a wife and eight children on his army pension and suffering from fits as a result of sunstroke while serving in India. Loder determined to help promote the career of his jockey son, William junior.

# THREE

# Embittered Servant

William Saxby spent most of the winter of 1912–13 at Foxhill riding work for Jack Robinson. The weather was cruel and the trainer's preparations for the coming season had been so interrupted that regular gallops reports for his string didn't appear in the trade papers until February. Even then conditions were frequently described as 'dull and wet' or 'frosty' with 'cold winds'.

During the first week of March, the trainer put on a brave face when visited by the 'Travelling Correspondent' of *The Sporting Chronicle*. In a piece subtitled 'The Capital Progress of Craganour', Robinson purred:

'I have been on some good ones, such as Seabreeze, Kilwarlin and others during my riding days, but neither as jockey nor trainer have I ever before been associated with one equal to Craganour. Come and see him.'

It is but fifty yards from the house to the two yards – the old one made wonderfully picturesque by the thatched roofs and the ivy-covered walls of the boxes. It is here, in a corner box so large that it permits a loose horse to take walking exercise, that Craganour is at home.

'Take his rug off and turn him loose,' said Robinson to the boy who was doing him when we walked in. No sooner was this done than Craganour wheeled round, trotted to the back of his box and became busy on the sliced carrots and handful of grass he clearly knew he would find there. Those disposed of, he began to investigate his visitors with a look in his eye that at first I did not quite like. I soon found, however, that Craganour was to be trusted, his nibbling at his trainer's coat and attempts to appropriate the pocket handkerchief being high-spirited playfulness without vice, of which he gave no sign while we examined him from all points at close quarters.

'What do you think of him?' asked Robinson.

'Why,' I exclaimed in astonishment, 'he looks three-parts trained now.'

'Well, if the Derby was to be run in a fortnight I think he would have an advantage in condition over most of his opponents. I kept him going until December; since then he has had three canters a day, missing but one day, and you will see how he goes in a good half-speed gallop in the morning when we are going to have a field day.'

The day Craganour missed galloping was about the middle of January, and that was owing to the lameness which caused a scare. That he was lame that day is true but it did not last more than three hours and there was no suggestion of infirmity about it. It was caused by a too tight shoe and when that was replaced he became all right again. His legs and feet are now as clean and sound as even the most critical could desire, his arms and second thighs being particularly good. The poise of his head and neck is, perhaps, a little 'flash' or 'cocky'; it gives the impression that if he could speak he would say 'I am an aristocrat, and don't you forget it.' His quarters have two aspects. Viewed broadside on they appear to cut in too sharply below the rump, which gives him the appearance of falling off a little behind the saddle. It is different, however, when one stands directly behind him. From that point of view his quarters are tremendous.

He has beautifully sloping shoulders. Power in his forelegs is denoted by them not being too long from shoulder to knee or from knee to fetlock. He has not grown up much since last year, but being 15.1½ he is big enough. In other respects he has improved. He is bigger in his second ribs, and altogether he looks thicker, more robust, heavier and stronger than last year. That he is better than then – when he was always a little backward – is Robinson's opinion.

Robinson is not satisfied that ordinary stable boys ride his horses at exercise even in the off season. That is why he has had William Saxby in residence throughout the winter. And not merely for ornament – at exercise he had six rides. The most interesting of these spins was the last, in which, at a good half-speed gallop over five furlongs, Craganour galloped in great style, pulling over his companions, Allegretto, Eton Boy and Bonnie Bird.

The star of the stable is Craganour, a 'great doer' as to food and a 'great doer' in action.

In the same issue of the *Chronicle* that carried this Foxhill piece, Robinson was able to catch up on the well-being of Craganour's main rival for Classic honours, Shogun, who featured heavily in a second stable report:

It would be impossible for a Classic candidate to have made greater improvement during the recess. Once looking overgrown, somewhat leggy and light of thigh, he is now really good to follow with muscle in all the right places. His knees were on the small side and his cannon bones rather narrow but whilst his shins have lost their bumpy appearance his knees and metacarpals have increased in symmetrical volume. He has splendid oblique shoulders, a lengthy and very muscular neck, deep girth, short back, and lengthy high-class quarters. He was always a long strider and one can readily credit that if he stays Craganour's great advantage as a quick beginner will not be so pronounced over longer distances this year as last. Shogun's immense stride will go a long way to equalise matters before the winning post is reached.

Suitably forewarned, Robinson soon had Craganour in regular work over five or seven furlongs with older work-mates

Marchwind and Moorland Lad and Ismay's two-year-old Ballyoukan (in the words of the *Life*'s gallop watcher, 'at a nice pace') to ready him for Liverpool's Union Jack Stakes over a mile on Thursday 3 April, barely a week into the new campaign. Twenty-four hours prior to the race it seemed as if Craganour would be granted a walk-over but four eventually elected to take him on. The Guineas and Derby favourite left paddock watchers divided in their opinion. According to *The Times* he had 'not grown much' although he had 'thickened out'; others saw this excess condition as evidence of him being backward and well short of full fitness, Edward Moorhouse going so far as to describe him as looking 'punchy'. Craganour ran like it. Sent to post at odds of 5/2 on, he failed by a length to concede 7lb to Flippant, already match fit from a race at Kempton Park. At no stage of the race did Craganour demonstrate the free, flowing, action that had distinguished his juvenile career.

The press left Liverpool in a quandary. Had Craganour failed to train-on from two to three? 'Flippant held Craganour helpless when he challenged,' said the *Life*. 'Apparently Craganour's Derby prospects have now faded completely out.' Craganour's Derby odds went out to 8s as Shogun assumed favouritism at half that price. What had troubled most onlookers was the loss of the smooth action so admired throughout the previous summer. Was it simply just a case of Robinson leaving him something to work on – or Foxhill's soggy gallops leaving him no option – with the 2000 Guineas still over three weeks away? Had the extra quarter of a mile found him out? It was the first time he'd been asked to race beyond six furlongs. 'The faith of the majority concerning his ability to stay is shaken, and there are suspicions of temper,' declared *The Times*.

There are times when the race for the 2000 Guineas is merely a demonstration of something that has seemed scarcely open to doubt; the best two-year-old of the previous generation has again given proof of his superiority. However, the general impression is that this year's race must be considered exceedingly open.

When Craganour reappeared at Newmarket on 30 April for the season's first Classic his appearance had undergone a transformation from one extreme to the other: 'He stripped in much more business-like trim than at Liverpool and carried the Foxhill polish to perfection,' said *The Sportsman*. Edward Moorhouse, conversely, was alarmed by the 'scarcity of muscular tissue on his quarters and thighs' as he watched him canter to post with his head in the air. 'When he was stripped for this race he might almost have been likened to a scarecrow.' Stable confidence in Craganour remained undiminished, especially following a sparkling gallop four days before the Classic. 'Craganour Riddle' ran the headline to *The Sporting Life*'s preview.

> Craganour is an enigma. If he had done what he was asked to do at Liverpool and done it in a manner giving no cause for quibbling the position would be far different. Yet it would be foolish to take it for granted that his chances can safely be ignored despite there being reason to believe he is nowhere near fit even now as Robinson's training ground of late afforded anything but good ground.

Nonetheless, even though a welter of late money briefly elevated Shogun's stable companion Fairy King into favouritism, it was Craganour who was sent off the 3/1 favourite to beat fourteen rivals. 'Craganour came out of his box all on his toes and was generous in his heel play,' said the *Chronicle*. 'But this was in pure exuberance of spirit.'

Fairy King (100/30), another son of Desmond, had demolished a big field in the Wood Ditton Stakes over course and distance earlier in the month. The form was nothing outstanding, but Fairy King had shown he'd trained on, and at least he offered punters the bonus of never having met Craganour – unlike other leading candidates – and he'd reportedly trounced Shogun in a recent home trial. So, he was entrusted with the first colours of the publisher of *The Sporting Chronicle*, Edward Hulton, instead of Craganour's old whipping boy, who, despite winning Newbury's Greenham Stakes effortlessly, was now offered at an insulting 25/1 along with Louvois. The participation of the latter had been the subject of rumour and counter-rumour after Walter Raphael's colt had trodden on a nail a fortnight before. His earlier work brought forth glowing reports from the Newmarket gallops but, on the Saturday and Monday before the Guineas, he was left behind by a couple of 'platers', causing 'the shrewd Newmarket men to drop him like a hot potato' in the words of the *Life*: 'I fear he can no longer be considered a fighting factor.' Serious expectations of winning the Guineas were abandoned, despite the French-based American Johnny Reiff being engaged to ride him. His dispirited trainer, Dawson Waugh, counselled withdrawal to await the Derby since he was plainly 'not ready'.

Thus Craganour's most dangerous rivals, and the two animals only recently first and second favourites for the Derby, were relegated to forlorn outsiders. Bookmakers conceded Craganour's other old adversaries, Day Comet and Radiant, had no chance of turning the tables on him and elevated Lord Rosebery's Sanquhar (who'd taken the Craven Stakes over course and distance on his seasonal reappearance) to third favourite at 5/1 despite a recent history of wind problems.

The violent thunderstorm which rocked Newmarket for an hour the night before the Guineas presaged a race deemed 'most unsatisfactory' (*The Sportsman*); 'hardly up to the best traditions of the race' (*The Sporting Life*); and won by 'a horse against which the cognoscenti of Newmarket ranged themselves as one man' (*The Sporting Chronicle*).

This unsatisfactory outcome stemmed from something as rudimentary as the exceptional width of Newmarket's Rowley Mile. The fifteen runners had lined up in the centre of the track but, after getting the favourite off to a flyer from his allotted berth nearest the stands side, Saxby gradually made his way across to the rail. The field had split so that by the time Craganour entered the last half mile of the race a gap of some thirty or forty yards separated him from the other runners away to his right led by Sanquhar and Fairy King. It was impossible to tell how far in front he was. Observers at the Bushes, roughly two furlongs from the finish, swore he was leading by four lengths and racing into the Dip, just above the furlong mark; it looked impossible for him to be caught. Saxby was not riding him hard. He appeared to have plenty in hand. Out in the centre, Louvois, after swerving under the initial impact of Reiff's whip, reached and then mastered Fairy King and Sanquhar, and yet, in the *Chronicle*'s words, 'looked little like being concerned with the end of the race.' Still Saxby failed to apply stern measures, 'betraying not the least anxiety'. Racing up the hill to the winning post it appeared Louvois closed to within half-a-length of Craganour with Saxby 'continuing to ride as though under the full impression that he was riding the winner'. People standing on the rising ground immediately behind the winning post, as fine a spot to judge a Newmarket finish as there was, agreed with him, declaring Craganour the winner by at least a neck. From the stands, however, *The Sportsman*'s representative declared 'the finish could not be judged with any presence of certainty'.

The judge was C. E. Robinson. No relation of Jack the trainer, 63-year-old Charles Robinson was originally a tenant farmer from Lincolnshire who inherited the job after marrying Catherine, the daughter of John Clark who was the third generation of Clarks to hold the position. Robinson began assisting his father-in-law and took over his role in 1889. With no semblance of delay, Robinson gave Louvois the verdict. According to a story that swept through Newmarket the next day, he'd told his boardman to raise the number of Meeting House into the frame as the second horse until his assistant asked where he was going to place Craganour. Robinson replied that he hadn't seen Craganour's colours. Told that if Craganour didn't win he was certainly close up, Robinson ordered the favourite's number be placed second and gave the winning distance as a head; Meeting House was placed third, two lengths back, a neck in front of Sanquhar, Fairy

King and Shogun. 'That Louvois was a fortunate winner will not be disputed by any who had a clear view of the finish,' opined the *Chronicle*.

The explanation for Robinson's gaffe lay in the judge's box being sited on the stands side, where Craganour had run right under his eyes while they were concentrating on the horses finishing down the centre. 'They've made a bloomer!' exclaimed Dawson Waugh upon spying Louvois's number in the frame. 'They'll damn soon take it down!' The excitement proved too much for Walter Raphael, who took ill and was removed to his Newmarket residence.

Saxby brought back Craganour wreathed in the smile of a man believing, like nine out of ten people on the Heath, he had won his first Classic. When Robinson began berating him for getting beaten he could not disguise his shock. He was adamant he'd one-and-a-half lengths to spare. Why else had he not bothered even to shake-up Craganour at the finish? The Stewards would surely hold an enquiry into the obvious error and revise the verdict. The three men with the power to put matters right were Lord Wolverton, the Hon. Frederick Lambton and Major Eustace Loder. Saxby, Jack Robinson and Bower Ismay waited and scrutinised the flagpole for the blue flag that denoted an objection. Rule 170 of the Rules of Racing gave the Stewards sweeping powers to object on their own initiative 'without deposit'. They could have cited Rule 10 empowering them to 'adjudicate upon the conduct of all officials', in this case invoking Rule 39 which afforded the judge licence for 'correcting any mistake'.

A mistake like this had happened before; in exactly the same circumstances. In 1875 Claremont passed the post beneath the judge's box of Robinson's father-in-law on one side of the track while Camballo headed the rest of the field on the other. Not only was Camballo declared the winner but Claremont was not even given a place. Clark had plainly not spotted him at all. 'Mr Clark's decisions,' wrote a contemporary chronicler, 'owing to the confidence which his rectitude of character and singular physical qualifications ensured, were invariably received with a respect which forbade dispute and open dissatisfaction.'

Neither did Clark's successor take kindly to his professionalism being questioned. 'They are saying that Saxby won on Mr Ismay's horse,' Robinson later told Sidney Galtrey. 'What they should say is that he *ought* to have won.' Galtrey, for one, believed him:

> I think Saxby was deceived by the angle. He rode with the confidence of one who is satisfied he has got the issue safe beyond any measure of doubt. Louvois was wide of Craganour on this very wide course. If he had not been (deceived) he would have realised the seriousness of a critical situation. He would have asked for more from Craganour because there was certainly more to give. He would not have been lulled into such a false sense of security.

The *Chronicle* went further: 'The old and bitter lesson will thrust itself on any reflection of his upon this unlucky venture that on Newmarket Heath, and placed as he was, wide of the horse which he thought he was beating comfortably, 'tis better to let out an extra length of reef and make assurance doubly sure.'

Galtrey's point about the deceptive angle was franked just forty-eight hours later when Danny Maher reckoned he won the 1000 Guineas on Prue, only to be told they had been beaten ¾ length into third. Nor would Galtrey's colleague at *The Times* lend credence to an error on the part of the judge: 'No one who dimly realises the deceptiveness of what may be called racecourse angles, particularly on such a wide course as that at Newmarket, will for a moment heed such an insinuation.' The *Life* preferred to dwell on Reiff's contribution: 'The American's powerful jockeyship contributed not little to the result and he felt Louvois would have won by more had he not swerved when whipped.'

The requisite fifteen-minute timespan for lodging an objection after the winner had weighed-in came and went. No blue flag was raised. A Classic had been won. And lost. Bower Ismay walked away. He could have lodged an appeal: he chose not to. If Robinson's verdict was ever going to be challenged it could only have come in its immediate aftermath. There was no photo-finish camera evidence to call upon; no newsreel testimony. Once instantaneous recall had passed the game was up. As Lord Rosebery recorded in his diary: 'Two Thousand won by Louvois, or, as some say, by Craganour. Anyhow a fine race.'

Wild rumours soon began reaching Ismay. Eustace Loder bore him a grudge and had set against him. He had instructed Saxby to lose the race and ordered Robinson not to favour Craganour in the event of a close finish. Ismay's mind must have presented fertile soil for such rumours to take root in the spring of 1913, but even he would have been hard-pressed to believe Loder capable of acting so completely out of character as to coerce a jockey and an official into fixing the result of a Classic.

Perhaps the problem was much simpler. Ismay was merely in need of a new jockey, a top jockey instead of a journeyman like Saxby. Robinson fed the flames, reminding Ismay how Saxby had been out-foxed by Maher in the Molecomb. Saxby's fate was sealed at the Chester spring meeting on 7 May. He was beaten a head in a desperate finish to the Badminton Plate on Ismay's Ballyoukan after getting into all manner of scrapes on the tight, turning, Chester track. The Stewards called him in to 'explain his erratic riding and severely cautioned him as to his future riding'. Robinson had seen enough. Ismay was persuaded and, as was his wont, once he'd made up his mind, he acted swiftly and decisively. Saxby was sacked and never rode for him again. His dream of a Derby victory was destroyed.

☞

All jockeys ache to win the Derby. The 1913 season saw 213 men holding a full licence from the Jockey Club. Only one of them was destined to earn immortality by riding the winner of the Derby. Many great jockeys had retired without experiencing it, even champion jockeys. Many great jockeys had waited years and years for a single success: George Fordham won on the nineteenth of his twenty-two attempts. Set against Fordham's name, that of Jack Morris means nothing in terms of jockeyship but the story of his victory on Galopin in 1875 when the hard-of-hearing jockey was exhorted by Fordham himself 'Go on, Deafie!' will live on so long as the history of the Derby is related. Morris died penniless but is not forgotten. Victory presented enduring fame to sixteen-year-old John Parsons. In 1862 Jem Goater chose to partner Spite instead of Caractacus, enabling the teenager to win a Derby on his solitary ride. Parsons sank back into obscurity; but years later he still merited pointing out as he led a yearling round a Newmarket sale ring. Parsons's fame was assured; Goater never would win a Derby despite riding in twenty-eight of them.

Thus, it's impossible not to feel some sympathy for Saxby. Craganour should have been his shot at immortality after his four previous Derby mounts performed as their long odds suggested they would. Compounding his bitterness at losing the mount on Craganour was the knowledge that he'd already been denied a Derby winner owing to the caprice of an owner. In May 1908 he was invited by the breeder-owner-trainer of the filly Signorinetta, the Chevalier Ginistrelli, to partner her in a trial with a view to taking the mount in the Derby. During a lethargic piece of work Saxby gave her a crack with the whip. Suitably stirred, Signorinetta won the trial and booked her place at Epsom. On dismounting, Saxby was asked to come up to Ginistrelli's house. Instead of praise for his performance in making the filly buck her ideas up, he was asked by the Chevalier whether he had used his whip. Saxby excused himself by saying that the filly was so lazy that she wasn't doing a tap. He was not ready for the Chevalier's response: 'Then you will never ride my beautiful mare again.' Signorinetta was the last of her sex to win a Derby at Epsom for sixty-eight years until Empery in 1976. Two days later she added the Oaks.

In the spring of 1913 Saxby was twenty-six years of age and at the crossroads of his career. He was born an 'Army Brat' in September 1886 at Bolarum, a cavalry base in Hyderabad, India, where his father was a Troop Sergeant-Major with the 12th Lancers. As a boy he was apprenticed to Sam Pickering at Kentford House, on the outskirts of Newmarket. The allowances for apprentices were still somewhat eccentric, with boys entitled to claim 5lb in handicaps for 365 days after their first winner. Thus, all promising apprentices were afforded a bit of practice in advance of that initial success in order to make hay during the ensuing year. Saxby had three dozen rides in 1902–03 before riding his first winner at Warwick in the third week of the 1904 season. What with his claim and being able to scale 5st 9lb, he duly went on to accumulate forty-nine winners (including the Liverpool Autumn Cup on Wild Lad) to finish eleventh in the jockeys' list at the age of seventeen. The following year yielded twenty fewer winners owing to the loss of his allowance, but another notable handicap was secured when Pickering's Imari took the Chester Cup; in 1906 Saxby added the Northumberland Plate and the Manchester November Handicap. He won these carrying between 6st 7lb and 7st 5lb. With maturity came extra weight: the 1909 Manchester Cup on Cargill, the 1911 City & Suburban on White Eagle and the same year's Northumberland Plate-Ebor double aboard Pillo were added under weights gradually rising to 8st 9lb.

Such headline victories brought Saxby rides on quality horses. In 1909 he won two of the top juvenile events, the July Stakes aboard Atty Persse's Prince Rupert and the Richmond Stakes on Charles O'Malley for the band of fearless punters known as the Druid's Lodge Confederacy. A year later he overcame two champion jockeys in Frank Wootton and Danny Maher to win Ascot's Triennial Stakes on Admiral Hawke (Pretty Polly's full brother) in the colours of his father's comrade-in-arms Eustace Loder. It appeared Saxby was on the verge of making his mark in the weighing room, but after finishing fifth in the list behind

Frank Wootton with a total of sixty-seven winners in 1909 his totals dipped alarmingly, to forty-seven, forty-three and thirty-eight, as he lost his battle with the scales. At the opening of the 1913 season the lightest he could do was 8st 7lb.

One of Saxby's greatest allies in the trainers' ranks was one who knew from personal experience the value of a lean and hungry youngster: Jack Robinson. It was Robinson who prepared Pillo and it was largely thanks to him that Saxby continued getting his leg across better horses, quality demonstrated by three more victories at Ascot's Royal Meeting in 1912. At one time or another he partnered three of the two-year-old colts who were bound to figure prominently in the 1913 Classics. He won York's Gimcrack Stakes on Flippant for Mr Edward Hulton and partnered Mr Walter Raphael's Louvois to three of his four victories, notably the Dewhurst Stakes at Newmarket.

Towering above both Flippant and Louvois was one of those Ascot victors: Craganour. He could be the great horse to write Saxby's name in the annals of the Turf. He was convinced he'd done nothing wrong in the Guineas and had won the race. Losing it was no fault of his. But he'd heard the rumours. Robinson was less than happy with his performances and it was a fact that he'd been beaten on a second odds-on Ismay-owned favourite at Liverpool, in addition to Craganour and another short-priced animal of his at Newbury. The 2000 Guineas proved a mistake too far for Robinson. Saxby could no longer be trusted to deliver. It didn't seem things could get any worse for Saxby after the Guineas. Yet they did.

The debacle on Ballyoukan at Chester that finally cost him his job with Ismay was swiftly followed by another at Haydock a fortnight later when his mount Rouleau, the 5/4 favourite, lost a race in the Stewards' Room for 'bumping and boring'; that the horse was blamed came as no consolation. After thirty-five rides in the first five weeks of the season culminating in the 2000 Guineas, he had partnered just nineteen horses in the five weeks leading up to the Derby – and despite winning two races on Sir Ernest Schiff's Melton Flier he was replaced with Frank Wootton for the opening race on Derby Day. It seemed as if Saxby couldn't buy a ride – and it bit into his finances as well as his confidence.

Saxby's income came from four sources: riding fees, retainers, presents and betting. A jockey received three guineas a ride plus his travelling expenses and £1 subsistence per day away from home; riding a winner brought an extra two guineas. Presents from grateful owners (and, albeit illegal, back-handers from bookmakers and punters 'tipped the wink') and the fruits of his betting (placed through his leg-man) were a bonus viewed as a divine right. A retainer from a big yard or wealthy owner like Ismay was every journeyman jockey's nirvana. Of course there were expenses to cover – equipment like saddles, boots, whips and the services of a valet – but those thirty-eight victories from 208 mounts in 1912, for instance, contributed a basic revenue of around £735 in fees (about £32,000 today). To that could be added generous presents arising from wins in lucrative events such as the New Stakes (worth £1,962 to the winner), Windsor Castle (£997), Alexandra (£1,570), Gimcrack (£935), Champagne (£1,680), Middle Park (£3,275) and Dewhurst (£1,557).

However, the new season was yielding nowhere near those returns. While the leading jockeys had already registered more than a hundred rides (Albert Whalley was the current leader with forty wins from 165 mounts), Saxby had partnered only fifty-four and won on just nine of them, and was obliged to look up in the table at the new wave of fashionable apprentices led by Walter Buckley and Ernest Huxley (both on fourteen wins) and the latter's brother William (twelve). Although he could hardly quibble with earnings of £200 for three months' work when the country's urban labourers were asked to exist on £60 per annum and farm hands eked out a living on £47 per annum, he'd lost his foothold in the promised land. He'd been robbed of a substantial present after Ismay had been deprived of the £6,800 pot for the Guineas. And he was only human.

So, though it should have come as no surprise, Saxby was bitterly disappointed to learn that when Craganour was sent to Newmarket for his Derby prep run in the Newmarket Stakes over 1¼ miles a fortnight before the Classic, he wasn't only overlooked for this ex-partner but also for other old allies in Louvois and Flippant. Saxby's commitment to Ismay's horse had prompted Walter Raphael to seek alternative partners: Frank O'Neill and Frank Wootton. In fact, Saxby couldn't muster a single ride on the seven-race Newmarket card. As May closed, the scales gave him worse news: he'd gained another 4lb. To his way of thinking each one of them equated to ten more lost rides. Another 120 guineas had gone begging.

The prized mount on Craganour instead passed to Danny Maher, another American, but at least an English-based American; indeed, an Anglophile who eventually sought and gained British nationality. More pertinently, Daniel Aloysius Maher was the acceptable face of American jockeyship as far as the English Turf Establishment was concerned.

Maher was the son of Irish emigrants from Nenagh, County Tipperary. He was born in Hartford, Connecticut, in 1881 and rode his first winner aged fourteen, weighing 4st 9lb. Within three years he was near the top of the American jockeys' list (one day riding a perfect five-timer from five mounts) and registering victories in some of the East Coast's premier events, although he hadn't won any of the American 'Classics', the Kentucky Derby, Preakness or Belmont Stakes. He left America for England in September 1900 (with a winning percentage of 26.1) principally to ride for the American tobacco millionaire Pierre Lorillard (owner of the 1888 Derby and St Leger winner Iroquois) and won on his first two mounts. Lorillard's death in 1901 left Maher to establish himself on two horses belonging to Sir James Miller: Aida in the 1000 Guineas of 1901 and Rock Sand in the Derby and St Leger of 1903.

While many of his compatriots had alienated the Establishment by their brattishness, Maher could charm a vulture off a corpse and jealously guarded his good name. It was said, for instance, that he had deserted his homeland because one afternoon his riding was unjustly, he felt, called into question. After he had been beaten at Leicester on a horse called Sallust – and his riding subsequently referred to the Jockey Club by the local Stewards – he refused to ride at the track ever again.

In truth, something of the snob lived within Maher and he was happy to be accepted into the Establishment fold on its terms rather than his own. Debonair and rakishly handsome, he married the actress Dorothy Fraser and for a spell lived at Cropwell Hall, near Nottingham, and was regularly to be spotted out with the local hunt. In short, Maher quickly came to appreciate the usefulness of forelock-tugging in affecting advancement in his adopted country. Right well could *The Sporting Life*'s Meyrick Good write of him: 'Danny was the "aristocrat" of all the jockeys I have known.'

Key to Maher's exalted status was the patronage of several Turf notables, and none more so than that of Archibald Philip Primrose, the 5th Earl of Rosebery, one of the truly charismatic personalities bestriding the Turf in 1913. The most glamorous Liberal politician of the late Victorian era, he was a gifted orator and wit, a man of charm and intellectual achievement. Yet he was a complex figure, often riven with self-doubt and loneliness, once described as 'a bundle of antagonistic personalities wrapped up in one skin like a mass of writhing snakes in a bag'.

After leaving Oxford voluntarily (he was asked to forego racehorse ownership or his college place), Rosebery was said to have set himself three outrageous ambitions: to marry the richest heiress in England, become Prime Minister and own a Derby winner. By his mid-forties he'd accomplished all three.

In 1878 he married Hannah, the only child of the banker Meyer de Rothschild, with a fortune of £2 million and an annual income of £80,000 (£240 million and £9.6 million respectively); since she was regarded as less than plain it was assumed Rosebery married for money not love. But Rosebery was hardly short of cash. She was his one true love and her early death at the age of thirty-nine was the greatest personal tragedy of his life from which he never recovered: when he did overcome his insomnia he'd frequently dream of Hannah.

He achieved the second of his ambitions following Gladstone's retirement in 1894 with these words of his former leader ringing in his ears: 'I do not know whether he really has any common sense.' His sixteen-month premiership was marked, in the opinion of Algernon Cecil, an authority on Victorian Prime Ministers, by 'so much display and left behind so much reputation with so little actually to his credit in the way of accomplishment'. Or as his former tutor phrased it: 'He is one of those who like the palm without the dust.'

Rosebery completed his 'set' by winning both the Derbies run during his premiership with Ladas and Sir Visto; adding a third in 1905 with Cicero. The string of Classic winners carrying his colours encompassed at least one victory in each of the five. Despite the Classic successes, it remains conjectural whether he liked racing for its own sake. 'Racing is the strangest of all amusements,' he once said. 'It consists of an endless series of painful disappointments varied by a rare ecstasy.' But it was 'politic' to feign love of the Turf. The 'Newmarket Lord Rosebery is an artificial creation', averred one cynical contemporary, 'to obtain that mixture of the sportsman and the politician which has always been warmly appreciated by the English people'.

Rosebery's reputation as a paragon of the Turf therefore begs some scepticism. Wherever one stands on this issue, it's plain that by 1913, at the age of sixty-six and severed from politics – his 'crown of thorns,' as he put it, laid aside – he'd become disenchanted by racing and seldom attended. 'I am kept in total darkness about my horses,' he wrote to Percy Peck, one of his trainers. 'I never go to see them as they are not worth the journey.'

Regardless, his attitude did not harm his status as the elder statesman of the Turf, a member of the Jockey Club for over forty years. An aura cloaked him as surely as the many material and intellectual gifts (he'd written biographies of two Prime Ministers, Pitt and Peel) with which God had blessed him. Viscount Esher thought 'Oligarchic rule was what he understood.' In other words, Rosebery was born to be a Steward – even though he felt his increasing apathy and deafness rendered him unsuitable. And it wouldn't pay to cross him.

Danny Maher could count him as a friend. A genuine affection seemed to have developed between jockey and patron: Rosebery invited him to cruise on his yacht and stay at Dalmeny, his Scottish country seat, was witness at his marriage and stood guarantor when he applied for British citizenship in 1913. Rosebery paid Maher an annual retainer of £4,000 (£176,000): in return Maher rode him the winners of the 1905 Derby (Cicero) and 1910 2000 Guineas (Neil Gow). Beside Rosebery, Maher could call on the horses of mining millionaire A. W. Cox, for whom he won the 1909 St Leger on Bayardo, Lord Derby (1906 Oaks on Keystone) and even Eustace Loder for whom he won the 1906 Derby on Spearmint; he also won the 2000 Guineas in 1912 on Sweeper II for the American H. B. Duryea (plus an Irish Derby on Civility during his one and only visit to the land of his forefathers). Boasting this calibre of patronage, Maher could hardly fail to become champion jockey, which he did for the first time in 1908: on six occasions between 1906 and 1913 his winning percentage exceeded 26 and once reached 29.17. 'He was the most stylish finisher,' said Meyrick Good. 'I have seen him ride races that almost made one's hair stand on end.' Sidney Galtrey called him 'the true artist'.

Maher had successfully adapted the Yankee style to English tracks. He realised that a method honed on the dead-level left-handed American race bowls demanded refinement if it was to cope with undulating courses – including right-handed ones – on which maintaining a horse's balance became an infinitely tougher proposition. He also had to overcome sterner opposition from the home-based jockeys, who themselves had started to come to terms with the American style. To outride them consistently as he did caused trainers like George Lambton, Charles Morton, Jack Jarvis and Sam Darling to rate Maher far and away the American jockey par excellence. 'His seat was the perfect mixture of the old and the new style,' said Lambton for whom Maher had ridden Keystone. 'His patience was wonderful and nothing would induce him to ride a horse hard unless he had him going as he wanted.' Rosebery's trainer Jack Jarvis, though open to a charge of bias, put the current pecking order into sharp perspective: 'Frank Wootton could be very effective, but to compare him with Danny Maher was like comparing a T-Model Ford with a Rolls Royce; they both got you there in the end, but you had a far better ride in the Rolls.'

Every jockey had his weaknesses, however, and Maher's 'patience' was one of his. He was often accused of overdoing the waiting tactics – which notably cost Bayardo the Goodwood Cup of 1910 and quite possibly the great Pretty Polly her unbeaten record in France in 1904. Nor was he said to excel at Epsom: he considered Tattenham Corner positively dangerous (a bad car accident in 1903 leaving him with a fracture at the base of his skull inducing caution) and kept well away from the rails. Other weaknesses came courtesy of his fiery Irish temper and his weight. The former led to much conflict with Frank Wootton. The latter (8st 7lb was as low as he could manage by 1911) combined with his heavy smoking was to leave him virtually speechless through shortage of breath after a strenuous ride. By the end of 1913 he'd secured his second championship but the 115th winner would be the last one of his distinguished career: the flushed cheeks, abnormally bright eyes and rasping cough marked him out as a victim of tuberculosis. Within three years he was dead, at the age of thirty-five and, considering his monumentally successful career, not as wealthy as he ought to have been thanks to an ill-fated investment in a New York hotel.

Nevertheless, in the early summer of 1913, he was still the jockey at the top of every owner's list and Bower Ismay turned to him after sacking Saxby. Immediately after the Guineas, the Derby betting bracketed Craganour, Shogun and Louvois as 5/1 joint favourites. Shogun waited for Epsom but the stamina of Louvois and Craganour was going to be tested over the extra quarter mile of the Newmarket Stakes. If Maher could get Craganour back to his best, there could be no doubting his choice of mount in the Derby. 'Louvois's improvement may be balanced by Maher's skill,' warned *The Times*. 'It is acknowledged that many horses will do more for Maher than any other jockey.' The *Life* rubbed it in: 'Maher's jockeyship will be an important factor and one can write this without in any way reflecting on the ability of Saxby, as he himself would admit.'

The Newmarket Stakes was the only recognised Derby 'trial' between the 2000 Guineas and the race itself, even though the course lacked the twists and undulations of Epsom and the trip was a quarter-mile shorter. The race was perfectly scheduled, coming three weeks after the Guineas and a fortnight before the Derby and, at £2,290, merited winning in its own right. The *Life* considered Craganour to be 'brighter in his coat than on Guineas day, lighter in the back ribs but with muscle in all the right places, his quarters and shoulders – in a sentence he was altogether harder trained'. Dawson Waugh was full of bullish optimism: 'Louvois won the Guineas on practically four good gallops. None of the rest will beat him now.' Nevertheless, the market favoured Craganour at evens with Louvois, who galloped to post with his mouth wide open, on 13/8; punters could name their own price for the remainder.

The race could not have been more straightforward for Craganour and Maher, but less so for Louvois and Frank O'Neill (whom Raphael had enticed over from Paris) once the runners set off on what *The Times* cryptically described as 'an eventful journey'. The two principals were drawn alongside each other in the centre of the track and passing the Bushes could be seen disputing the lead. However, ranging up on the outside of Louvois came Sun Yat and Flippant, and O'Neill suddenly found himself short of room, resulting in the Guineas victor taking a severe bump; he appeared not to like the firmer ground either. Maher was far too sly a fox to miss an opportunity: he set Craganour alight instantly and his horse 'shot to the front in particularly impressive style' to pass Charles Robinson one-and-a-half lengths ahead of Sun Yat with Louvois, whom *The Sporting Chronicle* decided 'gave a moodish display,' trailing a further four lengths behind. 'Craganour's thick-and-thin adherents are naturally jubilant,' observed the *Life*. 'Had this been his first race of the season all would be rosy.' Robinson told reporters his colt 'never went so well before' and stated unequivocally his wish to secure Maher's services for the Derby. The worth of the Guineas form had been exposed, although a few were still unconvinced. The proximity of Sun Yat (unplaced in a humble Plate last time out) was argued to devalue the form, and the scrimmaging had diverted the attention of many. As *The Times* observed: 'It is strange that on the wide Newmarket track where there is so much room, seven horses cannot race without bumping.'

Two days previously, Craganour and Louvois were quoted as 5/1 joint favourites for the Derby, followed by Shogun at 8/1 and the likeliest French challenger Nimbus (who had first appeared in the market on 26 April at 25s) at 100/8 and Great Sport at 20/1. The day following the Newmarket Stakes the betting read: 5/2 Craganour, 5/1 Shogun, 8/1 Louvois and Nimbus and 20/1 bar those four. The true merits of Craganour and Louvois had been franked. Craganour had beaten each of his main rivals or had the better of them on collateral form lines. There seemed nothing standing in his way. The undoubted presence of Maher in the saddle on Derby Day was, almost literally, the signature on the bookmaker's cheque. Money poured on the favourite. Bower Ismay was too much of a pragmatist to start counting his winnings in any case but on this occasion he could hardly ignore one glaring reason why such speculation was unwise. The reason went by the name of Prue.

Prue was one Derby entrant that Craganour hadn't met. As far as the Classics were concerned he was unlikely to come across her. She was a filly and fillies seldom contested the Derby – even with their 5lb sex allowance – principally because they had their own 'Derby' in the Oaks two days later. Sex allowance notwithstanding, they're not meant to be capable of beating the colts, but the success of Tagalie the previous year was still fresh in the memory. Prue was entered for the Oaks; she'd won two of her three races as a two-year-old, having been beaten a length by Shogun on her debut before collecting the huge prize of £4,357 for winning the calendar's richest event for juveniles, Sandown Park's National Breeders Produce Stakes. She then gave Lord Derby's useful colt Light Brigade a stone and beat him a neck in another £1,000 race at Hurst Park. That stamp of high-class performance, plus her close third in the 1000 Guineas, might give her some sort of chance in the Derby. More significantly, her trainer, Fred Pratt, seldom had anything good enough for the race and was keen to run. On 27 May all the trade papers declared Prue a probable runner.

Thus, it was the fate of Prue to be cast in the role of Joker. Or, to be more accurate, it was the role allotted to Danny Maher. For she was a home-bred filly belonging to Lord Rosebery. If Prue ran in the Derby, Maher insisted he rode her. While it's true he was retained by Rosebery, his patron was prepared to release him. Bower Ismay and his wife Connie went to Foxhill on 28 May 1913 to watch Craganour gallop seven furlongs with Eton Boy (winner of the previous year's Royal Hunt Cup) and so well did the colt work that Ismay determined to press Maher to maintain the winning partnership. Eustace Loder had paid Maher £3,000 (£132,000) to partner Spearmint in the 1906 Derby. Bower Ismay now offered the American £2,000 to stick with Craganour. The jockey turned it down, citing his allegiance to his principal employer. Though if one was being less generous, his decision owed more to an incurable habit of currying favour with the English Establishment.

Rosebery was nobody's fool. He knew his filly's chances in the Derby were slim. Nor was it a case of chasing a lifetime's ambition, as he'd already bred and owned three Derby winners. Yet this man of forthright opinion didn't overrule his trainer and declined to scratch his filly with the Oaks in mind. He did, however, release Maher from his obligation to ride her. The entry in his diary for 29 May reads: 'Hot. To London. Long and gloomy talk with Maher. Tried my best to get him to ride Craganour, but in vain.'

Rosebery made no secret of the fact. After all, he was a politician who knew the impact of bad publicity. He wasn't about to allow himself to be falsely labelled the party-pooper at Bower Ismay's forthcoming beano. He wrote to Sidney Galtrey, who broke the story in the *Daily Telegraph*:

> I have tried my very best for two days to get him to ride Craganour and let me find a jockey who would do for an outsider like Prue. But he says he insists on riding Prue if she runs, and her trainer is very anxious she should run, while I cannot give up even an outside chance of winning the Derby. That is how the matter stands, and as I am afraid will continue to stand.

Yet Rosebery must have known the awestruck American would decline his offer, thus frustrating Craganour's owner. Did Rosebery, too, wish to see Ismay denied a Derby winner? It needs little stretch of the imagination to visualise another senior member of the Turf's oligarchy sharing Eustace Loder's distaste for the womanising parvenu Ismay. Why make it easier for Ismay to lead in a Derby winner by presenting him with the one jockey everyone would have loved aboard their runner?

With Maher ruling himself out of contention for the mount on Craganour, Billy Saxby prayed for reinstatement. It was a forlorn exercise. 'An Ismay never goes back!' the press were fond of saying. Ismay snubbed him. He cabled Paris. He sent for Johnny Reiff. The overture had been leaked in the press as early as 27 May, 'but not on authority as Maher is still mentioned'. Reiff must have smiled. Back in 1907 he won his first Derby after

Maher had declined the ride on Orby in order to honour his commitment to Lord Rosebery's Bezonian. News of Craganour's continuing progress on the training ground (ten furlongs at 'a good pace' on 30 May, a mile 'nicely' on 1 June and a final spin of six furlongs before departing for Epsom on 2 June) only served to underline his good fortune.

However, the press was right to exercise caution about the name of Craganour's partner. Clearly, someone had got wind of continuing moves to get Maher aboard the favourite – as Johnny Reiff revealed in a letter to Bower Ismay after the Derby.

> I received word from Lord Rosebery, through Baron de Rothschild, if I would not mind changing my mount on Craganour for that of Maher on Prue. To this request naturally refused, which caused a little unpleasant feeling.

'Unpleasant' was too weak a description for the 'feeling' beginning to darken this Derby faster than ink on blotting paper. Ismay, Robinson and Reiff couldn't have whipped up a stronger undercurrent of ill-feeling had they set out to antagonise. In the Stewards' Room was the disinterested figure of Rosebery, nursing his declining faculties; alongside him was a tetchy Loder, nursing his loathing for Ismay; the judge's box contained an insulted Charles Robinson; and in a weighing room bursting with xenophobia, Saxby seethed even more.

Saxby had managed just four wins since the 2000 Guineas and was existing on a handful of rides. Then a morsel was thrown his way. Walter Raphael had been as unimpressed with Frank O'Neill at Newmarket as the American had been with Louvois. Neither was anxious to continue the association at Epsom. Saxby found himself reunited with Louvois. He arrived at Epsom with as much bile as nervous anticipation. It hurt that he'd been sacked by Ismay. Rejection in favour of an American hired gun like Johnny Reiff made him crave revenge. He'd lost a prized mount to this mercenary once before. Camisard was no Craganour but he'd been Saxby's ride. He won on him at Derby only to find himself 'on the ground' when Camisard ran for a bigger prize at Newmarket next time out. Reiff was beaten a head. Saxby would not have been human had he not rejoiced.

The sum that Maher had been offered to partner Craganour was common knowledge in the weighing room. Reiff was no Maher, but he had to be picking up a four-figure sum for merely crossing la Manche and throwing a leg across the favourite. Saxby hadn't earned that all season. He wanted to win this Derby on Louvois. But if he couldn't, no damn American mercenary like Reiff was going to win it.

# FOUR

# The American Disease

Johnny Reiff was a lightning rod for the resentment festering in the weighing rooms of England toward foreign-based riders, especially the ubiquitous Americans: Frank O'Neill, Matt McGee, Milton Henry, 'Skeets' Martin, Lucien Lyne, Nash Turner, Guy Garner, Jay Ransch, George Archibald, Jack Sumter, Winnie O'Connor. The list seemed endless.

'Many people,' said Classic-winning trainer Charles Morton, who brought over the French-based but English-born George Stern to win the 1911 Derby on Sunstar, 'strongly disapprove of trainers engaging imported jockeys, but every trainer knows that the supply of competent horsemen is so limited nowadays that it becomes practically imperative to engage the best man you can get irrespective of his birthplace.' Another training stalwart, John Porter, lamented: 'Where are our jockeys? We are stranded with little native talent and prey to American talent.'

Johnny Reiff had yet to sit a horse in anger when this hostility was born. In his case it was not the sins of the father that visited him on 4 June 1913, but quite possibly those of elder brother Lester – combined with those of the most remarkable American of them all, James Forman Sloan. The same boats that brought Lester Reiff and 'Tod' Sloan to England carried a cargo of gamblers and hangers-on eager to feed off their genius on a racehorse – and an equally astonishing inclination to flout the Rules of Racing. Both jockeys had been shown the door by the time the 1913 Derby was run, but their legacy was to pollute it. They had introduced the virus that contaminated relations between English and American jockeys.

Lester Reiff landed in England first, in 1896, beating Sloan by a year. He arrived on the coat-tails of William Duke Jnr and Enoch Wishard. They operated a team of ten horses from Red House, in Newmarket's St Mary's Square, that a scribe from *Racing Illustrated* described as a 'string of very useful horses in unpretentious quarters'. The hawk-faced Wishard had been a blacksmith; the walrus-moustached Duke made a fortune from oil and lumber. Wishard thus knew the value of good shoeing and imported lighter aluminium racing plates from the US (made to order at Tiffany's) which were thought to be the equivalent of four lengths over a mile. He was also a shrewd stableman. His boxes were airy and cool with open doors, the opposite of their stuffy English counterparts which often had their ventilation holes deliberately blocked up. The clock, rather than weight, ruled on the training ground. 'Our cousins from across the pond,' stated C. R. Acton, 'were able to teach us something about training as well as riding.' But they also taught the natives something about dope.

Wishard's English rivals recognised the threat. 'They knew their business upside down,' conceded Morton, 'and except that Wishard used dope on some of his horses, nobody had anything against either of them.' George Lambton seconded him:

> He was a remarkably clever man with his horses. There is no doubt he supplemented his great skill as a trainer by making use of dope but in those days there was no law against this pernicious practice. I always thought it a great pity that Wishard ever took to doping, for he was somewhat of a genius with horses, and would, I am sure, have made a great name for himself without it.

Red House quickly established a trend: its first winner obliged at odds of 8/1 'entirely ignored by all except the stable'. More followed at regular intervals, all well-backed at remunerative odds – 100/8, 100/12, 6/1, 4/1. By November the stable had won fifteen races. All were partnered by the freckled, red-haired, tall – he was 5 feet 7 inches – and lugubrious nineteen-year-old born in Americus, Missouri, known to his brothers as 'Reddy' but to the world as Lester Berchert Reiff.

Lester's father, John Wesley Reiff, was a restless hardware merchant who roamed the Midwest and pronounced his name as 'Reef' rather than the Germanic 'Rife' of his forebears. Lester was soon riding a wild bronco pony and, spotted by a neighbour who owned a quarter-horse, was offered a job. At the age of fifteen he graduated to the big tracks of the East and within three years he was winning stakes races, such as the Lawrence Realization on Bright Phoebus. A newspaper report of the latter stated:

> The course was a veritable quagmire and it was pouring down rain but the plucky little jockey urged his steed to its best endeavours. Early in the race the boy had held his horse five lengths behind the leaders. At 100 yards from the stand he was head and head with the first choice and then came thundering in, a close winner by a neck, his first taste of fame.

There was also bad publicity. Lester drew two lengthy bans for 'pulling' horses. Just as it seemed the youngster was not keeping the right company, William Duke gave him a way out. However, the Red House triumvirate did not return for the 1897 season. Thus, when Lord Rosebery concluded his speech to the Gimcrack Club at York by saying: 'The sport we honour tonight was never better and purer than at this moment; never more honest in its followers,' his optimism may not have been entirely groundless. But he'd spoken too soon: 1897 signalled the arrival of James Forman Sloan.

Time shouldn't be allowed to dim the brilliance of 'Tod' Sloan's meteoric flight through the firmament of the English Turf: even trying to do it justice is like trying to replicate a flash of lightning with the end of a wet matchstick. Sloan took English racing by storm. But if a man is judged by the company he keeps Sloan was on trial from the moment he set foot in England. He was too vain and conceited to realise he was being played for a fool by the parasites he brought with him from America. 'I didn't own the boat,' he bleated, 'so I was in no way responsible for what people afterwards called "The American Invasion".' But these spongers certainly owned bits of Sloan. At first, the Turf Establishment was unsure whether to celebrate his genius and forgive his indiscretions: within three seasons it had no choice but to put its house in order. Rough riding, race fixing, doping. All had to be stamped out.

America was to blame. The country had expressed revulsion with the evils of gambling – and, thus indirectly, the Turf. Evangelism was on the march. 'Salvation' demanded the rejection of the Devil's tools: none more than gambling. Diehards sought refuge on the 'outlaw' tracks of the South where they acted as bookmakers, fixing the races and fleecing mug punters. But the tide of reform inexorably swept state after state, and the Yankee gamblers were forced to look further afield: England. They brought old habits. Massive betting coups were routinely planned, all engineered by the judicious application of dope and willing co-operation from the saddle.

Gamblers like the cadaverous former bell-boy Riley Grannan and Chicago hotelier John Drake soon became synonymous with corruption. Thanks to the American jockeys allegedly in their pockets, the Yankee gamblers were reputed to have fleeced £2 million (a staggering £88 million in modern money) from the Ring by the time they high-tailed it out of the country in 1901, leaving behind debts of £500,000. When asked if there were many crooks on the American Turf, one of their trainers, John Huggins, as straight as many of his compatriots were bent, replied with no hint of irony in his voice: 'No. They have all come over here to England.'

Much of the mud slung during this tumultuous period clung

to the tiny polished boots of Sloan. He was brought to England in October 1897 to partner horses in the Cesarewitch and Cambridgeshire. That Autumn Double gamble came unstuck, but when he returned the following September to ride for American tobacco baron Pierre Lorillard and Lord William Beresford his impact was instant and sensational. He won on no fewer than twelve of his sixteen rides at Newmarket's first October meeting and within six weeks he put forty-three winners on the board at an astounding winning percentage of 43.8. He resumed at the start of the 1899 season and rode a further 108; in 1900 his score was eighty-two. That same year his stock was so high that his principal American patron, W. C. Whitney, paid him $5,000 (around £50,000 today) to go back to New York just to ride one race. Sloan won. When he met Whitney afterwards, the owner offered to give him everything he had in his pockets as a 'present' and promptly pulled out a bankroll of $9,000 – and threw in his watch for good measure.

Far outweighing Sloan's innate corruptibility was the legacy he bequeathed English race-riding. He revolutionised English jockeyship. John Porter maintained he had been privileged to see three geniuses in the art of jockeyship during a training career that had spanned half a century: George Fordham, Fred Archer and Tod Sloan.

> From the long stirrup and long rein we passed to the other extreme – the short stirrup and short rein. He not only set a new fashion in riding races but showed us a new way in running them. Instead of the slow, muddling way of waiting, we had races run as they should be. In this, Sloan showed his superiority by his knowledge of pace. He did not ride from pillar to post as others are apt to do, but at a pace that would give his horse a chance to carry him to the end of the race.

Charles Morton went further: 'He found most of our jockeys fast asleep, and was openly contemptuous of our horsemen.' *The*

*Sporting Life* recognised him as 'a great jockey who has brains as well as boots' – even if those brains were not always wired to them.

Trainers found Sloan's streamlined style to be worth 3–7lb over five furlongs. 'As his mount comes head-on to you,' said the *Life* with a mixture of awe and sarcasm, 'the jockey's cap is hardly discernible above the horse's ears.' He also capitalised on his seat to encourage, or pacify, his mount by whispering in its ear. 'Once he had been on the back of any horse,' said George Lambton, 'he had an uncanny intuition into its peculiarities and nature.' English jockeys were made to look silly. 'If I were an owner,' opined Lambton's jockey Fred Rickaby, 'I should not run a horse unless Sloan rode it.'

The betting public loved him. One London newspaper ran a poetry competition in his honour. The winning entry began:

> Of Toddy Sloan now let us sing,
> Whose praises through the country ring,
> Undoubtedly the jockey king,
> Proclaimed by everybody.

Sloan even emulated Eustace Loder by winning the accolade of a place in Cockney rhyming slang, viz 'Tod Sloan – alone', which gave rise to 'on your tod'.

Sloan did not share Lester Reiff's youthful empathy with horses; he grew up fearing them. A pudgy-faced, abnormally short man with stumpy legs and tiny feet, Sloan's shape drew the name 'Toad' from his father – soon altered to 'Tod' at the insistence of his teenage fists. He was built for horses, however, and he bummed around riding exercise until finally being given his first race-ride at New Orleans. By 1894 he was on the verge of giving up any hope of making it as a proper jockey: 'They used to say,' he wrote later with no hint of irony, 'that if a man didn't want his horse to win all he had to do was send for Sloan!' Then a horse bolted with him on the way to the start: he got up out of the saddle and crouched behind its neck to pull it up.

> I couldn't help noticing that when I was doing that neck crouch the horse's stride seemed to be freer and that it was easier for me too. I put two and two together and thought there must be something in it. Once a race had begun, by the strength of legs, the 'crouch' would be assumed and there would be an immediate difference in the action of a horse and his speed. The time came when I determined to put it into practice. Everybody laughed. But I was too cocksure to be discouraged. I persevered, and at last I began to win races!

Sloan arrived on the premier circuit of the East Coast tracks in 1896. No one gave the newcomer much attention until he'd won the Manhattan Handicap and began winning on one out of every three rides. The following year big wins followed in handicaps and stakes races alike. By 1898 his winning percentage rose to a scarcely credible 46 per cent.

Sloan could resist everything bar temptation. He quickly became the 'mark' of bad-hats of every description and paid dearly for it. At his peak, Sloan was rumoured to earn $100,000 a year and be worth half a million dollars (almost £5 million); he was said to be the inspiration for Yankee Doodle ('came to town, riding on a pony') in the Broadway musical *Little Johnny Jones*. Fat cigars, flash clothes and expensive champagne were to Sloan like plankton to a blue whale – and promised only one outcome. He went bust. Even then, only the best was good enough for him. Even down to his last $11 he still ate dinner in one of New York's finest eateries, refused to allow anyone else to buy a drink and gave his last quarter to the hat-check girl on the way out. Sloan's fall from grace inspired a different kind of story: he became the model for Joey Butler's father in Hemingway's short story *My Old Man* about an ex-jockey on the skids who makes an ill-judged comeback that results in his death.

Sloan eventually handed the Jockey Club his head on a platter thanks to his two greatest flaws, gambling and boasting. In the autumn of 1900, he made far too much noise about a mighty punt he and his cronies had engineered on his mount in the Cambridgeshire. The Stewards were looking for any excuse. Sloan was told not to bother applying for a licence for 1901. He was washed-up at the age of twenty-six. In less than four seasons in England, Sloan had won 253 races from 801 rides for a winning percentage of 31.6 that left stellar contemporaries like Lester Reiff (27.7), Danny Maher (25.3) and Frank Wootton (22.8) trailing. He'd learned a painful lesson: inside the velvet glove of the English aristocracy lurks an iron fist. Too many influential people had been on the receiving end of Sloan's Yankee indifference.

However, the authorities had to be on their guard if the virus was to be kept at bay. For the next fifteen years Sloan annually applied for his licence and fifteen times he was annually rejected – though he was never charged with any offence or 'warned-off' and continued to ride work on the Heath. He did make a brief return at a new track in New Orleans, riding a handful of winners but generally ridiculed, before whiling away his time in France in anticipation of regaining his licence to ride in England. He was arrested for card-sharping, raced motor cars, ran a bar on Paris's Rue Daunou, indulged in pigeon-shooting on the Riviera and managed horses until he was warned-off for 'knowingly abetting reprehensible conduct' involving the mare Rose de Mai: rumours of her ill-health were circulated before the 1903 Prix de Diane in order to secure better odds (she drifted from 2/1 to 14s). When war broke out he volunteered as a sharpshooter or a machine-gunner on the grounds that he made 'a smaller target': he was rejected and joined the Red Cross Ambulance Corps instead. In 1915 he was arrested in London for running a gaming house and deported to the USA. There, he managed a billiard hall; Oscar Hammerstein got him a one-man show delivering monologues in vaudeville and he even tried acting in the movies – two of his three marriages (both ending in divorce) were to actresses. At his lowest ebb he advertised himself for dimes on a street corner as 'the strangest dwarf in the world'. Later on, he was spotted working as a gateman at a racetrack on the Mexican border. Eventually he wound up behind a bar in Los Angeles, and, finally in a bed in the charity ward of the city hospital. His last words to a reporter who tracked him down were: 'Hell! There's nothing wrong with me! Be out of here in a week!' A week later, on 21 December 1933, he was dead, killed by cirrhosis of the liver at the age of fifty-nine. He was inducted into the Hall of Fame at the National Museum of Racing in 1955.

Sloan's immediate legacy to the English Turf was less honourable. The atmosphere toward American visitors had grown increasingly hostile. In his memoirs Sloan had recognised this:

> Black clouds were appearing. Some of them were very small certainly, but they were indications of a coming storm. The Americans were openly discussed, and it was well known that certain inquiries were pending, chiefly on the charge of dope. All those connected with American stables were dragged into the talk … the great topic of the American invasion and its consequences. There were plenty who were ready to say anything that could be suggested about horses who had run curiously well or unaccountably badly.

Robert Sievier knew a rogue when he saw one. He was one himself. He wasn't a man to curb his tongue or censor his pen, and he took an instant dislike to these American visitors. Sievier had accomplished more by the age of thirty than most men manage in a lifetime: appeared on the West End stage; served with the Frontier and Mounted Police in South Africa; fought in the Kaffir War; and made a living in Australia as a bookmaker and card-player. After one such card party at his house a guest was found dead beneath the balcony. Sievier never furnished an entirely plausible account of the incident. Bankruptcy followed on his return to England and, not entirely unconnected in all probability, Sievier then married into money: his bride, Lady Mabel Brudenell-Bruce, was a step-sister of the Marquess of Ailesbury. His many enemies in the Jockey Club saw to it that he was warned-off for a time and he turned his hand to running a newspaper he called *The Winning Post*: most of his journalism was of the outspoken kind and frequently landed him before the courts for libel. 'Is it a fact that you are a gambler pure and simple?' an exasperated counsel once quizzed him. 'I may be pure,' replied Sievier deadpan, 'but I'm not simple.' Despite the aforementioned, Sievier might be summed up in one sentence. He was the man who bought Sceptre for £10,500, trained her to win four Classics and £25,650 in stakes yet was still forced to sell her to settle his gambling debts.

Sievier let rip:

> The English Turf was infested with what I can only term an invasion of the scum of the States. Tod Sloan's remarkable success in the saddle was no doubt the attraction which, like a magnet, drew these men to our shores. The way these Yankee adventurers played battledore and shuttlecock with the Ring, or, for that matter, with anybody and everybody when an opportunity arose, is marvellous. They would stand in a cluster, or, as they would themselves term it, a 'bunch', until the numbers for a race were hoisted, and then would step down and back indiscriminately with every bookmaker they could get credit from. The price was no object to them! If it was even money they betted in thousands.

When the money was down, the Yanks in the saddle gave no quarter. 'I am sorry to say that since the American jockeys appeared amongst us we have had more complaints of foul riding than we had for years before,' observed Porter. 'I see it is suggested by some that it is impossible under the American style of riding to keep a horse straight. Well, I have watched races closely, and I have come to the conclusion that there is method in their manner of swerving, as they invariably swerve to the side where danger threatens, be it left or right.'

Apart from Sloan, there can be no doubting the American jockey uppermost in the minds of Sievier and Porter. Lester Reiff had adapted American styles and strategies to English tracks with aplomb. 'Lester Reiff has become almost as familiar to racecourse habitués as any of the leading English jockeys,' *The Sporting Life* observed during Reiff's second English season of 1899. The last day of the season saw him ride a four-timer to raise his total to fifty-five at a strike rate of almost 30 per cent. 'It does not need much perspicacity to see that the highest place in the list will be occupied next year by Reiff if he remains in England,' averred *The Times*. 'The odds at which his horses have started being, as a rule, sufficiently long to yield a considerable profit to those who have followed his mounts.' There was one caveat: 'On the assumption that the Stewards of the Jockey Club renew his licence.'

Doping; race-fixing; rough riding. The Jockey Club's authority was being tested as never before by the American disease spread by Tod Sloan and Lester Reiff.

# FIVE

# Hired Gun

Tod Sloan's success ensured every English owner who raced on a grand scale clamoured for the services of an American jockey. Thus, when Lester Reiff returned to England in the June of 1899 he brought with him his fourteen-year-old kid brother Johnny. Little Johnny was brown-haired with baby blue eyes and a round face; he stood barely four feet and weighed 4st 7lb. He looked like a cherub but he'd been mentored by a master in all the arts of jockeyship – including the darker ones. He became an overnight sensation.

Born on 29 January 1885, John William Reiff began riding exercise for Enoch Wishard at the age of twelve. The 'thorough, severe and relentless' regimen that made him into a jockey was described by a visiting reporter from the *Oswego Daily Times*:

The boys sleep in a stable loft over the horses. Summer and winter they are awakened at daybreak by a groom pounding on the boards. They jump into their clothes, shivering in the early morning's chill and hurry to a pump, where a douse of cold water sweeps away the cobwebs of sleep. Then to the horses, and for two hours each boy exercises his string. A string consists of two horses and exercising means walking them about the track until they are agreeably warm. After breakfast the youngsters exercise another string and employ an hour or more in doing chores. The afternoon they spend at the track and by 8 o'clock in the evening they must be abed. Plenty of time is allowed them for recreation. The trainer encourages the boys in such sports as swimming, running and ball-playing.

The youngster had had his first race-ride – and first win – only the previous year. He was so miniscule (less than 4st) that the winning trainer had to carry his saddle back into the weighing room on his behalf. 'The women on the grandstand and the clubhouse lawn were the most enthusiastic cheerers,' reported the local newspaper. 'It seemed like a baby riding!' Later that year he rode winners in Chicago before journeying west to San Francisco. 'A child wonder of the pigskin!' declared one local reporter. 'Johnny is a good-looking little fellow and bright as a new dollar. He is absolutely fearless and will take chances that Tod Sloan would not accept for $100,000. While his mounts are necessarily restricted to good actors, there is no horse at the track that Johnny would not ride if allowed by his older brother.' He left having won thirty-three races, including several stakes and two trebles. 'Master Reiff is a perfect little gentleman and a great favourite with the ladies.'

Sloan was as enthusiastic about young Johnny as he'd been about Lester:

> He was quite a little kid when he came over to England. He was such an infant that some of the jockeys used to complain about his being allowed to ride; they were afraid of hurting him. Johnny liked to hear me talk and used to ask me different things, which I told him freely, but the kid had already any number of ideas of his own, was a born rider and had developed it with his own intelligence. Johnny had the instinct for jockeyship, and from every gallop and race he rode in he seemed to learn something.

Whatever self-confidence Johnny Reiff possessed, he made less noise about it than Sloan. His grandson John Hackett Reiff recalls:

Grandaddy once told my wife and me that 'A horse is the dumbest creature that God ever created.' So much for that mystical connection of a jockey and his steed – at least this jockey and his steed. That didn't prevent his being able to control a horse well enough to do his bidding. But he was a modest man who never shouted about his accomplishments.

Within a week of crossing the Atlantic, Johnny gave the English press its first opportunity to sing his praises: he won the New Biennial at Ascot on Bettyfield. The *Illustrated Sporting and Dramatic News* commented:

> It is a fact that he is not big enough to unsaddle his own horse. There was a terrible lot of dead weight under his saddle and he was quite unable to carry it into the weighing room. He adopts Sloan's style of riding to a certain extent, and it takes some looking to see him at all as the horse he is riding comes up the course. But he rides a good race, and in spite of his body weight, is much stronger than he appears to be. He is a quiet well-behaved lad, and respected by his employers.

Elegant ladies cooed over the little boy. 'How is it your horses win so often?' one asked. 'Pineapples, ma'am,' he replied, instantly gaining his first nickname 'Pineapple Reiff'. He soon gained another. One of his regular mounts was the colt Knickerbocker. The association – and his smart knickerbocker breeches – saw him dubbed 'Knickerbocker Reiff'. Admirers queued for an audience. Lord Rosebery was kept waiting while the boy finished a game of marbles; when someone would ask him 'Are you ready?' he'd playfully reply 'No! I'm Reddy's brother!' The Duchess of Marlborough introduced him to the Prince of Wales. Johnny didn't allow his years to curb his American temerity. He told reporters:

> The Prince said 'I am pleased to see you' and shook hands with me just like any American might do. He then asked me what my

weight was, and also asked me my age and some other questions, which I answered. But it was getting time for me to be mounted and I could not wait any longer, even for the Prince of Wales. So I hopped on Knickerbocker and was off.

The hysteria peaked at Newmarket on 7 September after he rode Bishopswood to win the Alexandra Plate. The horse had not run all season and as soon as he went to post everyone knew why: he was a brute of a beast made to appear all the bigger and nastier by the mite trying to control him. Reiff fought him for furlong after furlong of the one-and-a-half-mile trip, sometimes in and sometimes out of the saddle, until, by dint of steering him against the rail, he settled the colt – and got up to win. 'How can this boy control the big and high-spirited thoroughbreds on whose backs he is thrown?' asked the *Life*. 'But he does control them; and not only that, he handles them artistically and rides cool and determined finishes.'

Then, as the 'boy wonder' slipped exhausted from the saddle, a handsomely dressed woman rushed up, caught him in her arms and kissed him rapturously. Hugging and kissing little Johnny swiftly became the fashion. His picture adorned the pages of every sporting journal, alongside all manner of human interest stories. 'It was amusing,' said the *Illustrated Sporting and Dramatic News*,

> to see the youngster lugging a big box off the racecourse at Lewes with a couple of Persian kittens in it, a present from an admirer. Johnny is very fond of kittens and took as keen an interest in his new charges as the usual English schoolboy does in his first brace of white mice. Although Johnny has an old head on young shoulders, he retains the charm of boyishness which renders him so great a favourite.

With tongue planted in cheek, *Vanity Fair* added:

> He is a good-looking little fellow and has not yet succeeded in

making himself unpopular. He means to be quite unspoiled by success. He likes sweets and he loves his mother.

The younger Reiff completed the season acknowledged as 'the peer of the midget jockeys of the world'. Before returning home to visit his parents he enrolled at an English school to fill the gaps in his education resulting from a life in stables. Behind him he'd left a burning fuse. Just two of his winners had been for Wishard. Other trainers were starting to snap up his services. English jockeys began to grow resentful. Nor had it escaped their attention that the 'boyishness' of the younger Reiff might be acting as a convenient smokescreen for those manipulating him for their own ends.

As the new century dawned, American jockeys began routing the opposition, with brother Lester leading the charge: 'For the first time in the history of our Turf,' said the *Life*,

> has a horseman who is not an Englishman succeeded in heading the list of winning jockeys. Great as was the sensation caused by the successes of Tod Sloan when he first came over, there was never any fear that he would ride more winners than any of our native horsemen, but from the middle of last season it became evident that Lester Reiff would make a great fight with Sam Loates for the premiership.

Reiff beat Loates by six with 143 winners; Johnny rode 124 to finish third.

None of the 1900's Classics fell to the Reiffs, but they collected a host of other elite events. Johnny was the star turn, scooping the Epsom Cup, Princess of Wales's Stakes, Royal Hunt Cup, Stewards' Cup, and Ebor Handicap; he even rode a treble at the Curragh on his first visit to Ireland. The brothers won seven of Ascot's twenty-eight races – with their compatriots Tod Sloan, 'Skeets' Martin and Ben Rigby contributing ten more. This was meaningful. Ascot was far more pre-eminent in 1900. The average prize-money of a British race was £274; and, if one excluded the five Classics, only fourteen of the calendar's 1,924 races offered prizes in excess of £2,000. Ascot hosted six of them, plus a further seven worth over £1,000. Their hot streak continued at 'Glorious' Goodwood where the Reiffs won twelve of the twenty-two races, Johnny landing no fewer than eight of them.

The statistic that worried some, however, was the number of those successes where the brothers occupied first and second – and the number of times the American gamblers backed the right one. It's not difficult to understand why English jockeys were fast becoming envious and resentful of American rivals viewed as profiteering. Lester was now so wealthy he'd acquired some Pennsylvanian oil wells. And even fifteen-year-old Johnny had raked in £5,000 (£250,000) during 1900.

There were other worrying signs. The Wishard-Duke partnership had been dissolved amid some acrimony. Once it emerged that the principal backer of Wishard's new stable was Richard Croker, the threat to the integrity of the sport heightened immeasurably.

Croker was born in County Cork, his family crossing the Atlantic during the Great Famine when he was seven to settle in New York. Barman, blacksmith and professional prizefighter were his occupations prior to becoming the boss of Tammany Hall, the organisation that controlled the Democratic Party in the city. 'He was the King and New York was his kingdom,' commented one of his political rivals: even a murder charge brought against him for shooting an opponent during an election campaign failed to stick. For seventeen years 'Boss' Croker was alleged to have used his position to amass considerable wealth by skimming 'off the top'. Ultimately, an investigation into the sale of public offices and legislation prompted his departure overseas. Croker maintained his wealth derived from real estate and railway stock. Few believed him.

Croker's arrival in England was greeted with awe. 'The leonine head, the mighty jaw, the penetrating eye, the deep chest and the commanding voice all bespoke the power,' wrote T. P. O'Connor in the *Daily Telegraph*. Ever-present cigar clamped firmly in his mouth, Croker had money to spend and plenty of time on his hands in which to do it. He settled on racing: he loved anything on four legs, be they racehorses, trotters, donkeys or bull-dogs, for which he was quite prepared to spend up to £1,000 on a champion specimen. More significantly, Croker spent £4,000 obtaining first call on the services of Lester Reiff.

Equally ominous was the appearance of John W. Gates, the Chicago millionaire. Gates's first venture into business was corn-husking; thereafter, it was threshing, woodcutting and manufacturing barbed wire. These yielded the clout to play on the stock market and led to the *New York Times* saluting his astuteness with the words: 'Gates is a born bull.' Along with the grand mansion and the yacht came the racehorses. 'He picks winners with the same ease and certainty that has long marked his deftness with stocks,' continued the *NYT*. 'He knows horses as he knows men and tells you frankly that he likes them better!' A bet was irresistible to Gates. One year he stopped in Memphis for the Tennessee Derby. Word of his presence soon spread through the gambling fraternity and, wishing to take on the 'man', a group of local dudes made up a pot and knocked on Gates's hotel door. 'Want to gamble a little?' said Gates. 'Fine! I'll betcha a million! How much coin did you boys bring? Fifty thousand?' Gates took a coin from his pocket. 'Still, I can use a bit of chicken feed. I'll match you. Call it. Heads or tails?'

Dope was the other currency underwriting the racecourse gambles. Doping was not illegal. Administering a slug of port was a popular Victorian ploy to give a recalcitrant animal a 'gee-up' and was said to have been instrumental in Taraban's Goodwood Stakes-Northumberland Plate double of 1871; George Fordham actually finished the bottle given to Digby Grand before the 1872 City & Suburban Handicap. Whisky was also used: trainer Tom Cannon reckoned his mount Melton was sozzled on it when beaten by another Derby winner, St Gatien, in the 1886 Jockey

Club Cup. And a Bishop Auckland vet named Jimmy Dean used to market 'speedy balls' that he claimed could improve a horse by 14–21lb – then sold the names of those who had partaken!

Nor were doped horses exactly undetectable: 'A desire to imitate the feats of the whirling Dervish, to climb trees, or lie down with the restful, happy expression of a pig in clover, accompanied by heavy sweating and bad attacks of the shocks,' observed *The Sporting Luck* drily, 'is foreign to the well trained thoroughbred.' The 'Yankee Alchemists', as Sievier dubbed them, had honed their methods to a fine edge. Cast-offs were bought for a pittance, so long as they had been fully exposed to the handicapper. Then, suitably energised with quantities of stimulant, generally cocaine, they were placed in superior company so that Gates and the rest of the 'bunch' could back them at fancy prices.

The 'Alchemists' had every right to be confident. By 1900 they had elevated the art to a science. The practice originated from the week-long American meetings that turned into the survival of the fittest. Trainers resorted to cocaine or strychnine as a pick-me-up (as opposed to an opiate as a 'stopper'), diluting it in a mixture of carbolic acid and distilled water (sometimes even with a solution of nitro-glycerine added for good measure!) and given hypodermically. But the swelling or wound left by the syringe could be detected under careful examination. More sophisticated methods involved administering the drug in capsules coated with a gelatine whose thickness varied according to the time when the dope was to take effect. The times of trial gallops were used to ascertain the precise effect of varying amounts of dope and the dosages required for each individual animal.

The career of Royal Flush was a celebrated instance of an exposed animal showing abnormal improvement. The six-year-old had shown decent form in the early part of 1899 to win four of his first five races before making no show in the Cambridgeshire. Since he'd carried the colours of Fred Lee – a man about to become a Jockey Club handicapper – it's reasonable to assume the horse had reached the limits of his achievement when he was sent to the Newmarket December Sales. Wishard paid just 400 guineas for him. Once he got to work on the horse in 1900 it won both the Royal Hunt Cup at Ascot and the Stewards' Cup at 'Glorious' Goodwood, two of the most competitive handicaps and two of the biggest betting opportunities in the calendar. Johnny Reiff rode him on each occasion, winning the former by a head at 100/7 and the latter by six lengths as the 11/4 favourite. At Ascot, Drake boasted he'd bet £5,000 on Royal Flush at 40/1 and 15/1, landing £275,000 – the equivalent of £12 million in modern money. At Goodwood the 'crew' allegedly took the bookmakers for a further £100,000, although one only has the word of the Americans to go on: it's impossible to believe the Ring could actually have stood those amounts.

When necessary the American horses could run 'cold' as well as 'hot'. Croker's Americus was once opposed by a single rival whom he'd slaughtered a month previously. The Yanks piled their cash on the no-hoper, which duly obliged. The selfsame ruse was put into operation when Wishard accepted the challenge from the connections of Eager, one of those beaten off in the Stewards' Cup, to a match race with Royal Flush. Eager was now 2st better off. The match only had one likely outcome, which the Americans knew full well: so they ran Royal Flush minus dope and backed Eager to win.

As the 1900 season closed, it's hard to know whether Johnny Reiff was a superstar or a scallywag – or both. *The Sportsman* insisted: 'Johnny Reiff is now the favourite jockey in England. He has supplanted Tod Sloan in the affections of Turf-loving Englishmen. His riding was quite one of the features of the past season.' By the same token it would be naïve to think some of that cash won by the 'bunch' didn't wind up in his pockets. 'That many of our jockeys bet, and not always in half sovereigns, there is reason for believing,' commented *The Sporting Life*.

It is not as if a jockey always backed the horse he is riding, that would imply an assurance that he would do his best to win, but unfortunately the money is at times on some other horse or against his own mounts, which is the simplest form of making winning sure. So many excellent people are convinced that the American contingent were playing an underhand game that an exhaustive inquiry is as necessary as welcome.

To describe comments like these as a delicate hint to the Americans would be committing a grave injustice to the word. This amounted to a notice of eviction being held to their door, in readiness for the hammer and nail to complete matters should they continue to thumb their noses at the racing authorities. They did – and the Establishment struck back.

Few people in racing were in any doubt as to the identity of the driving force behind this crackdown. Easily the most powerful and most charismatic figure in the Jockey Club – not a difficult accolade to win – was George Lambton's elder brother John, the 3rd Earl of Durham.

Known to his detractors as 'Determined Jack', Durham was obsessed with upholding the integrity of the sport. Nobody was immune. Back in 1887, as a Jockey Club tenderfoot of thirty-two, for example, he'd drawn attention to the inconsistent running of the horses belonging to former Senior Steward Sir George Chetwynd – which resulted in his being sued for libel. Even though he lost the suit, the award of a farthing in damages left him feeling vindicated.

Now Durham turned his wrath on the Americans and their malpractices. In October 1900, he referred to Newmarket as 'a dumping ground' for American jockeys during a Jockey Club meeting (Americans occupied five of the top ten places in the jockeys' championship), and his remarks were placed in the public domain by the racing correspondent of *The Times* – and roundly criticised. Durham refused to concede:

I have never condemned the 'style' of riding of American jockeys or of American training. But I do disapprove of 'the methods' of American jockeys and I do not welcome as a benefit to the English Turf the influx of their 'followers'. These can be dismissed in a sentence. They consider horse racing as merely an instrument for high gambling.

Many were shocked that Durham escaped litigation, especially from Lester Reiff, whom he'd specifically targeted. The inference was clear: Durham's accusations were grounded in fact. Durham received support from Leopold de Rothschild, fellow member of the Jockey Club and one of the most respected and best-loved men in the sport. In a letter to *The Times*, de Rothschild stressed the urgent need to deal with the menace of doping, race-fixing and the lax attitude of American riders toward betting and race-riding. He concluded with a powerful plea: 'I think that if one or two of the chief offenders were severely dealt with the others would be amenable to reason … if guilty, no mercy should be shown to them.'

The Jockey Club's stance needed to harden. It did. Before the start of the new season, the Jockey Club read the riot act: foul and/or rough riding would not be tolerated. Any jockey caught receiving presents from persons other than the owner of the horse they had ridden would lose their licence. Any jockey 'who may be proved to have been engaged in any betting transaction will have his licence withdrawn at once'. Any hint of corruption would result in the culprit being warned-off.

Straight away the authorities went gunning for the Reiffs. It took time. Normal service had resumed. Johnny won the Liverpool Spring Cup, the Great Metropolitan and then the Victoria Cup; Lester took the Chester Cup. In the Derby, Lester partnered the favourite Volodyovski, who'd been trained by John Huggins especially for the race, and took the lead early in the straight to hold-off all challengers. The first American to be crowned champion jockey had become the first American rider to win the Derby. Lester seemed unstoppable.

But there was one thing that could stop him: the witch hunt.

It intensified after he partnered The Scotchman, the 5/1 second favourite, to victory in Epsom's Craven Stakes on 4 June. 'The attention of the Stewards' was called to the 'variation in form' shown by the winner and Holstein – the 7/4 on favourite beaten 1¾ lengths under Johnny – compared to their running in the Stockil Stakes at Doncaster a fortnight earlier, when Holstein won comfortably. The Stewards pronounced themselves 'quite satisfied' with the explanations given by their respective trainers, Wishard and Huggins. On 17 July, at Newmarket, it was the facile success of Arizona II in a selling plate that came under scrutiny: the Wishard-trained colt justified odds of 7/4 on by three lengths, despite making no show as an unconsidered outsider on his only previous run. Once more, the Stewards could find no evidence to take the matter further.

The Jockey Club wouldn't give up. It finally struck gold with the New Barns Plate at Manchester, on 27 September. In a humble £100 race contested by four runners, Johnny, on the 7/4 second favourite, Croker's Oaks third Minnie Dee, beat his brother on Whitney's De Lacy (5/1) by a head. Despite Wishard and Huggins expressing total satisfaction with the riding of their horses, the Stewards were dissatisfied with the 'manner' and 'suspicious riding' of the champion jockey on the runner-up, and reported him to the Stewards of the Jockey Club. Four days later the Stewards decided Lester had not done his best to win, withdrew his licence and warned him off Newmarket Heath.

And Lester Reiff's version for reporters?

Johnny was penned in rather closely on the rail, and I was next to him. I saw that he would go down if I did not pull out, and naturally I did so. This caused the argument, although there is hardly a boy riding that would not have pulled out under the same circumstances. Even had it not been my brother, I would have pulled out rather than have caused an accident that would have resulted in the crippling of a boy.

In the pages of *The Sportsman*, 'Vigilant' expressed what the majority were thinking:

> The warning-off of Lester Reiff was only what was anticipated by those who have carefully watched his riding for the last few months. I could give half-a-dozen instances in which his performances have been more than suspicious, the worst features of the case being that they were foreshadowed by the state of the market. It cannot be said that he has not been given every chance. Indeed it is the opinion of most people that no English jockey would have been allowed so much rope. It is to be hoped that the lesson will be taken to heart by all his compatriots. So long as they conduct themselves properly they are welcome in this country. The Stewards of the Jockey Club and public opinion will not, however, tolerate unfair dealing.

The racing Establishment had snuffed out Lester Reiff's career on the English Turf, just as it had Tod Sloan's. Perhaps it also hadn't taken kindly to a less publicised action of Reiff's: he'd snubbed King Edward VII, rejecting an offer to ride his horses as the methods of the Royal trainer, Richard Marsh, were 'too severe'. *The Times* declared: 'It is certain he will not appear in the lists again, for apart from the improbability of his licence being restored to him, it is known that he will not ride again.' (He did, but very infrequently; and never in England, despite the Jockey Club cancelling his warning-off notice. He returned to California, married the daughter of a San Francisco veterinarian and won the Los Angeles Derby; after buying a small string and racing with moderate success he eventually gave up the Turf and entered the real estate business in Alameda, on the edge of San Franciso Bay, where he resided until his death on 10 October 1948 aged seventy-one.)

The message was writ large: Johnny would be next. He rode out the season (winning the Cambridgeshire and Dewhurst) to end up with eighty-nine winners, the last coming on Archduke II for Wishard. The gelding wore Drake's colours, but he'd already fled the country along with the rest of the 'bunch'. The American exodus was joined, for now, by Johnny Reiff. Wishard's horses were sold off: Sievier actually paid 240 guineas for Scotchman II 'partly out of curiosity … his neck showed the puncture scars where the hypodermic syringe had been inserted'.

In years to come, Johnny Reiff revisited these turbulent times with his grandson, John Hackett Reiff:

> In regard to the allegations of improper activities with gamblers, he told my wife and me: 'I didn't do anything of that sort, but I sometimes felt that I could not fully trust Lester to do the right thing.' He didn't clarify the statement further. But, of course, 'If one lays down with fleas, one can expect to wake up with fleas.' The brothers were sometimes employed by known American gamblers of questionable character and were, therefore, in danger of 'waking up with fleas' in the public's eyes.

It only remained for the scourge of doping to be eradicated. Half-hearted efforts to arouse awareness of the problem had come to nought. A meeting under the auspices of the Animals' Aid Society and Institute to discuss the issue ended in farce. None of the invited trainers and jockeys appeared; nor did the chairman or the Professor of Veterinary Science. It soon became clear that nobody among the 100 present either knew anything about the subject or were prepared to divulge what they did know, and the desultory conversation that ensued was notable for frequent outbursts of laughter.

George Lambton eventually took responsibility after watching a heavily drugged horse win a race in 1903, and then crash into a wall and kill itself because the jockey was unable to pull it up. Playing havoc with form-lines and, by masking infirmity, menacing the future soundness of the breed, was bad enough but endangering human lives was too much. Lambton obtained six bottles of dope and administered five of them to horses he described as 'some of the biggest rogues in training'. None had a scrap of form: four of them won, including Ruy Lopez, who'd defied the best jockeys in the country but now streaked up in the Lincoln Autumn Handicap in the hands of an apprentice. Lambton gave away the sixth bottle to the Duke of Devonshire, who used it to win with a horse of his called Cheers the following week.

Lambton had proved his point. Rule 176 (i) came into operation for the 1904 season:

> If any person shall administer, or cause to be administered, for the purpose of affecting the speed of a horse, drugs or stimulants internally, by hypodermic or any other method, he should be warned off the Turf.

It appeared as if the Jockey Club had relegated Croker, Wishard and Reiff to the role of bit players. Then, three years later, a colt of Croker's called Orby won twice to put himself bang in the Derby picture. Having been refused permission to keep horses in training at Newmarket, Croker had switched them to the Curragh. No Irish-trained runner had won the Derby and the English press scoffed at the possibility. Even Croker nursed reservations. Nonetheless, Irish money poured on Orby and Croker let him run – with the proviso that a top rider should be engaged. Danny Maher couldn't be tempted to abandon Lord Rosebery's Bezonian. Lester Reiff was no longer an option, but Croker hadn't forgotten his younger brother. Johnny was available; and the tiny boy rider of dope-fuelled lightweights had matured into an astute and highly accomplished jockey of twenty-two.

A call that was to become increasingly common went out: 'Get Johnny Reiff!'

Controversy had never stopped snapping at Johnny Reiff's heels like the devil's black dog since 1901. But he'd come to terms with its company.

He had few complaints with life. Race-riding had made him a wealthy man; he had feathered his nest through wise investments on the stock market, he had a beautiful young wife and an infant son, John Robert. The boyish face of 1899 had filled out a tad, as nature dictated it must, but with the aid of a lengthy sweat-bath he could still do 8st. What marked out the mature Johnny Reiff were the eyes, no longer angelic baby-blues but cobalt sharp, full of knowingness, pools of ruthlessness.

He had returned to Europe in 1902 after the scandal of the previous autumn that saw the exile of his brother but his destination wasn't England. He followed the money. He went to France, accepting a retainer to ride for M. Maurice Caillault, whose horses had won every big prize in the last four seasons including a Triple Crown with Perth. Reiff had, of course, ridden a few times in France, advertising his abilities by winning the Prix du Conseil Municipal of 1901 on W. C. Whitney's Kilmarnock II.

Reiff's French adventure began splendidly, with victory in the Poule d'Essai des Poulains (the French 2000 Guineas) and Prix du Jockey Club aboard Retz for M. Camille Blanc, and successes for Caillault at home and in Germany; he even demonstrated his accustomed flair at Ascot with a couple of victories. At season's end he led the French jockeys' championship. Though he'd traversed the globe and earned enough money to spend the rest of his life in luxury, he was not yet out of his teens and youthful naivety was to cost him dearly. In the autumn Reiff's head was turned by Edmond Blanc, the owner of the most powerful stable in France. 'Being a youngster of seventeen, coupled with the fact that M. Blanc had the best horses in France, I signed the contract,' Reiff explained to American journalist Carleton Burke years later, with no concession to misjudgement or poor advice. 'I was also being offered much more money than the contract I had with M. Caillault.'

Like Tod Sloan before him, Reiff was to discover that jockeys were servants not masters and that he'd been foolish to alienate a man like Caillault. Within a month his licence was withdrawn amid vague allegations of 'unbecoming conduct' and 'associating with disreputable characters'. The incriminating evidence was passed to the French Jockey Club by the police after a number of American bookmakers and gamblers were charged with fraud. Reiff wasn't called to give any testimony. However, a weekly newspaper called *La Vie Au Grand Air* simultaneously published a story stating he had been 'ruled off' for pulling a horse called St Saulge, and he felt obliged to sue on a point of principle: for one franc and apologies in six different daily newspapers. At the court hearing, the trainer of St Saulge swore the horse was 'ill, unreliable and untrustworthy' and the owner declared that before employing Reiff he had 'examined his English references and found them to be excellent; they'd never had cause to complain of his riding and didn't believe he'd pulled the horse in question'.

Reiff won his suit. 'The Jockey Club stated that I was ruled off under a certain rule which stated that the Stewards could rule off a trainer or jockey without giving any cause.' Reiff's cry of innocence may have been justified on this occasion, but no one could say that he didn't have it coming in the wake of sundry others.

Reiff returned to America to spend the winter with his parents on their new Californian farm with every hope of resuming his French career in 1903. However, his licence wasn't restored: he went to Kentucky and Chicago instead. At first his fortunes seemed to be looking up when he landed the Kentucky Oaks, but this proved nothing more than a prelude to a disaster that almost proved fatal. He moved on to the Harlem racetrack at Chicago and suffered a terrible fall with an animal called Galba on 19 June. In addition to a broken collarbone, he was left with his left eye skewed eerily to the right, and a grotesquely swollen head resulting from a massive haematoma on the brain which necessitated extensive surgery and the insertion of a metal plate.

The immediate prognosis was that he would never ride again. 'If I had had my wits about me I would have stayed on the ground where I fell and the horses would have jumped over me,' he explained. 'But I got up too quickly. One of Galba's hoofs struck me in the head, and I was unconscious for three days.'

Reiff was not short of grit. In March of the following year he announced that although he would never ride in the United States again, he was prepared to consider returning to ride in France. Reiff got his wish. In July 1904 the French Jockey Club restored his licence, and Caillault gave him his job back. Reiff returned to forge a particularly lucrative partnership with Macdonald II, winning the Furstenberg Memorial at Baden-Baden and the French St Leger, the Prix Royal Oak. The pair went one better in 1905 by taking the Prix du Conseil Municipal, the biggest French purse of the autumn. His personal life was also in the ascendant. On St Valentine's Day 1906, in the English church on the Rue Aguesseau, he married into French Turf 'royalty', his bride being Maria Denman, the daughter of Richard Denman, the English-born trainer to Edmond Blanc. The French idyll didn't last long. More money was put on Reiff's table. This time the currency was the deutschmark.

German racing was experiencing a period of expansion. 'Berlin badly needs something which will elevate the sport of kings to the level it enjoys in other countries,' declared a member of the German racing authority. 'The immense salaries which American riders and trainers are commanding here does more than anything else to induce Turf patrons to reorganise the whole game on a better and higher level.' The pre-eminent stable of the von Weinbergs had secured another young American in Winnie O'Connor; its rival, the Seibertsche stable, headed by the Bavarian nobleman Count von Langpuchoff, sought their own Yank. They'd seen plenty of Reiff at the international Baden-Baden meeting every August, most recently when winning the Grand Preis in 1906 on Houtbois. Langpuchoff offered Reiff a £3,000 annual retainer. Reiff spent two-and-a-half years based in Germany but failed to bring his employers any better luck in the major races. 'The Seibertsche stable unfortunately did not have top-class horses,' he informed Carleton Burke.

> I very often was on the ground without a mount in the big stakes, because the stables with good horses seemed always to have their own boys under contract, which precluded them from signing me for special races, had they wanted to do so – and I believe some owners would have liked me to ride.

The outcome was never in question: Reiff returned to France and settled in Maisons Laffitte. His undiminished skills were soon evident. In a special article for *The New York Times* Pierre Rochecourt wrote:

> Reiff is a magnificent horseman, has a beautiful seat and is a good judge of pace. He has the ideal physique for a jockey, although he is beginning to get a little too heavy, and when he trains down too severely he does not ride at his best. His speciality is a waiting race. He will wait until everybody believes that the other horse is going to win and then he starts out and snatches victory from defeat. His success is all the more flattering to his prowess as a rider because no influence is brought to bear to pick his mounts.

More French Classics followed: the 1911 Royal Oak on Combourg; the 1912 Poule d'Essai des Poulains on De Viris, who also collected the Prix du President de la Republique, a £4,000-er at Maisons Laffitte. Reiff was snaffling major races seemingly at will. And not just in France.

Reiff's reputation as a gun for hire inevitably led to excursions across la Manche. In May 1907, for example, Querido was sent over for the 2¼-miles Chester Cup. The long-striding four-year-old had warmed up by winning a two-miler at Longchamp before confounding traditional wisdom that small horses were the *beau ideal* around Chester's tight racebowl. Whizzing round the Roodee was just like being back home in the States as far as Reiff was concerned, and Querido romped home to justify 9/4 favouritism. Just under 8st, he'd been a shoo-in, because Querido was no mere handicapper: later in the summer he and Reiff beat a field of top-class animals to win the Prix du President de la Republique.

Then, at the end of May, came Croker's cable. Croker wouldn't divulge how much he had paid Reiff to partner Orby, but it was widely bandied in the press that Maher had rejected as much as £1,575. 'I never wanted to win a race quite so much as I wanted to win that one,' Reiff recounted to Carleton Burke. 'The prejudice against American riders had forced them all to leave England a few years before, and had resulted in Lester being warned off. I knew and liked Mr Croker, from the years I had ridden for him, and I was anxious to do him a favour.'

Reiff rode Orby in light work round Tattenham Corner on the day before the race. His mount had been backed down from 50/1 to 100/9 by the weight of Irish money but was still only fourth-best in a field of nine behind the odds-on favourite, the 2000 Guineas winner, Slieve Gallion. The English remained aloof to the Irish challenge, their attitude encapsulated by Royal trainer Richard Marsh's words to Sam Darling after being taken to see Orby: 'I have seen a beautiful horse this morning, but I never saw one look much worse to run in the Derby.'

The favourite was in front entering the straight. Then his stamina ebbed away: his stride shortened and he veered to the right – allowing Orby to pass him on the inside. Although Orby also began to show signs of distress, Reiff kept him going to win Ireland its first Derby. Reiff rubbed it in. He told reporters Orby's success did not say much for the quality of the others, whom he reckoned were inferior to several colts back in France.

These two English visits won Reiff races worth £8,480, no sweeter way of exacting revenge for the slights of 1901. But his greatest English achievement was yet to come. In 1912 Walter Raphael owned a grey filly, Tagalie, of whom he thought a lot. At two she'd finished third in the Cheveley Park Stakes; once she'd surprised the pundits by winning the 1000 Guineas comfortably on her reappearance, Raphael set his sights on the Derby. She couldn't handle the colts in the Newmarket Stakes en route to Epsom, and her Australian jockey, Leslie Hewitt, took the blame. Once again the telegram was sent: Johnny Reiff was booked for the Derby.

Reiff proved money well spent, demonstrating sublime confidence in his own abilities. He rode a copybook race from the front, putting all the other jockeys to bed, to win by four lengths. Watching from the stands was Tod Sloan: 'English jockeyship is a disgrace,' he told *The New York Times* with, doubtless, considerable relish and not a little sourness in his voice. 'Their horsemanship was indescribably bad, showing neither skill or nerve.' Two days later the filly failed to make the places in the Oaks under George Stern at 2/1 on. Nor did she shine in the Eclipse, Reiff's only other English ride in 1912, or the St Leger – in which she was partnered by William Saxby.

Tagalie's success would have dramatic repercussions. Two Englishmen impressed by Reiff's masterly front-running exhibition were Jack Robinson and Bower Ismay. Their runner Hall Cross had finished down the field; his jockey, William Saxby, 'put to sleep' by Reiff. In addition, the filly's humiliation of the colts – the second instance in five years – would tempt the connections of another to have a go in 1913, and in so doing deprive Bower Ismay of the services of his preferred jockey, Danny Maher. Ismay would be forced to look elsewhere. Importing a hired gun for the job, however, might be provocative. Especially if his name was Johnny Reiff.

But when Bower Ismay made a decision he stuck by it. That's the way it was with all the Ismay menfolk.

# SIX

# The Spare

Bower (the maiden name of his maternal grandmother and pronounced as in 'power') was the male half of twins born on 24 January 1874 to Thomas Henry and Margaret Ismay of Liverpool. Sets of twins ran in the Ismay family: only two years earlier Margaret Ismay had given birth to twin girls and her husband had twin sisters. The Ismays clearly possessed powerful genes.

Bower's father was a remarkable individual who typified the Victorian ideal for 'getting on'. A small, dusky, intelligent man with dark penetrating eyes, Thomas Henry Ismay hailed from a seafaring family residing in the small Cumbrian seaport of Maryport and was apprenticed to the Liverpool firm of Imrie, Tomlinson & Co., shipowners and shipbrokers, at the age of sixteen. After completing his indentures he widened his experience by sailing to the west coast of South America before starting up in the shipbroking business on his own account in 1857 at the age of just twenty. In 1867, he acquired the bankrupt White Star Line of Australian clippers and two years later he joined forces with his former boss William Imrie to found the Oceanic Steam Navigation Company. In 1870 the firm took the momentous decision to compete for the Atlantic trade in addition to the Australian. The business boomed and setbacks were few. At Ismay's retirement dinner in 1892 the company chairman stated: 'I am sure it would not be Mr Ismay's wish that I should enter upon any fulsome eulogy of his services but I must take it upon myself to say that we owe the largest share of our prosperity to him.'

Ismay had gone up in the world and was determined to advertise the fact. He purchased Dawpool, on the Cheshire side of the River Dee, and spent £53,000 rebuilding the property in the style of a sprawling Elizabethan manor house (tended by a staff of thirty-two) as a bricks-and-mortar testament to his station; whenever a White Star steamer navigated the estuary she would salute the chairman with her siren. He rejected offers of a seat in Parliament and, in 1897, a baronetcy: he told son Jimmy that he was born Mr Ismay and intended going to his grave as Mr Ismay, but the truth may be that he would not settle for anything lower than a peerage.

Ismay did move in exalted circles. He visited President Grover Cleveland at the White House and entertained some of the most prominent people in Victorian society, including the Queen herself, the future King Edward VII and the German Kaiser. When he died on 23 November 1899, aged only sixty-two years, the Kaiser cabled his widow: 'The shipping world has lost one of its most illustrious members and the country mourns a life's work crowned with unparalleled success.' Ismay had become the most successful steamship owner in the world and left £1¼ million in his will (£60 million). His wife wrote: 'Shall we ever be able to live without him?'

Thomas Ismay was both a harsh taskmaster and a hard act to follow. Indeed, for a Victorian patriarch and self-made man like himself to have been anything else would be surprising. Growing up in his shadow must have daunted his children, especially his sons. He'd married Margaret Bruce, the daughter of another Liverpool shipowner, and they had nine children, two of whom died young. Life in the Ismay household, even in the palatial surroundings of Dawpool, was austere: it was granted no central heating and, whatever the weather, the fires were never lit until tea-time. The day began at 6.30 in readiness for family prayers conducted by Ismay himself at 7.30 before he left for the office.

Breakfast, like every meal, commenced in silence until such time as Ismay had spoken; the newspapers were of no concern to his four daughters; and any emotional succour for his children was provided by their devoted nurse, 'Mardie'.

The eldest of Ismay's three surviving sons was bound to feel the most pressure. Joseph Bruce grew up shy and prickly, a brusque defence mechanism that led many to view his personality 'overpowering'. Bruce left Harrow after only five terms to be privately tutored for a year and embark on a lengthy cruise to New Zealand. There followed an apprenticeship with the family firm during which he was obliged to endure the brickbats routinely administered by his father without complaint. Home was no sanctuary. One dressing-down came after he'd ridden his father's favourite hunter without permission and the animal broke its leg. Being sent to New York as the local agent for the White Star Line was seized eagerly. He proceeded to paint the town red for a few months until he met Florence Schieffelin, 'an undisputed belle' according to the New York papers. She was the petite and pretty daughter of a prominent lawyer and, swept off his feet, he determined to marry her. Mr Schieffelin insisted they must live in the United States; Bruce was assured by his father that if he wished to succeed him as head of the firm he must return to England. He did so and assumed active control of the White Star Line at the start of 1892.

From the outset it was as if Bruce Ismay was on a mission to manufacture a negative public persona. Years of paternal humiliation appeared to have corroded the kind and generous spirit frequently on show in private. His marriage became sexless and he more domineering. His public utterances tended toward the sarcastic and his manner of conducting business bordered on the autocratic, raising the possibility that the boy-bullied had become the man-bully. 'I have such a horrible undemonstrative nature, I cannot show people how fond I am of them. Very often a word would make things right, but one's horrid pride slips in,' he wrote to a friend. 'I absolutely hate myself.' Nevertheless, he'd learnt the ways of business at the feet of a master. In 1902 he capitalised on them to effect the inclusion of the White Star Line in the International Mercantile Marine Company, formed to control Atlantic passenger fares and cargo rates. Two years on he assumed the positions of president and managing director. One summer evening in 1907 he sat down to dinner with Lord Pirrie, one of the partners in Harland & Wolff, and plotted the construction of three super-liners to outshine those of their closest competitor, Cunard. The second of the three was launched on 31 March 1909. Her name was *Titanic*.

Jimmy Ismay was five years younger than Bruce – and his father's favourite son. He was the academically clever son who went from Harrow to Exeter College, Oxford, and took his BA degree before entering the firm. He was at ease in company and instantly likeable. The only thing Jimmy did which openly irritated his father was to marry into the aristocracy: Lady Margaret Seymour, daughter of the Marquis of Hertford. Her death in childbirth hit him badly, and after the IMM's formation he retired from the business to adopt the life of a farming landowner.

That left Charles Bower, the male half of twins (the female, Charlotte) born on 24 January 1874. We know next to nothing of Bower Ismay's childhood other than his introduction at the earliest opportunity to his father's circle of influence: at the age of eleven, for example, he was allowed to dine aboard the *Adriatic* when his father entertained the Prince of Wales. Within the year he was sent away to Cheam in preparation for entry into Harrow. Shortly before his fifteenth birthday in January 1889 he became one of forty boys enjoying the Spartan conditions of Small House. He shared a room furnished with one table, two chairs, a wash stand and two beds, folded against the wall when not in use. Any other comforts were his responsibility. Photographs of home and kin were discouraged. Other unwritten laws included trousers to be worn turned-up, hat tilted forward. There were to be no displays of unbridled enthusiasm except in applauding sporting prowess. The latter was the gold standard. Character not intellect was a boy's best currency. Wimps and swots lay open to ridicule and bullying: he might expect to be folded against the wall inside his bed or even poked with a toasting fork should his singing displease house elders after dinner.

There was no danger of the teenage Ismay being ridiculed as a swot. Apart from one report stating 'he has done well this term', he appeared to struggle academically, though not so badly as his contemporary Winston Churchill whom he encountered in the bottom form. Like Bruce, it appeared he didn't care overmuch for Harrow. His 'trade' background would have drawn taunts from peers raised to view wealth as inherited not earned. Birth determined status; one's breeding, one's folks, singled out a gentleman.

Bower Ismay spent three years at Harrow, leaving at Christmas 1891 shortly before his eighteenth birthday. Then, like Bruce, he was packed off on a four-month round-trip to New Zealand during which it was hoped he'd discover some direction in his life. The ploy backfired. A week after his return a worried Mrs Ismay wrote in her diary: 'Thomas, Jimmy and myself had a long talk about Bower.' The upshot of these deliberations was enrolment in an Oxford 'crammer', but he showed no sign of the progress necessary to gain him a place at the University itself. On 26 June 1893 his mother continued: 'Received a letter from Mr Hawkins saying Bower had not passed his examinations having failed in three subjects,' and a week later she confides: 'Thomas had a long talk with Bower this morning about what he would like to do as he does not want to return to Mr Hawkins. I advised Bower to see Bruce and consult with him.'

Given his own experiences in the offices of the White Star Line it's perfectly possible Bruce Ismay advised his youngest brother to seek alternatives. If so, he didn't look very hard. Business didn't interest him and he was well provided for. Bower's grandson Michael Manser expands:

Mrs T. H. Ismay's diaries were completely quiet about what Bower did afterwards. There are occasional mentions of him hunting or coming with friends. Her diary entries are quite brief and factual. She certainly does not go into her feelings, but you can nevertheless pick up certain things from them. Bruce and Jimmy were seen as responsible and conscientious and hard working. Bower, we worry about. Bower seems to have been allowed to do what he will.

Doing 'what he will' amounted to nothing more arduous than hunting, shooting and playing polo at the Liverpool and Wirral Polo Clubs where the *Liverpool Courier* recorded him as a 'noticeably accomplished rider'; this talent was further demonstrated aboard his hunters Cruiser and Colonial Girl in point-to-points. 'His unassuming personality has gained him a wide circle of friends,' added the *Courier*. He was also said to be fond of twinkling an eye in the direction of the ladies. Bower Ismay was approaching the end of his twenty-sixth year with nothing tangible to show for them when the outbreak of the second Boer War in September 1899 offered him the chance of adventure and excitement.

The Boer War has been described by its most eminent historian, Thomas Packenham, as 'the longest, the costliest, the bloodiest and the most humiliating war for Britain between 1815 and 1914' and lamented by Rudyard Kipling as 'where the senseless bullet fell'. It was the last of the old wars which saw young men flock to the colours with scant consideration for what that might entail. It was going to be a big-game hunt through southern Africa with the minimum of discomfort. However, it was the first time since the Crimea over forty years before that the British Army had been asked to fire on white troops. As one veteran commented: 'It was the worst run war ever – no transport, no grub, nothing…'

By the end of 1899 the British garrisons in Kimberley and Mafeking were surrounded and the relief columns were defeated. Reinforcements were a matter of urgency: in the absence of conscription the call went out for volunteers. The War Office was particularly keen on raising a force of mounted infantry drawn from the ranks of the country's existing Yeomanry, whose best men were the equal of any regular army recruit. Committees chaired by peers and fox-hunting gentlemen mushroomed throughout the Shires with the aim of enlisting 'men who could ride well and shoot straight … young fellows sportsmen to the core, sons of professional men, farmers, merchants, fellows in all stations of life with the true British love for sport strong in them'. Northumberland landowner Henry Scott proposed the recruitment of a hundred mounted volunteers and the setting up of a fund for the provision of horses and equipment, and a sum in excess of £50,000 was soon gathered – sufficient to raise three squadrons of Yeomanry. The first two were en route to South Africa within six weeks; by late February 1900, 'C' Squadron was deemed suitably equipped and trained to join them.

Among its 'young fellows and sportsmen to the core' was Bower Ismay, who had hunting and farming connections in the north east. The job description fitted him to a tee and he'd nothing better to do with his time. His mother was distraught. She was still mourning the loss of her husband and the thought of her youngest son rushing off to war was too much to bear. 'Bower went to Newcastle and arranged to go out with Lord Grey's troop as a trooper,' she wrote in her diary on Boxing Day 1899. 'I am very distressed about it and don't like the idea of him going out to South Africa at all.'

Unfortunately, once Bower Ismay reached a decision he tended to abide by it – and reject any debate. It was a character-defining trait of all the Ismay men. Free of his father's daunting presence he could be his own man without fear of paternal opprobrium. The following day he wired his mother to say that he'd passed the necessary medical, riding and shooting tests – none of which were remotely severe – and was accepted immediately. 'I fear he'll have to go now,' his mother confided. 'God grant that he may be spared to come safely back to us.'

Mrs Ismay was due another shock. Her son decided to get married before he left for South Africa. 'I was very surprised

and said I could not agree ... but Bower had already applied
for a special licence.' His bride-to-be was Matilda Constance
Schieffelin, the third of prosperous New York lawyer
George Schieffelin's four daughters, whose elder sister Florence
had married Bruce Ismay twelve years before. Their daughter first
set eyes on her future husband, she approaching seventeen and he
just fifteen, when he'd sailed to New York on the maiden voyage
of the White Star's *Teutonic* in August 1889, along with the other
Ismays, to meet the new in-laws. Constance was a tiny avian-like
creature whose combination of broad, straight mouth, wide-set
eyes, strong brows, nose and jaw nonetheless made a forceful
impression: this was reinforced, in the words of her great-niece
Pauline Matarasso, by a personality 'rebellious and voluble'.

The marriage took place at St Paul's, Knightsbridge, on
13 January 1900: invited guests were few as the family was,
according to *The Times*, 'in deep mourning'. *New York World*
settled for: AMERICAN GIRL WEDS A DEPARTING WARRIOR.
Neither mother attended. Mrs Ismay's diary entry states blandly
that she 'did not feel equal to it'; the reasons behind Mrs Julia
Schieffelin's absence remain conjectural. It was rumoured that
the Schieffelins had been anxious about accepting the first Ismay
brother into the family since they feared this was yet another
instance of bagging a 'Dollar Princess'. Upper-class English
gentlemen swapping kudos for cash by marrying American
heiresses was very much in vogue – despite xenophobes snip-
ing that 'Yankee' women dressed and talked too loudly. The
Schieffelin sisters escaped such bitchiness, Constance being
referred to as 'a transplanted rose' by one gushing reporter. The
Prince of Wales, who knew what he was talking about having
enjoyed the favours of one such interloper in Jennie Jerome, the
wife of Lord Randolph Churchill, had no doubts: 'American
girls are livelier, better educated, and less hampered by etiquette.
They are not so squeamish as their English sisters and they are
better able to take care of themselves.'

Whether Bower Ismay would have volunteered or married

had his father been alive is debatable. However, with T. H. Ismay in his grave, any thoughts as to his mother's feelings were brushed aside. The day after the ceremony the newly-weds left London for Newcastle, where Bower was due to complete his training.

Ismay's regiment sprang from a unit of volunteer cavalry raised to maintain order during the unstable years following the Napoleonic Wars. Although grandly re-titled the Northumberland Hussars in 1876, the regiment was locally referred to as 'The Noodles', a derisory term for simpletons, and lampooned as 'Fireside sowjers who dor'nt gan to war.' Indeed, even as it prepared for war, one of its own described them as 'never quite aspiring to be cavalrymen – they were too much like the fox-hunting fraternity'. However, if Ismay and his chums did regard the war as a sporting adventure they were destined for a rude awakening: ninety-seven out of a complement of 355 were left behind in South African graves when 'The Noodles' returned home in June 1901.

Coming through it all relatively unscathed was 3137 Private C. B. Ismay of 14th Company 5th Battalion Imperial Yeomanry. He didn't leave with the rest of his regiment but, as his bride sailed for New York to stay with her parents, he embarked from Southampton on 10 February aboard the Union Company's steamship *Norman*, 'a distinguished passenger', in the words of *The Times*: 'Physically the men were as fine a body as one could desire. They go to face the most serious work that men can do and put their lives at stake for their country they leave behind.' Apart from exercising the horses round the stable deck of a morning (Ismay received £40 for bringing his own mount) and participating in rifle drill in the afternoon, there was little to lift the tedium on the three-week voyage to Cape Town. Only a brief step ashore at Madeira, when taking on coal, and the rowdy 'crossing-the-line' celebrations at the equator broke the monotony.

Although British forces had employed tried and tested battle-field tactics to subdue the Zulu, their Dutch countrymen were proving a tougher proposition. The Boers were well-armed and, crucially, well-mounted – which enabled them to exploit their knowledge of the terrain with vulpine cunning. The first phase of the war had ended with the breaking of the sieges at Mafeking, Ladysmith and Kimberley and a series of set-piece successes for the British. Unfortunately for Bower Ismay, he arrived just in time for the next phase of the war, the impossible phase, that involved tracking and 'bagging' the wily forces under de Wet and de la Rey. These 'commandos' would scatter at the first sign of a pitched battle; there would be no glorious battlefield charges with sabres pointing to the sound of the bugle. This would be a dusty and dirty campaign characterised by vicious guerrilla attacks from the Boers and equally nasty reprisals on the part of the British. By the middle of May The Noodles were attached to Lord Methuen's column, combing the Orange Free State and Transvaal on a series of night marches that left Ismay nodding in the saddle, all the while troubled by the thought that 'Brother Boer' might just elect to play the part of hunter instead of fox, the only inkling of role reversal being the 'klip-klop' sound of a hail of Mauser bullets whining in his direction.

Ismay avoided 'the senseless bullet', but disease killed as many soldiers in South Africa as the Boers did. After almost a year on campaign, Ismay found himself in Lichtenburg's hospital with a slight fever. It proved impossible to shake. A month later he was hospitalised in Kimberley with what was described as 'ague' and then transferred south, out of the combat zone, to the Yeomanry's field hospital at Deelfontein, in the Northern Cape, with malarial fever. This 800-patient hospital largely comprised tents and prefabricated huts. British field hospitals had been roundly criticised and, though recently improved, conditions tested Ismay's mettle. He was placed on a low cot – still in his uniform – and issued two blankets to keep himself warm during the night. Twice daily he was visited by the doctor, who administered quinine. He wasn't permitted solids: sustenance amounted to condensed milk mixed with warm water, beef tea, rice and milk, watered lime juice and as much fresh milk as desired. He'd pray no dust storm blew up to fill the tent, his bed and his clothes with grit.

After a month's convalescence, Ismay was invalided home aboard the *Tantallon Castle* and reached Southampton on 13 April 1901 to find Jimmy on the quayside. The brothers reached Dawpool that evening. Mrs Ismay's prayers had been answered. 'It is delightful having Bower back,' she wrote in her diary. 'The farmers and our men took the horses out and pulled the carriage in. Bower spoke nicely to them and thanked them for their reception. He is looking well.'

Perhaps his harsh experiences had even conspired to make a man of him.

# SEVEN

# Black Balls and White Feathers

At the age of twenty-seven, Bower Ismay returned from the Boer War in the prime of life, unencumbered by children and the need of a job, never having to worry where the next penny was coming from. If he'd made enemies none seemed apparent as the opening decade of the new century saw him pick up the carefree threads of the last. Once more he surrendered to the life of a man without a care in the world: a man whose industry made a sloth seem hyperactive. 'My grandmother once said to me, perhaps frivolously,' recalls Michael Manser with a smile, 'that Bower went to the White Star office for one day, said he caught a cold, and never went again.'

That 'cold' and any other inconveniences during the dozen years leading up to the 1913 Derby failed to quash Bower Ismay's appetite for hunting, shooting or racing. Matters intellectual held no interest for him. His waking hours revolved around the pursuit of pleasure. Within months, he was competing at the Liverpool Polo Club and partnering his pony Leash to victory in the Eastham Plate at Hooton Park, the pretty little racecourse halfway between Chester and Liverpool. In the spring it was the turn of point-to-point races, his most productive mount being the chestnut gelding Toffee whom he partnered to victory in four successive years: after a Bedale victory, *The Winning Post* congratulated him on riding 'a splendid race on his gallant thoroughbred'. Naturally, there was also much fine shooting to be had, locally or at his Scottish hunting lodge of Dalnaspidal, a few miles from Pitlochry in Perthshire. Bower's scrapbook for two days in August 1905 proudly records him and two guests bagging fifty-eight brace of grouse and thirty-six brace of snipe; on the 'Glorious Twelfth' of 1911 he and three others bagged the biggest reported haul in North Perthshire: 150 brace of grouse.

The image of a wastrel gave him no immunity when he was tainted by scandal: and he was embroiled in not just one scandal but three. That only one of them might be laid directly at his feet is irrelevant: they enabled any enemies to view those feet as being made of clay – enemies who might be in a position to exercise their disapproval. For example, an enemy like Eustace Loder.

☞

Bower Ismay's fondness for hunting took him to the Shires and his love of shooting led him to Africa. And it was from this combination that the first scandal sprang.

Finding a place to put down roots had proved a challenge for the Ismays. As keen hunters, the prerequisite for any permanent home was a location in prime hunting country. North Yorkshire was their preference since the family had farming interests there. While they house-hunted, the couple lived in rented accommodation at Smeaton Manor near Northallerton, enjoying many days out with the Bedale and the Hurworth, but failing to find anything suitable they switched their attention south. In September 1908 they settled upon Haselbech Hall in the Pytchley country between Kettering and Northampton.

The Ismays were a valuable injection of fresh blood for the local 'set'. The invitations soon accumulated on the mantelpiece at Haselbech (pronounced Hazelbeech), triggering a merry-go-round of cocktail parties, dinner parties, shooting parties, rollicking hunt balls in Northampton Town Hall and the kind of long lazy country-house weekends to encourage illicit liaisons. Major race meetings like Liverpool, Newmarket, Chester, Epsom,

Ascot, Goodwood or Doncaster provided a wonderful excuse for the like-minded to congregate: to gamble and to gossip, to carouse and to cavort. Among the Ismay's fellow socialites were Reginald and Margaret Loder, who lived at Maidwell Hall, just two miles away across the Northamptonshire countryside.

Reginald Loder was Eustace Loder's elder brother by three years. He'd preceded Eustace through Eton and Trinity, and then served in the Royal Bucks Hussars. Inheriting Maidwell and a legacy of £200,00 in his father's will, he'd latterly become a respected member of the Northamptonshire community, acting as a Justice of the Peace, holding the office of High Sheriff in 1899 and being a generous patron of Northampton General Hospital. While Loder's public works may not have brought him into Bower Ismay's orbit, his membership of the Pytchley and the fact that its point-to-point course ran across his land most certainly did. And he had a comely and vivacious wife.

'Reggie' had vaulted several steps up the social ladder on 25 July 1895 by marrying 24-year-old Lady Margaret Hare, the elder daughter of the Earl of Listowel. Her mother, Ernestine Brudenell-Bruce, was the younger daughter of the 3rd Marquess of Ailesbury and a relative of the 7th Earl of Cardigan who led the charge of the Light Brigade at Balaclava. She'd split her formative years between the urban grandeur of the Listowel's Knightsbridge residence overlooking Hyde Park and the rural splendour of the Convamore estate beside the Blackwater river in County Cork. When in London her name was ever-present in the Court Circular of *The Times*. In May 1888 she was presented at court, to the Princess of Wales, and her life became a whirl of invitations to every grand house, from levees at Buckingham Palace and Windsor Castle to masked balls at the Earl and Countess of Ilchester's and Lady Londesborough's. In short, she represented quite a 'catch' for Reginald Loder. The guest list for the wedding added further confirmation of the groom's arrival in the top tier of the British aristocracy: it included a princess, a duchess, two earls, three marchionesses and no fewer than a dozen countesses; his best man was the son of a duke. Whether this conventional and rather staid autocrat was the kind of man who could keep a woman of his new wife's exotic plumage caged forever was questionable.

Maggie Loder was thirty-eight years of age when Bower Ismay arrived at Haselbech. Slim of shoulder and oval of face, she couldn't be described as a great beauty in the conventional sense: but her heavy-lidded eyes, strong straight nose and full mouth lent her a sphinx-like elegance that made her classically attractive. Her photograph featured in the society pages of the newspapers as often as Bower Ismay's did not. The 'Gossip' columns of *The Northampton Independent*, for example, referred to 'the charming wife of Mr Reginald Loder kindly consenting to distribute the prizes' or 'Her Ladyship's cheerful readiness in giving her influential help' to some worthy institution; the *Northampton Mercury* deferred to her as 'an expert horsewoman with a fine seat and beautiful hands, a fine shot, fond of fishing and an accomplished pianist'.

A mutual passion for hunting and shooting soon brought the Northamptonshire neighbours together – at home and abroad. Once the completion of the Uganda Railway from Mombasa to Kisumu in 1903 had thrown open the game-rich plains of the African interior, the continent became a magnet for couples like the Ismays and Loders. Affluent gentry devoured the regular photographic essays extolling the delights of a winter safari in journals like the *Illustrated London News* and answered the call of advertisements inviting them to board the so-called 'Lunatic Express' and billet in the Edwardian splendour of Nairobi's Norfolk Hotel. After enjoying a spot of pony racing at the East African Turf Club, they'd head out into the *pori*, the wilderness, that drew the hunter north past Mount Kenya into the Great Rift Valley toward Lake Turkana. These safaris amounted to a display of brazen colonialism that became an integral part of the Ismays' pursuit of pleasure. Big-game hunting provided the ultimate thrill of the Edwardian age without going to war. They'd be away for three or four months at a time (as many as seven in 1907–08), using train, boat and train once again to reach Nairobi via Naples, Sicily and Aden, or else sailing the Nile via Luxor and Khartoum.

Such expeditions were not to be taken lightly, even if the objective – transfer the entire lifestyle of the English upper class to Kenya, and then kill everything that moved – was simple. Before their first safari in October 1907, Ismay sought further advice from a seasoned practitioner, Lord Cranworth, and received the following accumulated wisdom: 'Take plenty of wine after sunfall, preferably burgundy and port, keep your spirits up, bowels open and wear linen next to the skin.' In order to 'keep spirits up' tents were laid out to resemble drawing rooms, often complete with writing desks and bookcases, and sported porches and verandahs; every hunter could be assured of returning to camp to find his, or her, own thirty-four-inch travelling canvas bath (with initials) full of hot reviving water. Ismay's list of provisions ran to five pages and included such diverse items as tins of Oxford & Cambridge sausages, plum pudding, sardines, cocoa and Quaker oats. Plus three bottles of liqueur brandy, sixteen bottles of Scotch and eighteen half-bottles of champagne. The entire order was repeated nine times. The list of equipment included the latest cameras from Eastman Kodak: while Bower shot game with his Mannlicher .256, Connie photographed them.

No thought was given to conservation of the species. The new settlers regarded every species as pests, vermin to be exterminated. If it moved it could be shot and invariably was: one aristocrat was even accused of resorting to a Gatling gun. The diaries of both Ismays testify to the accuracy of Bower's Mannlicher: on their first safari he shot thirty-two different species. The ritual would be completed with the white hunter posed over his kill for a triumphal photograph. Then the party returned to a fresh camp, or *boma*, pitched under a canopy of acacia for shade and girded by some rocky outcrop or boulder-strewn stream for protection, there to bathe, rid themselves of ticks, change for dinner and watch the sun set from beneath the green fly of the dining tent, sipping their lime cocktails or Tusker beer.

Safari quickly earned for itself a degree of notoriety, not merely for the slaughter of game but for the scandalous behaviour after sundown. The experience was positively seductive, an atmosphere heightened by the intense heat, the consumption of too much alcohol and the freedom from society's conventional rules and regulations. Safari could, and frequently did, lend itself to a spirit of waywardness. Morals loosened: women, especially, found the sexiness of safari utterly alluring. One favourite pastime involved the gentlemen sticking their manhoods through holes in a sheet so the ladies might vote on their favourite. Partners were routinely shared with no jealousies fanned or grudges held.

Bower Ismay and Maggie Loder began an affair. That was the opinion of Connie Ismay, who intimated as much to her grandson, Michael Manser:

> I knew my grandmother very well. She didn't die until I was twenty-eight and I spent a lot of time with her. It was always assumed that one knew of the affair with Maggie Loder. That's what I've always known. My mother, however, never discussed her father. She was fifteen-years-old at Bower's death and I think she idolised and idealised him. But I'm sure it was Maggie Loder.

The distinct possibility arises that the Derby of 1913 was lost on the plains of East Africa. It would have needed just one whispered aside over tea at the Ritz or a whisky at the Turf Club for the damage to be done. It's unlikely Ismay would have felt vulnerable to any repercussions from Reginald Loder. One of Loder's grooms, Arthur Sturgess, later wrote a memoir in which he recalled a briefing in Loder's study when he got too close to the desk behind which his employer was sitting: 'Get back on the mat!' Loder barked. Sturgess records looking into Loder's eyes and seeing 'nothing he need have any fear of'.

That the Ismays and Loders met on safari isn't questioned.

During the 1911 safari Connie Ismay's diary entry for 16 March records: 'Tea at Lady Cranworth's to see Lady Maggie Loder.' By 14 May she records: 'Wrote to RL today.' In themselves these read as perfectly innocent comments, but to Connie Ismay they must have carried far greater significance. Her diary entries are sporadic and brief at best. She fails to mention the birth of her own daughter on 21 July 1909, for example, and seldom does she make a note of her correspondence. Was 'RL' Reginald Loder?

Published references to Ismay's affair with Eustace Loder's sister-in-law stem from an unsupported statement to that effect in the book *Infamous Occasions* written in 1980 by John Brennan (a.k.a. John Welcome), an Irish-based Turf historian and solicitor who knew people familiar with every facet of Eustace Loder's story, among them Loder's stud manager Noble Johnson and his nephews Peter Burrell (Johnson's successor) and Giles Loder, who inherited Eyrefield Lodge. Unfortunately, Brennan declined to name the lady in question: he'd given his word to his 'well-connected' source.

There's no reason why Brennan's claim should not be treated as totally *bone fide*. As a solicitor he was unlikely to commit to print anything he couldn't substantiate in a court of law. Connie Ismay died in 1963, seventeen years *before* the publication of Brennan's book and she couldn't, therefore, have been influenced by its veiled allegation. One is left to draw but one inference: Brennan was confirming what Connie Ismay already knew to be a fact.

The remaining issue – mindful of its implications for Eustace Loder's actions on Derby Day 1913 – constitutes a crucial one: did the affair *pre-date* the race? Connie Ismay's diary for 1909 is hardly conclusive evidence, however loaded her unique refer-ences to someone outside her immediate family make them sound. Unfortunately, no diaries exist for the years 1910, 1912 or 1913. The absence of the last is less significant since it's known Bower was in England while Maggie Loder was in East Africa, but destroying such diaries on account of what they contained might be perfectly understandable if they referred to details of an affair. Connie may have adjusted to leading separate lives under one roof (she was never averse to holidaying without Bower) and had just grown indifferent to her husband's peccadillo. There is, nonetheless, evidence of a marriage gradually in crisis (as there is in the other Ismay-Schieffelin marriage between Bruce and Florence).

Michael Manser reflects:

My grandmother's character must have made her difficult to live with. She could be impossible. She was a tiny woman, only 4ft 11.5in. tall, who ate a large cooked breakfast every day and virtually nothing else. She had a fear of being buried alive and inserted a clause in her Will that a main artery was to be severed after her death! She used to tell me that she always wanted to please Bower and that was very difficult to do because he used to say she was the most extravagant woman in England and then immediately afterwards he would be telling her she was the meanest woman in England. She thought this was unreasonable because all she was trying to do was to please him by saving money. They worried constantly about their finances.

My grandmother had a great many virtues. She was lively and entertaining, whereas Bower was undemonstrative and rather introverted. She was intrigued by all forms of new gadgetry, cinematography and photography; she had her own dark room. She was academic and literary, learning Arabic and transcribing books into Braille for the blind.

But, she told me, Bower only ever read one book and that was on stable management! Shooting and hunting were their common denominators. In fact, she said she was convinced she and her sister had married the wrong brothers.

The Ismays did make a strange couple. It took eight years for the couple to put down roots at Haselbech, a decision which appears to have prefaced the birth of their only child, Florence

Delaplaine, in July 1909, when they were well into their thirties. This delay in starting a family, and subsequent failure to increase it, is surprising given the usual proliferation of children in wealthy families, not least the Ismays. Of course, difficulty conceiving or carrying a child to full term may have played a part. Yet, if so, it is astounding to find a 36-year-old woman tramping through the wilderness during the delicate early stages of her first pregnancy braving daytime temperatures soaring above 100°F instead of resting at home under the closest medical supervision. Moreover, any pregnant wife who did endure the heat and dust could be excused for being frugal with her marital obligations. A frustrated husband might find it impossible not to stray, even if his family motto was 'Be mindful'.

The absence of a divorce is no proof of fidelity. Divorce was never an option entered into lightly by the upper classes; financial settlement and the washing of dirty linen in public was far less palatable than the risk of an affair becoming public knowledge. More to the point in this instance, wives were not granted the legal right to divorce their husbands on grounds of adultery alone until 1923: additional faults such as cruelty, desertion or 'unnatural vice' had to be cited. In any event, the deeply religious Connie, who read a chapter of the Bible every week, may have just been the forgiving kind; a devout believer in the sanctity of marriage or else so hopelessly in love she turned a blind eye to her husband's indiscretions.

So, an affair between Bower Ismay and Maggie Loder appears certain. It began before the 1913 Derby, either in 1909 or, most likely, the following year when Bower's diary insists he went to East Africa without his wife (whose absence might be explained by the welfare of her infant daughter or the death of her father). Consequently, the affair becomes relevant to the outcome of the 1913 Derby. We do know, however, that any affair was forcibly interrupted in the months preceding the race. In August 1912 Maggie Loder was admitted to a London clinic for an appendectomy; subsequently, a month's recuperation in Scotland was followed by a lengthy spell in East Africa which didn't end until May 1913. This trip, declared *The Times*, was considered a 'great benefit to her health'. Her return even warranted a mention in *The Sporting Chronicle*: 'Her Ladyship's many friends are rejoiced to know that the chief object with which the trip was undertaken has been accomplished.' Both papers might have added that it also succeeded in keeping her out of the limelight.

Pauline Matarasso (Ismay's great-niece) was assured by an impeccable source that 'at one point Bower Ismay had installed his mistress in the house, forcing his wife to move out for the duration'. Whether or not this lady and Maggie Loder were one and the same, we may be sure that Ismay's philandering was a topic of conversation in the luncheon rooms and paddock bars of every fashionable racecourse from Hooton Park to Hurst Park until, with equal certainty, they reached the ears of Eustace Loder. To a strait-laced gentleman cut from Loder's cloth this brand of tittle-tattle was intolerable. Ismay's purchase of one of his stud's 'cast-offs' might be viewed as one of racing's ups and downs. But cuckolding his brother was beyond the Pale.

'I don't see Bower as a vindictive man,' declares Michael Manser, 'who would rub the Loder nose in it.' That assessment is surely correct; but Loder felt his nose tweaked nonetheless.

☞

Eustace Loder's ammunition to 'ruin' Ismay was reinforced in the spring of 1912 when the Ismay name suddenly found itself mired in a notoriety transcending marital scandal. At 11.40 p.m. on 14 April *RMS Titanic* struck an iceberg off Newfoundland. This maritime tragedy is so well documented that even its basic narrative needs no repeating. Yet the loss of the White Star Line's flagship, the Ismay family firm's flagship, was such a disaster that its ramifications can't be ignored and, in particular, the possibility the effects made themselves felt on Derby Day 1913. Indicative of the mud slung at the family was an American newspaper smear suggesting the emblem of the White Star Line should be changed to 'The Yellow Liver' and the mark of Cain instantly foisted on the Ismay name was reflected in the Texan town of Ismay taking immediate steps to change its name because it couldn't bear the stigma. Bower Ismay was open to vilification by association, if not to his face, most certainly behind his back.

Bower Ismay wasn't aboard *Titanic*: Connie Ismay had fallen ill shortly before the liner set sail and he stayed with her at Haselbech. Yet he may just as well have been aboard. Some sources did state that he was on the liner. This misconception may stem from Bower going to Queenstown to meet his brother Bruce on his return from New York aboard the *Adriatic* and accompanying him down the gangplank in a display of fraternal solidarity when subsequently it docked in Liverpool. This confusion serves to emphasise how the entire Ismay family was tarred by association. Many couldn't forgive an Ismay not being among the dead. During the American enquiry into the tragedy, Bruce Ismay was castigated as 'the officer criminally responsible for this appalling tragedy' and a US Congressman was said to have suggested he ought to be 'lynched'. At the British enquiry an MP stated 'It was his duty to remain upon that ship until she went to the bottom.' Another suggested in print that 'someone ought to hang over this business'.

Bruce Ismay's conduct was exonerated by both the American and British enquiries. But when the managing director of the White Star Line took a seat in collapsible boat 'C' he was one of the few men on his doomed vessel who knew there were no similar opportunities available for most of those aboard. If he presumed those he left behind to face the freezing water would soon be rescued by passing ships he was surely deluding himself, because in all probability he knew that the closest help was almost four hours away and life expectancy in water two degrees below zero might be as little as fifteen minutes.

In consequence Ismay was pilloried in certain sections of the press. As chairman of the line he'd played a part in the design of the vessel and its luxurious specifications. Why, asked the press, was passenger safety sacrificed in favour of opulence? Why, demanded the *Daily Mirror*, did *Titanic* only carry enough lifeboats for 1,178 people when she was carrying a total of 2,206 passengers and crew – in other words, room for only a little over half?

The simple answers were not good enough: *Titanic* was regarded as 'unsinkable' owing to her system of 'watertight compartments'; and, should the unthinkable occur, the shipping lanes of the north Atlantic were now so busy that rescue might be assured without need of lifeboats. Based on the Board of Trade safety regulations (which had not kept pace with the increased size of liners like *Titanic*), she was over-endowed with lifeboats in any case: the outdated formula used to determine lifeboat requirements meant she had only to carry enough lifeboats for 962 persons. Had *Titanic* been carrying her full complement of passengers her lifeboat provision would have fallen and the loss of life would have been even more calamitous. Faced with a tragedy of this magnitude the public demanded a scapegoat and the press were ready to oblige them. Ismay had never courted the press. Now it sensed a soft target.

Bruce Ismay was accused of everything from interfering with *Titanic*'s course and speed to dressing in women's clothes and jumping into the first available lifeboat to save his own skin. Unlike his father, Bruce Ismay seldom visited the bridge or conversed with his captains and his behaviour as the *Titanic* sank was attested by several eye-witnesses; after helping load and launch four lifeboats on the starboard side of the ship, Ismay entered the last boat lowered on that side of the stricken vessel at 1.40 a.m. Ismay had done his duty throughout the two hours following the collision, especially during the fifty-five minutes since the first boat was lowered. *Titanic* had only forty minutes remaining. With no other passengers – men, women or children – in the vicinity, Ismay became the forty-first and last person to step into collapsible 'C' which had places for forty-seven people.

Ismay's critics insisted this was the worst step he ever took. His apologists might argue it was a desperately unlucky step. He was said to be disconsolate later when told women and children had been left behind, and accepted he should have gone down with his ship; his torment was so obvious that Florence Ismay thereafter forbade any mention of *Titanic* in his presence. 'Perhaps I was too proud of the ships,' he wrote a friend, 'and this is my punishment.' Quite possibly, amid the bedlam that night, he was under the impression all of them had been evacuated. Certainly, if he thought the 'women and children first' maxim had been observed to the letter all 547 women and children on board would have been safely accommodated. Indeed, there were the best part of 300 empty places on the ship's twenty lifeboats. Had all the women and children survived the night, Ismay's own survival might have escaped the vitriolic censure it did.

The *New York Sun* stated what many were thinking: 'No one knows how Mr Ismay himself got into a boat; it is assumed he wished to make a presentation of the case to his company.' According to Ismay, it was for this very reason that he was persuaded to leave *Titanic* by Chief Officer Wilde (who, unfortunately for Ismay, did not survive the night). He confided to Connie Ismay that he felt it his deputed role to speak for the vessel, its captain and its crew – which he then declined to do to any great effect. The consensus of opinion, nevertheless, was that he should have stayed aboard and gone down with his ship like his captain. 'Who would not rather die a hero than live a coward?' challenged the *Denver Post*.

Society still expected a 'gentleman' to do the 'right thing' and set a proper example, in this instance, by leaning against the rail and puffing nonchalantly on a last cigarette. It was prominent members of society (all listed on the newspaper front pages when the *Titanic* set sail) who provided the public with their role models. Their conduct was expected to be beyond reproach, which, free from an intrusive media, it was believed wholeheartedly to be. Tragedies like that of *Titanic* exposed these glamorous folk to very public scrutiny. 'The Last Seat – Should He Take It?' was the rhetorical caption to an illustration carried by the *St Louis Post-Dispatch*. The correct answer was exemplified by cartoons such as 'Where Manhood Perished Not' in the *New York Herald*, which lionised the sacrifice of the 115 'gentlemen' in first class: among them American multi-millionaire banker Benjamin Guggenheim who, along with his secretary, changed into evening clothes, declaring 'we are prepared to go down like gentlemen'; and John Jacob Astor IV, from one of the four wealthiest families in America, who was immortalised in song as bidding farewell to his new bride with the words, 'Don't grieve for me. I would give my life for the ladies to flee.'

However, the public found the conduct of the surviving fifty-eight 'gentlemen' less becoming. It was not long before Bruce Ismay *et al.* who didn't choose death found their manhood questioned for leaving women and children to perish. The *Daily Herald* rammed home the point visually with a cartoon entitled 'The Tragedy of the *Titanic*' featuring a first-class male survivor (dressed in silk topper, frock coat and spats) sat puffing a cigar on a floating coffin bearing a plaque inscribed '134' – the number of steerage women and children lost. It demanded very little licence to view the survivor as Bruce Ismay. Other cartoons were openly scurrilous. The worst, full page in size, depicted Ismay crouching in a lifeboat watching the ship go down: the caption read: 'This is J BRUTE Ismay – a picture that will live in the public memory for ever, J Bruce Ismay safe in a lifeboat while 1,500 people drown.'

Perhaps the most succinct comment on the witch hunt and its flurry of white feathers came from George Bernard Shaw. 'There is no heroism in being drowned when you cannot help it.' In the final analysis it did not matter whether Bruce Ismay was a bullying coward or a convenient whipping boy, a recluse or an outcast: whether he left *Titanic* on the first lifeboat or the last, eagerly or obediently; whether he cared 'for nobody but himself, his pride and profit' (*New York American*) or 'by the supreme artistry of Chance was caught by the urgent vacancy in the boat and the snare of the moment' (*Daily Mail*). The damage done to the Ismay name was both catastrophic and irredeemable.

Bower Ismay was no more 'unsinkable' than *Titanic*. He and Bruce were the closest of brothers, a fraternalism forged under the hammers of Dawpool and Harrow. A slap in the face to one stung the cheek of the other. Stigmatising the elder brother branded the younger. Any ostracism endured by one was shared by the other. The injustice rankled.

By the same token, Eustace Loder knew people who died on 15 April 1912, as did his fellow Stewards on Derby Day, the Lords Rosebery and Wolverton: men such as John Jacob Astor, a close relative of prominent owner William Waldorf Astor. Rosebery, for example, was one of the first donors to the benefit fund for *Titanic* victims, and he'd aired his views on 'gentlemanly' conduct by expressing in print his admiration for the gallant manner of Captain Scott's demise in the Antarctic. Few of their social circle would have thought ill of these three men were they to redirect their disdain from one Ismay to the other. No need for fanfares, no back-slapping afterwards; those who mattered understood. Their course of action would be as unwritten as the code of honour it underwrote.

One can't say the prime cause of Bower Ismay's Derby ill-fortune lay in the icy depths of the North Atlantic. But it can be said with absolute certainty that had Bruce Ismay chosen to stay aboard *Titanic* and gone down with his ship, one item of baggage marking his younger brother out for special treatment from the Epsom Stewards would have been removed.

☞

The events of spring 1912 marked a watershed in Bower Ismay's life. Henceforth, no matter what he might do and how he might try, his name was tainted. No longer could he count on an Englishman's right to the benefit of the doubt. Human nature decreed the activities of any Ismay were now viewed with suspicion. Even on the Turf. A year later such prejudice gave Eustace Loder another stick with which to beat Bower Ismay. And who is to say this stick didn't derive some of its power from the *Titanic* fall-out.

This change in public perception arrived at an unfortunate time for Ismay; his racing commitments had been strengthening steadily since he first registered his colours of 'Neapolitan violet and primrose hoops, quartered cap' in 1898. He had become a serious challenger for the country's two greatest races.

Every devotee of the Turf desired to lead-in a winner of the Derby. Yet to a man like Bower Ismay, raised within hailing distance of Liverpool, the city with which his family had such strong links, there was a race perhaps even closer to his heart: the Grand National. Accomplished horseman though he was, Ismay considered riding in the Grand National beyond his capabilities, but owning the winner was well within the compass of a man with unlimited financial resources.

However, Bower Ismay would never win the Grand National – although he did collect the Scottish version with Theodocian in 1905 and the Welsh with Jacobus in 1912. His first serious assault on Liverpool's greatest race had come in 1910 with Bloodstone, trained by Tom Coulthwaite. Ismay's association with Coulthwaite was one he would eventually have cause to regret. It may well have cost him a Grand National victory.

Although Coulthwaite won races on the Flat as diverse as the Chester Cup over 2¼ miles and the Portland Handicap over five-and-a-half furlongs, his genius lay with jumpers. He applied principles learned as a noted athlete and rugby player in his youth; it was said he'd been thrown the only time he sat on a horse and vowed thereafter to stay on two legs. Despite this attention to detail on the training grounds, where he built a miniature line of National fences, Coulthwaite believed that 'races are won in the stable'. He somehow got into the minds of his horses, got to know their foibles and idiosyncrasies, and treated them as his individual children. Many would take food only from him, and he was known to set his alarm clock for two in the morning to get up to feed his Chester Cup winner, Rathlea, who would only eat-up at nights. Whatever his secret, or the source of his genius, it was sufficiently magical to ferment suspicion among the envious. Since 1899 he had been based in Cannock Chase, an area of central Staffordshire dotted with grassy hills and well-drained soils ideal for training horses, latterly at Flaxley Green, on the outskirts of Rugeley, where he directed operations from his bungalow christened 'The Castle'. Eremon and Jenkinstown had already given him two National victories to sit beside the six in Manchester's greatest race, the Lancashire Chase, the sixth via Ismay's mare Wilkinstown.

Bloodstone had announced himself as a proper National horse with what *The Times* described as 'the event of the afternoon' when he upset the odds laid on Cackler in the previous year's Champion Chase by eight lengths. Allotted 11st 8lb in the 1910 National, Bloodstone failed to get round in a race that eventually went to his inferior stablemate Jenkinstown. Two years later he returned to Liverpool after encouraging victories at Leicester and Sandown Park to carry 11st 6lb into second place, six lengths behind a National specialist in Jerry M, burdened with 12st 7lb.

Ismay could be excused for thinking success in the Grand National was tantalisingly close. He found himself an even better candidate in the Irish-bred Balscadden bought privately in March 1912 for a figure reputed to be in the region of 1,000 guineas. The five-year-old immediately won the Liverpool Hurdle before Coulthwaite successfully aimed him at three French races culminating with the prestigious Grande Course de Haies d'Auteuil worth £3,886 to the winner. After these triumphs it was decided that a horse blessed with such a combination of stamina and speed was too good to be left idle during the summer and Ismay sent him to Jack Robinson. Balscadden didn't disappoint, landing a pair of lucrative £1,000 handicaps, the Prince Edward Handicap at Manchester and the Newbury Autumn Cup.

However, if Bower Ismay thought the golden summer of 1912 gifted him by Craganour and Balscadden had somehow expunged all memory of *Titanic* and heralded the dawn of a glorious 1913 encompassing an historic Grand National-Derby double, he was soon disabused. The New Year heaped more scandal by association on shoulders already burdened with plenty.

On 17 February the Stewards of the National Hunt Committee called him, Coulthwaite, his racing manager John Fergusson and jockeys Bob Chadwick and Frank Lyall to London's Registry Office to answer questions regarding the recent running of his Grand National candidates Jacobus and Bloodstone. Chadwick had ridden Jacobus to a ¾-length victory in the Warwickshire Handicap Steeplechase at Birmingham on 11 February at odds of 7/2 a week after the horse had failed to finish in a race at Sandown Park where it had started as a 100/8 outsider. Bloodstone's success under Lyall in Hurst Park's Champion Steeplechase on 16 March was even more eyebrow-raising. Over the same course and distance the previous month he'd been trounced twenty lengths by Dysart, but, now, at the same weights, after the Ismay runner was sent off the 10/1 outsider in a three-horse contest, he'd beaten Dysart by a neck. 'Dysart's success was, indeed, anticipated with the utmost confidence,' commented *The Times*, 'but to the general astonishment Bloodstone won.'

Having listened to the explanations offered by the five connections

the Stewards considered them, with exception of F Lyall's, unsatisfactory. The Stewards strongly recommended Mr Bower Ismay to look more closely into the running of his horses. They considered that Mr Fergusson's conduct, as manager of Mr Ismay's horses, was open to grave suspicion, and he was severely censured for gross lack of supervision.

Lyall was 'completely exonerated' but both Coulthwaite and his stable jockey Chadwick were 'warned off'. The trainer protested his innocence and mounted an appeal: he only prepared the horses and any riding orders came from elsewhere – a finger pointing at Fergusson.

Coulthwaite could have saved his breath for there are grounds for suspecting that the Stewards had him in their sights. Only the previous year he'd been severely cautioned for the discrepancy in form shown by Great Loss in races at Newbury and Cheltenham. Rubicond of cheek and bright of eye, the white-moustached trainer was regarded not only as one of the canniest in the game but also a man of boundless generosity: on bus journeys he would often pay the fares of his fellow passengers and when the local pitmen were out of work he would send their families free gifts of poultry and meat – as he did every Christmas. He neither smoked nor drank alcohol, his only distractions being the cultivation of roses and pigeons – and perhaps ways of beating the odds.

But 'Old Tom', as he always signed himself, possessed a forthright Lancashire manner. That was no insurmountable barrier to Ismay, who would have encountered plenty of Coulthwaites in his circle of northern business associates, but it came across as blunt to the point of rudeness in the minds of his alleged superiors. He wasn't a man prepared to go along with the Establishment convention of portraying trainers as mere grooms or minor functionaries. He didn't come from a racing family and saw no reason to be deferential to anyone who did. Even if he was the future King. Coulthwaite became friendly with Edward, Prince of Wales after 'HRH' began using nearby Himley Hall for trysts with his mistress Freda Dudley-Ward. The Prince loved to school over the training fences: he took to addressing the trainer as 'Old Tom' and, in return, Coulthwaite called him 'Princey'. On one such visit the Prince found Coulthwaite occupied in his pigeon loft, and proceeded to pass the time by lighting one of his endless chains of cigarettes. Coulthwaite could not abide the smell of cigarette fumes, and certainly not within inhaling distance of his prized birds. He turned on his future monarch and barked: 'Put that thing out!' The heir apparent did as he was told without so much as a murmur.

If Tom Coulthwaite could address the Prince of Wales as if he was nothing more than a stable-lad it's not unreasonable to presume that the odd racecourse official and Steward had been similarly berated. Grudges could be borne in high places. Tom Coulthwaite had pulled off one 'stroke' too many and paid the penalty.

Unfortunately, he took his owner down with him. And it may have cost Ismay a Grand National. His string of nine jumpers were transferred to Frank Hartigan at Weyhill, but his principal National hope Bloodstone responded badly to the interruption. He went to Liverpool 'not pleasing' Hartigan – and performed accordingly, exiting after one circuit.

Once again Bower had reason to feel aggrieved. He seldom betted. He let it be known that any coup had been engineered without his connivance. But the racing parish knew better when it came to matters like this. People merely tapped the side of their noses and winked: everyone's at it. Ismay lacked supporters in high places. He'd shown his hand by demonstrating no aspirations to join the Jockey Club or National Hunt Committee which was the ambition of any serious owner and follower of the Turf. Had he been so inclined, however, the odds on his being elected were long. Of the Jockey Club's seventy-one members at the start of the 1913 season just twelve were untitled. Eustace Loder was one of four from the officer class, and it's absolutely certain Ismay's nomination would have fallen foul of the trap described by Sidney Galtrey, a journalist with deep Establishment connections:

> An individual, whether of rank or title, who might have offended
> one of the paramount in the court of racing, might rely on getting

one black ball too many. That Ismay might confidently expect a
black ball from Loder was unquestioned.

This only made it harder for Bower Ismay to digest a bilious sense
of injustice. And after the judge's verdict in the 2000 Guineas of
1913, he must have wondered whether the Establishment was
conducting some kind of vendetta against him. He consoled
himself with the prospect of Epsom glory. Nothing could stop
Craganour winning the Derby.

# EIGHT

# Sixes Bar the Favourite

What could possibly puncture Ismay's optimism? Aside from ill-luck, where might the favourite's downfall lurk?

The Derby was always stated to have been the most attainable target for Louvois but his hopes of turning the tables on Craganour following the Newmarket Stakes appeared slim to the point of non-existent and his odds drifted from 7s to 10s. So neglected had he become that on the morning Newmarket's candidates were all put through their final paces for the Derby none of the principal work-watchers chose to attend his gallop. The *Life* was left with hearsay which suggested 'he simply played with his companions'.

What of Craganour's other perennial sparring partner? 'If there should be a weak spot in Mr Bower Ismay's son of Desmond – and not a few of the sons of Desmond have proved deceptive,' averred *The Times*, 'Shogun is likely to find it out.' *The Sporting Chronicle* countered: 'Shogun would beat Craganour in the show ring but not on the racecourse.' Although the big white-faced chestnut had come out second best on each of his four previous clashes with Craganour he was generally held to possess a better chance of staying the one-and-a-half miles of the Derby than Craganour, who not only liked to race prominently but also seemed to race too freely at times – traits which might see him run himself into the ground. Nevertheless Shogun was still dismissed scathingly by *The Sportsman* as 'a colt more like winning a Stewards Cup at Goodwood than a Derby'.

Shogun was Irish and possessed a hint of romance in his lineage. He was half-bred. His sire was Santoi, a tough, albeit bad-tempered, animal who won the Ascot Gold Cup. But of Shogun's seventh dam nothing was known other than she was foaled in Ireland in the early part of the nineteenth century, which thus debarred Shogun's dam Kendal Belle from the Stud Book. This drawback did not prevent newspaper baron Edward Hulton paying 2,000 guineas for him at the Doncaster Sales.

Behind Hulton's gentle manner and soft voice hid enormous willpower. His titles included *The Sporting Chronicle*, the Manchester *Evening Chronicle*, the *Daily Dispatch* and the *Daily Sketch*, which he launched as a 'picture paper' to compete with the *Daily Mirror*. His outlook on life had undoubtedly been steeled by a stroke of fate as a teenager. He and his elder brother were ardent cyclists in the era of the penny-farthing and one day their father mapped out a route for them, promising to reward the first home with a sovereign. His brother won the race but then fell from his machine's high seat and was killed. It was he who had been destined for the newspaper business while Edward was bound for the priesthood. At the outset he raced under the *nom de course* of Mr Lytham and had his horses trained in the north with only limited success. It was not until he placed them with the canny Australian Dick Wootton at Epsom that he enjoyed major success with Marajax (Manchester Cup) and Lomond (New Stakes at Royal Ascot and the Gimcrack Stakes) in 1911 and a second Gimcrack with Flippant in 1912.

Richard Wootton – always referred to as 'Old Man' Wootton – trained in his native New South Wales and then South Africa before coming to England in 1906 and setting up at Epsom's Treadwell House. Meyrick Good regarded him as 'undoubtedly the most able of all colonial trainers who had sought their fortune on our shores'; Sidney Galtrey believed 'he may have lacked culture ... which never bothered him' but saluted his 'ability to train racehorses in his own enlightened way and in exploiting them he blended shrewdness, bluntness and boldness'.

Shogun would be his first representative in the Derby, for plotting coups rather than Classic campaigns was Wootton's forte – to this end he was aided by his jockey sons Frank and Stanley, plus a supporting cast of other willing stable apprentices led by William and Ernest Huxley, for he was freely acknowledged as a brilliant maker of jockeys.

Wootton's machinations soon led to him being challenged by his former friend, and the Turf's resident *enfant terrible*, Robert Sievier, in the pages of his weekly newspaper *The Winning Post*. Sievier's journalism was even more heavy-handed than his handling of Sceptre and frequently juggled with the laws of libel. A long-running feud with J. B. Joel, for example, led to the owner laying a trap that resulted in Sievier being charged with trying to extort £5,000 from Joel by proposing to abstain from publishing further attacks on him in *The Winning Post* – which were to include his portrait being printed between those of two murderers. After a melodramatic performance at the Old Bailey that did sterling credit to his one-time acting career, Sievier was acquitted.

Now, when Wootton could least afford the distraction with the 1913 Derby days away, he found himself in court defending Sievier's allegation

> of entering into a conspiracy with other trainers to win or lose races by dishonest and illegitimate means ... arranging as to which of the horses under his control should win by putting up jockeys or apprentices in his own service and ordering them to pull horses when he was not backing them.

Mr Justice Darling clearly took the view that this was very much a matter of 'the pot calling the kettle black' and awarded Wootton a farthing in damages. Wootton considered bringing out his own paper to rebut Sievier's scurrilous accusations. As Good said: 'He was a good friend but a bad enemy.'

As his sons couldn't ride in Australia until they were fourteen,

Wootton had blooded them in South Africa where Frank rode his first winner when he was nine years and ten months old. Like all Wootton's apprentices, the brothers were taught to go the shortest route by hugging the rails, which frequently led to problems in running and subsequent accusations of foul or reckless riding, especially in the case of Frank. 'Frank was the most lynx-eyed jockey that ever came under my notice,' added Good. 'He not only knew what his own horse was doing, but what the other horses and jockeys were up to. Consequently, Richard Wootton frequently profited by son Frank's fine judgement.'

Frank's first English winner arrived quickly, at Folkestone on 23 August 1906 and fourteen months later he secured some hefty Australian bets when Demure won the Cesarewitch at 4/1. Landing gambles for his father became more of a regular feature than riding Classic winners: for that Frank had to wait until his first championship season of 1909, aboard Perola in the Oaks for Sussex handler Saunders Davies. A Classic and a championship at the age of fifteen amounted to accomplishments beyond any other jockey in the history of the English Turf.

The young Wootton reminded everyone of the young Johnny Reiff. Mused *The Sportsman*:

> He is like him physically. He is regarded as a wonder for his inches; he is being made the target of the snapshotters; he is being lionised by the crowd; and, more important than anything else in a business sense, the similarity is further demonstrated by the fact that he is riding a remarkably high percentage of winners and attracting a big following among the speculative public, and signs are not wanting that anything he rides in the near future may yield a profit.

Wootton's first title came courtesy of 165 winners, forty-nine more than the reigning champion Danny Maher, and he retained his title in 1910, 1911 and 1912 amid a simmering rivalry with the hot-tempered Irish-American. 'There was not much love lost between them,' wrote George Lambton of two jockeys he used as often as possible. 'Frank Wootton was always a good-natured, easy-going boy when off a horse; but in a race, like all good jockeys, he was quick to take advantage of anybody or anything.'

In the 1910 St Leger, Wootton enjoyed upsetting Maher who was riding the favourite Lemberg. Wootton rode Lambton's Swynford, beaten by Lemberg in the Derby and at Ascot. Swynford subsequently improved to win the Liverpool Summer Cup in a canter and, believing the favourite to be a non-stayer, Lambton instructed Wootton to make the pace a hot one. Wootton obeyed orders but as he was still only a sixteen-year-old boy – weighing just 7st 4lb – the effort of so doing on a big, powerful animal like Swynford reduced him to near exhaustion. That night young Frank was heard shouting in his sleep: 'I won't let you up, Danny! You shan't get up!'

Wooton's Derby partner Shogun had not been seen in public since his sixth-placed run in the Guineas when he was adjudged to be backward. Both Hulton and 'Old Man' Wootton, however, were quietly optimistic because they were confident of his ability to stay the trip, which might not be said of the favourite, and aside from suffering the minor setback of a slightly cracked heel (rumours of a bowed tendon were dismissed as poppycock) they reckoned he'd progressed steadily since the Guineas. A mark of their confidence in Shogun was to be found in the decision to leave the Derby to him and save Fairy King for Ascot, even though he'd just returned to form with a wide-margin success at Hurst Park. To triumph, however, Shogun would need to overcome the Epsom 'hoodoo' because not since Amato, seventy-five years back in 1838, had a Derby winner been quartered in the town.

With Wootton taking over from stable apprentice William Huxley it was as certain as Wednesday followed Tuesday that Hulton's blue and orange colours would be seen hugging the inside rails for the whole one-and-a-half miles. The fear was ever present that the feel of the rail against his boot might lure

Wootton up a blind alley to a mugging he'd then contest tooth and nail. He was, after all, still a teenager and prone to rashness: his disciplinary record was atrocious and he was forever being left 'on the ground' as a result of misbehaviour at the gate or for riding that verged on the dangerous during a race. In the previous summer's Liverpool Cup, for example, he'd been reported for twice interfering with another horse – and then proceeded to repeat the offence in the act of winning the next race. He was duly reported to the Stewards of the Jockey Club who handed him a month's suspension for 'reckless riding about which he has been repeatedly admonished'. No sooner was he back in action than he was 'on the carpet' at Birmingham for 'crossing' and once again reported to the Stewards of the Jockey Club by the local Stewards.

Frank was good, very good; but when he was bad he was horrid. Which Frank Wootton turned up on Derby Day would depend on what kind of passage he and Shogun experienced along the fence, because everyone knew that is where they'd be.

On the opening day of the season, Mr Leopold de Rothschild's Hippeastrum had capitalised on his maiden's weight allowance to win the Easter Stakes at Kempton Park from a field that included various trusty yardsticks – plus an unconsidered outsider named Aboyeur. Since that race Hippeastrum had featured prominently in the Derby market. Consequently, when de Rothschild elected to put all his faith in Day Comet the message seemed loud and clear.

There'd be no more popular winner of the Derby than Day Comet, who carried the 'blue and yellow' colours of one of the Turf's most popular characters in the sexagenarian de Rothschild, whose thick white moustache and kindly expression made him an instantly recognisable face on the racecourse. A man quick to flare but apt to make amends with equal alacrity, he was born to vast wealth and was the first Jew elected to the Jockey Club. He was the grandson of Mayer de Rothschild (and the cousin of Hannah Rosebery) who emerged from the Frankfurt ghetto

to found Europe's premier banking dynasty; at one point Mayer
de Rothschild was worth 0.62 per cent of the entire national
income of Britain. A liberal and sporting patron of the Turf,
'Mr Leo' had his horses trained privately by John Watson at
Palace House in Newmarket by this point, though he ran them
in the most public fashion. Both his stud (Southcourt, close to
Leighton Buzzard) and racing operation were conducted on a
grand scale and in no fewer than fourteen years his winnings ran
into five figures, his best being 1896 when fifty-three races netted
£46,766. He involved himself at all levels with the stock he bred,
arranging the entries and all the trials, at which he insisted the
jockeys wore full colours, breeches and boots. St Frusquin won
him a 2000 Guineas in 1896 and his son St Amant achieved the
Guineas-Derby double in 1904, three years after Doricles had
won the St Leger. He was also known to be very fond of a bet.
Were Day Comet to prevail there would also be no more excited
owner to lead in a Derby winner. After his home-bred St Amant
raced to victory through a thunderstorm, the threat of a severe
drenching failed to deter his coatless owner from leading him in.
Nor was trainer Watson a stranger to Classic celebration, having
trained Norman III to win the 1908 2000 Guineas and Tracery
the 1912 St Leger for August Belmont Jnr, first chairman of the
New York Jockey Club.

Since his ninth place in the Guineas, Day Comet had allegedly
been shaping well on the Newmarket training grounds when
galloped with Tracery, especially on the Saturday beforehand
when the *Life*'s correspondent declared 'he went the best 1½
miles of his life'. The chestnut son of St Frusquin out of Catgut
would lack nothing in confidence from the saddle since he would
be ridden by Albert 'Snowy' Whalley, the current season's most
in-form jockey. He was setting a scorching pace in the title race
with forty winners – a dozen clear of his nearest pursuer. After
coming out of his apprenticeship, Whalley had obtained few
opportunities and abandoned the saddle for the stage. That, too,
met with scant reward, so he returned to racing and eventually

had to go as far as India to ride his very first winner, at the age of twenty-three in 1909. Once he resumed race-riding in England the following year of 1910 he made rapid headway to come third in the jockeys' list behind Wootton and Maher with ninety-nine wins. This season he had stolen a march on both Wootton (side-lined briefly by a series of operations on his throat) and Maher to lead them by twenty-one and thirteen respectively at the start of the Derby meeting.

Apart from Shogun and Day Comet, it seemed that France was the only other source of danger to the favourite. Thus far in his career Craganour hadn't encountered a rival trained in France – nor was there any collateral form by which to assess the relative merits of the current Classic crops. Nimbus was the sole French representative and although he'd at one time been favour-ite for the French Derby, he now wasn't even regarded as the best three-year-old colt in France. How could a French second-rater be expected to humble the best of the English on their own turf?

After all, no French-trained horse had ever won the Derby. The French-bred and owned Gladiateur had prevailed in 1865 but he was trained at Newmarket by Tom Jennings and even though French-trained animals had won other Classics, including the Oaks, Gallic misfortune in the Derby was legion and often tinged with tragedy. The memory of the giant grey Holocauste was still fresh: upsides Flying Fox and about to go on and win the 1899 race, he broke a fetlock. Much of this Gallic misfortune fell to the famed owner-breeder Edmond Blanc, who'd used an inherit-ance derived from the concession to run the casinos at Monte Carlo and Bad Homburg in Germany to build the most power-ful stable in France. He'd been dispatching challengers since 1889 when his French Derby winner Clover broke down during the early stages of the race; two years later Gouverneur chased home Common. In 1905 Blanc was rumoured to possess three colts good enough to win, but barely had the season commenced than coughing swept through his stable, leaving Jardy the sole candidate. However, Jardy was clearly carrying the bug and began coughing as soon as he reached Epsom: notwithstanding, he still ran Cicero to three parts of a length.

M. Alexandre Aumont would be praying for better luck. His light chestnut Nimbus, set to carry 'white jacket and green cap', definitely possessed the pedigree of a Derby winner, being a half-brother to Nuage who won the Grand Prix de Paris in 1910. Nimbus had run just three times, twice as a two-year-old, winning his second race over seven furlongs. The colt was believed to have made significant improvement over the winter and proved it by winning the Prix Greffulhe over 1¼ miles at Longchamp on 11 May. He won decisively but was said to have beaten very little by *The Sporting Life*'s French correspondent. Having displayed form over the longer distance, he missed a tilt at the French 2000 Guineas and was given plenty of fast work over one-and-a-half miles at Chantilly by his trainer George Cunnington in readiness for Epsom. Accompanied by Cunnington's brother, Charles, he arrived in England six days before the Derby and was stabled at Newmarket with Tom Jennings. Speculation that this lengthy stay would lead to him becoming unsettled by the change in weather was promptly assuaged when he impressed work-watchers with a sparkling display over a mile on the Limekilns, followed by another over the full Derby trip two days before the race. 'Sturdy and even-tempered, with a beautifully shaped neck and shoulders if lacking a little behind the saddle' said the *Life*. 'Full of life and play. A beautiful mover.' *The Sportsman* agreed: 'A real daisycutter.'

On his back would be Milton Henry, 'the dean of American jockeys in France' according to Parisian journalist Pierre Rochecourt, and no stranger to Classic success in his adopted workplace where he had won the Prix du Jockey Club three times in the space of five years. Increasing weight had been restricting his opportunities of late but 'though his turn to give place to younger men may soon come, nevertheless he is still a star ... the crack jockey will let the mounts seek him.' Nonetheless, Henry had yet to win a Classic in England and had little experience round Epsom, other than a trio of unplaced rides on Derby long shots. This year he could leave the 'no-hopers' to others. However forlorn their chances appeared on paper, there would be no shortage of jockeys eager to ride them in the race. Every member of the weighing room knew he could not win a Derby unless he had a mount. And, sometimes, miracles did happen in a horse race.

# NINE

# No-hopers

Every year in every big race there is a certain amount of what is generally regarded as rubbish, horses who seem altogether out of place in the fields which expectant owners have sent them to swell.

In spite of this scornful blast from the *Illustrated Sporting and Dramatic News* the Derby was unlikely to be run without a representative of Turf aristocracy like Leopold de Rothschild and Lord Rosebery. And there were always going to be others like Prue who owed their place in the field to the name of their owner rather than the level of their form.

Jewish owners, for instance, were in the ascendant on the English Turf and, in addition to the de Rothschild representative, the name of J. B. Joel prefaced two runners. Two years earlier Joel's Sunstar won a Derby in which there were so many runners with Jewish owners that one wag was heard to remark: 'We ought to thank God for the Jews or there'd be no Derby this year!' Jack Barnato Joel was the son of an East End publican who made a fortune by adroit exploitation of the diamond fields around Kimberley, before diversifying into breweries and collieries. Unless, that is, one paid heed to the opinions of his sworn foe Robert Sievier who insisted on calling him 'Ike' (stating Joel's real name to be Isaac) and referring to him as 'an illicit diamond buyer, a thief's accomplice and a fugitive from justice … who incited and engaged a man to beat and maim me, offering this desperado a minimum of £200 as a reward with an increasing scale according to the limbs he broke'.

Joel had demonstrated his business flair at an early age, buying a basket of homing pigeons, selling them in the street outside his father's pub to gullible passers-by, waiting for them to fly home and then re-selling them over and over again. Not unsurprisingly, for an individual blessed with such innate drive and infinite funds, Joel's racing interests soon burgeoned. Within eight years of registering his colours of 'black jacket, scarlet cap' in 1900, he became leading owner for the first time and began collecting Classics as he had businesses. These included the 1911 Derby with Sunstar, who'd previously won the 2000 Guineas; Our Lassie (1903) and Glass Doll (1907) won the Oaks, and Your Majesty (1908) the St Leger; all were home-bred. Joel's principal racing objective was relaxation but this didn't exclude gambling. Reputedly he landed a vast bet on Our Lassie to win the Oaks and another coupling her with Rock Sand to win the Derby.

Joel's first colours were due to be carried by Frank O'Neill on Radiant, but this son of Sundridge trod on a nail on the morning of the race, leaving a second son of the champion sprinter, Sun Yat, as Joel's unlikely contender. In five starts this chestnut had not added to his victorious debut in Kempton Park's Breeders Foal Plate of 7 September 1912, and had been roundly put in his place by Craganour in the Newmarket Stakes. Despite the unexpected availability of O'Neill, the apprentice William Huxley kept the mount on Sun Yat.

Great Sport would carry the blue-and-white checks of Colonel William Hall Walker, twice leading owner – and the leading breeder of 1912 thanks to Prince Palatine who won both the Gold Cup and Eclipse Stakes. His bay son of Gallinule and Gondolette lacked the credentials of a serious Derby contender, but Hall Walker was a strange cove who placed immense store in the mystic powers of astrology and may have been persuaded by what he'd seen in the stars. The exact foaling time of his horses, for example, was meticulously logged and sent to a female astrologer acquaintance who prepared an elaborate horoscope of each foal so that Hall Walker might best decide the direction of its future racing career. Sometimes he got it woefully wrong: he sold Prince Palatine, for example, owing to an unfavourable horoscope and he went on to win a St Leger besides the Eclipse, Doncaster Cup, Coronation Cup and two renewals of the Gold Cup.

Hall Walker came from a wealthy family of Warrington brewers and had been MP for Widnes since 1900. A distinguished rider in pony races and point-to-points in his trimmer days, he now devoted his considerable intellect and energies in matters equine to racing thoroughbreds and breeding them at his stud at Tully, on the edge of the Curragh. His home-bred filly Cherry Lass achieved the 1000 Guineas-Oaks double in 1905 and another Tully product, Witch Elm, took the Guineas two years later. Doubtless drawing inspiration from his horoscopes, he seldom outlaid much money on his bloodstock purchases. He paid just 500 guineas for The Soarer a matter of weeks before the gelding won the Grand National of 1896, and Gondolette was acquired for just 360 guineas as a three-year-old in 1905. However, after she'd produced Great Sport for him he must have read the heavens incorrectly, because he sold her to Lord Derby for whom she produced two Classic winners in Ferry (1000 Guineas) and Sansovino (Derby). Her great-grandson Hyperion won the Derby and St Leger in 1933, prior to becoming champion sire on six occasions. Perhaps at heart Hall Walker realised the capricious nature of his celestial advisors, because he could be a cantankerous devil who apportioned blame to all bar himself and his horses whenever anything went awry: 'I don't think the Turf has suffered very much for the connection I have had with it,' he once said haughtily. Nevertheless, his jockeys came and went; and his trainers found it inadvisable to unpack all their furniture at once. The current occupant of the perilous seat was John Smith.

Great Sport had made his seasonal reappearance on Whit Monday at Hurst Park, where with Herbert Jones aboard, he had made full use of a 12lb weight concession to beat Sanquhar by two lengths over a mile. As a juvenile he'd secured two victories from five starts, and in his solitary incursion into the top class he had finished down the field behind Prue in the National Breeders Produce Stakes. On Derby Day the *Life* thought him 'grand-looking, well enough to run for a kingdom.' Whatever help Great Sport received from the stars he could be sure of maximum assistance from the man in the saddle. Thirty-one-year-old George Stern was in his pomp, with few rivals throughout Europe, especially 'over a long course' as George Lambton phrased it. Tod Sloan thought him

> the best all-round rider ... a hustler ... never minds what sort of course it is ... fearless ... takes chances ... seldom, if ever, loses his head. One knows that he can get out of tight places and it would take any of the others all their time to outgeneral him, for he has forgotten more than many of them will ever know.

In 1913 Sloan considered Stern's only rivals in terms of ability to be Johnny Reiff and Frank O'Neill.

Despite labouring under a name many would apply to the expression of any man plying his trade two stones below his natural body weight, Stern was a chirpy thick-set little individual whose broad-shouldered physique would have done justice to a bantamweight boxer. If there was any funny business in a race there was no likelihood of Stern ever emerging second best. Born in France to English parents, he rode his first winner aged seventeen and steadily accumulated victories in every major event on the French Turf, in the process establishing himself as the country's premier rider and perennial champion jockey. The first of six winners in the Prix du Jockey Club came on Edward Blanc's Saxon in 1901 and the first of four in the Prix de Diane aboard Profane in 1904. In 1908 he achieved the remarkable feat of winning three European Derbies – the French, Austrian and German – and riding the runner-up in Belgium. Sea Sick II gave him no kind of ride at Epsom that year, but three years later he continued his successful association with Sunstar, having been brought over from France by J. B. Joel to partner the colt to victory in the 2000 Guineas. Stern had also won the 1906 St Leger on Troutbeck for the Duke of Westminster. Stern's regular sorties to England reinforced a deserved reputation as a tough no-nonsense rider whose penchant for the rails rivalled that of Frank Wootton – and often drew equal retribution from the Stewards. In 1907 he'd ridden Eider to dead-heat with The White Knight in the Ascot Gold Cup only to be disqualified for 'bumping and boring'.

Another rider from France would be assisting the 25/1 shot Aldegond. Birmingham-born George 'Tich' Bellhouse had served his apprenticeship in France with William Flatman but was no longer so miniscule as his soubriquet suggested. He'd partnered the lightly weighted French-owned Ob to win the 1906 Lincolnshire Handicap but nowadays struggled to control his weight following a number of bad crashes and long lay-offs due to wasting. One two-month indisposition had cost him the win in the 1908 French Derby on Sea Sick II, though he did win the previous year's French Oaks on Qu'elle est Belle II; and he drank from the Classic cup in his homeland when winning the previous September's St Leger on Tracery. His sole Derby mount was on Tracery, who ran third behind Tagalie.

Although Aldegond 'appeared little else but a pony' he did come to the race off the back of a victory, and a good one at that. The previous Saturday he'd won the Victoria Cup, a 'hot' handicap over seven furlongs at Hurst Park; before that he'd run Lord Derby's highly regarded Light Brigade to half-a-length shortly after beginning the season by landing another ultra competitive handicap, the Newbury Spring Cup. The single blot on his three-year-old record (after one win from three starts as a juvenile) came in the Burwell Plate at Newmarket when, hardly surprisingly, he failed to compete with high-class older horses Tracery, Jackdaw and Stedfast.

Bachelor's Wedding sported the patriotic 'white, royal blue
sash and scarlet cap' of Sir William Nelson, an Irishman by
birth, who had made his fortune from the meat trade (the *Daily
Mail*'s Robin Goodfellow referred to him as 'the dead meat
merchant') and his eponymous steamship company plying the
South American route. Bachelor's Wedding was bred by Joseph
Lowry at Oatland's Stud, Navan, and was the third product of
a mating between Lowry's stallion Tredennis, a handsome but
useless racer acquired for £100, and an unraced mare called Lady
Bawn. By a non-winner out of a non-runner, the colt's prospects
looked exceedingly dim. Furthermore, Lady Bawn possessed
a dished back like a hammock and her forelegs were so bent
it appeared she walked with her legs crossed. If that wasn't
enough, she was a twin and twins seldom prospered; but not only
did she and her sister, Lady Black, both have the fortitude to
survive this usually calamitous occurrence, they both went on
to produce good winners.

As a juvenile Bachelor's Wedding had raced for the Lowrys
and been prepared by Michael Dawson, the small bearded
wizard of Rathbride Manor on the Curragh, multiple champion trainer of Ireland and ultimately the winner of four Irish
Derbies. Following one win (a five-furlong Plate at the Curragh)
from four starts, Nelson paid £4,000 for the colt in March 1913
and transferred him to Henry Seymour Persse, invariably known
as 'Atty', the equally renowned Irish trainer who operated from
Chattis Hill, near Stockbridge in Hampshire. Persse's family
owned the Nun's Island distillery in Galway but after graduating
from Oxford he preferred the life of an amateur steeplechase
rider and proved very successful, winning the Conyngham Cup
at Punchestown and finishing third in the 1906 Grand National
on Aunt May. He commenced training in Dublin's Phoenix Park
and briefly joined Colonel Hall Walker's procession of private
trainers before setting up at Stockbridge. He was the obvious
candidate for Nelson's new purchase since he had handled much
of the English career of Bachelor's Wedding's close relative

Bachelor's Double. Bachelor's Wedding ran in the 2000 Guineas and did enough to convince *The Sportsman* that 'this lengthy powerful chestnut was more capable of improvement than any of the unplaced division and he should be made a special note of'. A fortnight later he won a Plate at Newmarket over the full Derby distance and if he demonstrated any kind of improvement to the degree of his elder siblings he might just have some role to play in the Derby.

The chestnut's prime asset would be his jockey. Persse's retained rider was a man who would quickly come to dominate the Derby, winning the race four times in five years and on six occasions all told. Steve Donoghue would be having only his third ride in the Classic but he'd already shown his remarkable aptitude for the Epsom track and the hurly-burly of its greatest race by coming third on Charles O'Malley and Royal Tender in 1910 and 1911 respectively (and second in the 1911 Oaks on Tootles). The 1913 season was only his third based in England, having been champion of Ireland in 1909 when retained by 'Boss' Croker.

The young Donoghue modelled himself on no less than Tod Sloan, though it was the more polished Danny Maher whom he eventually resembled most. Ever since the day Donoghue tamed a bucking donkey during a visit of Ohmy's Circus to his home town of Warrington, he had been consumed by a passion for horses. After being apprenticed to three English trainers (notably John Porter with whom he lasted four months) but finishing his time with none of them, he developed his talent with the American Edward Johnson in France, riding his first winner at Hyeres, a tiny, tight and tricky track in the Midi. Riding to the clock on Johnson's gallops and the experience of surviving these dangerous provincial tracks (less than three-quarters of a mile round, all sharp elbows and bends with scarcely any running rails), proved priceless when Donoghue encountered Epsom which consequently held no fears for him. Charles Morton went so far as to state he was worth 7lb to a horse in a race like the Derby.

Donoghue's copious gifts, which numbered daring, speed at the gate, tactical acumen, exquisite balance and judgement of pace, were underpinned by his God-given hands. He was capable of instilling confidence into the most timorous animal or mastering the most fractious of beasts. It seemed the reins must be made of gossamer. 'Stephen can find out more about what is left in his horse with his little finger than most men with their legs and whip,' declared rival jockey Brownie Carslake. Indeed, doctors actually X-rayed Donoghue's hands in the hope of discovering some quality not possessed by other mortals. Crack hurdle-race jockey and noted stylist George Duller tried to analyse Donoghue's uncanny rapport with the thoroughbred in a newspaper article, and, after listing all the usual qualities, ended by saying:

> If a horse tries to fight for his head, he will lean over and give him a reassuring pat on the neck or, dropping his hands, will take his ear. The effect is magical. The mount becomes calm and tractable immediately ... it is the Donoghue electricity which produces the soothing effect.

Donoghue himself explained it more simply: 'I love horses with all that is in me. Some people think of them as animals, I think of them as my friends, my greatest friends.' Donoghue would need to be worth those 7lb in the Derby – and Bachelor's Wedding be his greatest friend – if the pair were to trouble Craganour.

The same could be said of the 'nuisances'. At least one of them listed on the racecard was eliminated from calculations because Primrose Knight, the intended mount of 'Skeets' Martin, was a late withdrawal. That left five no-hopers.

Jameson's claim to fame was that he belonged to the man who taught Winston Churchill how to deploy his toy cavalry. Owner Sir John Willoughby was one of those late Victorian adventurers on whom fate bestowed more money than sense, and who seemed destined to wind up with a million pounds in the bank or a rope around his neck. The former appeared unlikely once Willoughby began paying exorbitant prices for yearlings (even though one of them, Harvester, dead-heated for the 1884 Derby) but he almost managed the latter after becoming embroiled in the political machinations of the man whose name was carried by his current Derby entrant. In December 1895 Dr Leander Storr Jameson, an administrator in the British South Africa Company, led a mounted force from Bechuanaland into the Transvaal with the intention of helping the non-Boer workers of Johannesburg (the Uitlanders) gain voting rights. It was nothing less than an attempted *coup d'état* orchestrated by Britain aimed at overthrowing the Transvaal government of Paul Kruger and seizing the Johannesburg gold fields. One of those on the 'Jameson Raid' was James Willoughby. The planned revolt failed to materialise and the raiders were all captured four days after crossing the border. Like his leader, Willoughby escaped a death sentence but served a prison term back in England.

The chestnut son of King James bearing the name of Willoughby's commander was housed at Newmarket in the care of Sam Pickering, and had an equally lamentable record. Jameson's one win from four as a juvenile was followed by placings this season behind two other Derby runners: Shogun had beaten him by four lengths in Newbury's Greenham Stakes in April and Anmer proved too good for him by a similar margin at Newmarket shortly afterwards. Willoughby's white jacket with the yellow cuffs would be worn by Elijah Wheatley, so diminutive he was nicknamed 'The Whippet' (inevitably shortened to 'Whip'), who held the distinction of becoming champion jockey in 1905 while still an apprentice and was presently lying third in the jockeys' table with twenty-one winners. Jameson was unlikely to make it twenty-two.

Agadir could lay claim to be the Derby 'dark horse'. Every prestigious event boasts one, and the term has nothing to do with the animal's colour. Agadir had only run twice in his life: once as a two-year-old when he was allegedly not quite right and once this season, winning a Lingfield Park Plate over the Derby distance from a horse who had been sent to the race in the belief that he was unbeatable. Consequently, in racing parlance, Agadir could be 'anything' and might just spring a surprise for rider Walter Earl, who told reporters that none of his stablemates could live with the colt over one-and-a-half miles. A Derby victory could not come too soon for his 23-year-old jockey who was fast outgrowing a career on the Flat (he'd only scraped together seven wins this year) and might not get many more chances.

The complete novices in the field were the duo of Sandburr and Henri Jelliss. Trained by Edward Craven, Sandburr ran in the colours of Mrs G. Foster Rawlins and had only run once in his life, and that unplaced in a maiden plate over a mile at Kempton Park on 9 May. No maiden had won the Derby since Merry Hampton won on his debut back in 1887 and Sandburr's participation owed everything to a cable from Foster Rawlins in New York insisting the horse ran 'at all costs'. Twenty-one-year-old Belgian-born jockey Henri Jelliss would need to have been a fantasist to contemplate victory on what was his first ride in the Derby.

The one horse Wheatley, Earl and Jelliss and the other jockeys must have been glad not to be riding, however, was Aboyeur. This black son of Desmond would run equipped with blinkers, the rogue's 'badge', and with good reason: he was reputed to be a savage. Every jockey was familiar enough with horses displaying nasty tendencies since they were far from rare. The claustrophobic, and frequently brutal, stable conditions – once criticised by Enoch Wishard – weren't yet a total relic of the past. A regime of persistent sweating and strapping, combined with barbaric practices like the application of vicious wire contraptions to prevent colts from self-abuse, and the merciless employment of spur and whip by jockeys when the animals were doing their utmost, was quite sufficient to convert a docile creature into an equine lunatic.

The story of Muley Edris pulling Fred Archer to the ground

and kneeling on him the better to savage him, is well documented, as is the tale of the 1835 Derby winner Mundig actually
killing a man and the many stories of pitched battles between
half-crazed colts on Newmarket Heath and Richmond Moor.
Both George Lambton and P. P. Gilpin wrote of horse fights
they'd witnessed on the Limekilns at Newmarket: the former's
concerned Prince Simon who, after throwing his rider and biting
at nearby trees, chased his trainer's hack while the said trainer
hid in the branches. Gilpin recorded watching three or four of
Colonel Hall Walker's animals 'fighting like a lot of terriers,
down on their knees, attacking each other with their teeth and
heels'. Gilpin confessed to having one savage in his own yard
whom he had to beat off with a broom after it had thrown its lad
and gone for him open-mouthed on the ground. He concluded:
'Once a horse becomes a savage he is rarely any good to anyone
afterwards, and least of all on a racecourse.' Others believed it
was this selfsame high-spirit that made high-class racehorses
and that, in consequence, this courage should not be diluted or
quashed. This was the philosophy of Richard Marsh throughout the torrid period he spent attempting to convert Diamond
Jubilee from a psychopathic delinquent into a tractable Classic
contender. The fact the colt won a Triple Crown perhaps proves
Marsh had a point.

The source of Aboyeur's antisocial tendencies, however, was
more hereditary than environmental: Desmond was temperamental himself and Aboyeur's dam, the maiden Pawky, was by a
Hunt Cup and Gold Cup winner, Morion, who was as nasty as
they come. Indeed there was little on the dam's side of Aboyeur's
pedigree to suggest any reason for optimism until one reached
Stamp, the dam of Fitz Roland, winner of the 1858 2000 Guineas.
In Aboyeur's favour, however, was the fact that he ran for a syndicate of owners known as the Druid's Lodge Confederacy, named
after its isolated purpose-built training establishment near
Stonehenge on Salisbury Plain, which had acquired the deserved
reputation of being one of the most feared betting stables in the

country: its stable staff were locked in at night and any touts foolish enough to sniff around this fortress for early morning clues on
'trial' days were sent packing with a thrashing.

The Confederacy comprised five men, each of whose colours
were represented among its horses. Aboyeur ran in the name
of Percy Cunliffe, owner of the land on which Druid's Lodge
sat, who acted as the burly, overall mastermind of the syndicate.
He was an Old Etonian and City financier (and brother to
the Governor of the Bank of England) with hands-on racing
insight as a director and shareholder at Sandown Park and a
Steward at Brighton. While out in South Africa exploiting the
newly discovered gold fields he met avian-featured Wilfred
Purefoy – known as 'The Nut' among the racing fraternity – an
Old Harrovian and ex-cavalryman from landed stock in County
Tipperary, with investments in the West End stage and an eye
for its female inhabitants, besides a penchant for collecting rare
orchids and water lilies. It was 'Wicked Wilfred', as his family
called him, who orchestrated the stable commissions. During an
era when detailed form guides were scarce and the day's runners
were often unknown until minutes before the off, so astutely
did he perform his task that bookmakers seldom determined
the actual weight of money being laid until it was too late. It
wasn't unknown for him to 'keep' a horse a couple of years before
launching it at unsuspecting bookmakers with perhaps a stone in
hand, always selecting a race where a strong market was assured.
Frank Forester was another Old Etonian who'd served in the
3rd Hussars with Purefoy and had inherited a fortune which he
used to fund his twin passions of hunting and racing; he was
Master of the Quorn and, like Cunliffe, a Steward – though he
was not averse to abandoning his role as gamekeeper and turning
poacher to ride as an amateur jockey when given the chance.
Forester's role was to scout talent. Edward Wigan was another
Old Etonian cushioned by inherited wealth, and possessed of
a personality demanding he use it stealthily. The fifth and final
member of this cabal was Holmer Peard, a tall and handsome

Irish vet, stud manager and racing administrator who acted as the Confederacy's Irish 'spotter'. Thus, the Confederacy lacked nothing in capital, guile and racing knowledge. It reckoned it couldn't fail in its aim of fleecing the bookmakers. And it didn't.

In 1913 the trainer's licence was held by Ulsterman Ted Lewis ('for years considered one of the cleverest men in his profession,' according to the *Life*) following the 'retirement' of fellow Irishman Jack Fallon, fortified by a nest egg (of around £3 million) which he squandered away inside a decade. Fallon's 'pension fund' was generated by the Confederacy – or 'The Hermits of Salisbury Plain' as others called them – landing huge, cunningly planned, coups. In 1903 it landed the equivalent of £4 million when Ypsilanti (an ex-Wishard animal bought out of a seller for a comparative pittance) won the Great Jubilee Handicap and a further, quite astronomical sum of £10 million when Hackler's Pride won the Cambridgeshire six months later after being backed down from fancy odds through 25/1 to a starting price of 6/1. Twelve months on another fortune followed as the filly won the Cambridgeshire a second time; then, in 1909–10 it was a case of déjà vu when Christmas Daisy also recorded the Cambridgeshire double.

However, despite the undoubted class of Hackler's Pride and Ypsilanti, the Confederacy wasn't especially synonymous with Classic contenders. Cunliffe's Lord Rossmore had taken the Irish Derby in 1903 but that Classic didn't hold anything near the status it does today – its runners, for instance, carrying weights based on prize-money won. Its best representative was Purefoy's home-bred colt Lally, a top-rated two-year-old who won the Eclipse Stakes of 1907 a year after starting a disappointing favourite for Spearmint's Derby when carrying huge Confederacy bets – which Lally later recouped by winning Ascot's ultra-competitive Hunt Cup with his ears pricked. Aside from Lally's participation, the Confederacy's contribution to the Derby was restricted to Sarcelle (also in 1906), and Charles O'Malley and Royal Tender who came third in 1910 and 1911.

Aboyeur certainly didn't share the same lofty profile as Lally: he received just 7st 9lb in the Free Handicap – 23lb behind the top-rated Craganour. And his seven-race career record going into the Derby read: unplaced, won, third, second, fourth, fifth and fourth. But, if the Confederacy thought Aboyeur worth running might he not stand some sort of chance despite his paucity of Derby credentials? 'Mr Cunliffe is not a sentimentalist,' said the *Illustrated Sporting and Dramatic News*, 'by no means one of those who like to see their colours in the field for a big race. He likes to see his colours when he thinks there is a strong probability of their being first in the finish.' Odds of 200/1 were 'offered and taken' about Aboyeur on the eve of the race; on race day itself the Confederacy invested a further £250 each way on the course at 100/1, hardly an extravagant wager by its own stratospheric standards but one set to bring in excess of £30,000 (over £1¼ million) if by some fluke Aboyeur were to prove successful. After all, Jeddah (1898) and Signorinetta (1908) had sprung the same surprise within living memory.

The Confederacy had acquired Aboyeur in the summer of 1911 when Cunliffe asked Purefoy and Peard to go and see three Desmond colts of the late James Daly's near Dublin. Suitably impressed, Peard purchased all three and passed the colt destined to carry the name Aboyeur on to Cunliffe for 1,000 guineas; the colt thus acquired his fourth owner in a year, having been sold to Daly by his breeder Tom Laidlaw. His name, literally the French for 'barker', emanated from the restaurant business – Purefoy was a director of the renowned West End restaurant Romano's – where it referred to the waiter who relayed orders from the dining room to the kitchen.

Aboyeur didn't see a racecourse until well into the 1912 season, making his debut at Newbury in June in the Kennet Plate over five furlongs against a dozen others that included one previous winner and an Ismay colt called Loch Garry already thrice placed second. Aboyeur neither featured in the betting nor the race, finishing nearer last than first. A month later he was sent to his local track for the Bibury Club meeting and the Champagne Stakes, again over five furlongs. The market made him the 10/1 fourth best in a field of thirteen which included two other representatives of Druid's Lodge in Gibbet Rath and Queen's Parade. Had the bookmakers known that Aboyeur had dropped his work rider (a tough former steeplechase jockey allotted the unenviable task) the previous morning and galloped the six miles into Salisbury's town centre before being caught, they may have extended those odds. Just as well they didn't, because it was a weaker field than at Newbury and Aboyeur beat the favourite by a half-length. As *The Times* reported: 'The winner came from an altogether unexpected quarter.'

Lewis had Aboyeur back on the track the following week at Sandown Park. However, the Great Kingston Plate looked a much hotter affair, featuring four-time winner Thistleton (the 5/4 on favourite) and Harmonicon, a dual winner who had been placed at Ascot. Furthermore, the race conditions ensured that Aboyeur had to concede the pair 5lb. Bearing that in mind, plus the fact that Thistleton would win his two remaining races and Harmonicon would go on to win again at Liverpool before being pitted against the very best of the generation in the Middle Park and Dewhurst, Aboyeur did commendably to finish third, two-and-a-half lengths behind Harmonicon. Aboyeur returned to Sandown on 5 August and finished a close second to another H. P. Whitney animal in the filly Fly By Night.

Encouraged by these last two displays, the Confederacy let Aboyeur stand his ground for the International Plate at Kempton Park on the 18th of the month, the most valuable race he'd been asked to tackle and one that included top-notchers such as Craganour, Shogun, Flippant and Meeting House among its possible starters. On the day, only the last two opposed Aboyeur but even they were unable to give lumps of weight away to the filly Research and succumbed in a blanket finish. However, close up in fourth, was Aboyeur, who had likewise given the winner the best part of a stone.

Aboyeur subsequently suffered a serious attack of coughing accompanied by a high temperature. Thanks to being inoculated he recovered quickly and after a long rest he reappeared on the first day of November. The event chosen was the Free Handicap at Newmarket and it marked his first attempt at six furlongs. The field was small and select: seven runners headed by Lord Derby's Light Brigade and J. B. Joel's filly Jest, both fresh from a win and evenly matched on previous form behind Prue at Hurst Park: the colt led on sufferance only until William Huxley was prepared to let Jest stride past him. Aboyeur, giving her 4lb, finished fifth. This, too, amounted to no mean performance on Aboyeur's part: in 1913 Jest would win both the 1000 Guineas and the Oaks.

Thus, Aboyeur went into winter quarters rated 23lb inferior to the best of his generation. 'The crack two-year-old is very rarely supposed to be as much as 7lb in front of his rivals,' Purefoy was to write later on. Possibly, Purefoy believed Aboyeur would prosper over longer distances as a three-year-old, as Charles O'Malley, another son of Desmond, had done three years earlier. Be that as it may, the Confederacy didn't scratch Aboyeur from the Derby during the winter and, moreover, was said to have invested the odd pound on him to win it. This was always assuming Aboyeur's temperament could be held in check.

No time was wasted in testing Aboyeur's Classic credentials. On the first afternoon of the 1913 season he went to Kempton Park for the Easter Stakes where he faced a battery of opponents between 5 and 15lb his superior on the formbook yet here conceding him only 3–7lb. Accordingly, there was not a penny for him in the betting ring. The desperately heavy ground acted against the top weights and enabled Hippeastrum (8st) to make full use of his maiden's allowance to beat Roseworthy (9st 7lb) by three lengths; Aboyeur (9st) came home fourth, just ahead of Flippant, Rock Flint and Sanquhar.

That was all the general public had to go on. Aboyeur wasn't subjected to public scrutiny again until the Derby. Unless, that is, one happened to be watching on Salisbury Plain the morning

Aboyeur repeated his trick that prefaced victory in the Champagne Stakes by unseating his work rider and investigating the road into Salisbury. What might have been construed as a favourable omen for the Derby immediately fell flat when the colt went lame in his final piece of work (he was always dogged by suspect tendons). His work rider was ordered: 'Get on the bugger and ride him back, he's too lame to run on Wednesday, anyway. He'll eat you before you get home if you try and lead him!' However, by some miracle or other, Aboyeur recovered in time to board the London train; the generous odds of 200/1 available the day before the race were reported by *The Sporting Life* as 'offered and taken'.

There was still one snag: as late as twenty-four hours before the Derby no jockey had been confirmed for Aboyeur. Having failed to entice Steve Donoghue to come aboard as Druid Lodge's retained rider, the Confederacy had increasingly taken to putting up Edwin Piper whenever he was available. The 25-year-old Piper had ridden Aboyeur in five of his seven races, including the victory at Salisbury and the Easter Stakes, but, surprisingly for an unsung jockey, his availability to take the ride in the Derby was in doubt for his name was being linked with other possible mounts. Piper was expected to partner 'Boss' Croker's Knight's Key, on whom he'd won twice and been narrowly beaten in the Chester Vase. Further muddying the waters was the fact that he'd also partnered Aldegond when Mr Broome's Derby contender won the Victoria Cup. By the time Knight's Key was taken out of the Derby at 4.40 p.m. on the eve of the race, the mount on Aldegond had passed to 'Tich' Bellhouse. So, at the eleventh hour, Piper was free to renew his association with Aboyeur.

Although Piper could claim to be having a decent start to the season with sixteen winners already recorded, this sudden popularity must have come as some sort of pleasant shock to him because he was in the same boat as William Saxby. His reputation was that of no more than a reliable journeyman: he'd won no Classics and his fifty-three winners the previous season, though his highest ever total, still placed him some way down the jockeys' list. Like his contemporary Saxby, he had one foot on the ladder but he needed a push from somewhere if he was to rise any higher. The patronage of a leading owner or trainer would suffice. Saxby had attracted Ismay; Piper won a retainer from George Edwardes, the impresario behind West End theatres such as the Gaiety and Daly's. Unfortunately, Edwardes possessed no Craganours for Piper to ride in 1913. The prospect of an association with the 'one good horse' all aspiring jockeys crave in order to make their mark seemed remote.

Piper had been raised around horses. His father and uncle ran a riding school and trained point-to-pointers from the tiny village of Lew Down, on the north-western lip of Dartmoor, where he was born on the last day of 1887. William Piper sired fifteen children in almost as many years, and young Edwin George (the sixth of eight boys) must have known hard times: four of his siblings didn't survive the cradle. Times grew even harder when Edwin was eight years old after William Piper's horse fell in front of a cart and his father suffered fatal stomach injuries. The teenage horseman cut his teeth competing in local show rings and with his elder brothers satisfying the labour requirements of the family business he left Devon in 1905 for Lambourn, and an apprenticeship with Harry Bates.

Piper struggled to make an impact. His first winner didn't arrive for two years and the scalp of a major handicap, where canny trainers were always eager to put up a promising claimer to assure a betting coup, eluded him until Hayden landed the 1908 Great Jubilee for Atty Persse. Hope flamed in 1911, however. His win on Maaz in the Chester Vase was one of forty-three that year and he secured the job with Edwardes (one of Bates's owners) – and the patronage of Druid's Lodge. But 1912 brought forth the same pattern: thirty-eight winners of no significance; no Classic mounts and just half a dozen at Ascot to showcase his talents. Aboyeur would be only his second ride in the Derby. At

least Aboyeur, for all his sins, held a better chance than his first
mount – Chili II was sent off at odds of 300/1 in 1911.

There was one more 'nuisance' in the field besides Aboyeur, in
an ownership as far removed from the Machiavellian world of
Druid's Lodge as one could possibly imagine, for this outsider
ran for the most pre-eminent owner of them all: His Majesty
the King. George V's leisure pursuit of choice was sailing not
horse racing, unlike his father, Edward VII, who loved the raffish
atmosphere of the Turf and won no fewer than three runnings of
the Derby: with Persimmon (1896) and Diamond Jubilee (1900)
as the Prince of Wales and, most memorably, Minoru in 1909
as King. No doubt conscious of his legacy, George V set about
trying to uphold family honour in the sport and his nation's greatest horse race. He took over the Royal colours to win six races
in 1911 and a further thirteen in 1912, when he fielded his first
runner in the Derby, Pintadeau who finished fourth. This year it
was the turn of Pintadeau's brother Anmer (named after a house
on the Sandringham estate) to carry the purple, scarlet-sleeved
and gold-braided jacket with the gold-fringed black velvet cap.

Anmer was a handsome bay sporting a white star extending
into a broad stripe, two white feet behind and a distinctive white
spot in front of his off-fore coronet. Unfortunately he lacked
matching ability and possessed next to no chance of breaking
the new King's duck the day after his forty-eighth birthday or
providing Royal jockey Herbert Jones with a third Derby success
to stand alongside that of Minoru and Diamond Jubilee.

Next to Danny Maher, who had ridden in eleven Derbies and
won three, 32-year-old Herbert Ebsworth Jones was the most
experienced Derby jockey in the field with ten appearances.
He'd been connected with the Royal colours all his life, being
the son of Jack Jones, an Epsom-based steeplechase jockey who
won the 1878 Grand National on Shifnal and later trained jumpers for the Prince of Wales before he became Edward VII. As a
result, Herbert, one of thirteen siblings, and barely able to read
and write, found himself at the age of ten an apprentice with

Royal trainer Richard Marsh at Egerton House. He rode his first winner, Good News, at the Newmarket Craven Meeting of 1896 and the following year registered his first big winner when taking the Liverpool Summer Cup on Brayhead. Nevertheless, chances were few for the doleful-faced boy and he'd recorded just three dozen winners by the spring of 1900.

In the ordinary course of his stable duties, Jones regularly rode the Royal colt Diamond Jubilee in his work. The 'Diamond' was a fiery son of St Simon who terrorised every jockey that came near him – and they included legendary horsemen like Morny Cannon and Marsh's stable jockey Jack Watts – yet in Jones's hands he was contrition itself. The decision was taken to geld Diamond Jubilee (reluctantly so since he was a full brother to Persimmon) but when summoned the vet discovered only one testicle had descended, so nothing was done. It's impossible to state with certainty whether this disability had anything to do with the colt's queer-tempered disposition but when he made his debut in Ascot's Coventry Stakes of 1899 he behaved deplorably throughout the preliminaries. In the paddock he lashed out with his hind legs and connected with the hand of a man standing nearby. It was recorded by Marsh, with indelicate relish, that what made the kick the more excruciating was the fact that at the time the unfortunate man's hand was buried deep in his trouser pocket. Diamond Jubilee went out and finished fourth under Watts; in five further outings he recorded one success, with Cannon in the saddle.

Cannon came down to Newmarket one morning the following spring to work Diamond Jubilee and on dismounting was promptly savaged: he excused himself from the mount in the forthcoming 2000 Guineas without further delay. Watts had already made his feelings known about ever again riding the 'Diamond', so Marsh decided to take a chance and put up Jones, who'd won just a handful of races since his first – and only two in 1899. Diamond Jubilee won by four lengths; then the new partnership won the Derby, followed by the Eclipse Stakes and, finally, the St Leger to complete a Triple Crown. At Doncaster it took Marsh fifteen minutes to get a saddle across his horse and the truculent colt spent most of his time at the starting gate up on his hind legs with Jones clinging on like a rodeo rider. Jones, wrote Marsh in admiration, 'won us not only the Guineas but the Derby and St Leger by keeping in check the colt's ever-present tendency to lapse from the paths of virtue and rectitude'.

Thereafter Jones was known to the public as 'Diamond Jubilee' Jones. To Marsh he amounted to much more:

> He was about the pluckiest and best rough-horseman I have ever seen and the cheeriest soul imaginable. He could do wonders with some horses that would do nothing for others. He may not have been the most artistic but many a horse he had persuaded to better ways that would have been useless.
>
> He had an almost mesmeric influence over Diamond Jubilee, due in large measure to the fact that the horse knew him and trusted him, and to the way Jones would be firm while at the same time 'kidding' to him.
>
> The natural ready wit and his gaiety, together with the absolute trust we had in him, appealed immensely to all of us. A better servant no man ever had and a straighter jockey never got on a horse.

Jones never rode a great number of winners a season (fifty-four in 1906 being his best score) because he seldom overtaxed himself with rides, but rarely did one pass without success in one of the great races. Besides his Classic successes on Diamond Jubilee and Minoru, for example, he won the 2000 Guineas on Vedas and the Oaks on Cherry Lass for Jack Robinson in 1905 and another Guineas on Gorgos in 1906 for Marsh. Nor did he ever lose his uncanny knack with a temperamental animal: Vedas was another with Diamond Jubilee tendencies on whom he excelled and he was the only jockey able to win on another tricky customer called Saxham. His brand of fearless horsemanship was also demonstrated on Charornac in the Great Eastern Handicap of 1903 whom he rode to all intents and purposes bare back. In order to make the weight he rode with only a pad with leathers and irons attached. The opening months of 1913 had seen Jones perform in customarily spare fashion, visiting the winner's enclosure on just three occasions, the last on Great Sport at Hurst Park over three weeks ago, since when he'd ridden less than a dozen races – indeed, the King's two-year-old Per Mare in the opening race on Derby Day was his first ride for a week.

One of those rare sightings was aboard Anmer at Newmarket on 22 May in the Payne Stakes over the full Derby distance, which was meant to advertise the colt's Epsom chances. On this Newmarket evidence those chances amounted to between slim and none because Anmer failed by one-and-a-half lengths to concede 8lb to Kleinfontein, whose previous best had been winning a lowly handicap carrying 7st 1lb.

Unfortunately Anmer laboured under the cross that burdened every Royal thoroughbred: lofty expectations. He was as blue-blooded as his owner, being a son of Florizel II, a full brother to Persimmon and Diamond Jubilee, who'd reached his racing peak at the age of four when victorious in the Ascot Gold Vase, Manchester Cup, Goodwood Cup and Jockey Club Cup before going on to sire Classic-winning sons in Volodyvoski, Vedas and Doricles. Consequently, Anmer was aimed at races in the highest company and made his debut in the Coventry Stakes, leaving no impression: Goodwood's Richmond Stakes yielded a similar outcome; ditto the Rous Memorial Stakes at Newmarket. Anmer had to drop into the humble company of Newmarket's Hastings Plate in the early weeks of the 1913 season to open his account (with Jameson, conceding 12lb, just over four lengths behind) and was spared the inquisition of the 2000 Guineas.

Thus, Anmer had no right to be in the field for a Derby and his odds of 50/1 were a more than fair reflection of his chances. Jones knew that right well as he sat in the weighing room in the Royal colours after coming back from partnering Per Mare in the Caterham Plate, doubtless pondering the dismissive words of *The Sportsman* stating he was among those Derby entrants 'far better in their stables than possibly interfering with some of the others, such as the hot favourite Craganour'.

Fate had conspired to await Herbert Jones throughout his life: both on and off a horse. Notwithstanding his experiences in the saddle with the demonic Diamond Jubilee, his first attempt at motor cycling necessitated four stitches in an ear; one of his earliest shooting experiences resulted in half-a-dozen shot embedded above an eye; and his first effort in a football match ended in his being knocked insensible.

Fate had one further surprise up her sleeve. The sleeve was blue in colour and adorned the arm of a 40-year-old spinster with no interest in racing.

# TEN

# Faire Emelye

By June 1913 Emily Davison was an outcast. Her impetuosity had seen her pushed to the fringes of the suffragette movement – which itself hovered on the margins of respectable society. She was not always so ostracised.

Like most of her comrades she was a rebellious product of the bourgeoisie. She was born at Roxburgh House, in Vanburgh Park Road, Greenwich, on 11 October 1872, the second child of Charles Edward Davison's second marriage. Davison's family hailed from Wooler in Northumberland, where in the early 1800s his grandfather was appointed armourer to the Duke of Northumberland, resulting in his father establishing himself as a gunsmith. Charles Davison furthered his inheritance through speculative ventures ranging from brewing to property speculation and marriage to a wealthy heiress he'd met while establishing a business in India. She presented him with nine children before an early death. Davison must have missed the pleasures of the marital bed because he fathered another daughter, Letitia Charlotte, prior to marrying Margaret Caisley, some twenty-six years his junior, on 3 August 1868. Within weeks of the marriage his teenage bride was pregnant with Alfred Norris; in 1874 Ethel Henrietta followed Emily. By now, having invested heavily in a London tramway company, Davison had brought his family south.

Soon after Emily's birth, they left Greenwich for an imposing Georgian mansion called Gaston House that dominated the hamlet of Gaston Green on the Hertfordshire-Essex border. It was here, in some splendour, that Emily Davison spent the first nine years of her life cosseted by a governess, nanny, two house-maids, a footman and a cook. She was a high-spirited, daring and mischievous child, always the leader in the nursery and its deputed emissary whenever more freedom and more sweets – or 'Weet' as Emily pronounced the word (thereby earning her childhood nickname) – were to be begged from the grown-ups. 'Miss Emily, would you please return to the nursery,' her nanny, according to Davison's first biographer Gertrude Colmore, would demand. 'Now, be a good girl and do as I ask.' The little girl would stand against the wall at the top of the stairs, fold her arms and firmly plant her feet. The bright eyes would spit defiance and she would deliver her stock reply: 'No! I don't want to be good!'

Her choice of childhood play was equally revealing. Dolls and dolls houses were not for her. She preferred to play soldiers. And her way was the only way. A funeral procession for dead flies, for example, couldn't get underway until flags had been manufac-tured. When the other children opted to get on with the game without them, Emily went off in a huff. In contempt, and with the inexplicable logic known only to the young, they called her 'Pem'. The ignominious nickname stuck.

She was a tomboy of the first magnitude with more than a trace of nonconformity in her make-up, 'a regular pickle' as one family friend phrased it. This didn't prevent her from develop-ing into a sensitive and highly intelligent young woman: by the age of five she was already reading from her father's copy of *The Times* and able to recite lengthy chunks of poetry. Her formal education commenced at a London day school once her parents had moved to 43 Fairholme Road in West Kensington after the rustic idyll of Gaston House ended in tragedy. In 1880 the chil-dren fell victim to an outbreak of diphtheria which claimed the life of Emily's beloved younger sister Ethel.

At the age of thirteen she transferred to Kensington High School. This new school was one of a dozen day schools lately opened in and around London by the Girls' Public Day School

Company, aiming to provide an academic education for 'girls of all classes' over the age of ten with the lowest of fees. Besides the obvious academic areas, these schools determined to provide the most stringent moral and religious education. Her new head-mistress Miss Agnes Hitchcock described the thirteen-year-old:

> Rather delicate ... without much colour but with bright, intel-ligent eyes and a half-shy, half-confident way of looking up with her head a little on one side and smiling at one which won my heart at once. Her father was evidently very much devoted to her and very much afraid she might be over-worked.

Charles Davison need not have worried. His daughter achieved a 'fair standard' in German, Latin and Mathematics, but excelled in English Literature, Drama and French. Her aptitude for French was sparked by spending one year in Lausanne and its grasp was honed to perfection later on by holidaying with Letitia in Dunkirk, where she'd settled after her marriage to a local shipbuilder Frederick de Baecker. Miss Hitchcock continued:

> She did not attract as much attention or inspire as many hopes as to her future career as other and more brilliant girls who were her contemporaries. But she had a way of coming out better in examinations than we expected, and her essays showed thought and originality above the average. She was an interesting pupil, quickly stirred over passages in history and literature that appealed to her sense of the noble and the beautiful. Under a quiet unassuming exterior there was a great fund of enthusiasm, and a surprising power of steady and persistent work.

Hitchcock remembered her as 'a very gentle-mannered girl' but beneath the placid exterior, the soul of the teenage Emily Davison was becoming imbued with religious fervour. She had always sung hymns with Ethel before consenting to sleep, and now she was seldom far from her Bible or without two prayer books, whose psalms showed key words and phrases underlined and remarked upon for constant reference. Yet there were no signs of this fervour getting out of control. She was even-tempered, easy to get on with and well liked by her peers. They called her the 'faire Emelye' in recognition of her devotion and resemblance to the golden-haired maiden in Chaucer's *Knight's Tale* whose wish for a life of virginal freedom was ignored when she was given to Palamon as a prize. She loved cats, grew to love the theatre, whether Shakespeare, Bernard Shaw or musical comedy; possessed a fine soprano voice and was a keen dancer. An aptitude for swimming (securing a gold medal at one championship) and the new craze for cycling and roller skating reinforced the notion of a young woman strong in both mind and body.

Davison successfully negotiated the Higher Certificate Examination of the Oxford and Cambridge Joint Board (English Literature, French, German, Scripture, Mathematics and Drawing – gaining a distinction in the first three) and in 1891 won a bursary at the Royal Holloway College in Egham to study for the Oxford Honour School in English Literature. An academic future of some kind seemed assured. Miss Hitchcock summed up her teenage pupil: 'She proved earnest, diligent and conscientious in any work she undertook and a power of steady persevering work made her teachers augur well for her future.'

The very existence of the Royal Holloway signified changing attitudes toward the provision of further education for women. Founded in 1879 exclusively for women students, it was the brainchild of multi-millionaire Thomas Holloway who'd invited suggestions of how best to spend £250,000; the successful idea came from his wife. Davison began her studies in January 1892 and flourished until the first crisis in her cushioned existence arose just over a year later: in February 1893 her father died. Shortly afterwards she was summoned to the latest family home in Priory Road, Kew – suburban comfort, yet far removed from the opulence of Gaston House – to be informed by her mother they'd been left financially embarrassed. Emily's bursary amounted to

£30 per annum (the equivalent of a housemaid's annual wage) and finding the additional £20 per term to fund her at the Royal Holloway was an impossibility. Davison gave up her place. Her decision was accepted with reluctance. 'She possesses considerable activity and great energy and perseverance,' wrote Holloway's principal in her testimonial. 'She is courteous, very good-natured in her relations to all about her and has already taken the Oxford Pass Examination in French, German and English, the latter with a distinction.' It's interesting to note, given her subsequent flouting of it, that the principal also stressed her 'respect for authority'.

Margaret Davison sold the house in Kew and moved back north, to Longhorsley, a small village on the road to Scotland out of Morpeth, where she bought the corner shop and bakery opposite the Shoulder of Mutton pub. Her daughter refused to let this setback scupper the academic career intended to underwrite her aspirations. Having safely negotiated the Oxford Second Examination for Women at the Royal Holloway, she took up a position as a governess while continuing to study in the evenings with a view to completing the course. This enabled her to save enough money to cover the fees (around £20–25) for one crucial term of tutoring at Oxford's St Hugh's Hall, immediately prior to sitting her Finals in the summer of 1895.

St Hugh's was one of five Halls at Oxford specifically for women students. It provided opportunities for women in poorer circumstances, having been founded in 1886, eight years after the creation of the Association for the Education of Women in Oxford ended centuries of male domination at the University. Even so, it would be 1920 before women were formally allowed to matriculate (enjoy full membership of the University) or graduate (receive the degree to which any examination success entitled them). St Hugh's clearly regarded Davison's situation as exceptional since students weren't normally allowed to reside for less than a year. Its faith and Davison's doggedness were suitably rewarded with a First in English Language and Literature. When the news reached Longhorsley, an unusually ebullient Emily grabbed a jar of humbugs from her mother's shop and flung the 'black bullets' to the children of the village. Besides her degree she could add a further short yet glowing reference to her portfolio: from Elizabeth Lea, her English tutor, who deemed her 'industrious and painstaking'.

Compared to what had come before in Emily Davison's life and what was to come after, the eleven years between 1895 and 1906 were singularly unremarkable. A brief flirtation with public education in a London state school saw her find discipline hard to maintain. She served one year (1895–96) in Birmingham on the staff of the Church of England College for Girls in Edgbaston (teaching Literature, Latin, Mathematics and assisting with Games) followed by two years at Seabury School in West Worthing, but spent the majority of this period in the private sector or as a resident governess in the homes of well-to-do families, such as the Moorhouses of Spratton Grange in Northamptonshire – just a few miles north of Bower Ismay's home at Haselbech Hall – whose teenage daughters Ann and Mary were more willing pupils even if they did consider her 'solemn and severe'; a picture of her successor in the family photograph album has a note by the side saying they liked her much better than Davison. It's possible Davison's 'solemnity' reflected her pining for the vibrancy of London to which she hinted in verse:

> Oh, London! How I feel thy magic spell
> Now I have left thee, and amid the woods
> Sit lonely. Here I know I love thee well,
> Conscious of all the glamour of thy moods.
> But it is otherwise amid thy bounds!
> Thou art an ocean of humanity!
> Embarked on which I lose my soul in sounds
> That thunder in mine ear. The vanity
> And ceaseless struggle stifle doubt and fear
> Until I cry, bemused by the strife,
> 'The centre of the universe is here!
> This is the hub, the very fount of life.'

Throughout this period she sought additional qualifications. In 1878 London University had become the first to graduate women and, in addition, offer external degrees that promoted learning while earning: in 1902 Davison began reading for a BA degree in Modern Languages and in time graduated with Honours (Class III) in 1908.

Despite the pressures of teaching and studying, Davison had shown no sign of rebellion during her twenties and into her thirties. Observed Miss Hitchcock:

> I never heard her complain or express anxiety about her own future or that of her mother. I never heard her utter a word against anyone under whom or with whom she worked, and no one ever had less thought of adopting a 'misunderstood' pose, or the role of the neglected governess. On the contrary, she spoke of her affection for her pupils and of the kindness she received from their parents.

But by this point in her life there was another, inevitable, outlet for a woman of her intellect and intransigence: the fight for women's suffrage. John Stuart Mill's presentation to the House of Commons in 1866 of a petition asking for the enfranchisement of all householders, regardless of sex, had marked the first significant step in the campaign for votes for women. However, the National Union of Women's Suffrage Societies under the auspices of Mrs Millicent Fawcett amounted to mild lobbyists rather than violent activists. It was not until Mrs Emmeline Pankhurst founded the Women's Social and Political Union on 10 October 1903 that the drive for female emancipation adopted a more forceful tone: 'Deeds Not Words' became both motto and credo. The name of the new society was chosen to highlight its democracy. But it was directed by an autocrat in Mrs Pankhurst:

> It is purely a volunteer army, and no one is obliged to remain in it, but we don't want anybody to remain in it who does not ardently

believe in the policy of the army. Any woman can become a member by paying a shilling, but she is required to sign a declaration of loyal adherence to our policy.

The WSPU aimed to rid society of the attitude 'the woman, the cat and the chimney should never leave the house' which left women bereft of marital as well as professional rights. Why should wives not have the same rights of divorce as their husbands? Why should women be excluded from professions such as the Bar or the top positions in the Civil Service? If women got the Vote it would surely benefit women of every age and class, declared the WSPU's leader. 'England,' stated Winston Churchill, 'is the best country in the world for rich men.' Emmeline Pankhurst determined to achieve the same for women and the poor.

'Emmeline Pankhurst was at once recognised by me as a force, vital and resourceful,' wrote one early convert, Teresa Billington-Greig. Another, Canadian-born Mary Richardson, known throughout the movement as 'Polly Dick', was to write: 'She was a grand speaker on the platform. She tilted back her head and her voice deepened as she began to speak; her face came alight, her fingers clenched.' Emmeline Pethick-Lawrence agreed: 'She had a temperament akin to genius. She could have been a queen on the stage or in the salon. Excitement, drama and danger were the conditions in which her temperament found full scope. She had the qualities of a leader on the battlefield.' Annie Kenney put it most succinctly of all: 'They adored her. There is no other word for it.'

Mrs Pankhurst espoused a radical shift in strategy, encouraging her 'spiritual army' toward more disruptive measures. Once a Suffrage Bill was tossed aside by Westminster in May 1905 such disruptions became more violent and led to the first imprisonments. The *Daily Mirror* referred to the women as 'notoriety hunters, featherheads and flibbertigibbets'. A letter-writer to *The Times* sneered:

The upsettings of her mental equilibrium are the things that woman has most to hear; and no doctor can ever lose sight of the fact that the mind of woman is always threatened with danger from the reverberations of her physiological emergencies. The woman voter would be pernicious to the State not only because she could not back her vote by physical force, but also by reason of her intellectual defects.

Lloyd George and Churchill called them 'mewing cats … hen-peckers … hornets allying themselves with the forces of drink and reaction'; the police christened them 'she-males'. The *Daily Mail* dubbed this new breed of violent activist 'suffragettes' as opposed to the mild-mannered 'suffragists'. The name stuck.

In October 1906 Emmeline Pethick-Lawrence sent a rallying call from her cell in Holloway: 'Women of England, we are going to prison for you and therefore we do it gladly. We call upon you to take up the standard and bear it on to victory.' Emily Davison, a 'young rebel' enslaved by the 'exploitation of emotion', to use the words of Billington-Greig, answered the call. She attended a WSPU meeting and discovered press reports of these meetings to be distorted accounts of the truth. She found a gathering akin to a revivalist meeting, ringing with religious fervour, rich biblical rhetoric and romantic chivalric allegory. In contrast to venal and corrupt politicians, these women were infused with noble passion and engaged in a new crusade, a 'holy war' in which they were willing to give their lives 'to buy the enfranchisement of women'. They were imbued with the spirit of martyrs, like their *beau ideal*, Joan of Arc.

This army had its own colours of purple ('standing for the royal blood that flows in the veins of every suffragette, the instinct for freedom and dignity'), white (purity in private and public life) and green (hope and the emblem of spring); put another way, Give (green) Women (white) Votes (violet). These colours ensured emeralds, pearls and amethysts were the precious stones of choice for women keen to declare their coded allegiance to the cause or, indeed, whenever suffragettes exchanged items of jewellery as love tokens. The colours were replicated in merchandise ranging from bicycles, crockery and the most comfortable corsets for marching in, to card and board games called 'In and Out of Holloway Gaol'. They had their own newspaper, *Votes For Women*, which had an average weekly readership of 160,000. This entrepreneurial spirit saw the equivalent of £3 million added to the suffragette 'war chest' in five years.

The army marched to its own music, a blend of religious fervour and emotional intensity stoking a feeling of sisterhood. The movement had its own anthem, 'The Women's Marseillaise' – in time superceded by the especially composed 'March of the Women':

> Firm in reliance, laugh a defiance –
> Laugh in hope, for sure is the end,
> March, march – many as one,
> Shoulder to shoulder and friend to friend

There would be renderings from *Women's Suffrage Songbook*, which included (sung to the tune of 'Auld Lang Syne'):

> They say we are so ignorant
> We don't know right from wrong,
> But we can tell them what we want
> And what we'll have ere long!

To the tune of 'John Brown's Body' a second popular marching song:

> Rise up women! For the fight is hard and long,
> Rise in thousands, singing loud a battle song,
> Right is might and in its strength we shall be strong,
> And the cause goes marching on!

Another favourite was 'Women Join Hands', which captured their passionate camaraderie:

> Heart upon heart that waited,
> Hands which feared to begin;
> Hands with hearts now mated,
> Hand in hand we shall win.
> Right is stronger than might,
> Higher than kingship stands;
> Truth with face to the light,
> Women join hands, join hands!

Emily Davison had found a cause worth fighting for and shortly after celebrating her thirty-fourth birthday in October 1906 she enrolled in the Women's Social and Political Union. In a letter to *Votes For Women* she confided:

> To me, who lately led an ordinary commonplace existence, there has come through my enrolment the most wonderful broadening out and enriching of life. Through my humble work in the noblest of causes I have come into a fullness of joy and an interest in living which I never before experienced. I had a power to look beyond the outward appearance of events, to see right into their hidden meanings. And this is the power which is gradually permeating all over the land, and filling its women with that old love of liberty and justice. When the women are free, then will Britain be able to say in truth that which is only partially true: 'Britons never, never will be slaves!'

At last Emily Davison could inhabit *The Knight's Tale*.

She'd joined the WSPU at a turning point in its campaign. Despite gaining widespread support its claims continued to be ignored by both Parliament and government. Militancy was about to escalate. What Mrs Pankhurst called 'the argument of the stone' began in earnest; 'the argument of the broken pane is the most valuable argument in modern politics'. Davison must have committed herself to the movement with vigour because on 21 June 1908 she was entrusted with her first official duty – and a very crucial one: chief Steward at Marylebone station responsible for shepherding thousands of women to a massive demonstration in Hyde Park. The crowd was eventually estimated at up to half a million, the largest public meeting ever held in Britain. Within a fortnight the first window-smashing had begun. 'The time for dealing gently with idle, mischievous women who call themselves "militant suffragists" has gone,' harrumphed the *Daily Express*. 'Such things cannot be tolerated … now the country will demand that these women, who incite to disorder and riot, shall be punished with the utmost severity.'

The reason why Davison's suffragette career led her to Epsom on Derby Day 1913 is her indomitable conviction. An active member of the Anglican Church League for Women's Suffrage, she believed herself to be obeying a direct call from God. She determined to convert one of her favourite sayings into reality at every opportunity: 'Rebellion against tyrants is obedience to God.' In consequence, she is best judged by her personal 'rebellion against tyrants' – her deeds – and less so by her words, and hardly at all by the words of others. As she was wont to say: 'Words are cheap and easy compared with deeds which are not.' Everything written about Davison by those who purported to know her is coloured by the manner of her death. The mythical figure they created metamorphosed into historical reality.

'There was little in her appearance,' wrote Sylvia Pankhurst, typically, in 1931, 'to suggest her cool, unflinching courage, or the martyr's fate which finally was to be hers; and of her deliberate choice.' Rebecca West wrote posthumously of 'her cheerfulness and her pyrotechnic intelligence, she was a wonderful talker, her talk was an expression of that generosity which was her master passion. But for her last triumph, when in one moment she, by leaving us, became the governor of our thoughts, she led a very ordinary life for a woman of her type and times.' Cecily Hale's is a more candid post-Epsom verdict upon Davison: 'A fanatic, smouldering, always waiting for the next thing to do.'

Davison's Northumbrian neighbours were equally divided. One who knew her commented: 'Emily Davison was pleasant to meet but had an air of reserve and was uncompromising until she was sure about anyone.' Another recalled her saying to his father: 'If you get me a flying machine and take me to the top of the Houses of Parliament I'll blow them up!' Yet a third: 'Miss Davison was very intelligent and talented, but a fanatic – really two people in one. She could be cool and calm one minute then some impulse would cause her brain to explode like fireworks the next.' One, calling herself an 'old friend', still referred to her as 'a fool'. Above all, there were damning epitaphs from anonymous suffragette leaders: 'she is a self-dramatising individualist, insufficiently capable of acting in the confines of official instructions'; 'clever but headstrong, she tends to walk alone'.

In 1909 Davison stepped onto the vicious treadmill of confrontation, arrest, imprisonment, hunger strike and forcible feeding that led to her Calvary. On 30 March she was arrested following 'great disorder' in Parliament Square when a WSPU deputation attempting to present a resolution to the Prime Minister disintegrated into the usual free-for-all. She was charged with 'assaulting the police in the execution of their duty'; it was alleged she had struck four police officers. In mitigation, she complained that certain MPs had jeered the deputation: 'That was not the act of gentlemen or men but of curs.' Ordered to find two sureties in the sum of £25 each for her 'good behaviour' or undergo one month's imprisonment, Davison chose the latter. She was about to attain, as the suffragettes dubbed it, her 'Holloway Degree' and earn the right to wear the 'Holloway Badge' – an arrow of purple, white and green mounted on a silver portcullis.

Holloway Prison's 'D' Wing was increasingly commandeered for suffragettes. On arrival Davison was asked her name, age, occupation, religion, her sentence and whether she could read, write and sew; this reception process was completed by a cursory doctor's examination. Then, ordered to undress in full view of the rest, she was body-searched, patted down and had her hair examined before taking her turn in a bath of old water. To wear, she was given a short cotton chemise, thick black woollen stockings marked with red rings (but no garters), long cotton drawers, a thick petticoat, a dark green serge dress (lacking pockets) daubed with white painted arrows four inches long that was secured by one button at the neck, and a blue-and-white checked apron. The colour of her dress denoted her status in the Second Division: those in the lowest rank, the Third, wore chocolate dresses; those in the First – those granted 'Political' status – were identifiable by grey dresses. A white cap, one handkerchief and a pair of hard leather tie-up shoes completed her wardrobe. This basic garb was only changed every six weeks, so Davison would serve her entire month's sentence in the same clothes.

She was given a mug of cold cocoa and a thick hunk of brown bread and sent down the stone corridors and up the iron staircases, bounded by trellis railings with wire netting strung from one side to the other to catch inmates driven to suicide jumps, to the tiers of cells. In her outstretched arms she carried a pair of coarse sheets, a Bible, a hymn book and a pair of 'uplifting' religious tracts entitled 'The Narrow Way' and 'A Healthy Home and How to Keep It'. The cell awaiting her was no more than a dark cubicle of seventy-five square feet with no seat other than a small wooden stool and a lid-less lavatory; there was one small barred window high up near the ceiling and a gas jet set into the wall under glass gave off a thick opaque light. Across one corner was a wooden shelf on which lay a wooden spoon, a wooden salt cellar, a tin plate and a tiny joint measure for the prison gruel, made of oatmeal and water and known as 'skilly'; beside these items lay a piece of hard yellow soap, a thin towel, a toothbrush, scrubbing brush and a three-inch comb; each item was passed on from one occupant to the next. She found a mattress and blanket rolled onto a lower, corner shelf; on the floor underneath were a tin dustpan, a small brush for sweeping, a water can, wash basin and a slop-pail. Her bed was made of planks, just two inches off the cold stone floor. Hanging from a peg was a disc of yellow cloth with her cell number on it which she had to stitch to her dress. She would be a number, not a person.

Holloway's daily routine was as numbing to the spirit as the bed was to the body. A waking bell clanged at 5.30, some one-and-three-quarter hours before a breakfast consisting of a pint of sweet tea, a small brown loaf and two ounces of butter (to last all day), taken alone in her cell. Thereafter, Davison was required to clean all her utensils, empty her 'slops', fold up her bedclothes and scrub both her floor and the planks of her bed ready for inspection before chapel. The thirty minutes spent in chapel were in silence; as was the one hour of exercise in the prison yard. She enjoyed one bath per week and two visits to the library, from which books might be borrowed. For the initial four weeks of a sentence, prisoners spent the rest of the day in solitary confine-ment and were allowed neither correspondence nor visitors. Lunch was at noon and supper at five (a pint of greasy cocoa and a small brown loaf); the cell light was extinguished at 8 p.m. A raft of offences rendering Davison liable to punishment included wantonly breaking windows; singing or whistling; being inde-cent in language, act or gesture; swearing, cursing or using any abusive, insolent, threatening or other improper language.

Davison knew what a 'Holloway Degree' entailed but the reality – the mental deprivation alone – must have hit her hard. Nevertheless, within three months she was back in Holloway for a longer and more traumatic stay after she was one of a dozen women who attempted to disrupt a political meeting addressed by Lloyd George in the Mile End Road on 30 July. Her prior conviction earned her a sentence of two months.

All suffragettes demanded to be treated as 'political prisoners' but Davison arrived at Holloway to be informed by the Governor she was to be placed in the Second Division: if she'd 'go quietly' to their cells she might keep her own clothes. She demanded to be treated as First Division. In a letter (signed 'Your loving and rebellious friend, Emelye') written shortly after being released having served only five-and-a-half days, Davison confided how she'd smashed her cell windows with a hammer 'I had concealed about myself … I fasted 124 hours and was then released. I lost 1½ stone and much flesh.'

Hunger-striking had been adopted as a means of effecting early release. Like every hunger-striker (241 in all between 1909 and 1913), Davison's sacrifice was recognised by the movement's Medal of Valour: 'We, the members of the Women's Social and Political Union,' said the accompanying scroll, 'express our deep sense of admiration for your courage in enduring a long period of privation and solitary confinement in prison for the Votes for Women cause.' Davison wasn't finished. In the first week of September she joined a demonstration against Lloyd George's so-called 'People's Budget' at Manchester's White City. She was one of five arrested for throwing iron balls (labelled 'bombs') through the windows of the concert hall, and accepted the sentence of two months in Strangeways Prison. Her incarceration was, naturally, marked by breaking window panes in her cell window (leading to her being handcuffed) and a hunger strike: she was released after two-and-a-half days. This action was meant to be, she described in a letter to the *Manchester Guardian*, 'a warning to the general public of the personal risk they run if in future if they go to Cabinet Ministers' meetings anywhere'.

The early window-smashers received instant notoriety and respect within the suffragette movement. Davison and fellow firebrand Mary Leigh were canonised as 'Saints of the Church Militant'. Yet much of this praise was bogus. Although never publicly condemned for their unilateralism, the leadership distrusted the pair of them. In turn, despite their differences with the leadership, both women refused to cut their ties with the WSPU, which they regarded as much their union as anyone else's. Thus, they continued as rogue elements: renegades, mavericks, who never sought approval for their plans. High-profile politicians were now pursued from one engagement to another.

When Lloyd George visited Newcastle on 9 October, Davison hurled stones at his car. She missed. Eleven days later she targeted another Cabinet minister, Walter Runciman, at the Liberal Club in Radcliffe, Lancashire. Some windows were smashed. Davison and two others accepted the prison sentence and made it clear from the dock that 'a hunger strike would be commenced at once, and if they were forcibly fed action would be taken against the authorities'. Davison was well aware of the possible consequences and had taken the precaution of making her will prior to setting out for the Liberal Club. She left everything to her mother. (When the will was finally read in the summer of 1913 her estate was valued for probate at £186 one shilling and seven pence – equating to just over £8,000 today. By comparison, at her death in 1928, Mrs Pankhurst left a mere £85 five shillings and sixpence.)

Enduring what was her fourth prison sentence in seven months, Davison was as good as her word. On the second evening the matron, two doctors and a posse of wardresses entered her cell. The senior doctor pronounced her fit and then announced his intention to feed her by force. She protested that this was illegal but the doctor's only reply was that it was no concern of his.

Forcible-feeding was the government's policy for combating the use of the hunger strike as an early-release ploy. Its solution to the suffragette problem was summed-up by the Home Secretary: 'One, give them the Vote; Two, deport them; Three, consign them to lunatic asylums; Four, let one or two die of self-starvation.' But the latter bluff was called and suffragettes were subjected to a barbaric practice which involved a tube (with a funnel at one end and a glass junction in the middle to see if the liquid is passing) being pushed through the nostril or down the throat; milk, sometimes egg and milk, was then poured in. This brutal process of penetration was akin to rape from the victim's point of view; indeed, there were recorded instances of tubes being inserted into the rectum and the vagina. This sense of violation was considered worse than the pain of sore and bleeding gums, broken teeth and the repeated agony of coughing up the tube before it could be successfully inserted. The legacy included pulled-out hair, bloodshot eyes, bruised shoulders and aching back. Exceeding the pain of physical degradation was the mental anguish each woman endured as she listened to the moans and cries of her colleagues in the adjoining cells as her turn slowly approached. One suffragette who feared she 'should go mad' actually did, subsequent to her release. The events were so traumatic to all involved that £250 was distributed to wardresses in recompense for the extra strain.

Between 1909 and 1914 this torture was inflicted on 130 suffragettes: Davison would suffer this brutal indignity on forty-nine occasions. After this initiation she was moved to an adjoining cell whose pair of plank beds she manufactured into a makeshift barricade. After she'd repeatedly refused to budge, a window was broken and a hose-pipe was turned on her for fifteen minutes. She was surrounded by six inches of water when the hose-pipe was turned off and the door was finally broken open. She described to the *Manchester Guardian* the impact of again being forcibly fed: 'The drums of the ear seem to be bursting and there's a horrible pain in the throat and breast. The after-effects are a feeling of faintness, a sense of great pain in the diaphragm or breast bone and bad indigestion. The next morning I could hardly rise.'

Davison was released after eight days. She'd kept the first promise made in the dock. Now she set about sticking to the second. She brought an action against the authorities. The medical profession was unanimous in its condemnation: 'This latest piece of official cruelty will quite possibly end in the insanity of some of the victims,' stated Dr Harry Roberts. Questions were being asked in Parliament and a full inquiry was promised. However, the Home Secretary appeared unflustered. He wrote to the officials at Stangeways and applauded them for their 'efficiency and good sense'. On 10 January 1910 Davison's action to recover £100 damages arising from the 'hose-pipe incident'

Emily Davison, the proud suffragette, wearing her Holloway broach and Medal of Valour. © Mary Evans Picture Library

The battleaxe she became by 1913 thanks to years of hunger-striking and forcible feeding. © Getty Images

They might have been brothers: 'Lucky' Loder and 'The Spare'. RIGHT © National Portrait Gallery, London

But their differences are evident in portraits by *Vanity Fair* and *Mayfair*. LEFT © Getty Images,
RIGHT © Michael Manser

Craganour at the end of his juvenile career with Billy Saxby up and Jack Robinson at his head.
© Michael Manser

Saxby reduced to playing golf instead of riding winners.
© Getty Images

BERGER
PHOTO

Tattenham Corner: Davison is pole-axed. © Getty Images

The injured Jones is carted away. © Press Association

The finish: from left to right the five leaders are Nimbus, Great Sport, Craganour, Aboyeur and Louvois; Day Comet's run up the rail is completely missed. One can deduce from Reiff's upright body position how Craganour is suffering from Aboyeur's drift to the right under Piper's left-hand whipping. © Getty Images

ABOVE LEFT Four heads in line: Craganour, Aboyeur, Louvois and lastly, against the rail, Day Comet. © Press Association

ABOVE RIGHT Winner's enclosure: Bower Ismay leads in his short-lived Derby winner. © Getty Images

"The Suffragette," June 13, 1913.

Registered at the G.P.O. as a Newspaper

# The Suffragette

Edited by Christabel Pankhurst.

The Official Organ of the
Women's Social and Political Union

No. 35—Vol. 1.     FRIDAY, JUNE 13, 1913.     Price 1d. Weekly (Post Free 1½d.)

IN HONOUR AND IN LOVING, REVERENT MEMORY
OF
# EMILY WILDING DAVISON.
## SHE DIED FOR WOMEN.

"Greater love hath no man than this, that he lay down his life for his friends."

Miss Davison, who made a protest at the Derby against the denial of Votes to Women, was knocked down by the King's horse and sustained terrible injuries of which she died on Sunday, June 8th, 1913.

Davison's canonisation. © Getty Images

TOP Davison's cortège brings central London to a standstill.
© Press Association

The final resting place of 'Faire Emelye'. © Author collection

was heard at Manchester Crown Court. The defence maintained that she'd gone to prison 'with the avowed intention of breaking every rule … in a way that gave the most trouble and anxiety to those who had to deal with her'. Judge Parry awarded Davison 'nominal damages' of £2: 'the plaintiff had had the satisfaction of providing herself with copy for a vivacious and entertaining account of the affair in the press; and advertising a cause in which she and many others were greatly interested.'

Davison's mood darkened following the events of Friday 18 November – that came to be known as 'Black Friday'. A mass demonstration outside the House of Commons degenerated and a riot ensued. 'As a rule,' said *The Times*, 'the Police kept their tempers very well but their method in shoving back the raiders lacked nothing in vigour.' The women saw things differently: they saw organised gangs of policemen, 'bully-boys dressed in plain clothes like roughs', who manhandled them in the most appalling way. Over one hundred women received injuries of some sort and four died during the coming months as a direct result, and led to suffragettes receiving instruction in jiu jitsu from Edith Garrud, the country's first female expert – a few even took to practicing on a miniature shooting range with Browning pistols: for self-defence or acts of premeditated violence toward politicians it's impossible to tell. Davison was not among the 115 women arrested then, but she was on the Saturday after breaking a window at the Commons. She pleaded guilty to the charge and accepted a month's imprisonment in Holloway – and a further cycle of hunger-striking and forcible feeding that saw her sentence curtailed after eight days.

The WSPU talked of resorting 'to a state of war'. Such tension demanded a truce. Nevertheless, the census of 3 April 1911 yielded a peaceful opportunity for suffragettes to cock a snook at the government by avoiding enumeration. Davison was reported in *The Times* as saying: 'As I am a woman and as women do not count in the State, then I refuse to be counted.' Most chose to avoid the enumerator by staying away from home all day and all night.

But that was too simplistic for Davison: she planned a grander gesture – secreting herself in the House of Commons in order to have herself enumerated within the Palace of Westminster.

Davison was already well known to the Palace authorities: her name frequently crops up in reports filed by Chief Inspector Scantlebury, Head of Police in Parliament, and she had been on the *Index Expungatoris* of banned personages for almost a year. She'd been apprehended inside Westminster the previous April, having spent thirty hours hidden in a hot air duct (sustained by two bananas and some chocolate) with the intention of eventually putting a question to the Commons. Leaving her hideaway in search of water, she was apprehended by a watchman and released without charge. Three months later she broke two panes of glass in the Crown Office and left some scrawled messages for Asquith: 'Be wise. In time women will not be trifled with.' Davison's choice of gaol was no surprise, but later that day her fines were paid by 'a lady' and she was recalled to the dock to be told she was at liberty to go. 'I protest against going!' she railed, stamping her foot in a fit of pique. 'I protest! I protest!' The following day, the Serjeant at Arms received a letter from the Speaker describing Davison as 'evidently not a desirable personage to have hanging about' and requesting she be placed on the excluded list.

Davison was undeterred and on the night of the census she did achieve her objective. Discovered in a broom cupboard off St Mary Undercroft Chapel, she was duly listed on the census form as 'Sole Occupant: Found hiding in crypt of Westminster Hall.' unbeknown to Davison, she was also registered by her landlady at 31 Coram Street, (and described as a 'Political Secretary'), so she doubly undermined the accuracy of the census.

There were still more ducks-and-drakes with Scantlebury's men. Two months later she was found tiptoeing up the Members' staircase at 2.23 in the morning, carrying her shoes and a mineral-water bottle 'containing some liquid'. Her stated intention was to have said when the House re-assembled: 'Gentleman of the

House of Commons, vindicate your own liberty and do justice to the women of England by passing the Women's Enfranchisement Bill in 1911.' Davison was deemed 'foolish' but having committed no criminal offence was discharged.

Goaded beyond reason by months of political indifference and state-sanctioned torture, her 'foolishness' would soon reach fresh heights.

# ELEVEN

# Into the Vortex

On 4 October 1911 Mrs Pankhurst set off on an American tour and Davison was one of a party who gathered at Waterloo station to bid her farewell. Every mile Mrs Pankhurst travelled proved symbolic, putting more than mere physical distance between them. Never again would Davison be so close to her leader in spirit. When the government reneged on its promises to further some form of women's suffrage an uneasy WSPU ceasefire was immediately lifted, and Davison launched a fresh initiative that brought her into conflict with Mrs Pankhurst. From being someone with the leader's ear, she was marooned on the periphery. Her actions came to be regarded as those of a self-aggrandising maverick feeding on the oxygen of publicity. She grew to be a thorn in the leadership's side. In short, a liability. The salaried workforce of the WSPU now exceeded a hundred women but Davison was soon no longer one of them.

Davison's latest bout of impetuosity landed her in the dock of the Central Criminal Court on 10 January 1912 charged with attempting to destroy the contents of letter-boxes. 'The obvious next step after window-breaking was incendiarism,' she declared. She'd manufactured miniature fire bombs by wrapping boxes of wax matches in linen soaked with kerosene, which over a period of six days she lit and dropped into letter-boxes in the streets adjoining the Houses of Parliament. When Davison promptly surrendered to the nearest policeman she was ignored – until one eventually caught her red-handed. 'She has given the police a great deal of trouble,' the arresting officer informed the court. She replied: 'I contented myself with doing just sufficient to make my protest. I ignored pillar-boxes in Aldgate because the people there are of a poorer class.' One further comment is telling: 'I did this entirely on my own responsibility.'

If Davison's claim to acting independently hadn't inflicted enough damage by exposing her to accusations of being a maverick and a renegade, the tactic itself backfired spectacularly. Her trial resulted in the draconian sentence of six months' imprisonment. Quite possibly she hadn't curried favour by informing the Court:

> I stand here for justice, although I feel it is impossible to expect perfect justice in a court where every single official and person, from the judge to the public, is composed of men only. Women, your mothers and sisters, stand side by side. I stand for the justice you deny us.

If that tirade wasn't enough to get under the judge's skin, she ended by stating: 'Justice cannot be perfect when the prisoner is very often judged by a judge who was not in the highest possession of his faculties.'

As a long-term prisoner in Holloway she enjoyed greater privileges than before, especially as outside pressures had ensured some relaxation in the prison's regime. The daily exercise hour became positively joyous, with the women, who included Mrs Pankhurst and Mrs Pethick-Lawrence (jailed for being the leaders of the WSPU and therefore held responsible for the recent spate of incendiarism), even playing 'Here we go gathering nuts in May on a cold and frosty morning' and impromptu games of football – played 'with especial vigour by Davison who became very hot and tired' according to a fellow inmate. During the evenings there were now opportunities for singing, storytelling and reading aloud; a scene from *The Merchant of Venice* was performed, Davison adapting Shylock's 'If you prick me...'

speech by substituting 'Woman' for 'Jew'. A mock election was organised and even a fancy dress ball. The scene painted by more than one suffragette chronicler is redolent of a dormitory of a girls boarding school resounding to jolly japes.

A book of songs and poems written by the incarcerated suffragettes appeared in due course. Entitled *Holloway Jingles*, Davison's contribution, dated 28 April, was called 'L'envoi?':

> Like the pilgrim in the valley,
> Enemies may oft assail us,
> Enemies may close around us,
> Tyrants, hunger, horror, brute-force.
> But the glorious dawn is breaking,
> Freedom's beauty sheds her radiance;
> Freedom's clarion call is sounding,
> Rousing all the world to wisdom.

This comparative idyll – by Holloway standards – was shattered by Mrs Pankhurst insisting on a hunger strike in protest at the denial of first-class status to the majority of the suffragettes. This was the first prison term in which Davison hadn't initiated a hunger strike from the outset. Even so, she'd been forcibly-fed for a week when her health was deemed to be declining. The strike was called for 19 June. Three days later, just days before her due date of release, Davison was once more threatened with being forcibly-fed. In light of what was to happen at Epsom, her response was significant:

> I got up and smashed out the remaining panes of my window, then lay down again until I was able to get out into the corridor. In my mind was the thought that some desperate protest must be made to put a stop to the hideous torture which was now being our lot. Therefore, as soon as I got out, I climbed on to the railing and threw myself out onto the wire netting, a distance of between twenty and thirty feet. The idea in my mind was 'one

big tragedy may save many others' but the netting prevented any severe injury.

I was put into the ward but when the wardresses relaxed their watch, I was able to get out and realised that my best means of carrying out my purpose was the iron staircase. When a good moment came, quite deliberately, I walked upstairs and threw myself from the top, as I meant, onto the iron staircase. If I had been successful I should undoubtedly have been killed, as it was a clear drop of thirty to forty feet. But I caught once more on the edge of the netting. A wardress called on two of my comrades to try and stop me. I realised that there was only one chance left, and that was to hurl myself with the greatest force I could summon from the netting on to the staircase, a drop of about ten feet. I threw myself forward on my head with all my might. I knew nothing more except a fearful thud on my head.

Davison sustained two injuries to the head, two of her vertebrae, the right shoulder blade and the sacrum. She was released on the 28th, ten days early, with an endorsement from Dr Craig ringing in her ears. 'Don't do any more for your cause,' he said, shaking her hand. 'You have done more than enough.'

Craig's official report makes some interesting observations worth highlighting:

She is run-down and her physical health has evidently declined since her fall and continues to suffer. She conversed freely and answered the questions asked of her. Her mental condition and intellect is clear, but *I do not regard her as suicidal in the ordinary sense of the word* as she has never attempted to injure herself in her cell, neither at present is her mental condition sufficient to suggest confusion of mind. She is evidently a most determined woman and *she considers she is right to do anything for the cause and is evidently reckless in what she does for the movement.*

Davison could be credited with forcing not only the release of her fellow hunger-strikers on 6 July, but also the broader public debate of the issue in general. Yet she received scant recognition from her movement other than an additional bar to her Medal of Valour. In the light of subsequent events at Epsom, her claim that her actions in Holloway's stairwell graduated from a gesture into a serious suicide attempt has tended to be accepted with little scepticism, an interpretation fuelled by her adoption of highly charged phrases like 'one big tragedy may save the others … quite deliberately … I should undoubtedly have been killed … as I meant'.

But this was not the case. Many among the suffragette leadership viewed her boast as spurious at best, showboating at worst. Hers was a 'suicide attempt' confessed with the benefit of survival; there were no farewell letters to loved ones or the kind of valediction for posthumous publication that a self-publicist like Emily Davison would've surely left. Others pointed out that a woman of her intellect would have known the netting was stretched along the galleries specifically to prevent suicides so that she was bound to be unsuccessful.

Significantly, Davison's account of her latest 'sacrifice' in Holloway went unrecognised by her movement. It was printed in the *Daily Herald* on 4 July, but not in *The Suffragette* until after her death. Sylvia Pankhurst later confided:

> Her deed was represented as a news item in *Votes For Women* but the usual eulogy of all militant acts was in this case omitted from the editorial columns. Her statement was not published for there had been a general desire at headquarters to discourage her in such tendencies; some of her colleagues even suggested her attempt had been a sensational pretence.
>
> She was condemned and ostracised as a self-willed person who persisted in acting upon her own initiative without waiting for official instructions. She was far from the inner circle of the Union. Her action was cold-shouldered and was the precursor of a new and terrible struggle.

This latest spell in Holloway had, without question, transformed Davison, both physically and mentally. She'd never endured a sentence longer than a month in the past and it's probable that five months of undernutrition and malnutrition had weakened body and mind in equal measure. Holloway's foundation stone carried the inscription: 'May God make this place a terror to evil doers.' In her case it had done its very best. She'd entered Holloway weighing 9st 12.5lb; she came out weighing 7 stone 8.5lb. She looked haggard; nearer sixty than forty.

Henceforth, her struggle would indeed be 'terrible'. Three years on this treadmill of fasting and forcible-feeding was driving her to the brink of insanity. Now, more than ever, once her blood was up, one action inexorably fed another, each one more irresponsible, illogical and unreasoning than the last. What began rationally veered toward the irrational. She really was out of control, in grave danger of running amok. One line in Dr Craig's report screamed out: 'She is impulsively inclined and might do any rash act.'

Davison's descent into the vortex was triggered by Mrs Pankhurst's demand for heightened militancy at a Royal Albert Hall rally on 17 October 1912 which she concluded by 'inciting this meeting to rebellion'. She went on: 'Some women are able to go further than others in militant action and each woman is the judge of her own duty as far as that is concerned.' Her leader had effectively given a 'freelance militant' like Davison carte blanche to do as she wished.

Davison's loosening grasp on reality in the final months of her life may be gleaned from two unpublished essays. The first, dated 10 February 1912 and thus written in Holloway, was entitled 'The Real Christianity'. In it she stated 'the civilised world today is living a hideous lie! It professes to be Christian, but the teaching of the new Revelation is deformed and misrepresented.' The second, more famous discourse was entitled *The Price of Liberty*. This revealing document, running to seven pages and undated but likely also written while serving this latest sentence, remained, like the account of her Holloway 'suicide-bid', unacknowledged by her movement until after her death, appearing in *The Suffragette* of 5 June 1914 (a week *after* it had been printed in the *Daily Sketch*). In this tract Davison resorts to language that, taken at its every word, implies a mind if not actually set on martyrdom, then at least in the early stages of disintegration and self-destruction. It reads like a strange hybrid of Bible-bashing fire-and-brimstone and chivalric fantasy, full of religious rhetoric and crusading ideals. However, to Davison and other like-minded suffragettes this brand of florid tub-thumping was the language of choice. One can be sure that Emily Davison believed every word of it.

She transforms Jesus's parable of the 'Pearl of Great Price' into a suffragette war cry, referring to 'the true suffragette ... the true warrior ... the perfect Amazon ... who will sacrifice everything in order to win the Pearl of Freedom for her sex ... the Vote'.

> The glorious and inscrutable Spirit of Liberty has but one further penalty within its power, the surrender of life itself. It is the supreme consummation of sacrifice, than which none can be higher. To lay down one's life for friends, that is glorious, selfless, inspiring! But to re-enact the tragedy of Calvary for generations yet unborn, that is the last consummate sacrifice of the Militant!

What was required to secure this 'pearl' is nothing less than a modern-day Joan of Arc, inspired by the call of God and empowered by His constant presence. Someone like Emily Davison.

Words gushed out of Davison with the constancy of a burst water-main. She bombarded the press with her assorted ramblings. No fewer than fifty-five of her letters and articles were published during the five months following her release from Holloway. The outlets ranged from nationals such as the *Sunday Times, Daily Graphic, Daily Herald, Manchester Guardian* and *Evening Standard* to provincial papers like the *Newcastle Daily Journal, Birmingham Evening Dispatch* and the *Aberdeen Daily Journal*. One letter, drafted in September, discusses the kind of 'sacrifice' required to win the Vote: 'The sacrifice varies according to circumstances. It may be loss of livelihood, position, wealth, relatives and, not least common, loss of health or even possibly life.' Another, which appeared in the *Manchester Guardian* on 26 August, ended with a prophecy: 'But a time will come, which some of us may not see with our bodily eyes, when the nation will have exacted a sufficiently terrible crucifixion … but the price will have been gladly paid.'

Before that price was 'paid', Davison's exploits plumbed farce. In late November she travelled to Edinburgh and then on to Aberdeen, being lent the money so to do by the firebrand Scottish suffragette Ethel Moorhead: there she was intent on disrupting a speech to be delivered by Lloyd George on Friday 29th. The following morning Lloyd George was due to leave on the 10.20 train to Kirkcaldy amid heavy police protection. Davison inveigled her way onto the train and sat down in his compartment where he was stood talking to a woman passenger. When her target made to leave shortly before the train was scheduled to depart, she leapt to her feet and drawing a dog-whip (the suffragette standard weapon of defence) from her skirt dealt him a series of stinging blows across the face, exclaiming 'Villain, traitor! Take that – and that!'

Unfortunately, the man she was lashing wasn't Lloyd George, but the Reverend Forbes Jackson, of Aberdeen's Crown Terrace Baptist Church, who was seeing his wife off on her journey to Glasgow. With his thick moustache and silver curls, Jackson did bear a striking facial resemblance to the Chancellor of the Exchequer, but even after he revealed his identity Davison continued to pummel him. 'Oh, it's all right, I know you are Lloyd George,' she screamed. 'You have disguised yourself but you cannot hide yourself!'

Davison was dragged from the train by policemen and passengers, though not before managing to strike Jackson twice more with her fists. Possibly, Jackson was lucky, for the police later found a carving knife secreted in her skirt. Davison gave her name as 'Mary Brown' (Mary Leigh's birth-name) and was bailed to appear in Police Court. In the interim she told the *Aberdeen Daily Journal*: 'You people in Aberdeen may think you are up against a soft thing in dealing with the suffragists, but you will find the wall harder to get over than you believe.'

The trial was notable for Davison's long-winded oration. It elicited numerous outbreaks of laughter at her expense from the court officials and the public gallery. The Baillie fined her £2 or ten days' imprisonment. She took the latter and left the dock shouting 'I protest, sir!' and, waving to the gallery, 'No Surrender!' However, there was a surrender of sorts, because after fasting for four days in Craiginches Prison her fine was paid. Although her action had degenerated into a shambles, Davison still got her publicity, particularly in America where the story was carried in newspapers from Oakland to Atlanta.

This Aberdeen episode raises another obvious question besides that of Davison's grasp on reality. Why go so far north as Scotland to harry Lloyd George when, as she'd proved before, opportunities presented themselves all over England? The answer may lie with personal attachment rather than political principle. And in so doing raises the issue of Davison's sexuality and its role in manufacturing a militant suffragette.

Davison preferred the companionship of women. Of that there can be no doubt. At the time of her death we know for a fact she was enjoying a relationship with an 'intimate companion'. The point is franked by this lady being sat alongside Davison's mother and sister in the leading carriage of the Morpeth funeral cortege and being identified as such by the *Morpeth Herald*. She was referred to as 'Miss Morrison'. There are reasons to believe she may have had an Aberdeen connection.

Tainting Davison with the 'love that dare not speak its name' may seem gratuitous. However, the possibility can't be ignored because lesbianism was certainly rife among the suffragette sisterhood and undoubtedly accentuated the ferocity of its anti-Establishment, i.e. anti-male, attitudes and behaviour. Davison lived among a community of passionate women; united by passion and driven by passion. Their gatherings were drenched with religious fervour; their marches evoked images of crusaders leaving for the Holy Land. They saw themselves, and were viewed by the public at large, as revolutionaries, law-breakers and outlaws, a persecuted minority. In this highly charged atmosphere the boundaries separating camaraderie and love might easily become blurred, and then crossed in the quest for emotional solace. These passionate women needed relationships to sustain them during times of enormous physical and psychological pressure and tension. It would be ridiculous to believe anything otherwise. And if that relationship was with a member of their own sex, so be it. After all, unlike homosexuality, lesbianism was not illegal despite all female sexual activity outside wedlock still being deemed immoral in the eyes of the public.

Even in the first decade of the twentieth century both politicians and the popular press weren't averse to stooping to smear campaigns with regard to the sexuality of suffragettes. Since first being described as 'she-males', the press had taken to stating how WSPU organisers tended to be unmarried, as were 60 per cent of its subscribers; after one disturbance at the House of Commons, for example, the press made capital of the fact that eighty of the 108 arrested women were listed as 'Miss'. The inference was crystal clear. In time, one writer would go so far as to describe the suffragette movement as the 'pre-war lesbianism of daring ladies'.

These insinuations made no concession to prominent members of the movement. Many never married and several lived quite openly in single-sex relationships. One couple, Mary Gawthorpe and Dora Marsden, founded a journal called *The Freewoman* which actively discouraged marriage and condoned homosexuality. Mrs Pankhurst herself was pursued by the outlandish bisexual composer Dame Ethel Smyth who provided the music to *March of the Women*. Smyth's preferred dress was tweeds, deerstalker and tie, making her look, as one writer put it, 'forever poised for an assault on the Matterhorn'. Smyth drooled over her *beau ideal*'s 'well-knit figure, the quick deft movement, the soft bright eyes that could emit lambent flame … if you were to come to me now all I could do would be to hold you in my arms … and be silent'. Mrs Pankhurst's noisy, cross-dressing one-time chauffeur, Vera Holme, was another often mistaken for a man. She was known as 'Jack', and the bed she shared with the Hon. Evelina Haverfield had the initials 'V.H.' and 'E.H.' carved upon it.

Two of the Pankhurst girls were also objects of desire. Sylvia enjoyed a close relationship with the American Zelie Emerson that was described as 'very intense, possibly even sexual'. However, it was Christabel, her tack-sharp intellect complemented by a set of chestnut curls and full-lips that might have been lifted from the finest Roman mosaic, who made many a female heart flutter. 'Hundreds, perhaps thousands of young women,' wrote her sister Sylvia, 'adored her to distraction.' None adored her more than Annie Kenney, an exceptionally pretty, blue-eyed and golden-haired ex-mill worker from Lancashire who had initially attached herself to Pethick-Lawrence, a woman of self-confessed confused sexuality. Pethick-Lawrence did marry, but her attraction to Kenney 'was so emotional and so openly paraded' that it frightened Teresa Billington-Greig. 'I saw in it something unbalanced and primitive.' In time Kenney switched her attention to Christabel Pankhurst. 'Annie's devotion,' wrote Pethick-Lawrence, 'took the form of unquestioning faith and absolute obedience, and the surrender of her whole personality.' Others acidly referred to Kenney as 'Christabel's blotting paper'. Mary Blathwayt, supplanted in Christabel's affections by Kenney, reacted cattily by alluding to Kenney's promiscuity, recording in her diary that 'Annie slept with someone else last night' or 'There was someone else in Annie's bed this morning'.

Of course, women 'sleeping' together didn't necessarily make them lesbians in the Edwardian sense of the term, let alone the modern: none of the sexual contact by which lesbianism has become defined may have occurred. Preferring the company of women and loving them to the exclusion of men may have involved nothing more erotic than holding hands and walking arm in arm. Furthermore, many suffragettes, like Davison herself, were short of funds; sharing accommodation and beds offered a material benefit to go with the emotional. Until the publication, and banning, of the lesbian novel *The Well of Loneliness* in 1928 the general public was largely ignorant of the physical aspects of female relationships.

Davison's sexual orientation might be argued an irrelevance, yet it adds another combustible element to an already combustible personality. Certainly the issue has tended to be skirted, as it has in the context of the Pankhursts. The fact that by the age of forty Davison seemed to be living Faire Emelye's 'desire to be a maiden all my life, never will I be a lover or wife', or that she'd spent her entire working and personal life in the company of women, in school, college and prison, doesn't make her a lesbian. Indeed, cynics might argue that Davison's expulsion from the WSPU's 'lesbian-dominated' inner circle constitutes a strong case for her not being so inclined. Conversely, a well of Sapphic love might have served to intensify her passion for emancipation. If, as Dr Johnson suggested, patriotism is the last refuge of the nation's scoundrels, then fanaticism may constitute the final port of call for its misfits, outcasts and outsiders. To those of a particular temperament this kind of unjust ostracism must be met with an equally outrageous response. In that context, Davison's sexuality has significant relevance. Even in denial. There is a known correlation between denial of one's sexuality and a propensity to self-destructive behaviour.

Fate and the WSPU had left Davison primed and ready to detonate; her actions might be acknowledged or they might not. How that knowledge must have rankled with someone described only a few years earlier as one 'who has given up her whole life for the cause'. Bruised in body and soul, how she must have seethed.

In January 1913 she wrote to her college friend Rose Lamartine Yates from Longhorsley:

> At present I have no settled work. While here I busy myself writing my experiences and doing what I can to help mother. I wish I could hear of some work though. My mother is glad to have me and to know that I am not too battered. The long imprisonment last year, and the terrible finale did not, of course, do me much good but somehow I come up smiling. This last four days' hunger strike in Aberdeen found out my weakness, and I have some rheumatism in my neck and back where I fell on that iron staircase.

The letter ends with the plaintive thanks of an increasingly troubled soul:

> I was indeed glad to get your card, and to find that you were still willing to 'own me'! I had not heard from you for so long that I had almost come to the conclusion that you, like many others, had got to the pitch of thinking I was *too* militant.

Davison signed the letter 'Emelye'. Her lifelong identification with Chaucer's virginal Amazon showed no signs of waning. 'Faire Emelye' remained a male chattel. Davison still wished to be the Amazon who broke free; she even altered a key phrase in the first draft of *The Price of Liberty* to read 'the perfect Amazon' instead of 'the perfect warrior'. But 'Faire Emelye' was consigned to the past. Prison had seen to that. Her golden mane was surrendering to grey; the skin stretched across her cheekbones like so much aged vellum; the dentures filling the gap on the right side of her mouth where two teeth were missing no longer fitted as snugly as they ought. However, she refused to yield. Every opportunity to spread 'the word' was seized, assailing passers-by from a grass verge, holding forth from an upturned tub in a farmyard, debating fiercely with her doctor and priest or addressing organised gatherings throughout the north. She pursued paid outlets for her writing talents at the *Manchester Guardian, Daily Citizen* and even the *Nursing Times*. Every day she filled fat sixty-page exercise books with essay after essay but not one editor deigned to offer her a job, considering her style too verbose and florid. 'You can write, no doubt of that,' replied the editor of the *Daily Citizen*. 'You have only to learn the rules of journalism.'

Back in London, Christabel Pankhurst's fire-bombing campaign was in full swing. Arsonists were deployed with rags, paraffin, wood shavings, candles and matches; the targets were empty, isolated buildings – rural railway stations, cricket pavilions and racecourse grandstands were tailor-made (though many of these blazes may have been insurance scams, with suffragette literature left as a smokescreen). So was the villa being built for Lloyd George adjacent to the golf course at Walton Heath; on 19 February it was ripped by a blast that rattled the window-panes of an inn 300 yards away. This outrage was attributed to Davison by Sylvia Pankhurst, but only after her death. Her participation seems unlikely. Home Office files omit any mention of her. More significantly, Davison's modus operandi relied upon bare-faced defiance, the caught-red-handed attitude that had gained her the reputation as a publicity-seeker and earned the opprobrium of her leaders.

Mrs Pankhurst, as usual, accepted full responsibility and was sentenced to three years' penal servitude. *The Suffragette* announced a policy of 'Guerilla Warfare – A Fight to the Finish.' Houses were fired; empty railway stations and carriages bombed; the grandstands at Ayr and Cardiff racecourses were burned. On 7 May a bomb was discovered in the chancel of St Paul's Cathedral. Suspicion immediately fell on the suffragettes. None claimed responsibility and the police failed to uncover any leads. This became another outrage with which Davison's name was linked, but only once she was dead.

Nevertheless, Davison had no intention of being left on the sidelines even if her life continued to be nomadic during the first half of 1913. Her correspondence places her mainly in London: she was active on the streets of the East End collecting for the wives and children of the dockers; and served on the executive of the Marylebone branch of the Workers' Educational Association that devoted itself to bringing higher education within reach of the masses. After years of living at 31 Coram Street in fashionable Bloomsbury, her London domicile was now 133 Clapham Road, the home of Mrs Alice Green, where she gratefully received the occasional contribution from her 'loving sister Let' – even if those letters did rub an open sore:

> I enclose a postal order to keep you going for a bit. I hate to think of you without work and feeling as you do. I do think the Militants might remember your services and give you something. I hope you enjoyed your little holiday up north. Poor old dear. If you get hard up, let me know. I can always manage to squeeze something out! I do wish you could have some luck.

None came. Davison was reduced to applying for a job as a secretary with the Women's Tax Resistance League. On Tuesday 3 June, the day before the Derby, she received a reply informing her the vacancy was only for a junior shorthand typist rather than a secretary; her testimonials were enclosed.

Thus, politically and personally, Davison could hardly sink any lower. If nothing could alleviate her private woes, something had to be done to relieve the political pressure. Parliament was blocking all hope of the Vote. Prison was endangering the lives of her colleagues. If their deaths were to be prevented it would only be as a result of public revulsion at their present treatment. In order to attract that public sympathy, only the most dramatic expression of suffragette zeal would suffice. Davison conceived plans for just such a demonstration. It would be the first of its kind. A copy-cat was not good enough. This escapade would forever be associated with her, and her alone. She saw how prominently sport figured in the mind of the average Englishman; she knew that his mind would be centred on the Derby. She would turn his excitement and expectation against him, forcing him to confront the crying needs of women instead of the selfish pleasures of men.

Stories abound concerning the motive, planning and execution of Davison's actions: until any corroborating documentary evidence comes to light not one can be accepted with confidence. In his book *One-way Ticket to Epsom*, John Sleight recounts one Longhorsley slice of folklore referring to Davison being summoned to London by a mysterious telegram and discussing some kind of demonstration at Epsom with her mother before departing; Sleight quotes her cousin as asserting she left appearing 'rather depressed and was not her usual self'. He goes on to relate how local suffragettes had drawn straws to decide who should carry out the demonstration and that the group saw Davison off at Morpeth station. None of this tallies with Davison's known modus operandi by this late stage of her militant career viz planning and executing her actions in isolation. Nor was the story paid any kind of lip service by the WSPU on Davison's death – which it surely would in its climate of manufactured martyrdom. Stanley and Morley's book recounts a further Longhorsley tale of Davison practising for her forthcoming escapade on local horses. While this story might be taken to exemplify Davison's penchant for meticulous planning, if proved to be true it merely serves to illustrate her declining grasp of reality since horses out in a field bear no relation to thoroughbreds racing at speeds approaching 35mph. The story's veracity doesn't pass inspection.

Whatever course of action Davison had in mind, we can be assured she kept it to herself. That Tuesday afternoon of 3 June she went to the WSPU's grand summer fete, 'All in a Garden Fair', at the Empress Rooms on Kensington High Street where she met Mary Leigh. Her plans for the following afternoon weren't even divulged to her closest friend and ally. They admired the hard work of the organisers; they smiled at the children dressed as brownies, elves and butterflies helping to serve strawberries and cream teas; and they laughed at the pillar-box marked 'guaranteed safe'.

Finally, they paused before the large statue of Joan of Arc and Davison laid a wreath at its foot. Together they read the words of the movement's patron saint carved on the pedestal, 'Fight on and God will give the Victory'. According to Gertrude Colmore, Leigh asked Davison whether she would be attending all week.

'I shall be at the fair all day every day except tomorrow. I'm going to the Derby tomorrow,' replied Davison.

When pressed as to what she was going to do Davison cocked her head in that tantalising manner Leigh recognised as a precursor of impending mischief.

'Ah!' Davison replied. 'Look in the evening paper and you will see.'

# TWELVE

# The Pieces in Place

For a woman with a fragile hold on the tiller of reality one may yet imagine Davison striding down Kingsway in the direction of the WSPU headquarters at Lincoln's Inn House with a firmness of purpose on the morning of Wednesday 4 June 1913. After glancing at its window display (including postcard portraits of leading suffragettes – though not one of herself), she went inside and demonstrated her high spirits via an exchange as cryptic as that with Leigh in the Empress Rooms. She requested two flags. When asked their purpose, according to Colmore, she cocked her head to one side. 'Perhaps I'd better not ask,' said the knowing suffragette behind the counter. 'No,' Davison replied, 'don't ask me.'

Davison tucked the suffragette tricolours under her arm. On reaching Victoria station she counted out eight shillings and sixpence to buy a third-class return ticket to Epsom Downs. After presenting it at the barrier, she boarded one of many Derby Day 'specials'. She placed the return half of her ticket inside her black suede clip purse. In her other pocket, a handkerchief competed with her door key and a black 'memo' book whose well-scuffed appearance reflected frequent usage and testified to her thrift. Each page was tightly packed with meticulous entries of her daily expenditure. Wedged between the pages were two loose postal order counterfoils; a railway insurance ticket (issued on 10 May: 25 shillings per week if she should be disabled and £200 to be paid in the event of death); some stationery and stamps;

and her helper's pass for that day's 'All in a Garden Fair'. She had to be back in Kensington for the evening session.

Davison joined the multitude that had been building since dawn. The manual worker had either walked the sixteen miles from London or come by charabanc; the tradesman had kept her company on one of the 'specials'; the businessman and gentleman had taken to the road in their chaise, carriage or fashionable (albeit unreliable) motor-car, seeking periodic respite from the choking dust to wet their whistles at The Swan in Clapham and The Cock in Sutton. She braved the odd spot of rain to complete the final uphill leg of her trek on foot just as the King and Queen stepped from their special train at one o'clock to conclude theirs in a landau. King George looked splendid in black silk topper and dark grey frock-coat, a white carnation in his buttonhole and wearing the Guards tie; Queen Mary was dressed in navy blue *crepe de chine* over white, and a hat trimmed with pink and red roses. The King received a round of cheers, to which he and Queen Mary responded with limp waves born of protocol. One or two called out 'Happy Birthday, Your Majesty!' Yesterday was the King's forty-eighth birthday and George could be excused if his mind was already contemplating the evening's banquet at Buckingham Palace.

Epsom was now so congested that roads leading to the course were closed at 11.30. The panorama greeting Davison was one to take her breath away: this was a fete in stark contrast to the refined sort she'd frequented the previous evening in the Empress Rooms. The Downs resembled a vast ant-heap of humanity, its busy army of punters impersonating 'workers' while the profusion of carriages, motor cars and motor-omnibuses edged around more sedately in the manner of so many stray beetles. Every person had his or her place: each enclosure was distinguishable by its dress code, a tell-tale sign of the English class system. The flat caps, mufflers and cigarettes cupped furtively in backs of hands that predominated at the bottom of the scale on the Downs gave way to boaters and mackintoshes neatly folded

over arms in the Silver Ring; then bowlers, stiff collars and
umbrellas in the grandstand; until, finally, top hats and morning suits held sway in the Members' enclosure. Stretching out
up the straight against the inside running rail was 'Charabanc
City' where some 200 scarlet motor-omnibuses provided mobile
grandstands; between them were rows of trestle tables laden with
food and drink at which sat countless Pearlie kings and queens,
their heavy, button-encrusted coats bringing rivulets of sweat
to their jolly red faces. The Downs's beating heart was the gypsy
encampment, the annual summer congregation of Romanies,
tinkers and travellers from all over the British Isles. Washing-
lines pegged-out with clothes were strung between the brightly
painted caravans; motley collections of ponies were tethered
to stakes; goats, chickens and dogs roamed at will. Groups of
women, their faces burnt nut-brown by many summers on the
open road, their shiny plaited and pigtailed black hair just visible
beneath colourful bandannas and headscarves, gold hoops swing-
ing from one ear and a pink carnation behind the other, toiled
over a succession of large black cauldrons while their menfolk
played pitch 'n' toss and their children spun tops.

Davison was assailed by the overpowering sensations of sound
and smell. The aroma of rich fare wafted across the track from
the distant grandstand. In one massive kitchen alone chefs were
cooking 400 lobsters, 130 legs of lamb, sixty-five saddles of lamb,
130 shoulders of lamb, 150 ox tongues, 100 sirloins of beef, 500
spring chickens and 350 pigeon pies. Closer to hand, stalls offered
fish 'n' chips, pie 'n' mash and jellied eels to feed the working-
class stomach while occasional banners declaring 'Behold the
Lamb of God' offered mobile mission stations prepared to feed
their souls.

Cutting through this fug was the noise of Babel. There was no
charge for spectators on the Downs and it was a raucous play-
ground for the proletariat to enjoy their unofficial holiday. There
were grinding hurdy-gurdies; shrill organ music accompanied
the carousels enabling would-be jockeys to sit a horse. Touts like

'Donkey Jimmy' fished for mug-punters with desperate promises of 'an outsider to beat the field'. Three-card tricksters enticed the gauche with insidious patter; the proprietors of boxing booths bellowed challenges to the foolhardy; rifle galleries, menageries and peep shows competed for custom just as raucously. Ventriloquists and fiddlers, negro tap-dancers and banjoists, strong-men, acrobats and magicians: all readily entertained at the toss of a coin into a welcoming hat. Noise assaulted the senses from every angle. It was enough to make anyone's head spin. Especially if, like Emily Davison, they were unused to it.

Not for her the limelight of the biplane trailing its advertising banner; or the man on the cross-bar suspended beneath a balloon who was throwing out handbills. She knew her spotlight would glare from a newsreel camera.

&#x261E;

Eustace Loder had seen it all before, yet he felt on edge as he drove into Epsom with his nephew Merrik Burrell. He needed another Classic winner, preferably a Derby winner; moreover, unlike Spearmint, one of his own breeding. Loder would have needed cast iron for brains to deaden the recurring chorus in his head: if only he and Noble Johnson had kept Veneration II, it would be his colours, not Bower Ismay's, that Craganour would be carrying in the Derby.

Although his loathing for Ismay remained constant, the issue gnawing deepest, as it had for over six months now, was an occurrence dreaded by every breeder of bloodstock: disease. The previous autumn an influenza epidemic had erupted on one of his stud farms, Old Connell, located just three miles from Eyrefield Lodge.

Loder acquired the 560 acres of rich Liffey floodplain for £12,500 in 1906. He spent the same amount again to transform a run-down cattle farm into an up-to-date stud farm, constructing stallion boxes, foaling units and stabling for visiting mares.

The six-feet of alluvial soil at Old Connell yielded lush grass ideal for mares and stallions and became home to Spearmint. On 10 November 1912 Loder heard from Noble Johnson that one of his mares at Old Connell, Glimmerglass, had gone down with a high temperature and a distressing cough. She recovered, but on the 28th of the month May Race (the Irish Oaks winner of 1900) was struck by the same symptoms and died eight days later. By this time a third mare, Gallantry, was also afflicted and she, too, succumbed. Then a fourth mare, Martellina, died. 'Every possible precaution was taken to keep the affected animals isolated from the rest of the stud,' Johnson wrote later, 'and the men tending them were not allowed to go near other stock.' Even so, a fifth mare, Sweetbread, was to die on 18 January.

Eyrefield Lodge, home to Pretty Polly and the choicest mares, was unaffected. One of those mares was Auspicious and, early in December, she was sent to England to be mated with the 2000 Guineas winner of 1910, Lord Rosebery's Neil Gow, who stood at the Adstock Manor Stud in Buckinghamshire, belonging to Charles Prior. One other mare from Eyrefield accompanied Auspicious to England along with six from nearby Conyngham Lodge. Prior expressed surprise that the mares had been sent so early and, in due course, that no indication of any epidemic at Old Connell had been provided by Johnson or Loder at that juncture. When he queried why mares were being moved a good eleven to fourteen weeks before their foaling dates – and thus earliest covering dates – Johnson confined his answer to insisting 'he liked to get the mares away early as the weather was uncertain'. Auspicious had been at Adstock for a month when she fell ill; within weeks twenty-four mares on Prior's farm went down with contagious influenza, six of them fatally.

Prior made no bones about expressing his views. He said that despite numerous letters and telegrams, he was not informed of the problems at Old Connell until as late as 24 February, and that, self-evidently, Loder had sent him an infected mare. More to the point, he suggested Loder must have known Auspicious might be infected before he sent her to England. The Old Connell outbreak had begun, he declared, as early as September – which accounted for her being sent away before Christmas for a covering season that never commenced before 14 February. Why else, he asked, would the priceless commodity that was Pretty Polly be moved on 5 December to the Fort Union Stud in Adare, well in advance of her intended covering by Desmond, if it were not for Loder and Johnson being fully alert to the dangers of the epidemic spreading? Prior demanded £20,000 in damages – the equivalent of winning all five Classics in one season, or very nearly £1 million in modern currency.

Loder was appalled. It was an unforgivable slur on his personal and professional integrity to suggest that he, a breeder of Classic winners and a Steward of the Jockey Club, might stoop to such subterfuge and endanger other breeders' stock. He pointed out that none of the other mares sent to England with Auspicious had become ill. Therefore, she must have contracted the sickness at Adstock. Moreover, he disputed Prior's claim that her symptoms were the same as those exhibited by the sick animals at Old Connell. Prior stated Auspicious 'had turned very queer and had a sort of fit and suffered total loss of appetite'. Loder maintained this seemed commensurate with an old liver complaint Auspicious developed whenever over-fed. 'It never entered into Major Loder's or my head there was the slightest danger in sending these mares from Eyrefield,' said Johnson, 'and we acted in good faith.'

Prior wouldn't be mollified. The dispute was bound for the High Court, alleging 'breach of implied warranty and negligence in sending a mare … when she was infected with contagious influenza', and that his business was 'greatly injured … completely ruined and closed'. He saved his most damning indictment until last: 'If a man knew, or ought to have known, of any infection or vice in a horse which he sold or sent to another man's stable, and did not disclose it, he was liable for the consequences.'

Eustace Loder was stymied. Settle or counter attack? Eyrefield owned a name beyond reproach, even before he acquired the property, and thanks to the exploits of Pretty Polly and her kin, he'd built on that reputation to the degree that there had never been the slightest breath of a suspicion or suggestion against the management or conduct of the stud or of his horses. Now their names were being traduced. Pay up, concede Prior was correct, and his reputation was besmirched. But if he fought back, only to lose the case in the courts, he would face losing even greater kudos among his peers. The situation was intolerable.

'Major Loder was about the very last man in the world to run any risk of damage to any stud,' wrote Johnson, 'and I think through all the subsequent worry of the lawsuit nothing troubled him more than the action of Prior in accusing him of this very act.' Johnson's recollection of a meeting with Loder in London in early 1913 isn't without significance for subsequent events:

> I noticed the greatest change. He felt very keenly the action Prior was taking. His health was causing anxiety to his relatives and friends, and this impending lawsuit was not helping matters; he took it all so very much to heart, worrying over it night and day. He was a very sensitive man and he fretted day and night over the lawsuit.

In fact, Eustace Loder hadn't been feeling well. The occasional headache was hardly cause for concern, but the dull ache that frequently made itself felt at the base of his back and into his groin most definitely was. Even more so when he found blood in his urine. His doctor confirmed Bright's Disease, an affliction of the kidneys. No money could buy a cure. It was a disease that had claimed the life of Czar Alexander III and President Arthur of the United States, Lord Rosebery's wife Hannah and Bower Ismay's own mother six years earlier. Blood-letting, diuretics and laxatives were all the medical profession could offer beyond advising complete bed-rest in preparation for the inevitable. Loder's breathing and eyesight would fail, his blood pressure would rise, his face would grow puffier through oedema, the aches and vomiting increase. He was a dead man walking.

First Ismay's shenanigans with his sister-in-law. His home-bred Craganour in another man's colours. Then Prior's accusations. Now failing health. On Wednesday 4 June 1913, it's fair to say that Eustace Loder had a lot on his mind.

☞

The course over which the race would be contested posed the supreme test of a thoroughbred, demanding a blend of speed and stamina, adaptability and agility in equal balance. Balance, in point of fact, was a key requirement for any Derby candidate, for the vagaries of the Epsom course had long since led it to be regarded an unsuitable venue for identifying the country's best three-year-old. 'It is a singular Turf anomaly,' the *Illustrated London News* had once observed, 'that the greatest race in the world should be run over perhaps the worst and most dangerous course we have. Jockeys dread it not a little.'

Nothing had changed. The track still went up and down, demanding horses to gallop uphill one moment and then, with the ground falling away beneath their hooves, downhill the next. It switched one way and the other, right and left. In places changes of gradient and direction came simultaneously. The inherent dangers to man and beast were obvious and were exacerbated by Epsom's racing surface. The chalk sub-soil of the Downs was highly porous and, in an age lacking any form of artificial watering and next to no track husbandry, promoted only the shortest cover of grass which by high summer could ensure hard underfoot conditions akin to a road. To make the situation worse, the Downs were public land, much walked over and ridden on, which compacted the cover and did little to assist turf growth. Finally, in addition to these physical demands placed on its participants, the Derby insisted on mental toughness, the equable temperament to absorb this fusillade of physical challenges amid a barrage of noise from 250,000 spectators and their engines of entertainment in the centre of the course.

The gauntlet to be run started opposite the grandstand, across Langley Bottom, alongside the trees in front of Downs House. Before the introduction of the starting gate in 1900, the start could be shambolic: there were no fewer than fourteen false starts in 1830, for example, and in 1857 the field was at the post for an hour before a successful start was effected. Horses were now obliged to stand almost motionless behind the gate instead of approaching at the canter in anticipation of getting a 'flyer' when the starter let them go. Even so, a horse might still whip round and lose valuable ground once the tapes rose. From the gate the course dog-legs to the right through the opening quarter-mile before bearing left at Captain Durand's Corner and straightening out. All the while it's rising, attaining its highest point just short of the six-furlong pole where it's 134 feet above the start point. This is where stamina has been tapped: any horse that uses too much energy in the first, uphill, section of the race will have no reserves to fight out the finish. There follows 300 yards of level ground along the crest of the hill before the course begins the left-handed bend that prefaces the hair-raising descent down Tattenham Hill and its notoriously sharp corner into the straight. This critical section of the track was much straighter in alignment before the First World War and even more redolent of plunging down a cliff and turning sharp left on hitting the beach. Hereabout a horse needs courage; his rider must be fearless, nerveless. Fred Archer tackled the descent as if he were abseiling. His great rival, possibly even his superior, George Fordham, detested the Hill. Among contemporary jockeys in 1913, Danny Maher considered it dangerous whereas it brought the best out of Steve Donoghue.

When the runners swing round Tattenham Corner they have dropped forty feet inside 300 yards and are approaching speeds of 35mph. Early pace-setters will be dropping back while patiently ridden horses try to advance. Heels can be clipped and horses tumble, as happened to Sir Martin, the favourite in 1909. This is where agility and balance come into play. If a horse has travelled badly down the hill, time spent recovering balance at the top of the straight may cost the race. The three-and-a-half furlong straight that beckons continues to drop away in front of the runners until well inside the final furlong where there's a gradual rise to the finishing line which, though of just three feet, may assume the appearance of a mountain too far.

There's one more obstacle lying in wait: the straight is far from level, possessing a noticeable camber: the ground on the stands side of the track is some six feet higher than that on the inside rail. It's a trap waiting to ambush many a tiring horse or rider through the final surge to the winning post. Hit an exhausted animal on his right flank and he might easily roll down the camber into the rail or any opponents on his inside. This ordeal will take the winner somewhere between the two minutes 35.2 seconds recorded by Lemberg in 1910 and two minutes 45.4 recorded by St Amant in 1904, depending on the conditions and early pace. The track record stood to Pretty Polly, who clocked two minutes 33.8 in the 1905 Coronation Cup. If any horse was going to challenge that time it would surely be her kinsman Craganour.

☞

Tattenham Corner was the first location Emily Davison encountered that offered the opportunity she craved: direct exposure to the newsreel cameras. The 'Newsreels' of the day were known as 'Topicals' i.e. showing items of 'topical' interest. They usually ran up to five minutes and changed twice weekly along with the cinema main feature. The leaders in this field were Pathé's Animated Gazette and Gaumont Graphic (both from 1910), Topical Budget (1911) and Williamson's Animated News (1913). Coverage featured crowd scenes, parade, canter, start, Tattenham Corner, the finish and the lead-in. Since these companies jostled for the same locations there were few variations in camera angles or content. At just short of seven minutes, Pathé's footage was the longest, showing the start from both behind and in front of the tapes, but it lacked the detailed post-race scenes carried by Gaumont.

Davison chose to cross the track to stand on the inside of the bend, rather than on the outside, below the hordings lining Tattenham Corner station. She wove her way between the carriages pressed into service as makeshift grandstands that surround the flagpole, its Union Jack twitching limply in the occasional breath of air, to find a crowd some ten-deep barring her path to the rail. She waited for her chance to make inroads, which came between the first two races when the crowd thinned momentarily as punters wandered away to place bets. Gradually she edged forward with society's courtesies scrupulously observed. Boaters and caps were duly raised in her direction and the lady given the freedom to pass through to find a prime spot against the running rail, beside one of its supports.

She examined her race-card, or 'Dorling's List of Epsom Races' as it was still grandly titled. The horses in the first race, the Caterham Plate, dashed past on the far side of the track and, in due course, she marked her card with the result: a one beside the name Honeywood; a two for King's Scholar. In her under-standably heightened sense of anticipation, instead of a three beside the name of Sylva she inadvertently repeated its race-card number of nine. The second race came and went at five past two. Again she marked her card: first Marco Prunella; second Sweet Slumbers; third the unnamed daughter of Cinder.

☞

Far away to her left Jack Robinson was introducing Johnny Reiff to Bower Ismay. 'You have seen the horse, haven't you?' asked the trainer. 'Yes,' replied Reiff. 'Do the best you can, and ride your own race.' The jockey conferred with the owner before being legged up onto Craganour. Nearby, Stanley Wootton assisted his father in saddling Shogun under the attentive eye of Lord

Derby, while Leo de Rothschild was heard telling anyone who listened that 'Day Comet is a different horse to what you saw at Newmarket.' According to the market it made no difference to the outcome of the Derby. Craganour was being backed as if he was a certainty. Second favourite Shogun drifted out to sixes. It was 10/1 bar these.

Anmer led the fifteen runners for the Derby onto the track where they fell under the critical gaze of Robert Sievier:

> The field, all in all, did not reach in looks its average standard, there being considerable contrast among them.
>
> Craganour looked a gentleman, though he was not an ideal Derby horse to the eye, for while displaying much quality he is not truly balanced all round. He runs up a little slack behind the girth, though there is great power behind the saddle. His shoulders are symmetrical, while his neck is a mass of strength, but his head does not exactly fit.
>
> In contrast, Great Sport is a big, strong, well-grown colt, put together on excellent lines. His barrel is supported by well sprung ribs, strengthened by muscular quarters; he has a good forearm and is all over a picture of a Derby colt.
>
> Agadir looked a plater beside him, while in further contrast Aldegond appeared little else but a pony. Bachelor's Wedding stood out and held his own for looks as a very useful colt while Day Comet was more fine and symmetrical than at any period in his career.
>
> Louvois is cool and on his toes and still light of flank. Nimbus is quite a nice sort. Shogun sweated and showed signs of being treated for cracked heels, but was fit and well. Prue looked well but the fillies are undoubtedly behind the colts this season.

Bringing up the rear was number sixteen on the race-card (non-runner Radiant was number twelve). Aboyeur was so unconsidered that *The Sporting Life*'s correspondent did not bother taking any note of his appearance or well-being. With the benefit of hindsight, Sievier wrote in *The Winning Post*:

He is quite a good-looking black, possessing more substance than Craganour, for whereas the latter favours the aristocrat, Aboyeur has usefulness written all over him.

At the last minute Percy Cunliffe decided to encourage the Druid's Lodge contender with one final wager and instructed his commission agent Walter Fry to invest £250 each way; Fry sought out Ladbrokes's on-course representative Helen Vernet and placed the bet at 100/1.

The runners filed past the grandstand and enclosures before turning and cantering back past the winning post. Declared *The Times*:

> Nothing looked better than Shogun. Perfectly trained, hard and full of muscle. As was Prue, a handsome filly who evoked cordial admiration. None showed better in the canter than Prue who strode out with such brilliant action. Craganour, with his head in the air, was a less attractive mover, though Shogun must have delighted his adherents by his style of sweeping over the ground.

The *Life* disagreed:

> Wootton prevented Shogun from striding out but Craganour travelled with a nice low action; on looks alone he quite justified the strong favouritism showered upon him, winning golden opinions. It is hard to find a fault in him, excepting perhaps his temperament for there is an evil look about him at times which is invariably conspicuous with self-willed animals.

Sievier, as ever, was his own man: he awarded the 'palm' in the preliminary canter to Nimbus.

☞

The King re-adjusted his white carnation and chatted to the Crown Princess of Sweden. Queen Mary leant sideways to speak a few words to the Duke of Connaught. Through poised race-glasses, Prince Christian of Schleswig-Holstein focused on the runners going to post.

Bower Ismay seemed outwardly calm but his complexion – described, surprisingly so for a disciple of the African sun, as 'pallid' – implied otherwise; counterpointed by the darkness of his moustache and the solemnity of his frock coat, it lent him the aura of the principal mourner at a funeral – if not the undertaker himself. In the Jockey Club box, Eustace Loder unsheathed his race-glasses and suppressed the tensions coursing through his system, determined to exercise his authority and do his duty as a Steward.

Behind the tapes Johnny Reiff kept Craganour on the move, cluck-clucking at him as they circled to the right of the starter, eager to anticipate the break: he was drawn in the middle of the field at seven; Louvois (two) and Aboyeur (three) were on his inside; Shogun (eleven) and Anmer (fourteen) to his outside. Billy Saxby's brow furrowed in concentration upon Louvois: playing out in his mind the tactics necessary to secure victory for himself – or ignominious defeat for Reiff – but he needed mercury in his veins not to have cast a covetous eye at the favourite. Edwin Piper's priority was to prevent the blinkered Aboyeur's volatile temperament from cracking under the strain. Herbert Jones, meanwhile, sat proudly in the Royal colours aboard Anmer, hoping his slow-coach of a partner would not bring them into disrepute.

Meanwhile, down at Tattenham Corner, Police Sergeant Frank Bunn scanned the crowd for potential troublemakers – but saw none. Davison checked the suffragette flags pinned inside her jacket were still securely fastened, before closing her eyes and asking her God, in the manner of Joan of Arc, to sanction the deed she was about to commit for, as she frequently assured her mother, 'I never do any of the things except under the Influence.'

The Jockey Club's senior starter, Ernest Willoughby, pock-eted his timepiece. The sun slipped behind a cover of cloud encouraging the oppressiveness of the afternoon to assert itself. Women fanned themselves and men ran fingers inside collars. The tingle of mass anticipation was palpable. A monastic hush settled over the Downs, the stillness of an overnight carpet of snow. Ears strained for any sound suggesting the field had been sent on its way. A clap of thunder was heard in the far distance.

Finally, at one minute past three o'clock, the tension was broken. Like the swelling of a giant wave the traditional words swept over the course: 'They're off!'

# THIRTEEN

# 'I Will!'

**D**avison was not the only suffragette on Epsom Downs. Mary Richardson – 'Polly Dick' to her colleagues – had come to Epsom to sell suffragette literature. She'd climbed onto her folding stool and begun flourishing a copy of *The Suffragette* when, to her surprise, she spotted Davison in the crowd in front of her. In her memoir *Laugh A Defiance* she recounts how they had met several times and how she had formed the opinion that Davison was a very serious-minded person: 'That is why I felt so surprised to see her. She was not the sort of woman to spend an afternoon at the races.' Richardson recalled exchanging smiles with her. Davison seemed to have no interest in what was going on around her and Richardson felt a sudden premonition about her, noticing 'how beautifully calm her face was'. She was unable to keep her eyes off Davison. 'A minute before the race started she raised a paper, or some kind of card, before her eyes. I was watching her hand. It did not shake.' At that moment, according to Richardson, Davison was fully aware she 'was about to give her life for the cause' having assured close friends the previous evening that she would be 'the only casualty, no one else would be injured, not even the jockey'.

Unfortunately, considerable doubt must be cast on Richardson's entire account (italics author own). She says 'it was not until the *end of the third race*' that she saw Davison: yet the Derby was the third race on the card. She says she was standing 'near a man who was selling newspapers *at one corner of the grandstand*';

this would have placed her over 600 yards away from Davison's position at Tattenham Corner and she would have needed radar to pick out Davison in that throng let alone detect calm face and firm hand. Even those enjoying the best seats in the house, high up in the grandstand, such as the King and Queen, had neither sight nor inkling of Davison's actions until well after the race. Yet Richardson says she was '*unable to keep my eyes off her*'.

The kindest thing one can say for the veracity of the Richardson account is that it was written forty years after the event: yet she claimed that 'after nearly forty years it *remains as vivid*'. So much mileage was made out of Davison's 'martyrdom' by the suffragette movement at the time, and by subsequent waves of feminist writers, that one might reasonably assume baser motives behind Richardson's claim: to be the one who was *there*; to share the reflected glory. The story of her hasty flight from the track pursued by an angry mob, running 'in front of the King's carriage as he and the Queen hurriedly left from the back of the grandstand' (they didn't leave the track for some time), and hiding in a lavatory on Epsom Downs station before finally making her escape strikes one as equally fanciful. Would she – or any other suffragette in close proximity – have abandoned a stricken comrade or close friend? The cry 'Votes for Women!' was allegedly heard in the chaotic aftermath; a placard was said to have been hoisted bearing the same slogan. There must have been women in the crowd at Tattenham Corner with suffragette leanings, but that doesn't make them militants or associates of Davison. It is a fact that Davison wasn't formally identified until she had reached Epsom Cottage Hospital. Would friends and colleagues have left her lying on the turf had they been nearby? Sadly, the details don't square with the reality.

What we do know for sure is that the communal cry of 'Here they come!' failed to break the spell cast on Davison which had caused her to lose all rational thought. The policemen ordering those nearest the rail to stand back for their own safety were ignored. They were alert to the tradition of spectators spilling onto the track after the runners had passed to follow their progress up the straight, and were watching for anyone leaning too far over the rail and coming within reach of the boots or whips of jockeys hugging the inside.

Davison began to duck under the running rail ('still smiling', claimed the eagle-eyed Richardson) but those who actually noticed her were few. Every camera, newsreel or still, pointed toward Tattenham Corner and every image confirms the overwhelming majority on Davison's side of the track were transfixed by the colourful cavalcade streaking past them from right to left. Two men on the other rail, however, whose job it was to keep an eye open for troublemakers, subsequently maintain they had spotted the figure of a woman in the act of committing the unthinkable: Inspector Whitbread and PS 4NR Frank Bunn.

It wasn't unusual on Derby Day for upwards of 800 extra police to be drafted in from forces outside Epsom to assist Inspector Pawley's local men. Many of these 'bobbies' were reserves, signified by the 'R' following their division letter: along with PC 85NR Johnson and PC 59NR Eady, Bunn was part of the 'N' Division Reserve based at Waltham Abbey. The pencil-written account in Sergeant Bunn's pocket book became the most pertinent first-person account of events at Tattenham Corner, worthy of standing alongside frame-by-frame analysis of the newsreel evidence:

> I beg to report that at 3.10pm 4th inst I was on duty at Tattenham Corner near the tan path whilst the race for the Derby Cup [*sic*] was being run. Several horses passed by when a woman, supposed Emily Davison, ran out from under the fence and held her hands up in front of HM King's horse, whereby she was knocked down and rendered unconscious.

Bunn repeated this account to the subsequent inquest virtually word for word, adding:

I watched the horses come along in a heap, not strung out. She threw her hands up in front of the horses and was knocked down. Most of the horses had passed but there were about three still to come. The whole thing was too instantaneous to say whether she purposely allowed some of the horses to pass her.

Forty yards away on the opposite side of the track, near Pathé's newsreel camera, PC Samuel Eady was better placed to see what happened in those ten seconds:

I saw her head shoot out from under the bar on which she had been leaning just as the leading horses were passing. One of the leading horses seemed to swerve, as if it had narrowly missed her. She raised her hands before she was quite upright, facing the other horses which were coming on. I do not think it would be possible for her to pick out any particular horse the way they were bunched together.

Eady's testimony is supported by the newsreel evidence. From her position on the apex of the bend Davison could see no more than half-a-dozen yards in either direction, the run down to Tattenham Corner being straighter than its realignment post-1915. More significantly, both the previous races had been run on the five-furlong course, the straight arm of the track that extended up to the far right on the opposite side of the course. The runners had come nowhere near Davison on the inside of Tattenham Corner, on the round course used for the Derby. Those earlier horses she had seen. The runners in the Derby she could not see at all. Had she positioned herself on the other side of Tattenham Corner, on the outside of the bend adjacent to the railway hoardings, her task would have been made much easier. As it was she was forced to rely on sound and intuition.

Despite Richardson's belief, a genuinely 'calm' Emily Davison would have exercised patience and bided her time, waited for all the horses to have passed safely and joined the crowd as it spilled out onto the course in customary fashion to track the horses down the finishing straight. Then, and only then, would she have revealed her flags and carried out her demonstration. But that would have meant sharing the limelight. An overexcited Emily Davison, a temporarily unhinged Emily Davison, on the other hand, would have had only one thing on her mind. Grabbing the spotlight; occupying centre-stage. And she wasn't about to be dissuaded.

'Madam! You mustn't do that!' ordered a man standing next to her. To Emily Davison it was the command of a prison governor or magistrate; it was as if her governess and nanny were remonstrating with her outside the nursery back at Gaston House. She answered him as she once answered them.

'I will!' she responds tartly.

They were the last words anyone heard Davison utter. She shook herself free as the man tried to restrain her. One might venture to suggest other motivational lines were running through her brain as she did so.

*'Rise up women! For the fight is hard and long...'*

The wave of noise breaking along the rail to her right finally engulfed her and she began to move. She can clearly be spotted on film, stooping beneath the rail, the lighter shade of her hat betraying her progress. And she may be carrying something in her hands, something light in colour, white on film compared to the known grey of her hat, too large for her race-card but some kind of hand-bill perhaps. It's impossible to be conclusive.

*'They say we are so ignorant...'*

A tapestry of brightly coloured silks flew past. By the time the camera spots her again she's standing upright. Crucially, the leading nine horses have come and gone on her outside. If her intention has been to halt the race by standing on the track at the approach of the entire field she's far too late; a heartbeat sooner and she would have been kicked lifeless by this stampede and her place in history reduced immeasurably. She began to raise her arms as Prue galloped by, but Danny Maher, too, has no difficulty in passing her on the outer without the need to change tack.

*'We don't know right from wrong...'*

After hours of being cooped up with her secret amid thousands of other people, hours of manufacturing adrenaline in the build-up to this moment, the solitude of the greensward before her appeared to assume agoraphobic proportions. Despite her mental preparations the scale of moment itself was monumental compared to anything she had attempted in the past. In front of the biggest audience of her life she was crippled with stage fright. She took a couple more hesitant steps, totally lost in such unfamiliar surroundings, tottering like an absent-minded old lady trying to cross a busy road, bereft of drive or purpose.

*'We can tell them what we want...'*

Davison was unaware that as many as five more horses were careering down Tattenham Hill, through the fastest section of the course, and mere fractions of a second away. Hooves were heard and she turned to her right to see a brown shape hurtling toward her. It was Agadir, his blinkered profile looming over her like some bug-eyed devil. 'I was coming behind the leaders at Tattenham Corner,' Walter Earl told the *Daily News*. 'Suddenly a woman rushed out of the crowd and slipped under the head of my horse. I managed to pull Agadir up and get clear of her.' This manoeuvre, however, placed too much strain on Agadir's forelegs, causing lameness. His race was done.

*'And what we'll have ere long...'*

Davison had now wandered far enough out from the rail for Agadir to pass her on the inside. Having narrowly escaped one collision she then avoided another, registering the merest flash of the white jacket worn by Milton Henry on Nimbus as he brushed past her right shoulder, also between herself and the rail.

*'Firm in reliance, laugh a defiance...'*

Now she could plainly see another horse bearing down on her. If her resolve was ever going to flit away on the breeze it was then. But at times when it finds itself under extreme stress the human brain becomes tantamount to hermetically sealed, its owner trapped in the still, airless atmosphere of eternity. Instead of seeking the certain safety of the green void to her left Davison took firm steps toward the oncoming animal. She had no idea of its identity. The horse was moving at the speed of a locomotive, its colours a blur.

*'Hand in hand we shall win...'*

In fact, it was one of those hopeless outsiders the racing press believed should have stayed at home in its stable instead of getting in the way of others. This colt had already experienced a troubled passage, having collided with Nimbus in the back straight. That particular contretemps went largely unnoticed. The ensuing collision saw his name enter the history books.

*'Hands and hearts now mated...'*

Davison again raised her arms, and made a forlorn attempt to grab its reins or bridle as the animal ploughed into her. Was she attempting to attach the suffragette colours to Anmer's bridle? However, what the film seems to capture flying through the air after the collision behaved more like paper than fabric. It may be nothing more than a scrap of litter or even just a scratch on the negative. One can be no more assertive than that.

Had she chosen any one of the fifteen runners to be the instrument of her death, she couldn't have chosen a more apposite one. Though Davison wasn't to know it, her nemesis was the King's colt Anmer.

*'Right is stronger than might...'*

It is idle to speculate what might have been running through Davison's mind at this moment – yet somewhat unavoidable. Was she suddenly consumed with the spirit of Joan, the Maid of Orleans? Or even the other maiden she revered, the 'Faire Emelye'? There are certainly echoes of a scene from *The Knight's Tale*. Had she become so besotted with Chaucerian allegory that subconsciously she was attempting to stop the King's horse in the manner of the Theban women way-laying Duke Theseus's steed? Was she striving to convert literary fantasy into reality?

If any such fanciful notions flashed through Davison's head they must have been buried deep in her subconscious for she had no time to form them.

'*Higher than Kingship stands...*'

'A woman jumped out from underneath the rails and my horse hit her,' Herbert Jones mumbled later. 'Then the horse sort of rolled over, and I must have had a bang, for that's all I know.'

'*Truth with face to the light...*'

The suffragette's outstretched arms afforded no defence against the momentum of half a ton of racehorse galloping downhill at 35mph (a point the *Daily Sketch* was to make by printing a diagram of a train alongside a galloping racehorse). Anmer struck Davison almost head-on, and then cart-wheeled head over heels, rolling on top of Jones who had one foot momentarily trapped in a stirrup-iron, before sliding to a halt on his side and then struggling to his feet and standing nearby. Film footage suggests Davison escaped Anmer's hooves, a view endorsed by medical opinion. The two horses bringing up the rear, Jameson and Sandburr, easily negotiated the gap between the fracas and the inside rail, the rider of the latter, Henri Jelliss, turned round in the saddle to survey the carnage.

Davison was pole-axed, 'bowled over like a nine-pin' in the words of one nearby spectator, the force of the collision tossing her body through the air and her hat spinning across the turf, the back of her head hammering into the unforgiving ground with the impetus of an earthbound coconut. The Irish dramatist St John Ervine had been standing by the rail a few yards from Davison and later gave his account to the *Daily Mail*. Some key phrases merit emphasis:

> The horses had turned the corner and were running swiftly towards the winning-post. There was a curious silence, like the hush that always descends on a crowd at moments of great tension. Then I heard a woman saying 'What's she doing?' and I saw Miss Davison run onto the course.

I think that three or four horses had gone by when she ran out, or, at any rate, as she did so. The King's horse came up and Miss Davison *went towards it*. She put up her hand, but *whether it was to catch hold of the reins or to protect herself* I do not know. It was all over in a few seconds.

The horse knocked over the woman with very great force and then stumbled and fell, pitching the jockey violently onto the ground. Both he and Miss Davison were bleeding profusely.

From the opposite side of the track Davison's incursion was witnessed by a Mr Turner of Clapham Common. His account, given wide exposure in the press, is extremely clear; some of it again warrants emphasis:

I noticed a figure bob under the rails. The horses were thundering down the course at a great pace, bunched up close to the rails. From the position in which the woman was standing *it would have been impossible to pick out any special horse. Misjudging the pace of the horses*, she missed the first four or five. They dashed by just as she was emerging from the rails.

*With great calmness she walked in front* of the next group of horses. The first missed her but the second came right into her, and catching her with his shoulder, knocked her with terrific force to the ground while the crowd stood spellbound.

The woman rolled over two or three times and lay unconscious. She was thrown almost on her face. The horse fell after striking the woman, pitching the jockey clear over its head.

Davison came to rest flat on her back, her knees drawn up as if to protect her modesty. God chose to spare her blushes.

'*And the cause goes marching on…*'

# FOURTEEN

# The Bull Fight

Craganour and Aboyeur sped past Emily Davison's position just over three furlongs from the finish, appearing to have the destiny of the 1913 Derby between them: the hot favourite on the outside and the 100/1 plodder nearest the inside rail.

Both horses had been in the van from the rise of the two-strand barrier. Willoughby got the runners away within a minute of the scheduled time, indeed so swiftly that several jockeys were caught slightly unawares, none more so than Walter Earl aboard Agadir and 'Snowy' Whalley on Day Comet. Reiff, on the other hand, was urging Craganour from his central draw of seven under the tapes almost as they rose. He knew Craganour raced keenly and preferred a position with nothing but grass in front of him; and last year he had ridden the home jockeys to sleep by dictating the pace on Tagalie. He was confident he had the partner to do likewise this year. He had made it his business to discover what he could about his rivals, and he knew all about Aboyeur's temperament. Racing upsides with a tearaway might just make Craganour competitive too early; he might run himself out. Worse still, if the stories were correct, Aboyeur might prove a nasty distraction, an encumbrance even. Reiff took a pull and let Aboyeur forge clear.

To naked eyes in the grandstand, the field stretches out along the rise to Tattenham Hill like a string of coloured beads being dragged along a narrow green channel banked on each side by a solid phalanx of gesticulating onlookers. Only those holding

binoculars could identify the horses as Aboyeur now led a closing Craganour by three lengths, pursued by Aldegond, Nimbus,
Sun Yat, Louvois, Shogun, Prue and Agadir. They reached the
crest of the hill marking the half-way point in the race, having
completed the taxing uphill section of the course. Those lining
the rail suddenly heard an American voice cursing loudly. It's
Milton Henry. Someone had clattered into Nimbus, bringing
him to his knees. Henry lost his prominent position, and had
only three behind him on the perilous run down the hill to
Tattenham Corner. As the ground began to drop away so also did
Aldegond and Prue. Craganour moved up to Aboyeur's quarters,
pursued on his outer by Day Comet, while Shogun sneaked up
the rails in the channel previously occupied by Aldegond and
Prue. Behind him came Louvois and Sun Yat.

The runners accelerated whether they wanted to or not.
Gradient and the state of the grass – short, greasy, down-trodden
– saw to that. Wind singing. Horses panting. The muffled thud
of quickening hooves. Promptings; goading; whips cracking.
Some horses were tiring; others became unbalanced. Jockeys
need nerve and vigilance to keep their partners foot-sure, steer a
safe path and avoid clipping heels. It is a stage of the race fraught
with danger. 'The horses were not racing,' observed George Stern,
'but just tumbling down the hill.'

Craganour and Aboyeur pelted round Tattenham Corner side
by side as if hitched to a runaway chariot, Craganour on the
outer, Aboyeur on the inner. In their slipstream lurked Shogun,
running slap against the rail as everyone knew he would if Frank
Wootton had his way.

At this point the story of the 1913 Derby becomes mired in
conflicting accounts and begins its flirtation with notoriety.
However, photographs taken between the top of the hill and the
finish demonstrate a common theme: Reiff was constantly looking across at Aboyeur. His concern cannot emanate from any
fear of being beaten by the 100/1 shot. He was afraid of being
interfered with by an animal he knew to be bad-tempered.

Within a few strides two things happened. Aboyeur veered off a true line: either centrifugal forces pushed him wide so he could not hold the turn or he simply turned nasty. Either way, he ran into Craganour. Reiff's right arm rose and, feeling the whip sting his quarters, Craganour instinctively rolled away from it leftwards, down the cambered Epsom track toward the inside running rail; Aboyeur, conscious of another horse upsides him for the first time in the race, lunged sideways at this intruder with teeth bared.

Craganour's movement was entirely involuntary but in the mind of Aboyeur's English rider this was just the kind of 'dirty trick' he'd been anticipating from the Yank on his back. Once Piper whacked Aboyeur on his left rump, the evil-tempered animal responded in character by trying to bite Craganour, causing the pair of them to lurch back to the right. In mitigation, Piper might plead innocence on the grounds that his horse was in danger of rolling down the camber into the running rail if he hadn't resorted to a strong left-handed whip. But, with his blood up, it's far likelier he was determined to meet fire with fire and show Reiff that English jockeys were no push-overs.

The contest between 1,200lb of horseflesh and the 120lb of man on its back was demonstrably a one-sided affair, and in the process of executing this anarchic jig the leaders had hindered the progress of Shogun on their inside where Wootton, conducting his habitual romance with the rails in advance of launching his challenge, had forced Shogun's head level with Aboyeur's quarters. Shogun's supporters began to shout 'It's all over!' as they spotted him beginning his challenge exactly when and where they had expected. Their voices were suddenly still. Shogun looked to be full of running – until Aboyeur rolled onto him.

'What are you doing?' Wootton is alleged to have shouted at Piper. 'I can't help it!' Piper allegedly screamed back. 'It's the other horse!' If those comments are accurate in content one can be positive they are less so in the choice of vocabulary.

What had been distant figures to the occupants of the grand-stand now rapidly began to metamorphose into angry bundles of muscle and sinew. With just over a quarter of a mile left to race, the straight dips prior to ascending gently toward the winning post. Negotiating this slight depression at top speed has a tendency to unbalance a horse, causing him to lose his action. With a bunching field the result can be alarming. 'There was much skittle play,' averred Sievier. 'Louvois was one of the first and worst offenders, Shogun was shut in on the rails, Day Comet was knocked about and Great Sport was buffeted perhaps more than any.' Yet, acute race-reader he was, Sievier must have been blessed with ten pairs of eyes to make sense of everything that happened down the Epsom straight.

One thing is certain: Walter Raphael's dark blue silks and Shogun's big white face can be spotted once more seeking a path up the inside, a route that a revitalised Day Comet was also exploring. Shogun again reached Aboyeur's quarters before he received a further bump which forced him onto Day Comet and Wootton momentarily to ease him a second time. It is now evident that Wootton was shut in as surely as an eel in a trap as Louvois swooped by him to join issue with the lead-ing pair. Meanwhile, up the centre of the track, two horses were making equally rapid inroads on the leaders: widest of all was Nimbus, finishing faster than anything, and inside him Great Sport.

Passing 'Charabanc City' Craganour spurted and gained a half-length. Up went an open-throated roar of 'the-favourite's-won it!' Instead of inciting Craganour to greater effort the bedlam did the reverse. He faltered and Aboyeur drew level. Reiff fully expected the no-hoper to be waving the white flag by now. As, in all honesty, did Piper. But Aboyeur kept galloping resolutely. It was time for Reiff to earn his fee. He had no option but to test the questioned resolution of his own mount. He grabbed a firm hold of Craganour's head, steadied him and struck him with stinging force down his right flank. They went half-a-length to the good. No sooner had Craganour regained the slender advantage than he surrendered it again.

Entering the last furlong Craganour and Aboyeur looked as though they were contesting the final chukka of a polo match instead of the conclusion to a Derby. Piper realised his horse wasn't going to surrender unconditionally and that Craganour lacked either the class or courage to go past him. He actually had a chance of overturning the favourite and earning for himself a place in racing immortality – not to mention a hefty slice of the prize-money. Piper's riding became more demonic with every stride.

Despite now racing a safe distance from the inside rail Piper continued to carry his whip in his left hand and was seen to strike Aboyeur ten times without once entertaining the sensible option of pulling his whip through into his right hand. These repeated lashings inevitably and inexorably drove Aboyeur even farther to his right, taking the smaller Craganour with him, and, in so doing, blocking off and squeezing out the challenge of Great Sport whom George Stern was trying to thrust between them. With no option but to pull hard on Great Sport's head and yank him to the outside in search of safety, Stern inadvertently interfered with Craganour by clipping his heels before plunging toward the nearest space that lay between him and Nimbus.

The resultant gap along the inside rail was now wide enough for a squadron of dragoons to pass through in addition to Shogun. However, after the repeated buffeting he had received, Wootton's mount had nothing left in him to seize this opportunity and it was Louvois and Day Comet who exploited the opening to charge on. Saxby got behind Louvois's neck and administered a series of right-handers: he could smell retribution on the breeze, tasted revenge on his tongue.

Every second the colours appeared to be re-shuffling in the fashion of a wildly turning kaleidoscope as horse after horse closed on the two leaders who were locked in each other's embrace like a pair of amorous snakes, utterly oblivious to everything going on around them. Each time Craganour was barged by Aboyeur he responded by poking his head in front; and when they uncoiled themselves again he flagged again. 'These staccato movements,' declared Moorhouse in *The Bloodstock Breeders' Review*, 'seemed clearly to indicate that the spirit was willing but the flesh weak … probably occasioned by his inability to inflate his lungs.'

Then, as the line beckoned, it was as if Craganour's patience finally expired. Reiff was a picture of helpless resignation as, forced upright, he was quite unable to offer any last-ditch assistance owing to Aboyeur leaning into him, Craganour threw up his head and fly-leapt completely off the ground in the direction of his tormentor.

In the blink of an eye half-a-dozen horses were propelled past the judge in colourful line abreast amid a chorus of profanities and cracking whips, barely a half-length covering the lot of them. No race-goer who beheld this amazing scramble could possibly confess to anything but a hazy notion of what he or she had seen. If a dozen witnesses had been requested to write a summary statement on the subject there would assuredly have been a dozen conflicting accounts.

Charles Robinson was on a hiding to nothing. He had no photo-finish camera, no freeze-framed image. All he could call on was the instant assessment of his own eyes, plus years of experience and any input from his assistant, W. C. Manning. He had never been confronted by a Derby finish packed with so many possibilities. Not since his father-in-law called a dead-heat between Harvester and St Gatien in 1884 had the judge faced such a complicated task. His only point of reference was the controversial short-head decision he gave Minoru over Louviers in 1909. After some delay he posted his verdict. The number five was hoisted and hailed by a momentous cheer, 'volume not heard since the memorable afternoon on which Minoru won for King Edward', opined *The Sporting Life*.

Robinson awarded the race to Craganour by a head, with

Louvois a neck behind Aboyeur; Great Sport was placed fourth, a head in front of Nimbus and Day Comet sixth. The two sons of the derided Classic sire Desmond (his only representatives) had proved the bloodstock pundits wrong. The time of two minutes 37.6 seconds, on ground officially described as 'fair' (and matched by Jest in the Oaks two days later) was 0.8 seconds outside Spearmint's race record.

Quite patently it was a rough race. George Stern likened the finish to a 'bull fight'. The greatest sufferers were his own mount Great Sport, Shogun and Nimbus. Great Sport's challenge had been effectively snuffed out by Aboyeur's uncorrected drift to the right well inside the final furlong and he'd been beaten by barely a length: 'I think he won it!' his owner Hall Walker insisted afterwards. 'And I know he ought to have won it. He nearly fell over the fallen horse and the jockey lost his whip! Being a lazy horse his jockey could not squeeze him up in time to win.' Given that Great Sport was some way in front of Anmer at Tattenham Corner it is difficult to accept his first excuse.

In Shogun's case, however, his own jockey's role was critical. Wootton's paean to the rails turned into a suicide note. 'Did you ever see anything like that in your life?' Dick Wootton said to Charles Morton, fighting back tears. 'I thought he was an absolute certainty.' Morton looked Wootton in the eye and replied:

> Well, there you are. You teach your boys to keep to the fence and stick there. You cannot complain if they lose races by it. A good jockey can see a long way from home and he ought to be able to tell what he is going to do without getting shut in.

The Frenchman's case is different. Nimbus suffered no fewer than three bouts of interference, not one of them of his own making. The only observer to register the French challenger's misfortune was his owner, who had, naturally, been following his progress to the exclusion of others. M. Aumont was astounded to see Nimbus swerve away to the outside at Tattenham Corner and knew 'that something had happened'. Davison cost him ten lengths according to Milton Henry at a critical stage of the race three furlongs out; somehow he made up a dozen or more lengths only to be barged off a true line when mounting his challenge in the final hundred yards, owing to the knock-on effects of Aboyeur's flight from Piper's whip.

Equally hard done by, albeit ultimately in a different sense again, was another baulked in running, Day Comet. Testimony to the chaos of that last twenty yards is the fact that his finishing position was completely misjudged by Robinson: he clearly finished in front of Great Sport and, therefore, must have been fourth. Had Robinson recourse to the photographs of the finish freely available the following day he would have seen that, as at Newmarket in the 2000 Guineas, he had committed a major blunder. The side view of the finish, taken from the stand side of the course from a point just beyond his box, shows four horses whose heads are practically level. The nearest horse is clearly Craganour; next to him is Aboyeur; beyond him is Louvois. The fourth horse on the far rail is obscured but is wearing cloth bandages on his forelegs. Only one of the leading six horses wore bandages: Day Comet.

But Day Comet's ill fortune was nothing compared to what was about to befall Craganour.

# FIFTEEN

# 'He Has Not Won It Yet!'

Epsom Downs was in tumult. Rumours began spreading like bindweed. Even before Robinson announced his verdict some voices were heard muttering 'If Craganour has won he is sure to be disqualified.' By the time he was led into the weighing room enclosure the sensational prospect of an objection and possible disqualification had managed to spread. Ismay wore an unusually glum expression for a man at the head of his Derby winner.

Eustace Loder was already thinking along the lines of an objection. 'He has not won it yet,' he observed to Merrik Burrell as they descended from the Jockey Club box high in the grandstand. The identity of the 'he' in question – horse, jockey, trainer or owner – was as yet unclear. One can safely presume that Loder had seen enough to convince him an objection was in the offing from the connections of Aboyeur and he was eager to make contact with his fellow Stewards, Lords Rosebery and Wolverton. 'Never has there been greater confusion over the result of a race,' wrote Edward Moorhouse. The confusion was about to deepen.

Much of the detailed description of ensuing events in and around the winner's enclosure and weighing room comes via Sidney Galtrey's memoirs. Galtrey was a highly respected journalist, close enough to the Establishment to be cognisant of its feelings and opinions, if not to the extent of blind subservience. However, his memoirs were written twenty years after the Derby and even his memory for detail is self-evidently shaky:

he talks of 'coming across' Aboyeur's co-owner Wilfred Purefoy, for example, when Purefoy was 500 miles away and fast asleep on a train to Dublin at the time following a cattle-buying trip to Tipperary Fair. Thus, the passage of time is no guardian of the truth, merely a guide to the confusion reigning throughout those frenetic thirty minutes immediately after Craganour and Aboyeur passed the post locked together in a lover's embrace.

Craganour returned to racing's most hallowed patch of grass, Epsom's narrow unsaddling enclosure, for his coronation. His bay flanks were heaving and lathered with sweat as he leant on one hind leg, resting the other one as tired horses often do after a tough race. The mustachioed Bower Ismay and Jack Robinson accepted congratulatory handshakes and back-slaps; Ismay was even seen to break into a smile; a shout of 'Well ridden, Reiff!' was heard from the Stewards' stand.

'I've not won it yet. I've never had any luck in this race,' said Robinson, bowler hat in one hand while mopping a perspiring brow with the other. An aside from someone close by soon spooked him. 'What's the matter? There can't be anything wrong,' he exclaimed, fearing his eyes had not deceived him during that final-furlong barging match. 'They can't be objecting. You didn't see anything, did you?' Galtrey assured him there was no call for alarm. 'They were very close together and they came away from the rails. But it will be all right. They do not disqualify Derby winners.'

The men who might have been expected to object to the winner if there were any justification so to do had no intention of bothering. Percy Cunliffe, whom Galtrey insists was a man 'who would have had no qualms about lodging an objection if he thought that by doing so on grounds which he approved he might be awarded the Derby' and who stands to win over £31,000 (over £1¼ million) in bets in addition to the £6,450 (£283,800) in first-prize money, was prepared to accept the result. Indeed, contrary to the popular conception of a 100/1 no-hoper being friendless, several bookmakers reported Aboyeur to have been well backed

(Douglas Stuart – 'The Prince of Turf Accountants' – was hit particularly hard). In any event, no owner ever wished to object in a Derby; it amounted to 'poor form'. Equally, cognisant of Aboyeur's temper, Cunliffe knew objecting was a waste of time and he, a Steward himself remember, had no wish to be labelled a 'poor sport'.

Surely Piper would lay a complaint against Reiff if he had been so brutally treated all the way up the straight? He did not. 'One can only attribute this to the crowding of exciting incidents upon the brain of a comparatively young jockey who for the first time had been in the thick of a Derby fight,' suggested a journalist in *The Sporting Chronicle*: 'He may possibly have thought that the fault was really his at the outset in leaving the rails for it is true he was unable to hold the rails berth rounding Tattenham Corner.'

The journalist, Kettledrum, had raised a valid point. Piper was not about to disagree with his owner: he knew he had been more sinner than sinned against and feared disqualification from second place for not keeping his mount straight – he struck Aboyeur with his left hand no fewer than ten times in the last 200 yards so that he wound up six horse-widths off the fence. 'It was a most important point that no objection was lodged in the interests of those connected with the second,' Galtrey continued.

After some minutes, a shout of 'All Right!' – the shouter's identity was never confirmed officially – rang out and the red flag confirming as much was hoisted to the top of the pillar beside the number board opposite the grandstand, prompting many bookmakers to begin paying out. 'Thank goodness for that. Phew! I was beginning to get worried,' wheezed Robinson.

Events elsewhere, however, show he had cause to be 'worried'. Loder had been busy locating and consulting with his fellow Stewards, the Lords Rosebery and Wolverton. In Frederick Lambton's absence, Loder became the senior Steward presiding, and once it became apparent that the connections of Aboyeur weren't going to object he moved that the Stewards should take that initiative upon themselves. There were precedents. He had been on the panel that objected to and then disqualified Primrose Morn from first place in Goodwood's Singleton Plate the previous July, as he had at Newmarket when the apprentice-ridden two-year-old Loch Stack, the 7/2 favourite in a selling plate following the 2000 Guineas, was similarly treated for 'crossing'; the colt actually passing through the sale ring before the disqualification was announced. Commented *The Sporting Chronicle* of the debacle: 'The Stewards objecting provided a piece of quaint phraseology having regard to the fact that they decided their own objection.'

That it had been a rough race was blatantly obvious: Aboyeur, for instance, returned bleeding from two cuts above his near-hind joint, and immediately after passing the post Walter Earl jumped off Agadir who finished lame following his brush with Davison. It was incumbent on the Stewards to stamp out rough riding. There'd been too many instances of late where local Stewards had been judged lax in enforcing the Rules and whenever Stewards of the Jockey Club comprised the panel they were beholden to set a proper example. Cuthbert, for instance, had forfeited the Lincolnshire Handicap for 'bumping and boring' back in April; conversely, Jest kept the 1000 Guineas after a panel led by Loder had investigated an objection from the rider of the second on the same grounds, stating that 'both horses were in fault'. A similar judgement was reached after a race at York on 26 May in which the Stewards confessed 'there was a great deal of bumping' but felt 'they were unable to attach the blame to any individual jockey'. However, those judgements derived from objections lodged by connections not by the Stewards themselves.

There was a lull in the buzz of animated conversation. The *Daily Telegraph* said 'the sinking feeling returned with an awful rush to the Craganourites' and the *Life* recorded 'the word "Objection" falling like a bomb in their midst'. The ensuing couple of minutes did justice to a pantomime. Loder had the

Stewards' decision conveyed to the Clerk of the Scales. 'Before Reiff was out of the scales,' W. C. Manning, the Clerk of the Scales, later told the *Daily News*, 'the secretary of the Jockey Club came and told me I was not to pass the jockey.' In the winner's enclosure, the Lambton twins were making their presence felt. According to the *Illustrated Sporting and Dramatic News*, as Robinson's first Derby winner was being led away he was called back by Frederick Lambton while, according to Sydney Galtrey, the implacable figure of Lord Durham, barred the exit – 'looking rather fierce and terribly serious' – every inch the 'Determined Jack' of racecourse legend and dictator of the Turf even though he wasn't currently a Steward. Durham demanded to know who had given authority for the 'All Right' to be given, and ordered Craganour to be brought back.

The red flag, which had been fluttering in full view for a full five minutes, was lowered and replaced with the blue one denoting an objection. It transpired that the Stewards had lodged an objection to the winner on the grounds that 'he jostled the second horse' – which implied Rule 140 (ii). The full text of Rule 140 (ii) read:

> If a horse or his jockey jostle another horse, or jockey, the aggressor is disqualified, unless it be proved that the jostle was wholly caused by the fault of some other jockey, or that the jostled horse or his jockey was partly in fault.

Thus, in order for Craganour and Reiff to lose the race *all* blame has to rest with them: not even a scintilla of responsibility can lie with Aboyeur and Piper. Conversely, if both horses were equally to blame, their jockeys could be severely reprimanded but the result might stand – as happened after a race at Newmarket the previous October. That the Stewards felt obliged to lodge such an objection was tantamount to stating they felt they already knew the answer. So this wasn't going to be a fair hearing. Furthermore, the Stewards could also resort to Rule 140 (i):

A horse which crosses another in any part of the race so as to interfere with that or any other horse's chance is liable to disqualification, unless it be proved that he was two lengths in front when he crossed.

The key phrase here is *any part of the race*. Consequently, all those incidents involving Craganour and Aboyeur that occurred closer to Tattenham Corner than the finish were just as important as those in the neighbourhood of the winning post itself. This put Craganour's position in jeopardy. Yet such a strict interpretation of the Rule warranted clarification as to how early in a race, any race, can incidents be deemed result-affecting? In this particular race, scrupulous application of the Rule would as likely result in the disqualification of more than one participant.

An objection of this kind was unprecedented in the 132-year history of the race. The only three objections were all lodged later on technical grounds, and just the notorious Running Rein scandal of 1844 (the winner was found to be a 'ringer', namely a four-year-old called Maccabeus masquerading as a three-year-old) was upheld. Five years earlier the owner of the second horse, Deception, objected to the winner, Bloomsbury, on the grounds that he was entered as 'by Mulatto' whereas the Stud Book described him as being 'by Tramp or Mulatto'. In 1880 Robert the Devil's owner objected to the Duke of Westminster's Bend Or on the grounds that he was not Bend Or (by Doncaster out of Rouge Rose) but Tadcaster (by Doncaster out of Clemence) and their identities had been mixed up on leaving the Duke's stud as yearlings – subsequent information (that now encompasses DNA analysis) suggests Robert the Devil's owner was correct.

This was something else entirely: a unique objection arising from foul riding. The single winner to forfeit a Classic in such circumstances was Zanga, whose jockey, John Mangle, was found guilty of 'jostling' in the 1789 St Leger and the race awarded to the filly Pewett.

No official record was kept of the enquiry, the words of its participants, neither witnesses nor Stewards, ever divulged – which provided limitless scope for rumour. Rosebery, for example, has been widely reported as declining to take an active role in the enquiry, citing the fact that he had a runner in the race. This reluctance may appear to be rooted deep in the moral high ground of the aristocracy and the age, but it beggars belief. Prue was not among the sufferers, not involved in the finish and her fate as an also-ran should have had no remote bearing on Rosebery's view of proceedings. More significantly, and it's impossible to believe a stickler for the 'Rules' such as Loder was unaware of the fact, Rosebery's defection would immediately invalidate any enquiry because there was no longer the requisite quorum demanded under Rule 166. However Rule 167 states: 'If only two Stewards be present, they shall fix upon a third person, being a member of the Club, in lieu of the absent Steward.' Subsequently, it was suggested, but only after the judgement had been put under the spotlight, that Lord Derby may have taken Rosebery's place – albeit with Rosebery compounding the charge of spinelessness by staying in the room. One wonders where he sat. One can't imagine him skulking in a corner; if he sat behind the Stewards table his menacing silence alone should have counted for something.

But Rosebery was in no shape, physically or mentally, to act as Steward. Arguably he never had been: he'd no real understanding of horses; he disliked hunting and was a poor rider. The faculties of a man once dubbed 'The Uncrowned King of Scotland' by J. M. Barrie were now undermined by fading eyesight and memory, by piles and a weak bladder, and by recurring toothache in addition to the tiredness brought on by his insomnia. 'I am a well-preserved corpse,' he'd often told callers. Now he referred to himself as 'reduced to a point below being even a corpse'.

And it was an incontrovertible fact that he was out of practice. Until the opening day of the Epsom meeting twenty-four hours earlier, Rosebery had not officiated since the previous year's Derby meeting. However, the old politician in him hadn't lost all grasp of that 'common sense' Gladstone found so elusive in him. Always thin-skinned to criticism, he was far too shrewd to place himself in the eye of a storm he knew would howl for weeks following the disqualification of a Derby winner.

His diary clears up the matter, for even if silence was all he contributed, his entry for 4 June is extraordinarily illuminating; the insertion of italics highlights key issues:

> The most detestable day I ever spent on a racecourse. A woman ran into the King's horse, nearly killing herself and the jockey, the winner of the Derby was disqualified and Leo's horse Felizardo broke his leg nearly opposite the stand.
>
> I was called upon to act as Steward. *I should have preferred non-interference in such a race as the Derby as the second did not object.*
>
> But Loder and Wolverton declared necessity of an objection and, that granted, *the evidence seemed overwhelming*.
>
> The fact is I *ought not to act as Steward.* I go racing so little and am *so ignorant of its Rules* and practice, besides my *deafness*.
>
> Dined with the King. Sat between Londonderry and Enniskillen. Motored back with Sefton after.

Whatever view Rosebery may have held concerning the merits of an Ismay victory in the Derby, his reluctance to be associated with the enquiry – and thus the means of preventing it – is plain: it was not the 'done thing' to interfere with the result of the Derby. But it was he, not Lord Derby or even Frederick Lambton, who was the third member of the panel who gave it legitimacy – albeit as a silent partner. In addition, one of the most powerful men on the Turf confesses to being 'ignorant' of the Rules he is charged with enforcing and, to cap everything, would be hard-pressed to hear the evidence presented in any case. Therein lie the reasons for Rosebery's abrogation of responsibility to Loder for an enquiry and a judgement he sensed history would render notorious, not any public-spirited declaration on his part of a vested interest in the outcome thanks to his ownership of Prue.

With Rosebery effectively *in absentia*, Loder became the prime mover in the case against Craganour, for Wolverton was the junior partner on the panel, this being his first season as a Steward of the Jockey Club.

Frederick Glyn, the 4th Baron Wolverton, was obliged to scrape by on an annual income equating to £2¼ million in modern money. He was a partner in the firm of private bankers Glyn, Mills, Currie & Co. founded by his great-grandfather in 1753. In 1890 he was the senior partner when the bank prevented the collapse of Baring Brothers, thereby saving many of the City's financial institutions from ruin. He'd not expected to inherit his title but succeeded his brother in 1888. It was said he possessed 'a logical mind and a capacity for business'. But he had shown himself open to persuasion in the past: he presently sat on the Conservative benches in the House of Lords after once sitting as a Liberal. An owner who, like Loder, seldom bet, he was elected to the Jockey Club in 1899. On his elevation to Steward in the April of 1913, *The Sporting Life* was moved to comment:

> To the majority his personality is utterly unknown. Of medium height, well set-up and soldierly, he moves through life on the Turf as if his interest in the sport was more academic than personal. Behind rather tired looking eyes is an alert intelligence that misses nothing. He is a rare stickler for racing's purity and it will be a bad day for the evil doer who may come before him. He has a well-balanced and logical mind, qualities that have not invariably been associated with holders of this position.

Wolverton wasn't a successful owner: his durable handicapper Ugly did number a July Cup among his twenty-one successes but his best horse was probably Osboch, who won the Ascot Derby and Champion Stakes of 1901 after finishing third in the 2000 Guineas. Other than racing, his principal sporting interest, befitting the son of a vice admiral, was sailing, a pursuit that brought close friendship with King George V; he was a pillar of the Royal Yacht Squadron and in partnership with Lord Dunraven had mounted unsuccessful bids for the Americas Cup. Wolverton's acquaintance with Africa matched that of Bower Ismay. He fought in the Boer War as a Lieutenant in the North Somerset Yeomanry and was also a keen big-game hunter (he and another gun bagging seventeen lions between them on one tour) and published a book on the subject in 1894. Unfortunately, *Five Months Sport in Somali Land* was greeted with polite derision.

Rosebery, Loder and Wolverton: the three dusty-veined panjandrums now lording it over the red-blooded Ismay.

Having framed this indictment with or without Wolverton's compliance, Loder was now in a prime position to seek corroborative evidence and hand down the only possible sentence – disqualification. In effect, he had assumed the roles of prosecuting counsel, jury and judge. Finding that testimony wasn't going to tax his first role overmuch. Jockeys are unreliable witnesses at the best of times: tempers will be short; memories wayward; grudges surface. Biased evidence is endemic. There was a lot of money at stake and permitting wads of it to fall into the pockets of a Yankee mercenary like Johnny Reiff was never going to sit easily with the home-based riders. One in particular.

As the rider of the third horse past the post, Billy Saxby was one witness at the enquiry more than eager to steady a nail above Reiff's coffin while Loder drew back the hammer. He would certainly support Edwin Piper's account; as would Frank Wootton, whose lowly finish on Shogun (seventh past the post) was attributed to the 'jostling' he received earlier in the straight. Wootton had just lost a Derby he might have won. He was still only nineteen years of age and defeat was an indigestible meal for a volatile teenager reared on success – especially when the trainer involved was his own bitterly disappointed father. He had already been castigated by Leopold de Rothschild for the interference he caused Day Comet up the straight. 'He seldom came back with an excuse after a race,' wrote George Lambton of one of his favourite jockeys. 'When he was beat it was because the horse was not good enough.'

But this was not any old 'race' and Wootton had to cover his back. Thus, if events further from the finishing post, especially as described by a self-serving Frank Wootton, were going to be given weight in the enquiry, the position of Craganour became parlous. If ever a kangaroo court was assembled to try an objection this was it. The prosecutor, judge, jury and leading witnesses all had axes to grind. The outcome of the enquiry was scarcely in doubt, a view soon endorsed by George Stern who relayed as much to Jack Jarvis whom he bumped into outside the Stewards' Room following his interrogation: 'They're going to disqualify that bloody horse.' The tone of voice and choice of words betrayed both his incredulity and the Stewards' certainty of purpose. In 1913 Jack Jarvis, who was to become champion trainer three times and number a brace of Derbies among his nine Classic successes, was 26-years-old and recently forced out of the saddle owing to rising weight. Emboldened by Stern's opinion he walked along the rails where Aboyeur was 5/1 to get the race and backed him to win £5,000, 'a very nice sum for a young man in those days', as he related years afterwards.

Jarvis had watched the race from the top of the grandstand alongside the Epsom trainer 'Hoppy' Duller, who also proceeded to profit from the situation. Duller came across a bookmaker bemoaning likely losses of £20,000 on Craganour. 'I'll bet you £100 to ten shillings that it doesn't get the race,' said Duller. 'It might get disqualified.' The bookie agreed to take the wager. Once the enquiry had commenced Duller returned to his quarry: 'Now I'll bet you an even pony (£25) he doesn't get the race. And come and have a pint with me because I can tell you it will be disqualified.' The bookie consented; took the bet and the drink. Duller would collect his £125 while the bookmaker found himself £19,875 better off than he thought he would be.

George Stern had no axe to grind; but Messrs Piper, Wootton and Saxby had most definitely sharpened theirs.

Piper experienced a conversion of Pauline magnitude. The vanquished jockey, overheard expressing regret to Reiff for the rough ride they had, now contradicted himself before the tribunal. The contrite jockey disinclined to object some fifteen minutes earlier now emerged from his tête-à-tête with the Stewards to sing a different song for the waiting reporters:

> The facts I have already told the Stewards. What I told them they must have heard from other jockeys riding in the race. Craganour came up on my right and gave my horse the first bump some two furlongs from home. My horse then went over and shut off Shogun from coming up on my left. I heard Frank Wootton call to me and shouted back: 'I can't help it!'
>
> I did all I knew how to keep Aboyeur off the rails but once I got my horse going again I was cannoned into again by Craganour. This was after I re-headed the latter just as we reached the number board. Close home I was in front again but as we went by the post Craganour was right on top of my horse whom I was thus prevented from getting the last ounce out of.

So, plenty of emphasis on the 'jostling' that occurred two furlongs from the finish in which both Craganour and Aboyeur may have been equally culpable, and no reference to the fact that nearer the finish Aboyeur had forced Craganour completely out of his ground by coming six-horse widths off the inside rail, against the grain of the track, up the camber.

Wootton was never going to get the race but he wriggled mightily in an effort to suggest he would have won on merit had it not been for Reiff:

> Half-way down the straight an opening big enough to take a waggon through presented itself and at the instant I pulled my mount into the gap Aboyeur came rolling toward me. One more stride and I should not have been shut out.
>
> My shouts to Piper received the response that Reiff's mount

was causing the pressure and this seemed plain when I pulled behind them.

The same thing occurred half-a-furlong further on and after easing my mount again I could see my chance was hopeless, as the animals on the outside were so bunched together that it would have been useless for me to have tried to do any good by pulling out so far with the winning post so near.

Never before has Shogun impressed me so and he literally flew after taking the bend into the home straight.

The Stewards also placed great store in the testimony of their fellow officials, the judge and his assistant. However, from his position, by the winning line Robinson had no clear sight of the earlier contretemps that cost Craganour the race. The accuracy of his interpretation of the polo match in the shadow of the post is undermined by that other error of judgement on his part – on a par with that of the 2000 Guineas: he totally overlooked the run of Day Comet along the inside rail. Day Comet wasn't very big, and in the side-on photograph of the finish is obscured by Craganour, Aboyeur and Louvois, but he's nonetheless identifiable via his bandaged forelegs. Robinson initially failed to place him in the leading half dozen; only later did he award him fifth place. Yet it seems clear Day Comet passed the post ahead of Great Sport and should've placed third in the revised order.

Almost to a man, racing correspondents deemed Shogun the moral victor: the *Life*; *The Sporting Chronicle*; *Daily Express*; the *Illustrated Sporting and Dramatic News*; the *Daily Mail* ('never was there one which so palpably owed his defeat to bad luck') were notably unequivocal. However, Wootton's self-serving version of events is best put in its place by Charles Morton, who had watched the barging match unfold beside the jockey's shell-shocked father. 'They undoubtedly won innumerable races by this method and also lost many,' he said of the Wootton strategy to hug the rail, 'so it is probably six of one and half-a-dozen of the other.'

A lone voice belonged to 'Vigilant' in *The Sportsman*, who had obviously seen what M. Aumont had seen and reckoned that dubious distinction belonged to Nimbus:

> He acquitted himself of a startling performance and was travelling so much faster than anything else at the finish that a few more strides would have sufficed to give him the victory. Outpaced to begin with, he was soon so far behind that even his most ardent admirers abandoned all hope. Just when he was beginning to go, the Anmer tragedy occurred and badly baulked by the scrimmage, he lost more ground, so that when he came into the straight he must have been upwards of fifty yards behind the leaders. At the distance he was still half a dozen lengths away but, going great guns, and although placed fifth only, he was finally beaten by barely a length. In the circumstances it does not seem extravagant to suppose he was very unlucky.

Vigilant also took the time to extend some praise to Aboyeur, however:

> It appears to me there was not so much fluke about Aboyeur's performance as by many declared, for, to give him his due, he practically made all the running. It would be churlish, therefore, to belittle the credit of his achievement, the simple fact being that he is a much better horse than had been commonly supposed.

Saxby's account of the 'bull fight' was not printed verbatim but a *Daily Express* reporter who spoke with him said it

> gave very damning evidence against Reiff alleging that he interfered with almost everything in the race including Louvois and Shogun. He had just taken his position when the barging started and it robbed him of an opportunity to get going until too late and the fact that he was only beaten a head and a neck after 'coming from the clouds' shows how unlucky he was.

In its vilification of his replacement, Saxby's account is hardly surprising; in its logic far less so. Craganour had been too far ahead of everything else in the race to have interfered with them all and Louvois was, according to many neutral observers, one of the few involved in the finish to have been the beneficiary of a trouble-free passage. If Robert Sievier's report in *The Winning Post* is to be believed Louvois had caused trouble not suffered it and 'interfered with more than one opponent' amid the 'skittle play' in the vicinity of Tattenham Corner.

Reiff offered few words, as if he knew from the outset he was facing a 'stacked deck'. He said he admitted to the Stewards that he 'certainly did put Aboyeur back', which implies he felt Aboyeur had come onto Craganour first of all; and added that as this was acceptable in France he saw no reason to desist. 'If Reiff pleaded that the practice is such as obtained in France,' blasted Kettledrum in *The Sporting Chronicle*, 'then I for one say that the less we see of the French riding division over here the better.'

Later on Reiff confined himself to stating 'it was a bad decision' to disqualify his horse. However, on 5 August, when acknowledging receipt of his cheque from Bower Ismay, he provided the owner with his 'full account':

Dear Sir,

At the start I was well away. After having travelled about two hundred yards I let Craganour settle down behind Aboyeur, being clear from the rest.

On approaching Tattenham Corner a third horse came close on the outside of me. Not wishing to be pocketed by an outsider, I called upon my horse to pass Aboyeur, getting about three parts of a length advantage, when Piper suddenly came over on me causing my horse to drop back level with him.

When entering the straight line I again tried to pass Piper without forcing my horse. Having taken a half-length, I managed to push Aboyeur back in his place again. I did this to keep Piper from letting anyone take the rails having already noticed Wootton getting ready to make a rush through where he had no place (this was the only time I interfered with any horse).

Immediately after, Piper, releasing his hold, commenced riding Aboyeur hard with a loose rein. From then on Aboyeur was continually bumping Craganour from behind. The latter being a small horse could never get an action sufficient to get clear. With a straight run I would have won by two lengths. Then pulling-up I asked Piper why did he continually let his horse bump mine without trying to pull him off. He apologised, saying he could not help it and begged me to say nothing to the Stewards, not wishing to be disqualified for second place.

I told Piper that I intended to lodge a complaint for foul riding. After entering the weighing enclosure I told your trainer my intentions but he said let the matter drop, be satisfied we have won the race. I did not see Mr Robinson again. He left the enclosure with the horse.

Nothing was said about the race until I was nearly dressed when I was called in the presence of the Stewards. I was very much surprised when I found out they were accusing me whereas Piper was the faulty one.

The following jockeys were called in to give evidence: Wootton, Saxby. Whalley, Stern and Piper. Stern was the only one to give a true account of the race. Piper, when he saw I was the accused one, tried all he could to get the race, backed up by the others. Milton Henry was not called. I am sure he had a better view of the finish than either Wootton or Whalley. Mr Manning and Mr Robinson both gave convicting evidence against self.

After the Stewards' decision the jockeys became rather insult-ing by their remarks and not wishing to be the cause of any trouble I left the course at once.

Your very obedient, John Reiff.

One would expect Reiff's version of events to be as self-serving as Wootton's but it is not: he admits committing the very offence, namely '*to push Aboyeur back in his place again*' at the entrance to the straight, that prompted disqualification but asserts this followed Piper coming *'over on me'*. Stating the former in the Stewards' Room, however, was all the ammunition Loder needed under the full letter of Rule 140 (i) if Piper and his fellow jockeys denied the latter and were supported by the judge and his assistant.

Ten years later Reiff confided to New York sportswriter Frank Graham that 'the prejudiced testimony of English jockeys and the personal unpopularity of Mr Ismay, who had played an unenviable role in the *Titanic* disaster the year before, probably figured to some extent in the matter'. Although this quote makes Reiff seem as confused as many others regarding the exact nature of Ismay's role in the *Titanic* tragedy, the gist conveys the nub of truth: prejudiced jockeys and an unpopular owner – in the eyes of the Stewards at least – had tipped the balance. But for that Johnny Reiff would have gone into retirement boasting a Derby record of three wins from just four rides.

Decades on Reiff repeated more or less the same story to his grandson John Hackett Reiff:

> He said his disqualification for 'striking out with his riding crop' was in direct retaliation for the severe crowding and interference he had received from the other horse and rider.
>
> My grandfather told me his being 'ruled off the track' was a direct result of that political sentiment on the part of those officials who ruled the English Turf.
>
> I always knew him to be impeccably honest, not especially overly-impressed with his accomplishments and very candid in his recollection of those days.
>
> For example, I read an account of an incident in which he, as a young lad of only fifteen or sixteen years, stopped a runaway carriage on the streets of London. Because of his youth, small stature and fame as a handler of thoroughbreds, the account painted him as a hero, leaping astride the snorting beasts and subduing them. In recalling the event, he told me that the carriage

driver, in an advanced stage in inebriation, had simply fallen off the carriage, spooking the horses. He said the startled horses had only taken a few steps when he grasped the reins and brought the carriage to an easy stop.

I have always regarded this first-person account as a prime example of his being honest and candid.

Another jockey renowned for his probity was surprisingly not called to give evidence. Maher was the senior jockey riding and he had a good view of proceedings from Prue's saddle in rear; however, with Rosebery in the room, it's reasonable to assume his testimony would have toed the party line and been no help to Reiff. As it was, the witnesses called – Charles Robinson and W. C. Manning, Piper, Saxby, Stern, Wootton – seemed stacked against Reiff and drew accusations of bias; little wonder Rosebery was able to describe the evidence as 'overwhelming' in his diary. Only Reiff's fellow 'hired gun' George Stern might be expected to give him some sympathetic support. From his finishing position close up behind the leading bunch, Steve Donoghue enjoyed an even finer view of the shenanigans than Maher, but he, too, was not required; nor was Reiff's compatriot Milton Henry, even though he was involved in the finish.

Maher was dead inside three years and never wrote a memoir or aired an opinion. His protégé and successor Steve Donoghue did, albeit ten years after the event, in his autobiography *Just My Story*. From his position aboard Bachelor's Wedding (promoted to eighth) Donoghue enjoyed a fine view of the mayhem played out in front of him:

Nine out of ten of the onlookers considered Aboyeur to be quite as much to blame as Craganour. He certainly hung away from the rails badly and bored on to Craganour, and Reiff 'certainly did put Aboyeur back' as much as he was able to do, and that he considered he had every right to do so, as the other horse was hanging on to his mount. I should certainly have done the same in his place.

Saxby finished third in the race to him ... his evidence was taken by the Stewards. How could it possibly have been unprejudiced after – to say the least – the unfortunate way the jockey had been treated by the connections of Craganour?

Jockeys are like other people, only human, and here was surely a golden opportunity for anyone to 'get his own back'.

Another legendary figure of the Turf, Jack Jarvis took a different view, and was so sure Craganour would lose the race that he bet heavily against him. In his 1969 autobiography he stated: 'It was a barging match between the favourite and Aboyeur. It was Reiff on Craganour, though, who started the trouble and I have always been emphatic that the decision to disqualify Craganour was the right one.' In passing one might just add that Jarvis went on to train for Lord Rosebery and his heir. Another eminent trainer begged to disagree. In his autobiography Richard Marsh makes no bones about it: 'The cruellest disqualification in history,' he declares, 'a tragic decision that was not merited.'

Of these various eye-witnesses one cannot avoid returning to Steve Donoghue, a man who benefitted by being in both the race and the weighing room. He concluded his recollection of events, and Saxby's ultimately pivotal role in them, with the asperity of one who knew the score: 'Anyhow, Saxby's evidence certainly turned the scale against Craganour.'

Some thirty minutes elapsed before the board bearing the word 'Sustained' appeared in the frame beneath the blue 'Objection' flag as the runners for the following race cantered past on their way to the one-mile gate for the Stewards Handicap. The official statement issued by Loder's Star Chamber went as follows:

The Stewards objected to the winner on the grounds that he jostled the second horse. After hearing the evidence of the Judge and several of the jockeys riding in the race, they found that Craganour, the winner, did not keep a straight course and interfered with Shogun, Day Comet and Aboyeur. Having bumped and bored the second horse they disqualified Craganour and awarded the race to Aboyeur.

Craganour was thus placed last of the fourteen finishers and Bower Ismay denied even the £400 for second place. Jack Robinson fought hard to sport a brave face, telling the *Life:*

> I have nothing to add. All I know is that I am alive with the possibility of having other Derby candidates to train. It only shows what can happen in racing. It's no use saying anything. No matter what I say, it will make things neither better nor worse. I am, of course, a terribly disappointed man, but, who can tell, I may yet train the winner of the Derby.

Ismay took the blow with like stoicism, patting his trainer on the back and saying, 'Never mind, we shall win the Derby again some other day.' The adoption and significance of the word 'again' should not be underestimated. His comments to reporters were confined to the feeling that 'the disqualification was unjustified and all too tragic to discuss; my sympathy goes out to my trainer and the public must suffer considerably'. He ignored all further entreaties to discuss the Stewards' decision before leaving the racecourse. And his public stance on the matter never wavered until his dying day.

So, to frank Craganour's guilt, the Stewards had augmented the indictment against him to include crimes against Day Comet and Shogun. Aboyeur, by contrast, received a complete discharge. Where, when and how Craganour had come to interfere with Day Comet (presumably the horse Reiff mentioned coming 'close on the outside of me' on the descent of Tattenham Hill which he'd begun in third place) was never explained or challenged. Day Comet was owned by Leopold de Rothschild, clearly enraged by his colt's treatment at the hands of Wootton and doubtless swayed by his shifting all the blame onto Reiff. The interests of 'Mr Leo' had to be protected.

There's no record of Eustace Loder's demeanour in the after-math of the announcement. That very fact demonstrates him to have been as impassive as usual. Nevertheless, the disappointment of Eyrefield losing a Derby winner must have been assuaged by the feeling that Ismay's desolation plumbed greater depths.

But if Loder behaved like a gentleman and contained himself, outside the weighing room a jubilant Billy Saxby was seen to throw his hat in the air at the announcement of Craganour's disqualification. Had he shared Hall Walker's devotion to astrol-ogy he may have contained himself, for back at Imari House, the property he'd bought in Newmarket's Exeter Road and named in honour of his Chester Cup winner, a macabre sequence of events had begun to unfold. Saxby's father had foreseen Craganour winning the Derby and then having victory taken away. On hearing of the disqualification he'd retired to bed 'very excited'. The following morning 49-year-old William Saxby senior was found lying on the floor, one foot caught in the bed-rail, his head doubled grotesquely beneath him. During the night he must have accidentally tumbled out of bed, become entangled and fallen awkwardly onto his head, breaking his neck.

# SIXTEEN

# Rancour and Recrimination

Thanks to Emily Davison the press had a once-in-a-lifetime Derby story that gatecrashed the front page and thanks to Eustace Loder (or depending on one's point of view, Johnny Reiff) the racing pages were presented with a *cause célèbre* that would saturate them for a week or more and obsess racing's parish for decades to come.

Column inch after column inch was devoted to dissecting every aspect of the drama that had gripped Epsom and intrigued the racing community. Who was responsible for the 'bull fight' – Craganour or Aboyeur? Were the Stewards right to order an enquiry? Did they come to the just decision? Were the formalities of the enquiry properly observed? And inevitably: was there more to this scandal than met the eye?

If the answer to the last question was in the positive there was never any possibility of Eustace Loder revealing details or leaking clues, by word or deed. But his nerves must have been tauter than piano wire. This feeling is borne out by a revelation from Edward Moorhouse within his stallion biography of Craganour in *The Bloodstock Breeders' Review* of 1930. He recalled meeting Loder three weeks after the race when he seized the opportunity to raise the question of Craganour's disqualification.

The subject was broached with diffidence but Major Loder seemed to welcome the chance of discussing it, although as a rule, he was extremely reticent and shy. He intimated that it was he who spurred his fellow Stewards into action … striking proof of his strength of character. He was the breeder of Craganour and so deprived himself of a great honour. The feeling of the vast majority of sportsmen was one of regret, not indignation. The Stewards had not assumed an authority other than that imposed on them by the Rules of Racing.

Moorhouse concluded by recalling Loder's explanation:

> Rules are rules. They are made to be obeyed, and just as rigidly in the case of the Derby as of any other race. Whenever I am a Steward I shall do my best to see that they are obeyed. If the Rules are to be ignored when it may seem convenient, I must not be asked to serve as a Steward.

Abiding by the 'Rules' was second nature to a man like Eustace Loder. Despite many laudable human qualities – loyalty, generosity and industry chief among them – he was an inflexible servant to the 'Rules'. Manuals and rule books governed his life as a soldier and as a Turf administrator, and he used them to influence the lives of others. Such codes were issued only in black and white. There was no palette with the colours of compromise, no scope for turning a blind eye, little room for extenuating circumstances or hope of forgiveness. Already oozing with the implacable egocentricity of the middle-aged individual protected by a suit of emotional armour, this moral strait-jacket rendered Eustace Loder's actions on Derby Day 1913 doubly automatic.

Yet a number of questions are begged. Would he have been so eager to enforce the 'Rules' if the miscreants had been Prue and Danny Maher rather than Craganour and Johnny Reiff? Would he have been so proactive if the owner at risk had been Lord Rosebery and not Bower Ismay? And the acid test: how would he have reacted had the roles of Craganour and Anmer been reversed and it was Anmer tussling with Aboyeur? Is it possible to believe even the high-principled Loder would have dared instigate an objection hell-bent on throwing out a Derby winner owned by his sovereign? If this question is answered in the nega- tive, one final question is demanded: why, then, was Bower Ismay treated differently?

Hypothetical as they were, such critical questions as these were never put to Eustace Loder by any journalist – at least not 'on the record'. Nor did he seek to explain himself. There was no need. In 1913 there was no such obligation on the part of people holding positions of power to explain themselves. Even if Loder had felt so compelled, it's impossible to imagine him making a decent fist of the task. 'Stewards of the Jockey Club are not often called upon for oratory,' *The Times* once declared, 'and seldom equal to the occasion when it arises.' Loder was ring-fenced by the Rules and might retire behind them in complete safety; their sanctuary was inviolate. Any other reasons for choosing to apply them in this instance need never be revealed to a living soul. A statement giving the only official explanation of the Stewards' verdict was issued on the evening of the race to the effect that the Stewards did not disqualify Craganour simply because of bumping that took place in the last half-furlong, but because they were satisfied that Reiff had unduly interfered with other horses throughout the greater part of the race. Later on others fought Loder's corner for him, notably the two men closer than any to him in the racing community, Noble Johnson and Merrik Burrell.

In his book *Eyrefield Stud* Johnson writes:

The disqualification of Craganour troubled Eustace Loder very much. The public, most of whom had backed the favourite, were very hard in their criticism of the Stewards. From all accounts it was a very unsatisfactory race, and a great deal of rough riding took place, some going so far as to say Aboyeur was as much to blame as Craganour. As far as Eustace Loder was concerned, the last thing he would have wished was that Craganour should be disqualified. He had bred the horse, and to breed a Derby winner naturally is the greatest ambition of any owner or a stud and he, like his fellow Stewards, would eagerly have taken any advantage of any loophole that presented itself to escape enacting the extreme penalty. Apart from the hardship it entailed to the owner, Mr Bower Ismay, and Robinson, the trainer, the disqualifying of a Derby winner was bound to cause a great deal of public commotion. I know Eustace felt it all very much, and in a letter he wrote me shortly after he explained that anyone who listened to the evidence before the Stewards would never for a moment have hesitated in taking the course they did. One thing I am sure of, that the public have always given Eustace the credit of acting with nothing but the highest motives.

Johnson goes on to say that 'the sporting press nearly all wrote favourably of the decision' and that he sent Loder one such piece from the Dublin *Evening Mail* which 'I think pleased him very much.'

The article went:

A good deal of sympathy may be felt by many people. Especially by some who backed the favourite, with those who have suggested that the Stewards acted harshly in disqualifying Craganour. But we are glad to see that it is the judgment only and not the 'good faith' of the Stewards that is impugned. And it would be difficult, indeed, to impugn the good faith of the Stewards, seeing that one of them, Major Eustace Loder, is the man who bred Craganour, and his decision to disqualify the favourite was to deprive himself of the honour of breeding a Derby winner. It would seem, however, that the judgment of the critics is at least as much at fault as that which they criticise. They say that Craganour should be given the benefit of the doubt, because of the big amount of money at stake, the argument being that the loss of so much money on the part of the public will tend to make the sport unpopular. This, surely, is the most fatuous reasoning. The disqualification of Craganour was decided upon in the highest interest of the public and of sport, the interest of fair play. Surely there would be an end of public confidence if a jostling jockey got the benefit of the doubt because he was on the favourite.

The further suggestion has been made that the thing should have been looked over rather than involve the Derby in disgrace. Here again is the wrong-headed way of looking at things. The more important the race, the more necessary, surely, that it should be free from reproach. It has been asserted that the American style of riding, now universally adopted, tends to encourage jostling, bumping and boring. That may be so, but if it helps to win races there is no prospect of going back to the old style. And that only provides another argument for the necessity for prompt and drastic action on the part of the Stewards when a case of improper riding is reported.

A more legitimate complaint is that the shout 'Winner all right', which was not authorised, led to the fleecing of many bookmakers. Of course, if the bookmakers choose to pay out on a casual cry that is their own affair. But they are not, taking them all in all, exactly a class that need any fostering care or kindly guidance. If they cannot take care of themselves they ill deserve the reputation for astuteness they usually enjoy.

It is easy to see why Noble Johnson would have sent that particular article to his beleaguered friend: it diplomatically avoids any reference to the series of incidents that preceded the objection. Likewise, it is easy to see why Eustace Loder should warm to it. In his reply to Johnson he wrote:

Yes, I had an awful time over the Derby, but we could not act differently to what we did. It was a horrible job. So many people take a biased view of the affair, because of the money they lost, and the others lay too much importance on what occurred in the last 50 yards. The real mischief was done some distance before this. People seem to forget that disqualifying Craganour was doing me a lot of harm as well. Thanks very much for what you say about it. The cutting you send gives a very fair and proper view of the case.

In November 1955 the controversy was resurrected in *The Sporting Life* by the death of Dawson Waugh, the trainer of Louvois, who had told the writer Vincent Orchard that when the time came to pen his obituary he should state his belief that 'to my dying day I was positive Louvois won the 1913 Derby'. Waugh was lucky to win the 1913 Guineas verdict but certainly wasn't unlucky with the Derby decision. Orchard's devotion to duty sparked a response from someone who had watched the race from near the finish and insisted: 'Craganour no sinner.' In turn, this letter prompted a response from Merrik Burrell, which was given front-page prominence on 22 November under the headline WHY EPSOM STEWARDS DISQUALIFIED CRAGANOUR.

Forty-two years after the event Burrell defended his late uncle thus:

> The decisive cause was the deliberate interference which took place shortly after the horses had come round Tattenham Corner – not the dog-fight which took place between Craganour and Aboyeur in front of the stands. Reiff, on Craganour, was outside Aboyeur. He feared Shogun, but not the outsider Aboyeur, and he shouted at Piper riding the latter to close back on the rails. When he did not do so Reiff rode Craganour into Aboyeur in an effort to force him across.
>
> The evidence of the jockeys behind these horses was quite clear and was fully corroborated by a 'movie' picture which I saw later at a private view at Newmarket in order to report what it showed to Major Loder, as he had to go to a Jockey Club meeting.
>
> It showed, both when shown at correct speed and when quite slowly, Craganour charging Aboyeur so strongly as to very nearly cause Piper to fall off sideways. If Aboyeur had not balanced himself and rolled back again Piper would have been unseated.

The principal 'jockeys behind these horses' interviewed by Loder were George Stern and Billy Saxby. It seems Loder preferred Saxby's version over Stern's. No one could claim that either jockey was an angel. Saxby's recent offences at Chester and Haydock spoke volumes about his prevailing state of mind on a racetrack. Nor was Stern's record on his frequent sallies across the Channel exactly spotless but he was a Derby-winning rider, a multiple champion jockey – and a man whose testimony was not laced with bias.

It's only natural that Burrell should speak up for his uncle and godfather when his judgement, honour and very reputation were under attack. Burrell's description of the 'decisive' event 'shortly after' Tattenham Corner commences with 'Craganour *charging* Aboyeur' – thereby placing the onus squarely on Reiff for what followed and, as a result, making Craganour's disqualification justifiable under Rule 140 (ii).

How safe is that pronouncement? Fragile at best. There was no head-on 'movie picture' of events in the vicinity of Tattenham Corner for Burrell or the Stewards to view. This critical angle only existed for the final stages when Aboyeur is clearly seen to be the aggressor. Moreover, Burrell himself admitted that prior to this show of belligerence from Craganour 'Aboyeur had swung out from the rails' – as if this manoeuvre occurred in all innocence, the result of nothing more than centrifugal force. Yet while horses do have an innate tendency to roll down the Epsom camber toward the inside rail it is not feasible for them to roll involuntarily *up* the camber. Cue Robert Sievier, who, three days after the race, wrote in *The Winning Post*:

> There were few knowledgeable men who witnessed the Derby who did not see Aboyeur attempt to savage Craganour as he first came up alongside him, and this is serious interference, and in the case of Craganour, in our opinion, was the cause of Mr Bower Ismay's colt not going straight on and winning the Derby with ease.

If the Stewards have any doubt regarding the savaging, evidence could quickly set this at rest, for many owners of horses, members of the Club Enclosure at Epsom, and men whose word the Stewards would accept and whose opinion everyone respects, could corroborate all we have said.

So with Aboyeur the first offender as regards these two colts, it appears hard lines that Mr Bower Ismay should be deprived of a Derby.

There lies the technical conundrum at the nub of the investigation into the running of the 1913 Derby: that there was trouble in running is irrefutable but who started that trouble? Reiff or Piper? Craganour or Aboyeur? Whose version of events were the Stewards prepared to accept? Whose version does one accept now?

Burrell went on to shed some light on the 'All Right' issue:

Major Loder was expecting Mr Percy Cunliffe, the owner of Aboyeur, to object. The Clerk of the Course was warned that there might be an objection. But Mr Cunliffe had made it a lifelong rule never to object. In the interval I suppose the Clerk heard that Mr Cunliffe would not object, and, the jockeys having weighed-in, hoisted the 'All Right' flag without consulting the Stewards.

On that basis, the man Burrell, and thus Loder, identified as calling 'All Right!' was the Clerk of the Course, the generally disliked Henry Mayson Dorling, or some functionary doing so at his behest. Whoever he was, the culprit was deemed an 'irresponsible' or an 'unauthorised' person acting without 'official instructions' in all newspaper accounts; 'a circumstance which seems to show a certain want of discipline somewhere' in the pompous words of *The Times*. Yet while offering a plausible solution to one question, Burrell's account raises another: if Cunliffe was known '*never* to object' why would Loder, hardly a stranger to Cunliffe and his ways, be '*expecting*' him to do so?

Burrell concludes his letter by stating:

I had motored down with Major Loder from London, and on
the way back he told me the whole story, and on what evidence
they had based their decision. They were never in doubt, but very
worried at having to take such a step, which meant huge sums
laid on the favourite all over the world lost, let alone the thousands of pools, big and small, being upset. Major Loder never bet.

The phrase '*never in doubt*' might suggest the Stewards knew the
decision they wished to reach from the outset and it was merely
a case of posing the questions in such a way as to receive the
answers they craved in order to expedite that judgement.

In 1913 horse racing was a far bigger sport than it would
be a hundred years later, occupying a prominent place in the
consciousness of the general public that is almost impossible
to appreciate in the twenty-first century. In consequence, the
outcome of the 1913 Derby amounted to a colossal disaster for
the sport's public image, not least because the Confederacy's
windfall (which extended to the staff at Druid's Lodge receiving a bonus of two weeks' wages) spelt penury for a multitude
of others. Few had sympathy for firms like Ladbrokes, whose
profit and smile were both instantly wiped off when news of
Cunliffe's on-course wager (contributing to the biggest pay-
day of his betting life) reached its London office; his account
was immediately closed. Or the bookmaker to London's sporting clubs, Charles Villiers Chapman, who laid a £25 each-way
bet over the telephone at the last moment to a member of the
Beaufort Club that cost him £3,125; not to mention those who
had paid out on Craganour before news of the objection had
permeated the cheaper enclosures (an impromptu meeting
of the Racecourse Bookmakers Association decided to press
Weatherbys to address the problem of announcing objections
more effectively in order to prevent false pay-outs by sounding
an electric gong). Any strapped on-course bookmakers who

attempted to 'welsh' about Craganour were summarily dealt with in the traditional manner by irate punters before they could flee. Some layers were magnanimous to the point of being philanthropic: having already paid out one punter his place bet on Aboyeur, a bookmaker in Tattersall's by the name of Laubunum then paid him his win-money even though he had thrown away the ticket. Less fortunate was the group of Frenchmen who had backed Craganour and, reported the *Daily Mail*, 'entirely declined to understand the situation'. Sydney Holland, at the London Hospital, suggested a novel way for the bookmakers to atone for their unexpected good fortune: donate £3,000 to the Hospital in order to 'endow a bed as a bookmakers' memorial to the 1913 Derby and a fitting termination to a most unfortunate race'. A surgeon at Wolverhampton Hospital who held a winning ticket for Craganour in the nationwide sweepstake known as the 'Calcutta' would doubtless have cheered such a gesture. His misery was a City messenger boy's joy; he was given Aboyeur's ticket by his employer who'd drawn it in the Stock Exchange sweep – 'for all the good it'll do you' – and thus pocketed £1,875 (around £82,000). Mr W. T. Grover of the Bridge Hotel in Shawford, Hampshire, was an even greater beneficiary for he now held the winning ticket worth £5,500 (almost £250,000) in the Bouveret Turf and Sports Club sweepstake. Conversely, Lucien Stokvis, a one-time bookmaker and stockbroker, presently undergoing examination in the London Bankruptcy Court with debts of nearly £5,000, testified (to much laughter) that he would have cleared them had Craganour kept the race. On-course several professional backers gleefully seized the tempting odds offered about Aboyeur to hedge their Craganour bets: one was seen to place a £1,000 saver at 5/1 on Aboyeur to get the race. The bookmaker was glad to accommodate him, for his liabilities on Craganour were monumentally heavier. The revised result, presenting the race to a 100/1 'rag' was a heavenly outcome on the only race in the calendar that could rival the Grand National, especially as it was the third such instance in the last fifteen years following Jeddah (1898) and Signorinetta (1908). There hasn't been one since.

Noble Johnson's contention that 'the sporting press nearly all wrote favourably of the decision' warrants inspection:

*The Sporting Life*: A tragic Derby. Such a round of sensations never were; they have left us unstrung. The disqualification of Craganour, regrettable though it be, was inevitable. For what the Stewards had just cause to object was obvious to all those who saw what happened. The fact that the winner of the world's greatest race was disqualified must not be allowed to destroy the judicial mind. Much heart burning there is bound to be, but calm reflection must vindicate the Stewards up to the hilt. It is a point that cannot be unduly emphasised, the Rules of Racing are for the government of all races. We may not differentiate between the Derby or races for platers. I am with the Stewards entirely, as every sportsman is bound to be. They could not have adopted any other course than the drastic one they pursued and their courageous performance of a most unpleasant duty is recognised by all true sportsmen.

*The Sportsman*: The alertness of the Stewards is to be much commended and is bound to bear good fruit by convincing jockeys that even though they do not themselves protest against unfair riding the ruling authorities will on their own initiative interfere if they see good cause. Foul riding is one of the worst offences committed in race riding and the practice had reached such a pitch that it was high time somebody stepped into the breach to check it. While the decision of the Stewards has been cheerfully accepted, people are wondering why Reiff, who must surely be held accountable for Craganour having worked the havoc he apparently did amongst several of the other runners, has apparently escaped scot-free.

*The Sporting Chronicle*: A calamitous Derby. It will tax the memory of the oldest to recall a more remarkable Derby. It was won by the favourite, although he was reeling like a drunken man in the last furlong and a stride past the post almost fell 'all of a heap' on the despised 100/1 outsider, Aboyeur. The two, while engaged in some bumping on their own account, had been the means of obstructing others. An objection was generally anticipated but it was not made by those associated with Aboyeur. Some thought it not a little magnanimous on the part of Piper thus to allow the verdict to stand without at least asking the opinion of the Stewards. Presently the Stewards took up the matter on their own initiative. The disqualification of Craganour on such overwhelming evidence of repeated malpractices by Reiff after he reached the straight was undoubtedly the right verdict. The Stewards were there to see that the Rules of Racing were adhered to and if they are broken it is their duty to mete out justice and punish the delinquents. The worst of it is that Craganour was such a great favourite that his disqualification presses hard on his thousands of supporters who though entirely innocent of, and altogether unassociated with the circumstances, have to suffer more perhaps than the guilty jockey.

*Pall Mall Gazette*: The Stewards of the Jockey Club have it in trust to safeguard the interests of a noble sport, and to exert themselves unflinchingly on behalf of fair play. They had no hesitation in discharging that duty, in spite of the enormous disturbance and widespread concern which they must have known to be contingent on their decision. It is impossible to calculate the amount of money whose disposition hinged on the deliberations of the two or three men who are entrusted with supreme power in the constitution of the British Turf. In few circumstances can such enormous pecuniary issues be dependent on the decision of so small a number of individuals acting in intimate and informal conclave. An upright and inflexible administration is the cornerstone of prosperity in every sport, and racing, more than any perhaps, requires a clear head and a firm hand in its rulers.

Racing has always been able to place the highest confidence in the honour, high-mindedness, and capacity of those by whom so notable a despotism is administered.

Others disagreed:

*The Sporting Times*: The Stewards having become prosecutors, ought now to submit themselves to cross-examination. If Mr Cunliffe did not object and Piper had nothing to complain of, why was Craganour disqualified? Some sort of statement has been made to the effect that Craganour jostled Aboyeur. That there was some bumping is without doubt, but many thought when there was an objection that it was Aboyeur that was the culprit, and if there was any fault he began it before the other one. If they were both engaged in it, Aboyeur ought not to have received any benefit.

*Illustrated Sporting and Dramatic News*: It is a melancholy fact there should be a objection in such a race as the Derby and the disqualification of a red-hot favourite on behalf of a 100/1 outsider is nothing short of a tragedy. There had been some bumping, truly, but so far as could be made out Aboyeur, if not the aggressor, doing his fair share of it, the foundation for this opinion resting on the fact that he appeared to have driven Craganour from his position near the rails to somewhere near the middle of the course. A neighbour of mine remarked that 'if the second had won he wouldn't have got it.' I confess I thought Reiff was a vastly better jockey than to interfere with other horses throughout the race. It is quite enough for anyone to look after his own mount during the Derby and not to devote himself to interfering with others. We thought the bumping unavoidable. I suppose we were wrong, because it is impossible to imagine Stewards of the Jockey Club acting without what seemed to them not only ample justification but urgent necessity.

No one, least of all Loder and Johnson, would have expected Robert Sievier to adopt any other than a combative stance. In consecutive editions of *The Winning Post* he left nary a stone unturned in his dissection of events he described as 'a tragic page in the history of the Turf'. On 7 June he wrote:

> The winner of the Blue Riband was objected to after the owner, trainer and jockey of the second had not deemed it necessary to protest.
>
> The Derby is a race which franks the winner with international fame, and ensures a position for him at stud both unique and historical, according to his progeny.
>
> Moreover, there is an atmosphere about this great race which tacitly demands respect; respect from fraud, respect from unfair play, and equally respect for justice.
>
> Also, there is an unwritten law, and though such laws are not always commendable, it is nevertheless understood that, as at Ascot, it is not considered etiquette or sporting, call it what you will, to object; this, with equal strength, applies to the most important of all races, the Derby.
>
> Any breach of the Rules of Racing must be punished, no matter how important the event may be or, for that matter, how insignificant. But is it reasonable and within the spirit of common justice that the judges in such cases should be the actual accusers?
>
> To say they are not partially convinced before they sit in judgement under the circumstances described would be absurd.

The following Saturday he continued the attack:

> It must be conceded that the Stewards showed considerable courage in protesting against a winner of the Derby on their own initiative. Fearlessness, tempered with judgement, is a superlative quality, just as over-zealousness is a danger to justice.
>
> It is indisputable that whatever bumping occurred took place on Craganour's ground, and Piper on Aboyeur must have offended to have got there. If Wootton had a clear run on the inside, Aboyeur must have trespassed beyond even Craganour's ground and pressed him further toward the middle of the course.

It cannot be denied that it was an unsatisfactory race throughout. We would stand down every jockey who rode in the race for
a month so that the delinquents who were in the majority should
be punished.

Having regard for the interference of a suffragette and considering things impartially, the ordering of the running the race over
again would have been possibly a wiser course for the Stewards
to have pursued, and they have such power.

Sievier was indeed correct in stating the Stewards might conceivably have ordered a re-run, and his denunciation of the jockeys
found favour elsewhere in the press. 'There never was a more
disgraceful illustration of the depths to which modern jockeyship
has sunk when a number of horses are concerned in the Derby
with a scramble and scuffle altogether unworthy of the traditions
of the English Turf,' stated the *Daily Telegraph*. *The Sporting Life*
embellished the issue by returning to a well-worn theme:

Making full allowance for the laudable anxiety on the part of jockeys to win the greatest race of the year, it must be admitted that
there has never been a more lamentable exhibition of horsemanship – or lack of it. Derby competitors are ridden by the pick of
home jockeys and those who are at the head of their profession on
the continent. It has been demonstrated beyond all question that
imported riders are incapable of keeping their mounts straight, it
is to be hoped that the home product will be given a better chance.
There are enough and to spare of good riders in this country if the
necessary opportunity and encouragement are forthcoming, but
it cannot be expected that they will take a proper pride in their
profession if they are being continually called upon to make way
for 'fashionable' foreign jockeys in the very events which it is their
greatest and most natural ambition to win.

A laudable sentiment from the *Life* but it is remarkable how
quickly the paper had forgotten its praise for Reiff's swift, expert

and effectively race-winning correction of Louvois in the Guineas, now that he made the most convenient whipping boy for the whole rotten affair. Loose talk abounded. The gentlemen's clubs of London suggested the outcome of the enquiry might even be a relic of Public School enmity, a case of dastardly Old Etonian Stewards ganging up on the Old Harrovian for the benefit of Aboyeur's trio of Old Etonian owners – conveniently ignoring the fact that Purefoy was another Old Harrovian! Another story that gained currency involved Ismay owing money to one of the Stewards – presumably Loder. This seems equally derisory. Given his loathing of Ismay and Loder's litigious nature, Loder would have needed no second begging to drag Ismay's name through the mire in open court if that were the case.

The majority of contemporary reports in the popular press, on the other hand, preferred to dwell on the body-blow to the Derby's reputation and bemoaned the Stewards' decision.

*Daily Telegraph*: The most unsatisfactory, sensational and lamentable Derby in the history of the sport was added to the records. The result is too far-reaching and altogether beyond comprehension to be written in words. If there was any doubt at all, what a pity that the Stewards could not see their way to give the favourite the benefit of it!

*Daily Mail*: Sensations crowded thick and fast throughout the day, making a 'shilling shocker' tale of fantastic incredibility. Tens of thousands awaited the issue of the investigation that deprived Craganour of the Derby and caused Mr Bower Ismay and Robinson momentarily to ask themselves whether the game of owning and training horses was worth a candle. A lot of persons muttered uncomplimentary things about the Stewards, saying it was a case where they might have shut their eyes to things considering it was the Derby.

*Daily Express*: A mad-sad derby. The feeling that something was wrong was universal and the roar of cheering was almost entirely absent. The crowd was bewildered and resentful and there was an evident annoyance that the greatest of all races should have been marred by an unsatisfactory finish. The injury to the King's jockey and the rumours of the outrage caused something like stupefaction and, as if all this were not enough, the singular stupidity of the Stewards added to the day's discomforts.

*Daily Chronicle*: Although Epsom Downs have often provided the 'big scene' for melodramas and novels, no novelist or playwright would ever have been so extravagant with his material.

*Daily News & Leader*: Derby race outrage ... it was sheer sacrilege to challenge the first horse in the greatest classic race in the world. There was blank astonishment on thousands of faces.

The 'voice of the people' was heard occasionally. The *Life* was told in trenchant fashion by a Mr E. Lawrie of Hove that in its support for the Stewards it was 'entirely misinformed…if the Stewards were justified in adopting the course which they did, then all I can say is Minoru was extremely lucky not to have suffered the same fate which has overtaken the luckless Craganour'. But, Minoru was owned by a King not an Ismay.

The *Evening Standard* also published a letter highlighting the general public's unease:

Wherever I have gone since the disqualification of Craganour was made known, in clubs, in private houses, even in Hyde Park on Sunday, I have heard only one opinion – deep indignation that the whole tradition of the Derby should have been outraged by what is, rightly or wrongly, regarded as an academic disqualification of the winner. It is felt, moreover, as most undesirable that a purely judicial body to whom delicate matters of dispute must finally be referred, should have taken upon itself to accuse and prosecute. Even in law, the traditions of which are by no means so scrupulously fair as those of sport, the judge is not allowed to act as prosecutor.

The letter concluded tellingly: 'Hence, I think, the very deep and real indignation of the public which, *for some reason, has not found proper echo in the press.*'

In the *Daily Telegraph* Sidney Galtrey set down what he saw as the prevailing mood: 'In the endeavour to write honestly and without prejudice it is a duty to say that the disqualification meets with severe criticism and condemnation among many whose ideas of clean sport are beyond question.' Since Galtrey was very much an 'Establishment' man himself, those guarded words are tantamount to treason. His subsequent dissection of what he termed 'that crazy afternoon at Epsom' during the course of his 1934 memoir provides persuasive reason to believe he had more to say on the subject than protocol or the laws of libel permitted. He concedes the Stewards were 'right' but then adds the telling rider 'according to their statement overwhelmingly so' – suggesting the charge had been constructed to fit the punishment.

He goes on to add further caveats:

How much better it would have been if public opinion could have rid itself of the feeling that the parts of the prosecutors and judges had been merged. It is at best a dangerous principle and so easily liable to miscarriage of justice … the winner might so well have been given the benefit of the doubt, leaving the jockeys to be warned about their future riding. It was a most important point that no objection was lodged in the interests of those connected with the second. For the Epsom Stewards it can be pointed out that they were undoubtedly men of honour, who found themselves confronted with a most unpleasant task from the execution of which they could not flinch. They had seen what they regarded as a breach of the Rules … made to be obeyed and it was their duty to apply the unpleasant consequence. It mattered not that the jockey of the second, apparently, had no cause of complaint; ditto the owner. They had seen for themselves.

Galtrey's recollection of a 'disastrous day' mirrored the reaction of another Establishment writer, Edward Moorhouse, who wrote in *The Bloodstock Breeders' Review* for 1913:

> Historic! It is scarcely an adequate appellative. The dictionary, would, however, be searched in vain for one conveying all that it is desired to express. There have been many Derbys which could truthfully be described as sensational. That of 1913 must be added to the group. It was not only sensational; it was very nigh to being a travesty of a contest. After the race was over there prevailed a state of affairs bordering on chaos. Hardened campaigners were almost stricken dumb with astonishment and chagrin. They left the course in mournful mood because they had lived to see a winner of the Derby disqualified.
>
> Although the decision had been very generally anticipated its promulgation caused something like stupefaction. The public had hoped against hope that the Stewards would discover a method of exercising their authority short of depriving Craganour of the honours he gained ... we may be sure the Stewards would eagerly have taken advantage of any loophole that had presented itself. They could find none, and so the highly distasteful duty of disqualifying the winner was thrust upon them.

A third denizen of the press sounded more uneasy. In *Horse and Hound* its founding editor Arthur Portman, writing as Audax, called the proceedings 'A Day of Horrors'. He went on: 'I have a very strong opinion on the whole subject, but I consider it best to leave the matter as it stands without further comment.' Mindful of Portman's standing on the Turf (he edited *Horse and Hound* for fifty-six years), it is a pity he didn't feel able to add 'further comment'. Clearly he had something he wanted to get off his chest. One is left wondering whether his 'opinion' would have rocked a few privileged boats.

The legion of Doubting Thomases may have changed their minds had a written record been kept of the evidence placed before the Stewards. This omission was seized upon by *The Times* in a column entitled 'Novel Points Raised By The Disqualification – A Case For A Full Statement' on 6 June:

> The Stewards were convinced that the riding had been culpably reckless if not actually foul. And the evidence they called was held to confirm their impression. The great question is of what this evidence consisted.
>
> In the ordinary way it is undesirable that what witnesses say when Stewards are conducting investigations should be reported, but in such an altogether exceptional case as the disqualification of a Derby winner, who has also been a Derby favourite – it would [be] absurd to ignore the importance of this latter consideration – it seems urgently necessary that the multitude of those who are concerned, the world in general, indeed, should know precisely what was alleged, and by whom, and what reply was forthcoming to the allegations.
>
> A curious fact is that, though the colt was disqualified, no caution or reprimand seems to have been given by the Stewards to Reiff. The horse's owner is deprived of the race but, so far as what has come to light reveals, no blame is bestowed upon the rider, who is nevertheless accused of having done dangerous mischief throughout the contest.

Just in case its readership had missed the point it was made more forcefully the following day:

> It will always remain a circumstance to be regretted that the evidence given when the objection which the Stewards lodged on their own initiative was investigated should not have been taken down by a shorthand typist.

This evidence could not be collected again, even in the improbable event of the case being re-opened – it appears to have been finally settled that it will not be. Everyone who has experience of the duties of Stewardship knows how the statements of jockeys are apt to alter in the course of a few days. About matters concerning which they are certain when first questioned they not seldom become doubtful, and the reverse of this is equally true.

It is supposed to be the duty of a good sportsman to accept without cavil the decision of the Stewards, of judges, umpires or referees ... nevertheless the good sportsman may be excused for wanting to know on what a decision is based.

There was never any prospect of the Stewards revealing the details of their deliberations at Epsom. 'It is not the custom of the Jockey Club Stewards to publish the evidence they hear when adjudicating on cases of this sort,' stated *The Sporting Chronicle* in a piece titled 'Should the Stewards Give More Information?' It continued:

What was the evidence laid before them? Of what did this consist? We are strongly of the opinion that in most instances it is not politic or desirable that evidence heard by the Stewards inquiring into reckless or foul riding should be fully reported, but in this extraordinary case of the disqualification of a Derby winner the point arises whether it is necessary that something more than a short paragraph should be given out to the public.

Argument seems to increase in volume and intensity as the days go by. The unprecedented action of the Stewards – just and right as it must be – has raised a storm of protest. Seeing the importance of this unprecedented case, will the Stewards deem it desirable to enlighten the public?

We doubt whether they will be persuaded to depart from that custom.

The MP Walter Faber sent a strongly worded letter to the *Chronicle* and *The Sportsman* suggesting, rather grandly, that 'in the interest of the British public, and of what is the far greater importance, namely, the interests of the whole British Empire as regards the great Turf industry, the whole of the evidence should be published'. His argument ran:

> Lord Rosebery is far too good a public man and too good a sportsman not to know that the result of this race is not like that of a mere selling race which affects only Turf interests, but that the Derby is a national asset and that the Stewards are merely trustees. The owner of the second was too good a sportsman to object. A terrible blow has been dealt the public and they have a right to know the evidence.
>
> Reports are thick and furious and could be allayed or confirmed. Firstly, that the Stewards did not of their own motive propose an enquiry but that a leading owner more or less insisted on it and signed it. Secondly, that the Judge and the rider of Louvois were leading witnesses, the latter being a jockey who had been taken off Craganour. Thirdly, that Piper did not want to object.

For all his bluster, Faber left much to be read between his lines. Who was this 'leading owner'? The quick-to-rise Leopold de Rothschild would seem the likely candidate there. Is he impugning the probity of Charles Robinson and Billy Saxby? And is he saying Piper knew better than to object when he was the prime malefactor?

Other letter writers contained more novel suggestions. Harding Cox wrote to the *Life* wondering whether, in view of the bumping and swerving,

> horses might keep their proper line if they ran 'between strings' as their human counterparts do when sprinting. Better still, why have jockeys at all, revert to the methods of classic stadiums of old and let the galloping steeds run loose, each bearing a plume on its noble 'nut' advertising the colours of its owner.

The boss of Hurst Park racecourse, Joseph Davis, saw an

opportunity to stage a sweepstakes open to all those horses with Derby hard-luck stories: 500 sovereigns to enter and a £1,000 cup. Both initiatives fell on deaf ears.

If even *The Times* and Members of Parliament could be seen to be offering Bower Ismay covert encouragement to challenge the conduct of the investigation it was only natural that Robert Sievier would do likewise. In *The Winning Post* he devoted his infamous 'Celebrities in Glass Houses' column, written under the pen-name 'Tweedledum and Tweedledee', to the iniquities of Bower Ismay's ordeal:

> Sir, with every respect for you both as a sportsman and a gentleman, we censure you for not asking leave to appeal.
>
> On the fact alone that the informers were the judges you should have appealed. You should have had an opportunity of gathering fresh evidence and have been conscious of what was going on in place of standing dumbfounded outside closed doors.
>
> You are one of the best and most philosophical losers racing has ever known but as owner of the Derby favourite you owe the public a duty. Through you the public is entitled to a hearing before a second tribunal.
>
> At Epsom it was all so hurried, it was a Star Chamber hearing. Were you asked if you desired to call anyone? No. You were treated as nothing more or less than a cipher in connection with this enquiry.
>
> If you can yet find the ways and means to appeal, you will have the public and at least 99% of racing men with you. Not that you or the public desire Craganour to be reinstated if he has offended, but because the full case could hardly have been dealt with, for some who rode in the race were never heard, nor could you rebut evidence you were barred from hearing.
>
> If the objection was not made in writing there is at least a technical error committed if the Rules of Racing are printed in the English Language. The Jockey Club should make this clear.

Were you informed of the objection and the grounds for it? We venture to guess in the negative.

Sievier concludes his peroration with trademark mischievousness:

Whatever steps you have contemplated or may be able to take in duty to the public, nobody, not your worst enemy if you have one, will for an instant ascribe a selfish motive to you.

Your fault is rather your generosity, and you have a kindly feeling even for those who have taken the race from you. Even for your ungrateful groom, Saxby.

As a veteran acquaintance of the law courts, Sievier was alert enough to allow identification of Bower Ismay's 'worst enemy' to pass without further allusion. Jockeys might not sue for libel, but the likes of Eustace Loder most certainly would. By this stage Bower Ismay had wrapped the warm cloak of public sympathy around him and retired to nurse his bruises at Haselbech. The press was unanimous in praising his dignity and sportsmanlike behaviour at such a cruel reverse. 'He was naturally very much upset at the result of the Stewards decision and he felt there was little or no justification for the disqualification,' observed *The Sporting Life*. 'There must have been bitterness in his mind but he did not show it outwardly,' Sidney Galtrey said of his muted reaction. 'His attitude was that of the cynic.' There was, of course, every reason to hold this view. That Aboyeur would keep the race at a Jockey Club appeal was as sure as death and taxation because two of the Stewards sitting on that appeal would be the very pair who had disqualified Craganour at Epsom. Even if Frederick Lambton sided with Ismay he would still be out-voted by Loder and Wolverton.

However, it transpired that an appeal had been launched. The process quickly descended into farce. Getting wind of the move had prompted the *Life* to telephone Ismay on Monday 9 June for confirmation. He assured them he was not lodging an appeal and the paper printed his denial on the Tuesday. Then news broke that an appeal had been lodged with the Clerk of the Course on Saturday 7 June, alleging technical breaches in the drawing up of the objection: 'the formalities had not been complied with.' Since no more information proved forthcoming, racing correspondents began to speculate. Was it a breach of Rule 166, viz the enquiry had been conducted by only two Stewards and not three? If so, Ismay had no grounds here. Then there was Rule 168 (iv) which stated any objection 'must be made within a quarter of an hour after the winner has weighed in'. There was no basis for complaint here either. Lastly, there was Rule 169 demanding 'every objection shall be in writing, and must be signed by the owner of some horse in the race, or by his authorised agent, trainer, jockey or groom'. Here there may have been grounds. However, Rule 170 gave a Steward the right to object 'in his official capacity' – which appears to allow the Stewards carte blanche to ride roughshod over the other Rules if they so chose. Nevertheless, Rule 170 made no reference to a Steward having any right to waive the requirement of putting his objection in writing. Rumour, and process of elimination, insisted it was on this basis that the appeal was being lodged. But, asked the *Life*, who had lodged the appeal if Ismay had not? The paper contacted Ismay again and he replied by telegram, stating his telephone response must have been 'misinterpreted'. Odd, thought the *Life*, since he had been asked a question demanding only a 'yes' or 'no' answer.

It made not a scrap of difference. The Rules of Racing were observed to the letter. Rule 166 was quite specific: notice of appeal had to be given 'within 48 hours of the decision being made known'. Ismay's written notice reached the Clerk of the Course, Dorling, a day late – and did not reach the Stewards until the Monday. Thwarted on this front, Ismay then began legal moves in the Chancery Division to restrain Weatherbys from distributing any part of the Derby Stakes to the owners of the horses awarded places following Craganour's demotion. Ismay won an interim injunction but for some unexplained reason – repugnance over the whole affair, or possibly an over-whelming attack of that cynicism cited by Galtrey – this too was abandoned, on the 18 June. There was one final act in the Derby Day drama over which Ismay did have some control: he saw to it that every member of the staff at Foxhill received the same present as if Craganour had prevailed.

Despite Ismay throwing in the towel the controversy rumbled on. However many coatings of gloss one side put on the whole issue, the other side found acid to throw. Why wasn't Aboyeur thrown out as well as Craganour? His last-furlong lunge to the right had blatantly interfered with Great Sport. Yet there was no censure. If Reiff had been the sole malefactor why wasn't he handed a stiff suspension?

Said the *Life*:

Everyone suffered in one way or another on account of Craganour's disqualification with the exception of his jockey who has appar-ently escaped scot-free without even a reprimand. The Stewards decided to omit mention of their opinion of Reiff's riding. Yet there is no mention of Reiff being exonerated in the notice handed out to the Press and published in the Racing calendar. Some more explicit allusion to this phase of the affair is desirable and it is rightly argued that if Reiff was held to be blameless for the illegal behavior of his mount, the fact should be made known to the public, if only as an act of justice to the Franco-American horseman.

The *Life*'s request was ignored even though in recent months both Frank Wootton and Billy Saxby had been stood down for lesser crimes than Reiff was charged with. This latter question raised the prickly subject of inconsistency – which events at Goodwood two months later did nothing to assuage. In a four-runner race for the Nassau Stakes, Arda (11/4 second favourite) beat the 1000 Guineas and Oaks winner Jest (11/10 favourite) by a three-quarter length with Queen's Parade (owned by the Confederacy and ridden by Piper) four lengths back in third; the other runner being Eustace Loder's Addenda. The two jockeys disputing the finish were the bitter enemies Maher and Wootton. The latter objected to Maher on the grounds of 'crossing'. The Stewards interviewed all four jockeys and took forty-five minutes to pass judgement: the result of their deliberation was to find that: 'Wootton, whose orders were to wait, attempted to come through with Jest when there was not sufficient room.' Heading the Stewards' panel was Eustace Loder, owner of the fourth filly but, unlike Lord Rosebery on Derby Day, not prepared to sit idly. Afterwards Jest's trainer, Charles Morton, challenged Maher and the jockey openly admitted that he'd deliberately baulked Wootton. 'I had the right to do it,' he said. 'I would have done the same if I had been riding for you. What would you have done? Would you have let him through?'

From whichever angle one views this Goodwood objection and its outcome in the Stewards' Room it is impossible not to get an uneasy feeling. Was Reiff any guiltier than Maher? Why was the Steward with a runner disinclined to stand aside on this occasion? It is inconsistencies of this kind that provide fertile soil for those who interpret the decisions over the 1913 2000 Guineas and the Derby as demonstrating a distasteful bias against the horse owned by Bower Ismay. He was a Turf outsider who consorted with gambling trainers like Robinson and Coulthwaite and who, more to the point, as Galtrey observed, showed not 'the slightest desire' of entering the fold through membership of the Jockey Club.

For its part the Jockey Club moved swiftly; whether motivated by a desire to rescue Loder from the hole he had dug for himself or to rescue its own Rules from ridicule is impossible to judge. On 12 June, eight days after the Derby, the Racing Calendar printed a list of 'signals' it had issued to all Clerks of the Course designed to display 'uniformity' after weighing in, viz:

1. When the rider of a winning horse has passed the scales, an official signal shall be displayed to notify that the jockey has drawn the correct weight.
2. The words 'All Right' are not to be used. They may be misleading to the public in the event of an objection being subsequently made.
3. When an objection is lodged, an official signal shall immediately be shown, and a notice placed on the Number Board.

The instructions went on to insist that there should be uniformity in the signals used. A blue signal was to denote that 'the winner passed the scale' and a red signal 'should be used to notify an objection'. These colours reversed those used on Derby Day.

The now infamous Law 140 covering interference was the subject of much debate within the Club. A 'long discussion' at its meeting on the Monday of Ascot week resulted in proposals to amend 140 (ii) by restricting it to the actions of the horse and introducing a new clause, 140 (iv), to encompass the jockey. Rule 140 (ii) was to read 'A horse which jostles another horse in the race is liable to disqualification unless it be proved that the horse interfered with was wholly in fault' and 140 (iv) 'If a jockey jostle another horse or jockey his horse is disqualified unless it be proved that the jostle was accidental, or was caused by the fault of some other horse or jockey.' The proposals were printed in the Racing Calendar with the codicil: 'The Stewards claimed urgency.'

These revisions still proved too unwieldy for some members of the Club to accept and further lengthy discussion ensued during the Second July Meeting at Newmarket. On behalf of the Stewards, the Hon. Frederick Lambton assured members that the amendments conferred no more power on Stewards than they possessed previously; on the contrary, he maintained the alterations allowed them 'to exercise the quality of mercy which they were not able to under the old Rule'. Finally, a consensus was reached and the Rule was amended as follows:

Rule 140 (i): unaltered.

Rule 140 (ii): simplified to read 'A horse is liable to disqualification if he or his jockey jostle another horse or jockey.'

Rule 140 (iii): unaltered.

Rule 140 (iv): a new clause to read 'If the Stewards, on an objection,
find a jockey guilty of foul riding, his horse shall be disqualified.'

One might be tempted to describe this clause as the 'Reiff Rule'.

It is impossible to state conclusively whether Epsom's
notorious camber, equine fatigue, jockey error or plain human
vindictiveness was the root cause of the roughest and most
sensational Derby ever run despite forensic re-examination of
the controversy at seemingly every available opportunity. *The
Sporting Life* marked Bower Ismay's death in 1924 by saying:

> Whenever that Derby is discussed you are pretty sure to find some
> unprejudiced soul who considers that Craganour was unjustly
> dealt with when the Stewards took the race off him. So he would
> have been had the complaints which his jockey was called upon
> to answer merely concerned what took place over the last furlong.
> During the closing stages of that memorable scrimmage it was a
> case of six of one and half a dozen of the other. But the Stewards
> had seen farther down the course what had come clearly into the
> view of two or three of us who in those days preferred the roof of
> the stand to the then ill-arranged part of it which the press had
> to put up with. It was not long after the leaders had come into
> the straight that Reiff on Craganour saw Shogun creeping up
> on the rails. There was only Aboyeur between the two horses,
> and, as Aboyeur had swung a little wide at Tattenham Corner,
> Reiff conceived it to be his duty to bore Aboyeur back again,
> and so close Shogun out. And he did so. This manoeuvre was
> resorted to twice, and the second time Shogun had to be checked
> to the loss of a still bright chance, or go over the rails, but Reiff's
> explanation was that he thought he had a perfect right to put
> Aboyeur back again to the inside position, as he did in France,

and, to quote the words of a member of the Jockey Club uttered the same afternoon, Craganour's rider had, in so saying, '*made a clean breast of it*' [italics author's own].

Do those final few words explain Johnny Reiff's public reticence? Did his reticence confirm his guilt? He knew he'd indeed committed the manoeuvres deemed offences by the Stewards. Perhaps. But what if Danny Maher had committed those manoeuvres on Lord Rosebery's Prue? Would he have kept the race, as he did upon Arda at Goodwood?

There's every justification for suspecting that if Craganour hadn't been owned by Bower Ismay or ridden by Johnny Reiff he would have kept the race. Perfidious caveats such as these make it even harder to disagree with the sentiments of Steve Donoghue when he said 'The whole thing was a terrible tragedy, and the verdict was a most unpopular one.'

# SEVENTEEN

# Accidental Martyr

While Reiff, Piper *et al.* were playing their part in consigning the 1913 Derby to legend at the winning post, down at Tattenham Corner Inspector Whitbread and Sergeant Bunn were among the first to reach the prostrate figures of Davison and Jones. They were quickly joined by PC Eady and hordes of spectators from the Tattenham Corner station side of the track, where the crowd traditionally watched the race from the grass. The three officers immediately had their work cut out trying to hold back the gawpers before mounted police arrived to form a cordon: though there is no evidence to suggest – as has been stated on occasions – that the crowd was intent on inflicting further punishment on Davison for disrupting the race. According to *The Times*, a placard bearing the words 'Votes for Women' was raised by somebody in the crowd. If so, its holder was never identified. Some presume it to have been Mary Richardson, but she was nowhere near Tattenham Corner and any comrade of Davison would surely have rushed to her aid, not raised a placard and fled. The police on the spot were soon joined by senior officers, Superintendent Robinson of the Met and Superintendent McCarthy, who was in charge of the detective force.

Bunn records in his notebook what happened next:

Dr Lane of Banstead attended the woman and directed her removal to the Cottage Hospital, Epsom, where she was taken in a private motor car No LA7959 owned by JBV Faber Esq.,

Manor House, Ewell, who placed same at disposal of police. Mrs Warburg of 2 Craven Hill, Paddington, rendered great assistance to the injured woman and accompanied her in the motor car to hospital, she formerly having been a nurse. She was seen by the House Surgeon, Dr Peacock, and detained. The doctor stated she was suffering from concussion and was unconscious.

The jockey, Herbert Jones, aged twenty-eight of Egerton House, Newmarket, was thrown from the horse and rendered unconscious. Dr Percy John Spencer, 'Casa Pedro', Mellison Road, Tooting, attended to him and he was removed on police ambulance to the Ambulance Room on course by Inspector Whitbread and PC 85NR Johnson. Dr Coultard, Race Course doctor, and Dr Spencer there examined him and stated he was suffering from abrasions to the left of face, abrasion over left eye and shoulder, contusion of left elbow and shock. Mr Jones recovered consciousness and was left in charge of the doctors. Mr W Fenn of Egerton House, with whom he resides, took charge of him, stating he would have him removed to the great Eastern Hotel, Liverpool Street, on the evening of the 4th inst. And remove him home on the 5th inst.

The horse which pitched over onto its head had stopped on the course and was handed over to Mr George Prince, Egerton House, by PS 35T Lewis. It received slight cuts to the face and body and injury to its off-fore hoof.

Davison's only visible sign of injury was a bruise on her left temple and a trickle of blood seeping from her nose: a photograph has appeared in some works purporting to show Davison lying on the ground surrounded by policemen, a newspaper wrapping her head, but this photograph was taken after a later incident at Ascot when a suffragette sympathiser named Harold Hewitt determined to follow, almost literally, in her footsteps by step-ping out in front of the runners for the Gold Cup. Brandishing a revolver in one hand and a suffragette flag in the other, he shouted 'I will stop the race! Hold up!' seconds before 'Snowy'

Whalley drove Tracery straight into him to inflict the same injury that Anmer gave Davison: a fracture at the base of the skull. Unlike Davison, Hewitt survived. His possessions declared him to be certifiably insane. One of two Bibles doubled as a diary in which he had written: 'Oh! The weariness of these races, and the crowds they attract. They bring out all that is worst in humanity. I give my body as a protest against society conventions.' Then, as an afterthought, he adds what may have been at the root of his malaise: 'There are plenty of pretty girls, but none for me.'

It would be inconceivable for Davison not to have incurred some facial abrasions or grass burns but there were no signs of heavy bruising or broken bones commensurate with being struck by hooves. The blow to her head which ultimately proved fatal was likely akin to a 'whiplash' injury when her body struck the ground. She arrived at Epsom Cottage Hospital at 3.35 and was immediately identified by a name-tag sewn into her jacket. Initial reports suggested she was dead: indeed, the Central News Agency issued a statement to that effect during the afternoon. Subsequently, her injuries were variously reported in the press as 'severe concussion of the brain' and 'critical', and that she was 'in too weak a state to be examined'. The *Daily Chronicle* obtained an interview with the hospital's senior surgeon, Dr W. B. Peacock, and quoted him in full:

> So far as we have diagnosed the case, she is suffering from concussion of the brain and severe shock. At present she shows no signs of consciousness. From her present appearance I do not think she will regain consciousness for some hours, although, of course, she may relapse at any moment, in which case death would ensue. There are no signs of any injury at the base of the skull. I could find no trace of her having been kicked by a horse.

Sergeant Bunn itemised her possessions:

> On her jacket being removed I found two suffragette flags, 1½ yards long by ¾ yard wide, each consisting of green, white and

purple stripes, folded up and pinned to the back of her jacket, on the inside.

On person: one purse containing 3 shillings and 8 ¾ pence; one return half railway ticket from Epsom Race Course to Victoria Number 0315; two postal order counterfoils, one Number 790/435593 for two shillings and sixpence 'crossed' written in ink thereon, and one 20H/924704 for seven shillings and sixpence, E Gore 1/4/13 written in ink thereon; one insurance ticket dated May 10 1913 on GE Railways to and from New Oxford Street; eight halfpenny stamps; one key; one Helpers Pass for the Suffragette Summer Fete, Empress Rooms, High Street, Kensington, for 4 June 1913; one small black memo book; one race card; some envelopes and writing paper; one handkerchief with the initials EWD.

The solicitor husband of Davison's college friend Rose Lamartine Yates reclaimed these items on 10 June: the space on the police document where he had to insert the identity of their owner was denoted 'name of lunatic'.

Telegrams had been sent to Kensington (presumably to the Empress Rooms following the discovery on Davison's person of her Helper's Card for the Summer Festival) alerting fellow suffragettes to the accident but it was almost 10 p.m. before Davison was formally identified by Alice Green and her daughter. The lateness of their arrival suggests women caught totally unprepared for such an eventuality, proving that Davison had been working alone and in secret. Although the *Daily News* stated Davison later 'showed signs of regaining consciousness' and *The Sporting Life* insisted she did, she remained comatose.

The appearance of George Prince leading the befuddled Anmer past the winning post, just as the 'victorious' Craganour was being led-in, provided the first inkling to those in the vicinity of the grandstand – with the notable exception of M. Aumont who had seen his horse stopped by the incident – that something amiss had transpired. The stretcher carrying Jones soon followed, but was found to be too long to pass through either the jockeys' room or the passage leading to the back of the grandstand, and he was placed on the ground in full view of the crowd while it was decided how he should be conveyed to hospital. He regained consciousness after a couple of hours, his only major discomfort coming from the aggravation of an old rib injury, and, the *Chronicle* declared, 'expressed regret that he had not been allowed to finish the race'. He had no recollection of Davison rushing in front of Anmer and could offer no coherent account of the incident, as 'the whole thing had happened so suddenly', until Lord Marcus Beresford mentioned the word 'suffragette'. 'Oh, yes, I remember,' he then said. 'A woman jumped out from underneath the rails and my horse hit her, and the horse sort of rolled over and I must have had a bang, for that's all I know. I recall falling through the air but not hitting the ground.' The assembled doctors declared Jones to be 'as hard as nails'.

The next day he told the *Evening Standard*: 'I remember a woman running in front of me like this,' he said placing his arms over his head. 'I could not get out of her way, and my horse struck right into her. It is a wonder we were not both killed.' In 1934 the *Sunday Express* printed his 'official version' of the race, highly theatrical and clearly ghosted, under the title 'The Suffragette Who Died To Stop the Derby':

> Whose was that strange figure wandering uncertainly on the grass ahead? A woman. Silly woman! Heavens, she had hardly escaped being trampled down by the two horses in front of me. Thank goodness I should miss her. She was nearly in the centre of the course now. I was near the rails. But surely she was mad. She was running back into my path. She stumbled and nearly fell. I reined Anmer cruelly. And then with a great rush, she seized Anmer's bridle. Leaped at his neck with the movement of a matador. An awful scream. The crowd in the vicinity yelled. Women fainted. In an instant we were all three in a struggling heap on the grass.

Jones's 'account' went on to describe events elsewhere (that he couldn't have seen), and concluded:

> A sad story of wasted attainments in a fanatical cause. Hers, anyway, was a doomed life. For years she has suffered from a malignant disease and medical attendants had given her up as a hopeless case. It was only a matter of months, perhaps weeks before the end. They invited me to attend her funeral. I refused.

Letitia de Baecker sprang to her sister's defence. 'She had a marvellously healthy and robust constitution,' she wrote in response to the revived charge that madness must have sparked such actions, 'and was an excellent all-round athlete.' The *Sunday Express* declined to print her letter.

After vacating the Royal Box for the Jockey Club terraces where Superintendent McCarthy appraised him of the incident, the King was seen to trace a V-shaped gash on his own cheek when conveying news of his jockey to those around him. The Royal couple enquired as to the welfare of both injured parties before departing the racecourse. The King was hosting the evening's annual Derby banquet at Buckingham Palace for sixty members of the Jockey Club, naturally including Loder, Wolverton and Rosebery. In his diary the King recorded:

> We all left for Epsom at 12.40 to see the Derby. The police say it was the largest crowd that has ever been there, the road was blocked and it took some time to get on the course.
>
> It was a most disastrous Derby. Craganour, the favourite, won by a head from Aboyeur (who had made all the running) and was led in by his owner Mr Ismay, but was afterwards disqualified for bumping and boring by the Stewards and the race given to Aboyeur (100/1) with Louvois second and Great Sport third.
>
> I ran Anmer. Just as the horses were coming round Tattenham Corner, a suffragette (Miss Davison) dashed out and tried to catch Anmer's bridle, of course she was knocked down and

seriously injured and poor Herbert Jones and Anmer were sent flying. Jones unconscious, badly cut, broken rib and slight concussion, a most regrettable and scandalous proceeding.

In the next race Leo Rothschild's horse Felizardo fell and broke his leg and had to be destroyed, his jockey was not hurt.

A most disappointing day. Got home at 5.15.

Queen Mary confided:

> Went to Epsom to see the Derby. A most sensational one. The favourite Craganour was disqualified and Aboyeur won. A suffragette ran out near Tattenham Corner and got in front of G's horse Anmer which knocked her down, then fell throwing poor Jones who was much knocked about. The horrid woman was injured but not seriously. Back by 5.

Jones was soon in receipt of a telegram from the Dowager Queen Alexandra wishing him a speedy recovery and bemoaning 'your sad accident caused through the abominable conduct of a brutal lunatic woman': in 1996 the telegram sold for £2,415 at Sotheby's. Another telegram Jones received read: 'A woman of England sends her deep sympathy to you, and wishes to express her horror at the outrageous act of one of her own sex.'

Sympathy for his assailant was in short supply. The tone was set by a scathing *Daily Telegraph*: 'Deep in the hearts of every onlooker was a feeling of fierce resentment with the miserable woman'; 'Some wild woman,' declared *The Sporting Life*; 'A well-known malignant suffragette,' the *Daily Express* called her; 'The hottest of all suffragette hot-bloods, a notorious militant with a thirst for martyrdom,' stated the *Daily Mail* in its report of 'Mad Woman's Dash'. *The Times* called her 'demented'; *The Standard* labelled her 'entirely unbalanced' and insisted 'it is highly characteristic of the suffragette militancy that an attempt should be made to introduce a note of tragedy into a day of festival'.

The *Pall Mall Gazette* chose not to mince its words:

There can only be pity for the dementia which led an unfortunate
woman to seek a grotesque and meaningless kind of 'martyrdom'
in the fancied interests of a political cause and at the cost of
grave peril to the lives of others. The tragedy, or semi-tragedy
of Tattenham Corner was inspired by emotions that have more
kinship with the grossest pagan superstitions than with the
progressive intelligence of English womanhood. The public will
rather be confirmed in the view that political excitement has a
disastrous effect upon certain types of feminine nature.

The *Illustrated Sporting and Dramatic News* resorted to heavy-
handed sarcasm with a reference to the intended participation of
His Majesty's runner in the Oaks:

Miss Davison came to the conclusion it would be an excellent
argument in favour of votes for women if she could get hold of
the King's colt and chance the rest. No doubt this is quite as good
an argument as many of those advanced on behalf of the same
cause, though it scarcely seems to be logically convincing. She
will not be in a position to have another go at Princess Dagmar
when she runs in the Oaks.

The *Morning Post* tried to analyse the causes of the suffragist
'disease' which destroyed property and sent Davison to her death:

If we are to believe the leaders of the 'movement', the purpose
with which these things are done is to make men think. The
question is, what are we to think?
    There is an epidemic of the state of mind which produced
these instances. This frame of mind cannot possibly be considered
healthy. The acts which it produces constitute a war. The women
who go about setting fire to houses seem to have their thoughts
out of gear. In most respects apparently their minds work as other
people's do, but the epidemic of arson appears to be a form of
monomania.

These ladies say that women ought to have the same political rights as men. But it is unthinkable that a person who refuses to recognise the fundamental condition upon which every society is founded can be qualified for membership in that society. The person whose mind works in that way is inaccessible to reasonable arguments. There seems, therefore, no escape from the conclusion that society has to deal with an epidemic of monomania.

In short: if women can perpetrate such acts of folly they are clearly not worthy of the Vote. A sympathetic stance was hard to find. The *Daily Herald*, recently founded by the pro-suffragette George Lansbury, tried its utmost. Under the headline MISS DAVISON'S SACRIFICE it declared: 'In a normal nation, Miss Davison's life might have gone on from distinction to distinction, a record of fine achievement throughout. In the Britain that murders mind, and thwarts and degrades so much brave humanity, it was largely one of protest culminating in martyrdom.' The *Manchester Guardian* probably put it best: 'a futile tragedy.'

The first cross section of the general public in a position to draw some conclusions of their own were Wednesday evening's audiences in West End theatres like the Palace, Coliseum, Hippodrome and all the 'Empire' halls, plus several provincial houses. All of them were able to watch newsreel footage of that afternoon's drama.

On Thursday the 5th, as Emily Davison hovered between life and death, the hospital authorities were notified by the police that she was to be regarded as 'a prisoner'. She was placed under police guard, and a detective kept vigil at the foot of her bed in the hope of learning the reasons for her actions, because the Director of Public Prosecutions was already considering bringing charges of committing an 'act calculated to cause grievous bodily harm'. The *Sporting Chronicle*, for one, believed this would come to pass because, it had been informed, 'authorities are confident she will recover; during the morning she recovered partial consciousness and answered to her name'. While the detective waited, the poison-pen letters began to arrive. Someone calling himself 'An Englishman' wrote:

> I am glad to hear you are in hospital. I hope you suffer torture until you die, you idiot. I consider you unworthy of existence. For what you have done, I should like the opportunity of starving and beating you to a pulp. Why don't your people find an asylum for you.

A second, from 'A Roused of Richmond', arrived with a black border:

> I as sincerely wish for your recovery as I regret that it is possible. When you are fully conscious it may be that crazy fanaticism which drove you to break the laws of God and Man will have left your poor brain clearer. And in that case surely you will thank Him for sparing you the sin of murder! Of course, I cannot hope to touch the heart of a confirmed gaol bird.

According to Longhorsley folklore, Margaret Davison was not unduly surprised to hear of her daughter's accident. 'I had a premonition this morning that something tragic was going to happen today,' she allegedly told the messenger who relayed the contents of the telephone call from London. 'A magpie appeared on my window-sill and would not go away. When I opened the door to go out, the bird flew into the house. I knew it was a bad omen.' However, even she was moved to question her daughter's actions in a letter of 5 June delivered to Epsom. Addressing her daughter by her family pet-name of 'Weet Weet', her maternal *cri de coeur* reads as poignantly today as it did then.

> I feel I must write to you although I am in a terrible state of mind at the news which reached me last evening. I cannot believe that you could have done such a dreadful act. Even for the Cause

which I know you have given up your whole heart and soul to, and it has done so little in return for you. Now I can only hope and pray God will mercifully restore you to life and health and that there may be a better and brighter future before you. I would have come to you if I could but you will remember asking me never to leave home no matter what occurred as it would relieve your mind to know where I was.

Today I had telegrams from Mrs Penn Gaskell, Mrs Leigh and Mrs Green. They are all more favourable than the newspaper reports and I trust the next may be better still.

I need not tell you my heart is full of grief and agony and the thought you are so far away gives me much misery and pain. I know you would not wilfully give me any unhappiness and though it must have been some sudden impulse and excitement I trust you feel assured my earnest and devout prayers will be upmost in my mind until you will be restored to health again.

With all my love, from your sorrowful Mother.

Emily Davison would never read that letter for her 'future' grew dimmer by the hour. Though nominally in the care of Dr Peacock, it was Charles Mansell-Moullin, Harley Street doctor, fellow of the Royal College of Surgeons and the husband of her suffragette colleague Edith, who subsequently spent three days trying to save Davison's life. On the Thursday afternoon he found her pulse a little stronger but it was evident there was bleeding going on inside the skull from a fracture across the base, and from the injured brain. In his opinion it would be 'some weeks before she can leave the institution'. On Friday he operated and brought temporary relief. However, the damaged portion of the brain never recovered and the heart and breathing gradually failed. On Saturday the dying suffragette was again visited by a number of fellow suffragettes, Mary Leigh and Rose Lamartine Yates draping a suffragette flag upon the screen around Davison's bed and attaching a WSPU badge to the head of the bed. Letitia arrived from France to spend many hours at her sister's bedside, to be joined that evening by her elder half-brother, Captain Henry Jocelyn Davison – but not by her mother, who, according to the press, had sent a 'lady friend' to sit with her daughter. Davison never opened her eyes or uttered a word from the moment Anmer struck her until she took her dying breath at 4.50 in the afternoon of Sunday 8 June. Only hospital staff were with her when the end finally came. Back in Longhorsley her mother was said to have felt the fluttering of wings pass her by – but on this occasion saw no bird. As if in tribute to a fallen comrade, the grandstand at Hurst Park racecourse was set ablaze that night.

At 3 p.m. on Tuesday 10 June, the inquest into Emily Davison's death was opened at Epsom Court House: C. F. Gill KC watched the proceedings on behalf of the Stewards and Tom Yates, husband of Rose Lamartine, appeared for Margaret Davison and Captain Davison. The coroner for West Surrey, Gilbert H. White, opened proceedings by stating that Herbert Jones, though not seriously hurt, was 'not well enough' to give evidence.

The first witness called was Henry Davison. The opening question indicated which way the inquest was heading: did he know anything that would lead him to think that his half-sister was 'abnormal mentally'? Just how well Davison knew his half-sister is questionable: he had already given her age incorrectly as thirty-eight, not forty. Led by Yates, he replied to the effect that she was a woman of very strong reasoning faculties and passionately devoted to the women's movement, a devotion that caused her many talents 'to wither like Dead Sea fruit' if the *Daily Express* report is to be believed. Asked why she might have committed this act, he said that, from what he knew of her character, it was with the object of calling attention to the suffrage movement; acting alone, added the *Express*, was attributed to 'pathetic loneliness'. He concluded by stating he felt perfectly certain it was an accident, she realised the danger but accepted it, hoping she would be saved from it. Yates then asked him whether he thought she had done this 'by way of protest with a view to calling public attention to the fact that the government have not done justice to women'. The Coroner immediately intervened to prevent Davison answering, declaring he did not propose to allow any 'political questions'.

Sergeant Bunn was called next. He said he saw Miss Davison rush forward, throw up her hands in front of the horses and then be knocked down; the whole thing happened so swiftly that he was unable to say whether 'she purposely allowed some of the horses to pass her'. So far as he knew she was 'quite alone'. Constable Eady, who'd been stationed on the outside of the course about forty yards from the turn into straight, replicated Bunn's version of events. In answer to a leading question from the Coroner, he confirmed it wouldn't be possible for her to have picked out any particular horse since they were 'bunched together'. So, that removed any hint of a deliberate anti-monarchist gesture. It was then only left for Dr Thornely to reiterate Davison's injuries and cause of death.

White summed up thus:

> It was evident that Miss Davison did not make specifically for the King's horse, but her intention was merely to disturb or upset the race ... her object was not to take her own life, but it was an exceedingly sad thing for an educated lady to sacrifice herself in this way.

After an absence of an hour and twenty-five minutes, the jury returned a verdict that 'Miss Emily Wilding Davison died of a fracture of the base of the skull, caused by being accidentally knocked down by a horse through wilfully rushing on to the racecourse at Epsom Downs during the progress of the race for the Derby; death was due to misadventure.' That verdict, with all its detail, was duly entered on Davison's death certificate. The delicate issue of whether Davison had committed suicide was never discussed – for suicide was a criminal offence (and remained so until 1961).

Has time shed any light on what was running through

Davison's mind and what provoked the extraordinary sequence of actions?

We can dispense once and for all with the notion that she had an accomplice or that she intended to single out the King's horse and bring it down, forfeiting her life in the process. In the first instance, she'd now taken to acting alone: 'pathetic loneliness' played no part. She hadn't even told Leigh of her plans the previous evening in the Empress Rooms; none of her confidantes or closest associates, such as Leigh or Rose Lamartine Yates, would have left her lying alone on the turf. In the second instance, she couldn't have identified any particular horse. And the presence of her return ticket and her known plans for the rest of the week – helping at the Summer Festival; attending a lecture at the Bishopsgate Institute on the Saturday; then France to visit Letitia and her nephew and niece – plus the absence of any 'suicide note' (to her mother or any of her close colleagues) eliminates any likelihood of her death being premeditated.

So what did account for her actions? In light of Davison's known record as a militant suffragette one can discount the evidence of those racegoers whose instantly canvassed opinion was that she was merely trying to cross the track and thought all the horses had passed. There may be a grain of truth in this, however. Clearly she wished to disrupt the race but, equally clearly, she misjudged her location and, above all, the speed of the horses.

First, an objective analysis of those actions.

1. On hearing the horses approaching, more likely alerted by the rising roar of the crowd than the thud of galloping hooves, she ducks under the running rail.
2. The leading horses have already dashed past because she has misjudged their speed.
3. She walks onto the track, falters and stops, allowing Agadir and Nimbus to pass behind her, to her right, between her and the inside running rail she has just vacated.

4. The key moment: she continues into the middle of the course, to a point of safety where, for example, her concealed flags might be unfurled or revealed.

5. She spurns safety. She walks toward the next horse, which by pure happenstance is Anmer.

Second, to a reasoned consideration of the motivation and state of mind that sparked these actions. Although it is unthinkable for a woman like Emily Davison not to have planned her protest, it is evident she had not thought it through as thoroughly as she might. She had even bought a return ticket, for instance, which would have been entirely superfluous, since any kind of plan to disrupt the race would surely have ended in her arrest.

1. She's chosen the wrong side from which to launch her protest. The inside of the track offered the prime site facing the newsreel cameras but the worst site for judging the arrival of horses. She can neither see nor hear properly. She should have selected a position on the opposite side of the track, below the hoardings by Tattenham Corner station. Better still: she ought to have positioned herself at the start, where she could have walked out in front of the starting gate, in full glare of the cameras, while the horses were still safely behind the tapes, to delay and disrupt the race in complete safety. But Tattenham Corner was more photogenic and closer. Walking a further mile, however, would have saved her life.

2. From her chosen position, she misjudges the pace of horses thundering down Tattenham Hill and leaves her vantage point either far too late or too early – dependent on whether she intended halting the race or merely drawing attention to herself once the field had galloped past. It's not inconceivable that she was unaware from which direction the horses would be coming until almost the last moment: what would she, a middle-aged God-fearing spinster and political activist, be expected to know about the intricacies of horse racing at

Epsom on Derby Day? Significantly, both the earlier races she had watched were on the straight course, some forty or more yards distant to her left, and thus gave no hint of the problems she would face confronting horses galloping at full pelt out of nowhere from her immediate right.

3. Once she finds herself in the midst of galloping horses she is overcome by the same rush of blood which had swept over her on the staircase in Holloway. Her protest was going awry. Safety was still an option, however faint a possibility. She could have stepped away to her left. But she doesn't. She throws up her hands. Was she trying to protect herself? If self-preservation was her motive, she would surely have turned her back. But her very being demands a gesture of bravado to save face. She feels compelled to grab a horse, and moves toward the nearest one.

If Emily Davison believed she could 'petition the King' by stopping his horse she was as self-willed and delusional as the WSPU leadership suspected. Her glorious 'sacrifice' was nothing more than a protest that went gloriously wrong. It was always liable to go wrong because it was poorly planned and executed, like many of her earlier protests ending in fiasco – the Commons invasions, the letter-boxes, Aberdeen, even the Holloway 'suicide' attempt – owing to her innate impetuosity. Davison lacked nothing in intellect and courage – both moral and physical. She was clever with 'words' but her 'deeds' demonstrated flawed common sense. Her sense of intellectual superiority led her to believe she knew more about Epsom and the Derby than she plainly did. Whether this arrogance was stoked by an unhealthy obsession with figures like Joan or Emelye, it's possible her world temporarily fused fantasy with reality – and trapped within it, her 'deeds' were determined by it. Her action was only 'glorious' in terms of the incredible courage it took to walk toward a racehorse galloping at 35mph instead of away from it.

History proved kind to Emily Davison. Its view of her lost touch with the reality. One second earlier and she'd have been mown down by the entire field; one second later and Anmer would have passed and she would have collided with either Sandburr or Jameson. One second either way and history would have needed re-writing: her death was assured but the historical resonance provided by Anmer would have been lost. The best that may be said of Davison's demise is that if she did manage to register it was a horse carrying the King's purple jacket bearing down on her, she at least walked into the cold dark hereafter with heart warmed by a glow of satisfaction because a Royal executioner gifted her a level of immortality far beyond the compass of the fourteen other potential headsmen.

☞

Whatever the precise context of Davison's death, the cause of women's suffrage had its blood sacrifice: she became gold dust as surely as the 'martyrs' of the Easter Rebellion would be for Irish Nationalism; postcards of her were soon on sale in the WSPU shop. However accidentally it materialised, the WSPU wasn't about to forego the opportunity of using her death for political capital. It would have been politically naïve not to. In keeping with the movement's quasi religious leit-motif the tributes and calls for renewed commitment and vigour were laced with talk of 'Holy Wars', 'Crusades', 'Martyrs' and 'Saints'.

Emmeline Pethick-Lawrence instantly set the tone, being quoted in the *Daily News* the day after the Derby:

> It is a very extraordinary action and it shows the immense pitch of desperation to which women have been driven. There is no doubt that this plan was well thought out on the part of Miss Davison and it has been carried through with amazing coolness and resource, and almost superhuman courage. There is not the smallest doubt that she deliberately risked her life with the idea that by this action she would call the attention of her country and of the world to the great hardships and

privations endured by women by reason of their exclusion from any political status.

This aggrandising nonsense continued. The day after Davison's death Edith Mansell-Moullin told a WSPU meeting that it was

perfectly clear that Miss Davison went out with the express purpose of stopping the King's horse ... what she did was to challenge the very head of this country, the Government, and the press with an act that could not be kept out of the papers. She is worthy of the highest rank among the martyrs all down the ages who have voluntarily laid down their lives for a holy cause.

Mary Leigh saluted her great friend whom she believed had been 'welcomed as a kindred soul by the heroine of old time, "Blessed Joan of Arc". The dauntless heart of Saint Joan still beats in the women of this movement.' Rose Lamartine Yates believed she had 'felt the call, she knew that suffering and outraged woman-hood looked to her to do her utmost to release them from bondage ... and had given her life for us and all humanity, count-ing but not fearing the cost, for the cause she held more than life'. Mrs Pankhurst, never slow in making political capital, was quick to follow suit. She forgot any differences Davison had with her leadership and paid tribute to 'one of our valiant soldiers' who had

gladly laid down her life for women's freedom ... in our grief we rejoice that she succeeded by her heroic deed in calling attention to the great struggle for the emancipation of women. We mourn for the loss of a dead comrade, for to mourn is human, but we also rejoice in her splendid heroism. We who remain can but honour her memory by continuing our work unceasingly.

The WSPU rammed home the message by dispatching a tele-gram to the King:

Constitutional methods of approaching our King having failed, Emily Davison has given her life to call attention to the women's passionate demands. We call upon our King to give serious attention to this appeal of womanhood.

In its issue of 12 June 1913, *Votes for Women* began the process of canonisation:

> Waiting there in the sun, in that gay scene, among the heedless crowd, she had in her soul the thought, the vision of wronged women. That thought she held to her; that vision she kept before her. Thus inspired, she threw herself into the fierce current of the race. So greatly did she care for freedom that she died for it.

The following day the movement's sister publication, *The Suffragette*, accelerated the process in what amounted to a memorial edition of the paper. Its front page depicted an angel with unfurled wings and upraised arms standing before a running rail with shadowy figures of solemn-faced racegoers behind it; her halo read 'Love That Overcometh' and beneath her feet was a suitably religious dedication which read: 'In Honour and in Loving, Reverent Memory of Emily Wilding Davison: She Died For Women. Greater love hath no man than this, that he lay down his life for his friends.' Inside, next to a poem titled 'The First Martyr of Woman Suffrage', Christabel Pankhurst's editorial ran:

> So greatly did she care for freedom that she died for it. So dearly did she love women that she offered her life as their ransom. Miss Davison made a protest which has fired the imagination and touched the heart of people. Her act has proved to be an appeal infinitely more eloquent than all the words of all the speakers could be. She has taught the world that there are women who care passionately for the Vote. She has said 'I want the Vote, I care for it, more than my life, and I give my life as a pledge of

my desire that women shall be free.' Some day we will all be dead. Emily Wilding Davison resolved that she would strive by her death to purchase something for the people she left behind her.

The feminist journal *The Awakener* was equally florid. Its issue of 21 June contained an editorial emblazoned 'The Noble Army of Martyrs Praise Thee' in which it contrasted the Derby where 'selfishness and lust ride neck and neck' with the plight of women 'whose whole lives are pounded beneath the iron hooves of circumstances because they are too conventional, or too timid, to grasp the rein of their own lives'. The same page gave prominence to an appreciation of Davison 'By One Who Knew Her', A. E. Willson:

> It was my privilege to be acquainted with this heroic woman who has now joined 'the choir invisible of those immortal dead who live again in the minds made better by their presence'.
> Emily Wilding Davison most firmly held the opinion that every great cause needs its martyrs; and united with her beautiful capacity for self-forgetful heroism was a self-effacing desire for any acknowledgment of her many deeds of daring and enduring courage. Only those who knew her personally know that she was one of the women whose great natural abilities and lofty generosity of nature fitted her, like the woman of antiquity resting in the catacombs of Rome, to be 'a mother to all the world'.

Another feminist tribute came from Rebecca West in *The Clarion*:

> We belittle her if we think that her great decision can have made that decision to die an easy one; her last months before death must have been a time of great agony. To a woman of such quick senses life must have been very dear, and the abandonment of it a horror which we, who are still alive and mean to remain so, who have not even had the pluck to unseat the Government and shake it into sense, cannot conceive. And this decision was made by a

soul harried by a body whose state was such as would have killed the courage in most of us.

Surely it was the most merciful thing that ever befell Emily Davison that her death, unlike her life, was unshadowed by prison walls. To the end the sunlight was on her face. I was glad that for an executioner she had an unmalicious brute.

The months and years following Davison's death would see her 'sacrifice' elevated to messianic proportions. In her autobiography of 1914, *My Own Story*, Mrs Pankhurst wrote:

> Emily Davison clung to the conviction that one great tragedy, the deliberate throwing into the breach of a human life, would put an end to the intolerable torture of women. And so she threw herself at the King's horse, in full view of the King and Queen and a great multitude of their Majesties' subjects.

In her book *The Suffrage Movement*, published in 1931, Sylvia Pankhurst declared that Davison and a fellow militant in whose flat she lived had concocted a plan to wave suffragette flags at Tattenham Corner and stop the race – which implicates either Alice Green or her daughter. Yet neither of them attended the Derby. Not to be outdone, Christabel Pankhurst's memoir *Unshackled*, published in 1959, contained her own eulogy in which she stated her belief that Davison had acted completely alone, her plan divulged to not a single soul. This difference of opinion typifies the paradox surrounding Emily Davison's death and her status as a martyr to the cause of women's suffrage.

That Emily Davison was more valuable to the movement as a dead martyr than ever she was as a live militant is indisputable. Equally, it's widely acknowledged that the suffragettes had discussed among themselves the distinct possibility that someone in their number would have to die – Mrs Pankhurst's high profile making her the obvious candidate – before the Vote was granted. The consensus was that this would arise at the hands of a

hooligan during a demonstration or as a result of hunger striking and/or forcible feeding. However, the former had already
occurred in the guise of Mrs Pankhurst's sister, Mary Clarke – yet
no capital was made of her death in 1912. No thought whatsoever
had been given to any death by intention.

Martyr and martyrdom were words Davison never used in
the context of her own activities, even if her words and actions
clearly established her willingness to accept death should it strike.
Martyrdom should serve some purpose: did Davison's? One of her
Morpeth admirers, Connie Lewcock, confessed to being 'inspired
to even greater efforts' – which included contemplating blowing
up Durham Cathedral. WSPU sympathiser Lawrence Housman
was one prepared to believe many who had been 'careless or indifferent' to the cause of women's suffrage subsequently viewed it as 'a
serious thing'. The National Union of Women's Suffrage Societies,
which refused to participate in Davison's funeral, later conceded
Davison's death 'startled and indeed aroused the country … all over
the world people read about it … it was time the struggle ended'.

That the 'struggle' for the Vote was slowly being won now
seems obvious. However, the outbreak of a much greater conflict
in August 1914 delayed its victory. The Representation of the
People Act gave the Vote to women over the age of thirty (if
they were either householders, married to a householder, the
occupant of property with rent of £5 per annum or held a degree
from a British university) in time for the 'Coupon Election' of
December 1918. Countess Markievicz was duly elected for Sinn
Fein in Dublin, but she refused to take the oath of allegiance
and never took her seat. Thus, Lady Astor became Britain's first
woman MP a year later; the voting age was reduced to twenty-
one, and on the same terms as men, in 1928.

Even if Emily Davison was nothing more than an accidental
martyr, the WSPU were determined to ensure her funeral had
all the trappings of a martyr's farewell. She was to be interred in
St Mary's churchyard, Morpeth, on Sunday 15 June following the
removal of the coffin from Victoria to King's Cross, and thence

Newcastle, on the Saturday. The procession's route through London to King's Cross to meet the 5.30 p.m. train would be via a memorial service at St George's Church in Hart Street. Arrangements were put in hand to turn the London phase into a demonstration of suffragette might. The authorities responded accordingly. The Commissioner of Police advised the WSPU that 'as all reasonable facilities must be given to the ordinary traffic, the progress of the proposed funeral cortege may be greatly hindered. In order to convey the remains in a seemly and reverent manner, the hearse should be accompanied by a limited number of mourners only.' The Union ignored the letter. Its efforts were spectacularly successful, achieving what the *Manchester Guardian* called, 'the brilliancy of a military funeral'; another journalist declared 'they might have been saluting the corpse of some dead conqueror, instead of the dead body of a rebel heroine'.

On Saturday 14 June, the funeral procession assembled at 1 p.m. on the north side of Buckingham Palace Road, opposite Victoria station, to await the arrival of the hearse. It was a fine, warm day. The procession was due to set off at 2 p.m. but was delayed thirty minutes: somebody was missing. Mrs Pankhurst had expressed her intention of taking part in the ceremony and a carriage had been reserved for her, but as soon as she left the Westminster flat where she'd stayed since being released from Holloway under the Cat and Mouse Act on 30 May, she was re-arrested and returned to prison.

The procession numbered possibly as many as 6,000 and brought central London to a standstill as an estimated 50,000 people packed the pavements. Divided into eleven sections, marching in ranks of four, the procession slowly moved forward to the roll of drums and the muffled chords of Chopin's funeral march. At its head was Charlotte Marsh, carrying a huge wooden cross, her fair hair uncovered. Immediately behind came twelve white-clad girls with laurel wreaths and a banner inscribed with Joan of Arc's exhortation to 'Fight On! God Will Give The Victory'. Behind this group came sections comprised of London

WSPU members dressed in white (with tall Madonna lilies), black (carrying purple irises) or purple (red peonies) followed by a party of fifty hunger-strikers. Every woman wore a black crepe arm-band.

The coffin, placed on a low open bier, was draped with a silver-edged purple pall, held in place by three wreaths in the shape of prison arrows; eight suffragettes, Mary Leigh, Rose Lamartine Yates and Sylvia Pankhurst among them, provided the honour guard. The hearse was surrounded by the chief mourners led by Captain Davison, and then came a masterstroke – an empty carriage, symbolising the absent Mrs Pankhurst, a veritable Banquo's ghost. In its wake, trailed WSPU squadrons from the provinces; other organisations sympathetic to the movement; and finally the general public, with a phalanx of drummers bringing up the rear.

The memorial service at St George's was conducted by the Ven. Archdeacon Escreet assisted by two stalwarts of the Church League for Women's Suffrage, the Rev. H. Baumgarten and the Rev. Claud Hinscliffe. Hymns sung were 'Onward Christian Soldiers', 'Lead Kindly Light', 'Nearer my God to Thee' and 'Fight the Good Fight with all thy Might'. The printed valediction carried a photograph of Davison in academic dress on the front above a list of her academic achievements and suffragette ordeals, and the words of St John's gospel, 'Greater Love hath no man than this, that he lay down his life for his friend.' Inside, under the heading WHY DID SHE STOP THE KING'S HORSE? A PETITION TO THE KING, could be read the following, which was clearly composed with the general public in mind.

In 1906 Miss Davison became keenly alive to the many evils the country was suffering from owing to the exclusion of women from the parliamentary franchise, and to the inferior position thus assigned them. She realised, as do so many social workers, that no relief can come to the weak, the oppressed and the suffering until women have won their freedom and the full citizen rights possessed by men. To this end she worked unceasingly and fearlessly, with all the wonderful ability, literary skill and eloquence she possessed. Finding reason unavailing, she adopted other measures. Cheerfully she bore the horrors of the hunger strike; withstood the cruel ordeal of the hose pipe at Strangeways Gaol, and endured the tortures of forcible feeding. But as time went on she began to feel that to break down the walls of obstinacy and ancient prejudice, more even than this was needed. With her clear and unflinching vision she realised that now, as in days of old, to awake the conscience of the people, a human life would be needed as sacrifice – a human life freely given under circumstances of tragedy, the shock of which would travel round the world.

And so this marvellous woman, who, besides her brilliant intellectual gifts was a being full of health, vitality and the joy of living, heard within her heart the call which told her she must surrender the life which to her was so delightful and so precious. She heard the call and made answer, 'I come.' And so she offered up her life as a PETITION TO THE KING, praying that women might be freed to aid their sisters.'

However, this conscious demonstration of suffragette pride, might and right aimed at winning over the general public didn't pass without some signs of discord. One woman was arrested for trying to pull down a banner; pepper was thrown, as was a brick; there were isolated shouts of 'Three cheers for the King's jockey!'; and approaching King's Cross portions of the crowd jeered the hearse – leaving Rebecca West to wail:

Old men that looked like wicked little boys, little boys that looked like wicked old men, lively young prostitutes with bare arms scrawled with tattooing, old women putrescent with sin. I was glad that Emily Davison was killed by a horse and not by the kind of person she was fighting with.

Such had been the press that the train scheduled to bear the coffin north had to be held up as the coffin only arrived a minute or two prior to its scheduled departure; such were the floral tributes that over a thousand were loaded onto a later train. After being held overnight in a siding at Newcastle Central station, an honour guard that included Leigh, Yates and Marsh standing vigil in pairs throughout, the brake van containing the coffin was attached to the 10.40 train to Morpeth where a further 20,000 people had gathered on a bright sunny day.

This second procession, organised by the Newcastle branch of the WSPU, lost little in comparison to its predecessor, although the 'decorous and sympathetic demeanour' of Davison's own folk contrasted with the occasional oafishness shown the previous day. The other notable difference was the presence of mourners from Davison's immediate family. Five private coaches followed the coffin, the first of which held Davison's mother, her sister Letitia and her 'intimate companion, Miss Morrison'. Led by the Benwell Silver Band, the procession stretched half-a-mile and took forty-five minutes to wind its way past Station Bank and Mafeking Park to the parish church of St Mary. As the *Morpeth Herald and Reporter* was to observe: 'Last Sunday was one of the most noteworthy days in Morpeth history.' After a brief burial service, conducted by the Rev. E. R. Wilkinson, senior curate of St Mary's, the body was laid to rest in the family plot lying on rising ground to the west of the church amid blooming clumps of rhododendrons and sentinels of cypress and yew trees. Her final resting place, already containing her younger sister 'Darling Ethel', her father and his first wife, Sarah, was enclosed by a set of iron railings and presided over by a marble obelisk surmounted by a cross. Upon it had been added: 'Emily Wilding Davison. Died June 8 1913. Valiant In Courage and Faith.' In front of the obelisk was an eye-catching stone in the form of a large open book carved from marble which had occupied a similarly prominent position on the hearse throughout the procession from the station. Its pages bore the words: 'A Veritable Princess of Spirituality. From A Loving Aberdeen Friend.' The speed of its preparation and delivery matched the tenderness of its message, suggesting its donor to be that 'intimate companion' privileged to have shared Emily Davison's life and been seated in the leading carriage alongside her mother and sister.

Before the coffin was lowered into the grave a purple cloth embroidered with the words 'Welcome Northumbrian hunger striker' – presented to Davison years earlier – was laid on top at the express wish of her mother. Departing suffragettes cast flowers into the grave before wreaths were banked around the railings: 'With the love and admiration of a comrade,' said the card from Christabel Pankhurst; 'To honour my dear comrade,' said her sister Sylvia. Others came from such diverse sources as 'A Gambler's Wife', 'From a Jew to a Christian Martyr' and 'Two Baby Suffragettes'.

That evening a large body of suffragettes held a meeting in Morpeth's Market Square which was addressed by Mrs Arncliffe Sennett of the Actresses' Franchise League. 'I think Morpeth has every reason to be proud of itself today,' she told them. 'It has given to the world a heroine.'

☞

For some years afterwards Longhorsley children would chant a ditty in homage to that 'heroine' which began 'The Longhorsley lady's gone away/She's back from London another day!'

Yet Emily Davison has never really 'gone away'. She has never left the public consciousness. Her public sacrifice was the first of its kind to be immortalised by one of the twentieth century's most influential innovations. Those flickering black-and-white images captured by the movie camera offer an enduring monument to her actions. She even features in another modern medium, recorded music, in the form of a eulogy written by the American rock singer Greg Kihn, featured on his debut album of 1976. In addition to the tribute in the Palace of Westminster, Epsom's Cottage Hospital in Alexandra Road boasts a plaque commemorating the fact that 'Emily Davison, Heroine of the Women's Suffrage Movement was cared for here'; and the town has honoured her by naming the thoroughfare behind Tattenham Corner station 'Emily Davison Drive' – matching Morpeth's 'Emily Davison Avenue'. There have been moves to create an annual 'holiday' on 4 June: 'Emily Davison Day.'

Nor was she forsaken by her own. For the remaining sixty years of her own life, Mary Leigh either placed a wreath, or arranged for one to be so placed, on her friend's grave every 4 June. That grave had fallen into a state of disrepair by the 1990s, and in 1998 a public appeal was launched to raise an £8,000 restoration fund. A pink plate now adorns the wall of her mother's house in Longhorsley: bordered by 'Votes For Women' and Davison's motto 'Fight On! God Will Give The Victory', it states: 'From this house Emily Wilding Davison Suffragette set out for the Derby Epsom – June 1913.'

Another statement some way from the truth of the matter.

# EIGHTEEN

# Surplus to Requirements

The same papers that carried the news of Davison's death on Monday 9 June also announced the news of Craganour's sale.

Having 'won and lost' two Classics, poor Craganour seemed jinxed: straight after the Derby, negotiations were put in hand to sell him. Bloodstock dealer Ernest Tanner brokered a deal for the colt's sale to the Argentinian Señor Miguel Martinez de Hoz to stand as a stallion at the Chapadmalal Stud he'd founded on his forty-five square-mile estate bordering the Atlantic, 250 miles south of Buenos Aires near Mar del Plata: Craganour realised the handsome sum of £30,000. The South American bloodstock market was booming and Tanner specialised in feeding it, having already expedited the sale of the Gold Cup winner and dual champion sire Cyllene to the Ojo de Agua Stud for £25,000 in 1911; Ormonde and Diamond Jubilee were Triple Crown winners who'd also wound up in Argentina. That country's gain was likely England's loss for had Craganour received his due at Newmarket and Epsom, he almost certainly would have been aimed at the St Leger and the Triple Crown. That final Classic was won by his vastly inferior stablemate Night Hawk. Craganour had stayed the one-and-a-half miles of the Derby; there's no reason to suppose he couldn't have lasted the additional 572 yards of the St Leger. His younger full sister Glorvina, for instance, would win the Ascot Gold Vase over two miles and Desmond had already sired such doughty stayers as The White Knight and Charles O'Malley. As by far the best of Desmond's sons, Craganour had the potential to be an influential sire. Desmond was one of the most successful of St Simon's stallion sons and, if the 'sire-of-sires' adage possessed any credence, Craganour would have strengthened the St Simon line recently depleted by the death of Persimmon and Desmond himself.

Craganour would be unable to redeem his reputation on an Argentinian track. Bower Ismay's one stipulation of the sale was that he should not race again. Señor de Hoz gave an immediate interview to *The Sporting Life* explaining all.

It was a very few hours after the Derby was run that I bought Craganour. Mr Ismay decided to sell because he had reached the state of mind when he wanted to rid himself of a tragically unfortunate horse. I sympathise with him in those feelings.

I regard my new horse as the virtual winner of the Derby and the 2000 Guineas. A dual Classic winner even though you will not find it in the records of *Ruff's Guide*. Whatever may be handed down to posterity Craganour will always be regarded as the virtual winner of the first two Classics of the year and there was no question of his superiority to all other horses as a two-year-old. I do not for a moment believe his value could have gone down. You cannot regard him as anything other than a Derby winner and if he had gone on as he could have done and won some of the valuable races in which he was engaged, his price could only have gone higher. I think him a bargain upon which I can congratulate myself. I am only too glad to have him, and I am convinced that he is a cheap horse at the price I paid.

Of course it may be that Craganour will not be the success at the Stud that I confidently anticipate but that is the remotest possible chance. In every respect and particular he is the ideal horse for the Argentine, and his value is enhanced by the fact that he is ideally bred for mating with my mares. From the female side he gets the best racing blood extant, and on his male side it is superfluous to say anything because it is universally acknowledged that St Simon is the best breeding blood in the world. And if there is anything certain in breeding it is that Craganour will demonstrate his worth as a sire and do credit to the strain whence he comes.

In buying Craganour I was influenced by the knowledge of his great adaptability to the country in which he will find his new home. He has such beautiful feet and legs, and a rather light body; he does not carry too much burden on top, and we do not want big horses in the Argentine on account of our virgin soil. In my opinion, big-topped horses would not be of much service to us. The big-bodied horse is not of much use round the bends. I personally believe that horses for the Argentine should not be more than 15.3 hands. Good feet and legs are the first essentials and then comes height. Craganour has all these qualities.

On 11 July one of the unluckiest thoroughbreds in the history of the English Turf was crated aboard a steamer at Southampton bound for Buenos Aires. Acknowledged as the best of his generation at two and three, he had raced ten times and never passed the post worse than second; six victories and three seconds netted £11,565, no mean return on Bower Ismay's outlay of 3,200 guineas even before this £30,000 was added. Yet what could money mean to a man like Bower Ismay who was hardly on the breadline? The glory of two Classics, however, was beyond rubies.

If misfortune had denied him Classic laurels on the racecourse, Craganour was at least destined to stamp his Classic-winning class in the opulent surroundings of Chapadmalal. The residence itself was built in the style of a baronial Norman castle, with interior woodwork and panelling of imported English oak; its grounds held a pheasantry, a kennel of greyhounds, a polo field, golf course, riding school – besides thousands of sheep and cattle fit to grace any English show ring. Craganour's accommodation was equally luxurious and adjacent to a sandy beach so that he might relax in the sea after completing his obligations in the covering shed. Living the life of Riley like this, it was no wonder Craganour fulfilled his legacy as progenitor of the St

Simon line. He became an outstanding sire before dying at the age of twenty, on 21 August 1930, having sired 148 winners of 616 races, some sixty-three of which had come in elite events. His most successful offspring was the colt Buen Ojo, whose eleven successes included two legs of Argentina's Quadruple Crown, the Polla de Potrillos and the Premio Jockey Club, before he, too, became a successful stallion. Craganour's reputation was sealed by San Isidro racecourse naming a race in his honour.

Craganour's death was recorded in *The Bloodstock Breeders' Review* with the award of a six-page obituary in the Stallion section. Suitably entitled 'A Horse with a Chequered History', much of its content dwelt on the fates befalling Craganour at Newmarket and Epsom, with Edward Moorhouse re-asserting his opinion that Craganour had been robbed of one Classic by the judge but rightly denied the second by the Stewards. 'Because of the misfortunes that pursued him when he was a three-year-old,' he commented, somewhat wryly, 'he has always been regarded with a sympathetic interest in this country.'

Aboyeur was rewarded by the *Daily Sketch* with a front-page pictorial spread that showed him spending 'a quiet day at home trying to recover from his astonishment' and by Percy Cunliffe with being put on the market.

Doubtless keen to capitalise on the colt's new-found credibility before it might be exposed, Cunliffe lost no time in touting him for £18,000. It's fair to say he was not knocked over in the rush. Lord Dunraven, for instance, replaced the deceased Desmond at his Fort Union Stud with another, more tractable, son in the shape of Lomond, winner of the Gimcrack and two races at Ascot, rather than invest in the irascible Derby-winning Aboyeur.

Consequently, once his cut leg had healed, the colt was sent to Liverpool on 23 July for the St George Stakes over one mile

and three furlongs, worth £1,716 to the winner. Aboyeur carried
9st 10lb and was made 5/4 favourite to give weight to five rivals
for, however fortuitously the circumstances, he was a Derby
winner and, as *The Times* reported, 'few imagined that he could
be beaten, though a current of opposition was discernible'. He
looked well beforehand and led for a mile before being over-
hauled by Aghdoe (receiving 10lb) who went five lengths clear
of him, with the Jack Robinson-trained Night Hawk (receiving 24lb) beating him three lengths into third. This was not as
bad a performance as it seemed. Aboyeur came out by far the
best at the weights; Aghdoe had once been talked of as a Derby
contender and Night Hawk went on to win the St Leger by
two lengths. Nine days later Aboyeur was asked to carry 10st in
Goodwood's Gordon Stakes and found the concession of 24lb to
Eustace Loder's gelding Augur too demanding by three parts of
a length; the remainder were beaten off by five lengths or more.
This did not stop the press carping that he 'would have won had
he finished with determination'.

Goodwood proved to be Aboyeur's swansong. On 4 September
it was announced he'd been sold through the British Bloodstock
Agency to the Imperial Racing Club of St Petersburg for the
knock-down price of 13,000 guineas. His loss wasn't lamented.
'Aboyeur has an evil temper and a strong grain of cowardice,'
declared *The Times*. 'Vices are also transmitted and on the whole
there is little cause to regret the expatriation of Aboyeur.'

Aboyeur followed in the hoofprints of earlier Derby winners
Galtee More and Minoru, whom the Russians had acquired only
a fortnight earlier. With war and revolution in the air, however,
Tsarist Russia was no place for thoroughbreds and the fates of
Aboyeur and his fellow exiles are shrouded in uncertainty. Legend
has it that during the Revolution the two Derby winners were
harnessed to a cart and taken on a six-month journey of a thousand miles from Moscow to the Black Sea port of Novorossiysk,
only to be evacuated to Constantinople with the aid of the British
Military Mission. The presence of two stallions was corroborated

but their identities were not. Another story, the Cunliffe family version, insisted Aboyeur arrived in Novorossisyk in the midst of the Russian Civil War when it served as the headquarters of the White Russian counter-revolutionary army, and was commandeered by an officer as a cavalry charger – in which case the officer must have earned his pay.

Whatever the exact nature of his fate, Aboyeur returned to the obscurity from which he had emerged. Even the Derby trophy he secured in the Stewards' Room was stolen from Edward Wigan's family home of Conholt Park in January 1988 and was never recovered.

☞

And what of Anmer, the third leading actor in this equine drama?

Emily Davison's nemesis returned to the track on 18 June, just a fortnight to the day after his Epsom mishap, having suffered no lasting ill-effects. As was Anmer's lot, the race selected for him was no minor run-out but the Ascot Derby. He was partnered by Herbert Jones, who was likewise making his comeback. They made no impression behind William Astor's one-time Derby hope Pilliwinkie; nor did they behind Augur and Aboyeur in the Gordon Stakes at Goodwood. After a two-month break, Anmer returned to Newmarket and ran two of his best races. In the Newmarket St Leger he was only beaten by a head and three-quarter length giving weight away; and at the next meeting he failed by just a neck and a head to concede 10lb to Halos and Harry of Hereford in the Royal (Post) Stakes over one-and-a-quarter miles. He finally received an opportunity to gain a victory the end of October when he was dropped into handicap company, but the old Anmer resurfaced and even with only 6st 10lb to carry he failed to distinguish himself in the hands of an apprentice.

Anmer never ran again. In March 1916 the King presented him to Ontario's Department of Agriculture who, in line with

Canadian government policy, was seeking thoroughbred stallions for the purpose of improving the calibre of local draught animals. Anmer took up residence at the farm of former jockey and then director of the Canadian Thoroughbred Horse Society, James Fletcher, in Downsview, and later on at Major Palmer Wright's stud at Chaffey's Locks, near Ottawa. His fee was $10. He proved well worth the money. As a sire of racehorses he was always in the top three and led the Canadian list from 1925 to 1928. The most prolific of his winners was the mare Hoi Poilloi but the most notable was the filly Fairbank. Owned and bred by Fletcher, Fairbank won the important Coronation Stakes as a juvenile in 1924 before adding the following year's King's Plate, Canada's equivalent of the Derby, by a nose. Fletcher soon received a telegram of congratulations from the King but controversy had not finished with Anmer. Fairbank's dam, Rock On, had been bred to both Anmer and another stallion called Sobieski in 1919, and there was some talk that Fairbank was actually a daughter of the latter and not Anmer. Fletcher knew the stock of both sires and had sided with Anmer.

Epsom's innocent party lived on until the early 1930s. One of his progeny, the black gelding Wilfrid G, was still winning steeplechases in 1942.

☛

Aboyeur and Anmer typified the racing fortunes of those veterans of Epsom who resumed their three-year-old careers after the Derby; Craganour was one of three (along with Great Sport and Agadir) who did not. Of the dozen who competed in a total of fifty-three races, six managed a win – Sun Yat won three, Shogun, Nimbus and Prue two apiece and Bachelor's Wedding and Louvois one each – making a grand total of eleven wins from thirty appearances. In addition to Aboyeur and Anmer, the non-winners were Sandburr, Jameson, Aldegond and Day Comet (feeling the effects of his troubled run at Epsom he finished distressed on his only start).

Sun Yat's mid-summer treble included the Sussex Stakes at Goodwood. Louvois's form continued to be in and out. He ran up to his best to win Ascot's Prince of Wales's Stakes in the hands of Saxby and chase home Tracery in the Eclipse before running disappointingly in Liverpool's Atlantic Stakes. Despite a subsequent failure to convert odds-on favouritism into victory in Derby's Breeders St Leger, he was still made favourite to win the genuine article at Doncaster. Another deplorable display saw him a spent force before reaching the straight and he finished tenth of twelve behind Night Hawk – to whom he'd conceded 15lb and beaten three lengths at the Derby. Shogun boasted a perfect two-from-two, winning the Gold Vase at Ascot and the Knowsley Dinner Stakes at Liverpool on 24 July, before leg damage on the gallops brought his season to a premature end. Such is the romance of the Turf that it was the half-bred Shogun who left the most indelible legacy as a stallion. Put to a half-bred mare called Finale, he produced the outstanding filly Verdict whose eight wins included a memorable victory over the French champion Epinard in the 1923 Cambridgeshire and one in the following season's Coronation Cup. In her turn, Verdict produced Quashed, winner of the Oaks, and the Gold Cup in which she defeated the American Triple Crown winner Omaha.

The unluckiest horse in the Derby also received some measure of compensation. Nimbus received none in the French equivalent, finishing fourth. He was made to wait until the autumn, when he collected two valuable prizes in the space of eleven days: the Coupe d'Or worth £2,000 at Maisons Laffitte followed by the vastly more prestigious Prix du Conseil Municipal of £4,674 at Longchamp. The following spring he won in the hands of Johnny Reiff. Nimbus had earned his right to a career at stud, where he bred the Classic-winning colts Keror (Prix Royal Oak) and Le Capucin (Prix du Jockey Club).

Of the 'also-rans,' Bachelor's Wedding reappeared at the Curragh to win the Irish Derby in a canter by one-and-a-half lengths but after finishing third in the Eclipse he trailed in last in the St Leger. The rest of his domestic career added one small contest, but on being exported to India he reasserted his class with two victories in the Viceroy's Cup.

And the villainess of the piece who kept Danny Maher off Craganour's back? After forty-eight hours respite, Prue was hauled out for her authentic 'Derby', the Oaks. She never featured behind Jest, but in receipt of a stone, she readily accounted for the dual Classic winner in the Coronation Stakes at Ascot two weeks later. In her remaining five outings she was burdened by lumps of weight in three valuable handicaps and failing to give 2lb to her old adversary Light Brigade at York. She finished the season by finally winning her Oaks, albeit the Newmarket version rather than the Epsom one that really counted.

# NINETEEN

# All Debts Settled

The fortunes of the human survivors of Epsom's drama were immediately overshadowed by a carnage and desolation beyond anything felt on Derby Day. Even a minor actor in the piece such as Lord Wolverton found himself swept away: obliged to turn down his automatic stint as Senior Steward in 1915 owing to 'military duties', he lost £1,000-worth of possessions in a burglary at his London home and later suffered the indignity of being fined £10 for 'unlawfully using straw as bedding for horses' in contravention of the Hay and Straw Order. After the war he owned a useful animal in The Light Patrol but never owned another as good as Osboch. He died on 3 October 1932. His reluctant Epsom colleague, Lord Rosebery, won more Classics before 'the noble Earl, one of the outstanding figures of the Victorian era, statesman, historian and sportsman', as he was described in *The Bloodstock Breeders' Review*'s lengthy obituary, passed peacefully away at the age of eighty-three in May 1929.

Charles Robinson soldiered on as a judge until he was seventy-three. Embroiled in one controversy too many, at Liverpool in March 1923, he resigned. Members of the Jockey Club passed a resolution expressing regret, adding: 'They further desire to convey their thanks for the loyal and efficient manner in which he has always discharged his duties.' He retired to his home in Reigate where he died on 12 November 1927.

The Confederacy found their bookie-bashing capers curtailed by the restricted ration of war-time racing as Druid's Lodge

was requisitioned by the Army and its gallops used for manoeuvres. The quintet never re-united, though Percy Cunliffe and
Frank Forester enjoyed some success as individual owners.
Cunliffe won the 1924 Oaks with Charlebelle while Forester
stunned both himself and the bookmakers by landing the 1925
Cesarewitch with Light Dragoon, who started unbacked at odds
of 100/1. The Confederates went to their graves rich men, all
bar Holmer Peard millionaires by modern standards – Edward
Wigan was worth close to £7 million. Forester was the last to
go, in September 1942.

However, fate dealt harsh cards to the leading actors from 4
June 1913. Eustace Loder, Jack Robinson, Billy Saxby and Bower
Ismay were dead inside eleven years. Edwin Piper and Herbert
Jones reached old age but both died in sombre circumstances.
Only Johnny Reiff can be said to have enjoyed a long and happy
life but even the American scapegoat eventually sought refuge
in the bottle.

Reiff lost no time in returning to Paris and, while Emily
Davison lay close to death, he won the Prix de Diane aboard
Moia to give himself some Classic compensation, in monetary
terms, for the loss of the Derby. Reiff's last appearance on an
English racecourse came the following June, on Orsonville in
the Gold Cup at Ascot. They finished down the field behind
Aleppo. Within two months Europe was at war; French racing
ceased on 28 July. Reiff signed-off with a 33/1 winner, the two-
year-old colt M. de Camors at Chantilly.

Reiff returned to Maisons Laffitte in 1919. Two years later
there was some talk of him resuming in the saddle (in place
of the suspended Frank O'Neill) as first jockey to American
millionaire A. K. Macomber but nothing came of it. Reiff never
rode again, and when war once again blighted Europe he went
back to America for good, settling in Portland, Oregon. He died

on 4 February 1974 at the age of eighty-nine in Vista, San Diego, California, and lies alongside his wife in Portland's Riverview Cemetery.

John Hackett Reiff recalls his grandfather's latter years:

My wife tells me that he told her that ever since he was seriously injured in a fall and had a metal plate placed in his head, his youthful fearlessness was beginning to wane and he became more fearful of riding by 1914, especially given the fact he was a married man with a young son.

We would visit him around every Christmas time. He was very careful with his finances, having not worked since 1914, and he and my dad spent most of their time together discussing his investments, mostly in the stock market, which my dad managed on his behalf. He maintained a down-to-earth modesty. If my dad bought a nice new convertible family car, he would admonish him with the statement 'Don't act like a big shot!' I was once accused, as a college student, of being a 'playboy' because I drove a sports car, provided by my father, and didn't pay my own way through school by working. The one-bedroomed cottage that he and my grandmother occupied prior to her passing was so small that it was almost ludicrous. I don't believe he ever drove or owned a car.

My father told me that sometime during his adult years, Johnny developed an inordinate fondness for liquor, apparently disrupting his life. His constitution was so strong that, when he decided to quit drinking, he simply did so without, apparently, any professional help. I believe that this is an example of the strength of will and character that had made him so successful as a fierce competitor on the Turf as a young lad.

He didn't seem to follow racing avidly. The only references I recall were his verbal reference to 'Old Banana Nose' Eddie Arcaro, whom he disliked for some unstated reason, and his declared fondness for Willie Shoemaker.

When he was inducted into the American Racing Hall of

Fame in 1956 he didn't attend the ceremony or ever visit the facil-
ity. He just didn't think of himself or his accomplishments as a
'big deal'.

No parallel acclaim has been extended in England to the only
jockey first past the post in three of his only four rides in
the Derby.

☞

Given that 1913 should have encompassed a victory in the 2000
Guineas and conceivably another in the Derby (plus anything
Craganour may have won thereafter) yet disastrously included
neither, Billy Saxby's season still contrived to be one of his most
successful, in quality if not in quantity.

It was also one of perverse twists. At the same time as the
body of his dead father was being discovered in Newmarket he
was handed a gift horse in the form of Prince Palatine. The colt's
intended rider Frank O'Neill stayed in Paris when Radiant was
a late withdrawal from the Derby, and Saxby took the mount
on the St Leger winner in the Coronation Cup. The odds-on
favourite won in 'a common canter' to give him a tenth winner of
the season: 'I take 3/1 the second doesn't get it!' shouted a wag as
Saxby returned to much polite hand-clapping. This triggered a
recovery of sorts – he even picked up a late spare ride in the Oaks
aboard Jones's intended mount. He rode a further twenty-seven
winners which included a treble at Ascot in the Prince of Wales's
Stakes (on Louvois), the Alexandra Plate (Rivoli) and the Gold
Cup aboard Prince Palatine, unquestionably the best horse he
ever rode.

That week at Ascot marked Saxby's curtain call. Prince Palatine's
long-standing foot troubles flared up in the Goodwood Cup
and he struggled home out of the places. The first two restricted
war-ravaged seasons that followed saw Saxby accumulate sixteen
winners before he joined the Royal Field Artillery, and he didn't

resume race-riding until 1919. Two further seasons saw him scrape together just twenty-three successes, riding mainly for the small Royston stable of Roy Pope, and his only re-acquaintance with the Derby was the unplaced mount on the 33/1 shot Attilius in 1920. In March of that year he'd married a local farmer's daughter, Betty Davis. The following season Saxby's name disappeared from the lists. The reason soon became apparent. He'd contracted consumption and succumbed to the disease on 13 March 1922, at the tobacconist shop run by his mother Louisa at 139 Midland Road, Bedford. He was just thirty-five. His body was taken to Newmarket and he was buried beside his father. There were floral tributes from other veterans of the 1913 Derby in Snowy Whalley, Henri Jellis, Elijah Wheatley, Steve Donoghue and Herbert Jones. But there was nothing from Bower Ismay. *The Bloodstock Breeders' Review* didn't consider him worthy of an obituary. He rode 470 winners but would be remembered for the three that he didn't: 2000 Guineas stolen from him by an incompetent judge; a Derby on Signorinetta denied him by the whim of the Chevalier Ginistrelli; and surely another on Craganour, but for the caprice of Bower Ismay.

Herbert Jones belied his accident-prone nature to live until the age of seventy, when he felt compelled to take his own life.

He returned from his Epsom injury to partner Anmer at Ascot but by November had only managed seven wins from just 109 rides. The glory days of Diamond Jubilee, Minoru and Classic victories had become a thing of the past. The Great War saw him capitalise on his ability to drive by serving as a batman and, although his rides continued to dwindle once racing resumed, his reputation usually assured him of a mount in a Classic. Jones kept riding into his forties. His final mount was, aptly enough, on a Royal horse, King George V's Erne at Kempton Park on 16 August 1923. Soon afterwards he collapsed from a pulmonary haemorrhage and was forced to retire, suffering from tuberculosis. The King saw to it that he recuperated in the clear mountain air of Davos in Switzerland; while there, Jones suffered a collapsed lung.

Whether the Davison incident scarred Herbert Jones is debatable. It's said his wife joined Davison's funeral procession but if she did, she was only four at the time! It's also said that Jones sent a wreath to Mrs Pankhurst's funeral, bearing the sentiment 'To the honour of Mrs Pankhurst and Miss Emily Davison'. His suicide, some have maintained, was the result of a life 'haunted by that woman's face' but, if so, Jones took nearly fifty years reaching that conclusion. Like so many stories linked to the 'Suffragette Derby' these are fanciful – as his children attest. His daughter Thelma insists:

> They are all untrue as far as I can say. In many ways, he was a Victorian father, and didn't talk to his children about things like that. By the time I was old enough to talk about such matters with him he was so deaf that I couldn't get through to him. He was unwilling to cope with his deafness. He got very impatient. He refused a hearing aid and wouldn't read anything written down for him – except the football results for his pools coupon! He'd read his books – Wild West stories mainly – and tend his vegetable garden. He loved his pond and its goldfish: the first batch had come from Egerton. He loved his shooting: he had a pair of Purdeys. And he used to drive a three-wheeled Morgan.
>
> But he became very depressed after my mother died. There was a big age difference between them. He was forty-nine and she was only twenty-one when they married in 1930. They met when Doris was a fourteen-year-old housemaid working at the Fenn's house, where father lived, at Egerton. After mother died of peritonitis in 1943, aged thirty-four, he changed completely. Because she was so much younger than him, he never believed she would die before him. He never recovered. There was no medication then: depression wasn't regarded as an illness. Afterwards he often threatened to end it all.

He had a few mementos from his racing career: silver cigarette boxes; a set of Royal colours; a tie pin; a clock decorated with a horse-shoe from Minoru. But he had no money. A pension of £8 came each week from Hampton Court. I believe it came from a lump sum in Trust set up by Edward VII. But it wasn't index linked. It was the same in 1951 as in 1923.

John Jones has no truck with those who think his father was 'haunted' by Davison:

An utter load of rubbish! It's incomprehensible. I never knew my father to be tossing and turning at night, haunted by her face.

It would have been impossible to register the look on someone's face who'd suddenly rushed out when he was galloping down to Tattenham Corner at that speed. How anyone can think he might have seen her face is hilarious.

On 17 July 1951 Herbert Jones was found by John in the gas-filled kitchen of his home in Woodlands Park, Girton, near Cambridge. He lay on the floor, fully clothed and with an overcoat over him; in his hand he held a piece of flexible gas tubing connected to the gas copper. An inquest was held the following evening at which the coroner recorded a verdict of 'Suicide while the balance of the mind was disturbed.' Jones left a note which, the coroner added, made it 'abundantly clear that ill-health was behind it all'. Aside from his deafness, he'd suffered two recent strokes.

The *Newmarket Journal* recorded his passing under the headline JOCKEY, GENTLEMAN AND CHRISTIAN.

He will be remembered in Newmarket as the man who was always ready to help a friend, a man who could not refuse a request for aid. As jockey to two Kings, he might well have broadened his sphere of social life, and in the process forgot those who had been his friends. That was not in his make-up.

To the time he retired he was a sociable, likeable and completely modest person. His greatest thrill was to make other people happy. He helped the old folks when the seaside holidays came round and November 5th was an occasion for the children at Egerton, as he purchased large quantities of fireworks and personally set them off. He founded the Egerton Amateurs football team and also fostered cricket.

He never let racing interfere with his attendance at church and was known to dash from Manchester on a Sunday so as to sing in the choir at the private chapel on the Egerton estate.

Jones lies next to his wife in an unmarked grave behind Girton church.

☞

Edwin Piper followed Jones to the grave three months later in equally sad circumstances.

He had added another Derby – the Scottish version at Ayr on Pochard – to finish the 1913 season with forty-nine winners, but his career was another that stalled and nosedived thanks to the outbreak of hostilities. After completing war service at a Remounts depot in Redhill, he returned to race-riding in 1919 and carried on into his late thirties, scratching out an odd winner here and there, until the degrading return of just a dozen unplaced rides in the spring and summer of 1925 prompted him to quit with three months of the season remaining. His career haul numbered barely 300 winners. But no one could take away from him that one glorious afternoon in the Epsom spotlight. Piper's sixth and final ride in the Derby was on Silvanus in 1922, the colt's odds of 66/1 reflecting his jockey's standing in the sport just as those of his precursors had: 300/1 100/1; 66/1; 50/1 and 40/1.

Piper had met and married the daughter of a prosperous hotelier while serving in Redhill and they'd built a house in Epsom's Longdown Lane, which he named in honour of his

Derby partner. His own name, however, was that of one Derby-winning jockey destined to be largely forgotten and he ended his days in Epsom's psychiatric hospital, St Ebba's. Toward the end of his riding career he'd suffered a head injury in a fall and this triggered periodic bouts of depression. His nephews Cyril and Roy Piper visited 'Aboyeur' on a regular basis as boys in the 1930s. 'He was often in a world of his own,' recalls Cyril. 'Away with the fairies. I'm sure it was due to the head injury.'

Roy Piper's recollections paint a picture of a man whose final twenty years lacked real purpose:

> I don't think he ever did anything after he stopped riding. Thanks to his wife's money, they were never short. He'd given our father, Arthur, his youngest brother, who also became a jockey, a bunga-low in Epsom as a wedding present – then charged us rent! That was probably his wife's doing. She had the money, and perhaps she kept a firm hand on the finances owing to his problem.
>
> Cyril and me used to go over once a month to pay the rent money. In the summer we might cut his grass. He was pleasant enough but Aunt Nellie was a bit bossy. He was always doing the washing-up! And we were only ever allowed in the kitchen, never the living room!

In April 1951 Piper was admitted to St Ebba's as a voluntary patient suffering from depression; discharged after two months, he was re-admitted on 12 October and died of suppurative bron-cho pneumonia four days later, aged sixty-three. His ashes were buried in Epsom cemetery.

In a final irony, the local paper got his name wrong in its obituary, calling him 'William Piper'.

☛

Any discomfort felt by Eustace Loder in the weeks immediately after the 1913 Derby wasn't assuaged in the last fourteen months of his life. Both his health and the Prior litigation went from bad to worse.

Bright's Disease had taken such a grip on Loder by the opening of 1914 that on 14 February he felt obliged to inform Frederick Lambton he must resign his position as a Steward of the Jockey Club, thereby passing up his accession to the post of Senior Steward. Loder's decision was officially announced at the Jockey Club meeting held during Craven week at Newmarket in April. The Club's minutes record: 'Lord Coventry moved, and Lord Harewood seconded, a vote of thanks to Major Loder for his services, and expressed their deep regret at his illness.'

Loder's dispute with Prior reached court on 11 May before Mr Justice Ridley and a special jury. Each side had hired a team of legal heavyweights. Frederick Edwin Smith KC, later ennobled as the 1st Earl Birkenhead, led for Prior. Smith was a Conservative MP and great friend of Winston Churchill who referred to him as possessing 'all the canine virtues in a remarkable degree'. He was also renowned as a wag. A judge once asked his advice on sentencing a sodomy case. 'What do you think one ought to give a man who allows himself to be buggered?' asked the judge. Without hesitation Smith replied: 'Oh, thirty shillings or £2, whatever you happen to have on you.' Facing Smith across the courtroom in what amounted to an Anglo-Irish legal duel was another MP in James Campbell KC (later to become Lord Glenavy), the only Irish barrister who stood comparison with Sir Edward Carson. Campbell had served as both Solicitor-General and Attorney-General for Ireland.

Loder was too ill to travel to London and had already given his evidence on commission at the Shelbourne Hotel in Dublin. 'The worry of this lawsuit, without doubt,' wrote Noble Johnson, 'augmented his illness and hastened his death.' Following Smith's opening address setting out the basis for his client's claim for £20,000 compensation, Prior entered the witness box to give his account of Loder's 'negligence in sending him a mare with contagious influenza'. The second day started dramatically. Smith and Campbell immediately consulted and it was announced that a settlement had been agreed. Johnson, waiting to give his own evidence, wanted to fight the case – 'knowing we were absolutely guiltless' – but obeyed Loder's instructions to comply with any advice Campbell offered.

Smith rose to say that the 'matters in dispute had been adjusted' and that, as far as the allegations concerning the conduct of Loder and Noble Johnson was concerned, 'it was a condition of the settlement that every imputation be unreservedly withdrawn'. He admitted the plaintiff's case would be difficult for him to establish in light of the 'imperfect scientific knowledge with reference to the particular ailment' and the need to show that the defendant 'knew or suspected, or ought to have known or suspected, that the mare Auspicious was infected or might be infected'. Although there was no legal liability against the defendant, Smith told the Court that Major Loder had made 'a generous contribution to the plaintiff to compensate him for the very serious loss which he had suffered'. Each party was to pay its own costs. Though it was not made public, Loder had agreed to pay Prior £8,000.

Campbell then made the following statement:

Major Loder was for many years a very prominent gentleman on the Turf, and one who until lately, when his health compelled him to resign that position, filled the very highest position in official life on the Turf, that of Steward of the Jockey Club, a position which he never could have attained had he not been a gentleman of irreproachable personal honour and integrity. And having regard also to the fact that during all the years in which Major Loder has been engaged in racing matters there never has been even the slightest breath of a suspicion or suggestion against the management or conduct either by himself or Mr Noble Johnson of his stud or of his horses, in that view it was perfectly plain that so long as this case took the form of suggesting that Major Loder or Mr Noble Johnson had been guilty of concealing something which it was their duty to reveal, Major Loder had made up his mind and was determined under no circumstances could he consider the suggestion of a settlement at all.

But in the meantime, Major Loder had the advantage of being examined by anticipation in this action about a week ago in Ireland, stating in the clearest and most emphatic way upon oath that never from first to last had he the slightest idea or suspicion that Auspicious was in any way infected.

Therefore, having thoroughly vindicated his own personal honour and character, and that of Mr Noble Johnson, he did feel considerable sympathy for Mr Prior, who, through no fault of his own, had suffered such a material loss in connection with his Stud, and that it would not be unreasonable for him, or at least it would be a generous action on the part of Major Loder if he were to bear a portion of that loss.

Having completely exonerated Major Loder and Mr Noble Johnson from the slightest imputation of impropriety of any sort or kind, the case I respectfully suggest to your lordship has been settled upon terms that will meet with your lordship's approval.

Thus was settled a dispute that a century earlier would have prompted Eustace Loder to send his second to Prior with an invitation to meet him at dawn on Hampstead Heath to settle the matter with pistols. At this distance of time, his gesture of compensation seems excessively generous, possibly as if under-written by a smidgeon of guilt; a kinder view might suggest Loder's illness had robbed him of the will to fight.

Eustace Loder left the Shelbourne Hotel for Eyrefield to meet his death with characteristic military phlegm. The last of his 118 English winners on the Flat came via Glass and China at Wolverhampton over the Whitsun holiday, but it was a glimpse of his greatest winner that he took with him to the grave. Having rallied, as if by some alchemy during Derby week, he requested Pretty Polly be brought round onto the lawn in front of his bedroom and her head be put through the open window so that he might admire her one last time as he lay dying.

He died at 10.30 in the morning of Monday 27 July. He was only forty-seven years of age. His coffin was conveyed to England for interment in the family vault in Slaugham churchyard, Sussex, where he was laid to rest beside his elder brother Wilfred. The list of mourners included numerous members of the aristocracy in addition to old comrades from the 12th Lancers. Loder's abstemious lifestyle had made him a very rich man, enabling him to leave a personal estate valued at £295,938 (in excess of £13 million). After the deduction of a number of financial bequests to his family, former Regiment and staff at Eyrefield and Old Connell (Noble Johnson received a life annuity of £500), the residue of his property, including the two studs, passed to his nephew Giles Loder, Wilfred's eldest son. Eyrefield continued Eustace Loder's remit to breed Classic winners in Ireland and England; and in 1920 the ghost of Craganour was exorcised when Spion Kop, a son of Spearmint and Hammerkop, won the Derby.

Loder's death was marked by a two-column obituary in *The Sporting Life* in keeping with his status. It confined itself in the main to cataloguing Loder's successes on the Turf as a breeder and owner, and concluded with the sentiment: 'So a somewhat short but nevertheless glorious military, social and sporting career ended.' His obituary in *The Bloodstock Breeders' Review* befitted the owner/breeder of the 'Peerless' Pretty Polly and the owner of an outstanding Derby winner in Spearmint. It ran to six-and-a-half pages. Most of them were devoted to the exploits of Pretty Polly and Spearmint and their kind. But, as he would do on the death of Craganour and Bower Ismay, Edward Moorhouse seized the opportunity to re-state Loder's case for Craganour's disqualification at Epsom:

It was his absolute conviction that the course which he and his co-Stewards took in depriving Craganour of his honours was not only justified but the only possible one in the circumstances. He used particularly scornful language when he referred to the suggestion, made in certain quarters, that the Stewards might have refrained from taking action seeing that it was the Derby.

'If,' he said, 'I am entrusted with the difficult task of administering the Rules of Racing, I shall apply them without fear or favour, whether the race is the Derby or a paltry selling event.'

Moorhouse's opening is also worth quoting in full:

> As a sportsman, Major Loder was known by name at least, to the world at large and was greatly honoured and respected. As a man he was known to very few. The few held it a privilege to regard him and to be regarded by him, as a friend. His every thought and action was inspired by kindness and charity.
>
> But this lovable trait in his character was, as a rule, screened by an unconquerable timidity, and a reserve of manner apt to be misunderstood. His heart was not worn on his sleeve. The friendships he formed were mostly of slow growth, but once they had matured a severance was to him unthinkable. At all times, his word was his bond.
>
> Major Loder's shyness must often have been rather painful and embarrassing to him. It prevented him doing many things which inclination prompted. Those who moved within his immediate circle are aware that owing to this curious little idiosyncrasy he often refrained from inviting to stay with him people whom he would have been delighted to entertain. And yet, if by chance, these same people suggested that they should pay him a visit he at once, and gladly, agreed to the proposal, and was grateful for their society. Though not one who shone as a conversationalist or raconteur, he thoroughly enjoyed a good story. He was an excellent companion and a generous host.
>
> His opinion was always worth having, because it was formed only after he had regarded the matter under consideration from

every point of view. This habit accounted for the soundness of his judgment. To all appearance he was a somewhat unemotional man; there is, however, little doubt that he frequently suffered from suppressed excitement when a casual observer would suppose he was not in the least affected.

As one of his closest friends puts it, 'through and through, he was a white man, and his like are very few and far between'.

It's hard not to think that Moorhouse, subconsciously or not, is attempting to prove the old adage stating no man is completely as he seems. Yet, however much one admires Moorhouse's pen gliding over Loder's faults and smoothing the rough edges of his public persona, one is still left with a portrait of a 'cold fish', a lonely man who, if he took an ardent dislike to you, would have no compunction in seizing every opportunity to ram home the point.

☞

Whether or not Eustace Loder destroyed Bower Ismay is highly contentious, but his actions at Epsom went some way to destroying Jack Robinson.

According to Meyrick Good,

Robinson seemed to lose much of his interest in the sport after Craganour's disqualification. There are two things I will never forget: the elation on his face when Craganour was led into the winner's enclosure, and the utter dejection which took its place when, after the horse had actually been led out of the 'pen', an official arrived shouting 'Take him back!' When the news of the disqualification arrived Robinson seemed dazed ... hardly able to grasp the catastrophe which had befallen him. The Stewards' verdict was a terrible blow to him and he never recovered from the bitter disappointment of seeing his horse first past the post and then deprived of the fruits of victory.

Robinson had lost his star three-year-old but he still managed to win the season's final Classic with the maiden Night Hawk on behalf of Colonel Hall Walker at odds of 50/1. There have only been three longer-priced St Leger winners than Night Hawk (all in the nineteenth century), who failed to win another race. Robinson won twenty-three races for £16,993. Had he gained those two Classic wins at Newmarket and Epsom with Craganour he would have been leading trainer instead of finishing fifth behind Richard Wootton. He enjoyed another decent season in 1914, winning the New Stakes and the Dewhurst with Let Fly for Hall Walker. The following season he sent out Hare Hill to win the Chester Cup for Bower Ismay, but thereafter his fortunes waned. Then, ironically, he, too, became a victim of Bright's Disease. After spending much of the winter of 1917–18 in a London nursing home, he returned to Foxhill and was superintending operations in the hay-field on 1 July when the exertions taxed his depleted strength and he succumbed to heart failure. The trainer of over 600 winners was just fifty years of age.

His obituary in *The Bloodstock Breeders' Review* inevitably referred to his 'atrocious luck' with Craganour, 'the deprivation of Derby honours was a mortifying experience'. Robinson, of course, felt aggrieved, continued Moorhouse, 'but he took the blow like a man'.

☞

Contrary to some accounts, Bower Ismay didn't abandon racing in the wake of his disappointments of 1913. If anything he re-doubled his efforts to leave his mark on the Turf.

He returned to Doncaster for the yearling sales of 1913 and once more spent thousands. His targets were, yet again, the lots consigned from Sledmere and he paid an aggregate of 9,350 guineas for three of the choicest, going to 5,600 guineas for a son of St Frusquin. The one colt he avoided was Craganour's half-brother (by Symington), who went to Sir William Nelson for the week's second-best price of 6,000 guineas; just as well for Ismay because he developed a wind infirmity and never made the racecourse.

Those three colts were the only yearlings Ismay purchased at public auction in 1913, but privately he was also actively seeking to replenish his stock and in the early autumn he acquired the promising Irish stayer Hare Hill following the colt's victory in a King's Plate at the Curragh, his second win in three starts as a three-year-old. While Ismay's season would have prospered immeasurably from the stakes denied Craganour, he still finished the year with fourteen winners of £7,804 (with the benefit of £13,300 from the Guineas and Derby he would have finished third in the owners list). Balscadden did him proud by winning the Newbury Autumn Cup under Danny Maher and the juveniles Elgon and Radway contributed six and four victories respectively.

Ismay lacked a genuine Classic contender in 1914 and the potentially top-flight Hare Hill flattered to deceive, winning one decent handicap at Liverpool yet showing none of the ability necessary to hold his own in the Chester, Manchester and Derby Cups; Ismay's nine victories rewarded him with less than £3,000. Balscadden, on the other hand, was his dependable self, boosting his reputation with a win over fences in the Prix des Drags before bruising a foot after his prep race for the Grand Steeplechase de Paris that reduced him to a fast-finishing fourth on the day. Balscadden had more victories in him, although he never realised Ismay's dream of winning the Grand National. It was another case of what-might-have-been, because, after falling on the first circuit in the 1915 race, Balscadden was remounted and was finishing with greater gusto than any other horse. Bearing in mind Ismay's second string Jacobus was only beaten two lengths into second place by Ally Sloper, the performance of Balscadden was all the more agonising. 'As Balscadden was supposed to be very much better than Jacobus it was protested that only bad luck prevented his victory,' commented *The Times*. This most genuine and versatile of servants – he'd won fourteen races on the Flat, over hurdles and fences at distances from one mile to three-and-a-half miles – was rewarded with a place at the Broome Stud, near Swindon.

That same season of 1915 saw Hare Hill justify his purchase by winning the Chester Cup and Salisbury Cup. The former success – complete with its 'Champion Cheshire Cheese' – at the nearest track to his family home at Dawpool at least achieved one of Ismay's racing ambitions, but he was not present to see it. Ismay's year was earmarked for sterner campaigns than any racecourse might possibly offer. On the declaration of war Ismay had immediately sought action. Within weeks he held two commissions, one as a 2nd Lieutenant with the Earl of Chester's Territorials and another as a 'temporary 2nd Lieutenant' – a rank usually associated with pre-war part-time soldiers or ones in poor health – in the 12th Lancers. Ismay's attachment to the Chesters was cancelled on 9 October when he knew who would see action first: he went to France with the Lancers.

Serving with Eustace Loder's own beloved regiment may have been a poke in the eye for his former nemesis. Ismay wasn't a man believed to hold grudges but if his choice was so influenced one can hardly blame him. Leaving Constance, as the *Northampton Independent* declared, 'cheerfully undertaking the most menial tasks in YMCA canteens and hostels', he eventually joined up with the twenty-five officers, 523 men and 608 horses of the Lancers on 15 March 1915 at Merville on the River Lys, prior to deployment on mounted and trench duties. The Lancers were generally occupied in shepherding columns of ammunition and rations rather than conducting direct assaults and they were under constant threat from enemy snipers. The monotony was lifted by boxing tournaments, sports days and the novelty of an afternoon's boar hunting. In September 1916 the regiment moved south toward the Somme and Ismay found himself at Morlancourt, north-east of Amiens; shortly afterwards he fell seriously ill and was repatriated. It seems as if foreign climes of any description exposed some fragility in his constitution. Once recovered, on

26 November, he was gazetted First Assistant Superintendent in the Remounts with the rank of Temporary Captain and based at Ormskirk; subsequently promoted to Superintendent on 17 February 1918, he didn't relinquish the post until 8 March 1919. In the King's Birthday Honours list of 3 June he received an OBE (Military Division) for 'valuable services in connection with the War', and his temporary rank was later made permanent.

Ismay's war ended, however, with his personal life in some disarray. On 24 February 1917 a terrible fire (a housemaid left an iron burning) gutted Haselbech causing damage estimated at £20,000. Coincidently, a fire had also destroyed the Loder's Maidwell Hall a year or two earlier. Ismay rebuilt Haselbech more easily than he could mend his marriage, which, according to Michael Manser, 'was in trouble, whether because of Maggie Loder or someone, or something, else I cannot say'.

Nevertheless, there was still hunting and racing to be enjoyed. Winners had come in dribs and drabs after the war but this didn't stop Ismay from continuing to invest. In 1923 he came away from one day at the Newmarket July Sales having spent 2,760 guineas on four yearlings and he wound up the season with a highly respectable score of thirteen winners of £8,018 for eighteenth place in the owners' list that harked back to his pre-war days. His jumpers were now spread between Aubrey Hastings, Frank Hartigan and Tom Coulthwaite. The Flat animals were in the care of Atty Persse at Stockbridge and Fred Darling at Beckhampton. While it was true his horses had fallen short of the standards of old – no Derby runners, for instance, and only a single Grand National competitor in Garryvoe, who failed to get round in 1921 – there was much for him to anticipate in 1924.

Thus, as he settled down in a first-class compartment of the train from Kettering to St Pancras that would deliver him to a meeting of the T. H. Ismay Trust Fund in London on Friday 8 February 1924, Bower's thoughts would have strayed toward the forthcoming Flat season with a mixture of enthusiasm and optimism. In Heverswood and Beresford he had two excellent three-year-old prospects in training with Fred Darling. The two colts had won five races apiece as juveniles to earn weights of 8st 8lb and 8st 5lb (fifth and eighth place respectively) in the Free Handicap behind Mumtaz Mahal. Heverswood had no Classic engagements, but Beresford held a Derby entry and although his juvenile record wasn't nearly so impressive as Craganour's had been in 1912, some slim hopes of Derby compensation might be entertained. Who knows, the filly Hasty Catch, a winner three times, might even come to justify her nominations for the 1000 Guineas and Oaks. And he had that batch of promising youngsters laden with fancy entries. Perhaps one of those would eventually win the race he had been so cruelly denied in 1913.

Ismay's train journey may have been blighted by a headache. He'd recently come a nasty cropper out hunting; certainly he'd not been feeling himself of late, complaining of tiredness.

Any final thoughts were never communicated. He didn't arrive at the meeting. Bruce Ismay, growing increasingly agitated by his brother's tardiness, left the meeting to telephone St Pancras and was informed that a man found unconscious on the Kettering train had been rushed to the Royal Free Hospital in Gray's Inn Road.

Ismay had suffered a cerebral haemorrhage and was subsequently diagnosed as suffering from sleepy sickness. Not to be confused with the tropical disease of sleeping sickness (a parasitic disease conveyed by the tsetse fly), which Ismay might conceivably have contracted while in East Africa on safari, sleepy sickness is a viral disease affecting the upper layer of the brain. It tended to appear periodically in the form of an epidemic, especially in the spring. The onset of headaches and a sore throat prefaced a deep slumber, leaving victims lying like logs. Temporary consciousness might ensue but one out of every two cases proved fatal; some 1,470 cases were recorded during a 1921 outbreak. By 1924 the number of cases had doubled, leading *The Times* to state: 'Experts of the Ministry of Health and Medical Research are trying vainly to find some means of combating the mystery disease which is spreading at an alarming rate.'

Ismay briefly recovered consciousness on the Saturday and was removed to a London nursing home until being conveyed to Haselbech just before Easter. Expert medical advice was sought but despite frequent attendance by four London specialists (running up bills approaching four figures) his decline proved irrevocable. After a long period of unconsciousness he died at midday on Sunday 25 May surrounded by his wife, brothers and two of his sisters.

Ismay was no pauper but his estate appeared measly in comparison to Eustace Loder's. His personal estate of £106,053 (over £3 million) passed to Constance; a trust fund for his daughter had been set up from income derived from his father's Will. A few minor bequests were made – paintings to each of his brothers; £200 to his butler and £100 to his gardener – but there was no memento for Maggie Loder. Nor was she listed among the mourners at Ismay's funeral on 28 May or those who sent floral tributes – which did include wreaths from the officers and NCOs of the 12th Lancers. Ismay's ashes (unusually for cremated remains in a full-sized coffin rather than a casket) were interred beneath a grand oblong tomb of white marble beside the tower of Haselbech's parish church of St Michael. On its four sides were carved respectively game (lions and gazelles), greyhounds coursing hares, horses and hounds chasing foxes. Inside the church, the wall of its south aisle carries a painted tablet commemorating him.

Most of Ismay's racehorses went under the hammer on 15 July (his widow retained the juvenile Loddington who won two races for her), over half the £8,799 realised deriving from the sale of Heverswood, Ismay's final winner at Kempton Park, a week before his death. The colt went some way to fulfilling his juvenile promise by winning the Portland Handicap at the St Leger meeting in the colours of Sir Lewis Richardson under the then record weight for a three-year-old of 8st 12lb. While Ismay lay unconscious, his own silks were carried one final time around Aintree in the hope of achieving that Grand National victory, but the 60/1 shot Newlands ran as his odds suggested.

Ismay's passing drew mixed notices. In the *Liverpool Courier* he was once more described as a man whose 'unassuming personality gained him a wide circle of friends'. The *Northampton Independent* expressed 'profound shock' at his death before peddling the old myth that he was 'one of the survivors of the *Titanic* disaster'. It continued in sober vein:

> There is a touching and tragic pathos over the end of this gallant sportsman. He had everything that would seem to make life worth living, a beautiful home and wealth with which he loved to make his poorer neighbours happy, and a zest in life for indulging in his favourite pastimes of racing, hunting, shooting and fishing. He was a man who had won much popularity in town and county largely by reason of his ready sympathy and assistance to all good causes.

Aside from those carried by the newspapers of his home town and his adopted county, however, other obituaries made little or no reference to Ismay's personality whatsoever, preferring to dwell on the career of Craganour and the sensational outcome of the 1913 Derby. His 'Memorative Biography' in *The Bloodstock Breeders' Review* merited just two pages compared to Eustace Loder's six-and-a-half; that in *The Sporting Life* three inches compared to Loder's thirty. This balance can't be disputed on Turf criteria. Yet the *Life*'s heading 'Sensational Derby of 1913 Recalled' (not to mention its inaccurate sub-heading 'Death of Well Known Shipping Magnate') and three-quarters of Edward Moorhouse's space being devoted to the circumstances of Craganour's disqualification were tell-tale. Moorhouse concluded by reiterating his belief that his friend Loder had been correct to take 'the initiative' he had chosen which 'incurred the wrath of a whole host of people who considered his action monstrous and without justification'; and he related once more how Loder had referred 'somewhat bitterly to his critics'.

Even in death Eustace Loder had the last laugh.

# APPENDICES

# Appendix 1: Race Details

**Wednesday, 4 June 1913 at 3.00 (Off 3.01) Going Fair**

134th Renewal of the Derby Stakes of 6500 sov., by subscription of 50 sov. each, h. ft., or 5 sov. only if declared by the last Tuesday in March 1912, for entire colts and fillies foaled in 1910; colts, 9st, and fillies, 8st 9lb; the nominator of the winner to receive 500 sov. out of the race; if sufficient surplus be not obtained from subscriptions to give the second at least 400 sov., and the third at least 200 sov., the difference to be made up by the Race-fund; about one mile and a half (344 entries, forfeit declared for 120). Closed July 18th 1911. £6450 to the winner.

| Horse/Draw | Trainer | Jockey |
|---|---|---|
| 1. ABOYEUR (3) b.c. Desmond-Pawky | T Lewis | E Piper |
| Mr AP Cunliffe (white, black seams/cap) bl | | |
| 2. LOUVOIS (2) b.c. Isinglass-St Louvaine | D Waugh | W Saxby |
| Mr W Raphael (dark blue, scarlet hooped sleeves/cap) | | |
| 3. GREAT SPORT (6) b.c. Gallinule-Gondolette | J Smith | G Stern |
| Mr W Hall Walker (blue and white check, cerise cap) | | |
| 4. NIMBUS (4) ch.c. Elf-Nephte | G Cunnington | M Henry |
| M Alexandre Aumont (white, green cap) | | |
| 5. DAY COMET (9) ch.c. St Frusquin-Catgut | J Watson | A Whalley |
| Mr L de Rothschild (dark blue, yellow cap) | | |
| 6. SHOGUN (11) ch.c. Santoi-Kendal Belle | R Wootton | F Wootton |
| Mr E Hulton (pale blue/orange hoops, orange sleeves/cap) | | |
| 7. SUN YAT (12) ch.c. Sundridge-Angelic | C Morton | W Huxley |
| Mr JB Joel (black, scarlet cap) | | |
| 8. BACHELOR'S WEDDING (10) ch.c. Trendennis-Lady Bawn | HS Persse | S Donoghue |
| Sir W Nelson (white, red, white and blue sash, scarlet cap) | | |
| 9. ALDEGOND (15) b.c. Eager-St Aldegonde | JM Bell | G Bellhouse |
| Mr P Broome (salmon/olive green halves, white cap) | | |
| 10. PRUE (5) ch.f. Cicero-Prune | F Pratt | D Maher |
| Lord Rosebery (primrose/rose hoops, rose cap) | | |
| 11. AGADIR (1) br.c. Aquascutum-Poppits | E Martin | W Earl |
| Mr R Bunsow (blue, scarlet belt, gold cap) bl | | |
| 12. JAMESON (8) ch.c. King James-Alexandra | S Pickering | E Wheatley |
| Sir J Willoughby (white, yellow cuffs/cap) | | |

13. SANDBURR (13) b.c. Sandringham-Marshmallow          E Craven       H Jelliss
Mrs G Foster-Rawlins (maroon, primrose belt/cap)
Fell: ANMER (14) b.c. Florizel II-Guinea Hen            R Marsh        H Jones
His Majesty (purple, gold braid, scarlet sleeves, black cap)
Disq: CRAGANOUR (7) b.c. Desmond-Veneration II     WT Robinson  J Reiff
Mr CB Ismay (Neapolitan violet/primrose hoops, violet cap)

BETTING: 6/4 Craganour; 6/1 Shogun; 10/1 Louvois and Nimbus; 100/9 Day Comet; 100/7
Prue; 20/1 Great Sport; 25/1 Aldegond; 33/1 Bachelor's Wedding and Sun Yat; 50/1 Anmer; 100/1
Aboyeur, Agadir, Jameson and Sandburr. TIME: 2 mins 37.60 secs.

OFFICIAL DISTANCES PASSING THE POST: head; neck; head

# Appendix 2: Davison's 'Intimate Companion'

The prominence of Davison's 'intimate companion' Miss Morrison at her funeral has always sparked intense speculation. Who was she exactly? And what exactly was the nature of their relationship? Anything that possibly adds to history's understanding of Emily Davison, and the actions she took on Derby Day 1913, merits perusal and it would be remiss not to examine the facts as they are known.

Davison's lack of male companionship has been attributed by those colleagues who subsequently went into print to her all-consuming commitment to teaching, good works and the pursuit of suffrage. There's no mention of possible loathing, distrust or disgust for the male of the species – the charge often levelled at the suffragettes by their most misogynistic critics. As a role model for the male sex, her father had set the bar rather low, not only by obliging her to forfeit her college place and her mother to sell the family home but also by siring an illegitimate child. Davison often made plain her disgust at the manner in which women were degraded, professionally and personally.

If Davison did enjoy the pleasures of the flesh, the experience was likely to have been with a woman. The 1911 census lists her as 'boarder' with Charlotte Bateman, a fifty-year-old widow, at 31 Coram Street in Bloomsbury which she'd given as her London address for at least six months. At the time of her death she'd moved in with Alice Green and daughter at 133 Clapham Road. There's no evidence to suggest either relationship was anything other than domestic. And although her circle of women friends is frequently listed, it's seldom scrutinised for any relationship hinting at the sexual. Her closest friends were Eleanor Penn Gaskell, Rose Lamartine Yates (with whom she'd attended Royal Holloway) and Mary Leigh (with whom she'd shared gaol time in Holloway). All had married.

Leigh, however, had long since separated from her husband: she was born 'Mary Brown', the name Davison gave when arrested in Aberdeen. Also a teacher – and known as 'The Bandleader' owing to her role as drum major in the WSPU band – she was a dozen years younger than Davison, a working class girl from Manchester who'd married a local builder. She was mousy and soft-featured to look at, but chiselled from the same granite as Davison. Hers was the first hand to hurl a stone ('It'll be a bomb next time!'); hers the first body to be force-fed. 'She was notable among us for her great courage,' said Pethick-Lawrence. 'Her calm and quiet demeanour seemed to add to her moral strength. She was adamant in her resistance to injustice.' Like her friend, Leigh saw things in black and white, putting principles above WSPU internal politics and never afraid to act on them without informing the leadership. Her moral strength was matched by a physical courage belying her slightness (she was never averse to chasing hecklers) and earned her more prison time than Davison; she'd spent over six months of the previous year behind bars on three separate counts. Her standing in the movement was franked by her becoming one of the select few to adorn official WSPU postcards. In short, she was the kind of woman that Emily Davison wished herself to be.

Davison's intense feelings for Leigh are broadcast in the present she sent her in December 1912 (it has been suggested that this gift was never sent because it later appeared in the papers and possession of Rose Lamartine Yates). The gift was a small green book, a collection of poems by the American Walt

Whitman in the series *Pearls from the Poets*. On the title page
she underlined in black ink the words 'the institution of the
dear love of comrades' and added, in her distinctive large and
bold handwriting, 'from Comrade Davison to Comrade Leigh'.
Throughout the volume evocative phrases and couplets are likewise marked: 'None have understood you, but I understood you /
I only find no imperfection in you / There is no virtue, no beauty,
in man / Or woman, but as good as you / Dear friend, take this
kiss / I give it especially to you – do not forget me.' This speaks of
an affection greater than the platonic. Yet it wasn't Mary Leigh
who sat in the chief mourners' carriage in the funeral cortege
through Morpeth, alongside Emily Davison's mother Margaret
and sister Letitia, and was publicly acknowledged in the *Morpeth
Herald* as her 'intimate companion'; this was a 'Miss Morrison'.
And resting beside Davison's coffin was an open book carved
from marble, destined for the graveside, on which was written: 'A
veritable princess of spirituality. From a loving Aberdeen friend.'

The likeliest candidate for the book's donor is Katherine
Riddell, a prominent Aberdonian suffragette whose letters to
Davison reek of affection – which would explain how the tribute was commissioned and delivered so promptly: she simply
brought it with her to the funeral. Yet the same might be said if
'Miss Morrison' and the 'loving Aberdeen friend' were one and
the same.

'Miss Morrison' had been on close terms with Davison for
at least three years, because an unposted letter of 27 June 1910
written by Davison's cousin Isabella Bell includes: 'Do you
ever attend the suffragette meetings? Have you noticed Emily
Davison's name flourishing amongst them? We are expecting she
will be through here for her holidays soon with Miss Morrison.'
The Morrison family is certainly known to all the Davisons
because Letitia refers to them in a letter to her sister of early 1913.

The identity of 'Miss Morrison' has never been established
satisfactorily. The lady might be Edith Morrison, a clergyman's
daughter from Ulster, recently a student at Aberdeen University

and Vice President of the Women's Suffrage Association in Aberdeen. Described as slight, shortish and in her late twenties, Morrison was said not to suffer silliness or romanticism. It's no stretch of the imagination to envisage the junior intellectual in thrall to the senior. Morrison died an 81-year-old spinster in 1964.

A genuine soul-mate for Davison would have been 'Margaret Morrison'. This was one of the aliases used by the Scottish suffragette, Ethel Moorhead, the first suffragette to be forcibly fed in Scotland. Suffragettes frequently gave false names to protect their families. There is no question Moorhead and Davison were acquainted. Moorhead had recently spent time in Aberdeen's Craiginches prison with Davison following the 'Lloyd George' incident; Moorhead had thrown a stone at the Chancellor's car. And it was Moorhead who lent Davison the train fare from Edinburgh to Aberdeen.

Three years younger than Davison, Ethel Moorhead was an acclaimed artist who'd flung herself into the suffragette movement with the same headstrong indomitability as her English alter ego: window-breaking, egg-throwing, tax-dodging and assaulting male foes. Two months after her imprisonment with Davison she was arrested as 'Margaret Morrison' for throwing cayenne pepper into the eyes of a constable; while on remand she flooded the lavatories by running the taps and threw a bucket of water over the warder who came to restrain her. The prison governor called her 'insolent and defiant'; the medical officer described her as 'a weak minded person of defective self-control'.

Moorhead enjoyed a long relationship with the suffragette Frances Parker and, in her own words, 'we suffragettes snatched friendships as they rushed past on mad quests'. Like Davison's, her kudos was entirely self-generated; she was a self-made heroine of the rank and file. Like Davison in England, she held no official position within the WSPU in Scotland. But nothing concrete confirms this match made in heaven.

If one does accept that the 'Miss Morrison' of the Morpeth funeral cortege was the 'loving Aberdeen friend' it may seem puzzling that Mary Leigh, and not she, subsequently made the annual pilgrimage to Davison's grave. The 'Miss Morrison' who was Ethel Moorhead had a perfectly valid reason for not so doing: in the 1920s she moved to France and, eventually, on to Dublin, where she died in 1955. She never married.

Whether 'Miss Morrison' was the first or last 'intimate companion' enjoyed by Davison is academic. Yet the mere suggestion of lesbianism introduced by her presence does broaden the genesis of Davison's espousal of everything blighting the condition of the female sex – and the consequent lengths to which that fervour might propel her.

# Appendix 3: Davison's Flags

The number of flags carried by Davison at Epsom to advertise her 'Cause' has always intrigued; their present whereabouts equally so.

Colmore says Davison took two flags to Epsom: 'one round her body, under her coat ... another rolled tight in her hand.' Some newspapers (*The Sporting Life*, the *Morning Post* and *Daily News & Leader*) refer to Davison having a suffragette flag 'wrapped round her waist'. Neither claim can be verified. Davison was removed before any reporters arrived on the scene to see for themselves; neither photographs nor newsreels reveal evidence of a flag in her hand or worn as an apron.

Two flags, however, were found on Davison by PS Bunn when she was removed to Epsom Cottage Hospital, folded and pinned inside the back of her jacket, measuring 1½ yards (54 inches) by ¾ yard (27 inches). The Women's Library in Aldgate, home to the Davison archive bequeathed by her friend and colleague Rose Lamartine Yates in 1985–86, holds two flags (7/EWD/M/10), presumably those noted by PS Bunn and reclaimed by Thomas Lamartine Yates. However, when requested for examination on 14 April 2005 neither flag could be located.

The Museum of London also holds a flag some claim to have been carried by Davison at Epsom that measures 44.5 inches by 27 inches. This flag incorporates a pole that protrudes a further 5.5 inches: Davison definitely wasn't waving a flag on the day. However, this flag's provenance is excellent, having been presented to the museum by Davison's closest suffragette confidante, Mary Leigh, who was one of the last people to visit her before she died in Epsom Hospital and had draped a suffragette flag around her bed. Perhaps this is that flag. This might also explain the presence of the pole as Leigh carried this flag at George Bernard Shaw's funeral in 1950 (declaring he'd been a good friend of the suffragettes); at the re-dedication of Emmeline Pankhurst's statue in Victoria Tower Gardens; on the first Aldermaston 'Ban the Bomb' march in April 1958; and at annual May Day Parades in Hyde Park and suffragette gatherings in the Caxton Hall well into the 1960s before donating it to the museum. In addition, Leigh made an annual pilgrimage to Davison's grave on the anniversary of her friend's death and took the flag with her. So, this flag seems likely to have been associated with Davison, if not actually owned or carried by her on Derby Day, but seems unlikely to be either of the two flags described in the Yates collection. Adding to the confusion is an exhibit loaned by the Museum of London to the Derby Day 200 Exhibition at the Royal Academy of Arts (5 April–1 July 1979) which purports to be a 'Fragment of the suffragette flag carried inside Miss Davison's coat at Epsom'.

Then there's the sash claimed to have been worn by Davison at Epsom that is now on display in the Palace of Westminster. Acquired by the film-maker Barbara Gorna at a Sotheby's (New York) sale in 1997, it's not a sash at all but a suffragette motor scarf measuring 82 inches by 12 inches, in Japanese silk, lettered at each end with 'Votes For Women'.

Its provenance is questionable – as Sotheby's acknowledged. The catalogue stated:

Lot 550: A silk suffragette sash *reputed* to have been worn by Emily Davison during her demonstration in the cause of female suffrage at the Epsom Derby 1913. From the estate of the late Frances Annie Burton. On her instructions a draft affidavit was produced in March 1997 by Miss Burton's solicitors relating to the history of this sash. However, she unfortunately died before it was possible for her to approve and swear the affidavit. The sash is sold with a copy of Miss Burton's draft affidavit and another sworn by her solicitor verifying that it accurately reflected her instructions. The draft affidavit states: 'My father Richard Pittway Burton and my mother Alice Annie Burton were both keen supporters of the Suffragette Movement. On the day that Emily Davison threw herself under the King's horse during the Derby in 1913 my father was working as a Clerk of the Course at Epsom. He identified the body whilst it lay on the course since he knew Emily Davison personally due to his connections with the Suffragette Movement. My father gave me the sash when I was about six years old on his return from the First World War. I remember that he explained to me about the Suffragette Movement and that Emily Davison has sacrificed her life to bring the campaign of votes for Women to a head. He told me that he removed the sash for safe-keeping.'

The scarf is well worn, bearing, it is further claimed, the hoof prints of Anmer. According to the doctor who examined Davison, however, she bore no traces of being struck by hooves. A few newspapers, the *Morning Post* and *Daily Express* for example, did mention her wearing a 'sash' as others mentioned an 'apron'. PS Bunn's report mentioned neither. However, the Burton scarf could never be confused with a sash or a flag; a stickler for accuracy, as Bunn showed himself to be, would never have described either as a flag. Moreover, if she was wearing a scarf or sash brazenly declaring her suffragette sympathies, why was she bothering to conceal two flags inside the back of her jacket? Sotheby's were prudent to go no further than 'reputed' when discussing the item's whereabouts on Derby Day 1913.

This scarf may or may not have belonged to Davison. But whether she was wearing it on Derby Day is dubious. Quite apart from any qualms concerning the accurate recall of a lady in her ninth decade, who was, furthermore, apparently in need of funds to pay nursing-home fees at the time she dictated the draft affidavit, four areas demand attention:

1. What precise capacity did Richard Pittway Burton fill at Epsom? Henry Dorling was the designated Clerk of the Course.

2. How did Burton come by the scarf? Unless he was standing in the immediate vicinity of Davison at Tattenham Corner she would have been removed by the time he beat a path through the crowds to reach the spot. The time-line is quite clear: Bunn logged the incident at 3.10 and Davison was admitted to Epsom Cottage Hospital at 3.35. Finding, and getting her into, transport, before exiting a packed racecourse and reaching the hospital must have taken most of that time, so Davison barely spent ten minutes 'lying on the course'.

3. Davison was identified on reaching the hospital by the name tag sewn into her jacket, not by Burton, or anyone else, at Tattenham Corner.

4. Under the conditions of her Will, all her 'personal property' became the property of her mother. So keeping the scarf amounted to much more than 'safe-keeping'.

What we do know with absolute certainty is that when Miss Burton was born just nine days before the 1913 Derby at her parents' home, 283 Old Ford Road in Bow, East London, her father's occupation was given as 'Dock Labourer'. It amounts to some leap of faith to place Richard Pittway Burton in a position of influence at Epsom racecourse on Derby Day just over a week later. Until evidence far more convincing appears to the contrary, one's left with little alternative but to view the claims made for the scarf as bogus.

Once Davison was dead, however, her possessions – genuine or otherwise – assumed the status of religious relics and were valued accordingly. There may be as many Davison relics in circulation as there are parts of the true cross.

# Acknowledgements

I should begin by extending sincere thanks to a select number of individuals.

Bower Ismay's grandson Michael Manser gave me a lengthy interview and answered any amount of subsequent correspondence; he provided extracts from the diary of Mrs T. H. Ismay. Bower's great-niece Pauline Matarasso graciously shared her memories. The co-operation of Eustace Loder's great-great nephew Sir Edmund Loder is similarly acknowledged with deep thanks, in particular for providing extracts from Noble Johnson's memoir on Eyrefield Lodge. Lady Margaret Loder's granddaughter Verena Elliott took time to speak with me over the telephone, as did Bertie Jones's children, John and Thelma. The family of Edwin Piper went out of its way to offer assistance, notably Elizabeth Gayton (who provided material collected by her late mother Jill) and Piper's nephews Cyril and Roy, who knew him personally. Johnny Reiff's grandson John Hackett Reiff was another direct link with a leading actor from the Suffragette Derby: he recalled personal conversations with his grandfather during the course of lengthy correspondence. The 5th Earl of Rosebery's great-granddaughter Jane Kaplan was kind enough to provide relevant entries from his diary for 1913; Bryn Elliott did likewise with PS Frank Bunn's notebook entry for 4 June 1913; Carolyn Collette provided a copy of her paper on *Faire Emelye*; and David Boyd sent valuable information on William Saxby and Charles Robinson.

A number of archivists have treated my requests with the utmost courtesy and diligence. Special thanks are extended to two gentlemen across the Atlantic: Allan Carter at America's National Museum of Racing, who dug out the series of articles about the Reiff brothers; and Louis Cauz, at the Canadian Horse Racing Hall of Fame in Toronto, who provided the data on Anmer's stud career. Gail Cameron and Sonia Gomes expedited access to the papers of Emily Davison at the Women's Library; Beverley Cook, at the Museum of London, responded to my queries regarding Emily Davison's flags with the utmost patience and arranged a private viewing of the museum's flag. Others who rendered sterling service were the archivists at Eton (Penny Hatfield) and Harrow (Rita Boswell); Royal Holloway College (Vicky Holmes); Trinity College, Cambridge (Jon Smith); St Hugh's College, Oxford (Amanda Ingram); the Museum of the Northumberland Hussars (Roberta Twinn); and the 12th Lancers at Derby Museum (Mike Galer). Finally, acknowledgement is extended to the Royal Archives at Windsor Castle for the permission of Her Majesty Queen Elizabeth II to quote extracts from the diaries of King George V and Queen Mary.

Similar gratitude goes to the following individuals at Record Offices and Libraries. Jon-Paul Carr at Northamptonshire Studies and all the staff at the Northampton Records Office; Deborah Hopkinson at the Dept of Manuscripts, Nottingham University; John Rylands at the University of Manchester Library; Enid Jarvis of the Spratton Local History Society; Helen Keen at the Surrey History Centre in Woking; Linda Clark at the Epsom & Ewell Local History Centre; Kate Parr at Somerset Studies Library; Jo Patterson at Northumberland Museum Archives and Country Park; Jean Deathridge at the Suffolk Records Office; Terry Bracher and Carol Ashley at Central Library Northampton; Miss S. Worrall at Horsham Library; Sheila Young at Aberdeen Central Library; all those at Morpeth Library and, of course, the army of helpers at Colindale's National Newspaper Library without whom no researcher could function.

Finally, and above all, I owe a huge debt of gratitude to Paul Mathieu, whose account of 'The Suffragette Derby' in his 1990 book *The Druid's Lodge Confederacy* is second to none. Paul loaned me some of his research papers and read the first draft of my manuscript, making many valuable suggestions and tidying up the text generally. I cannot thank Paul enough for the generous gift of his time and expertise.

# Select Bibliography

**(a) Newspapers & Periodicals**
*Aberdeen Daily Journal*
*Aberdeen Evening Express*
*Cambridge Daily News*
*Daily Chronicle*
*Daily Express*
*Daily Herald*
*Daily Mail*
*Daily News & Leader*
*Daily Sketch*
*Daily Telegraph*
*Epsom Advertiser*
*Illustrated London News*
*Illustrated Sporting and Dramatic News*
*Manchester Guardian*
*Mayfair*
*Morning Post*
*Morpeth Herald*
*Newmarket Journal*
*New York Times*
*Northampton Independent*
*Pacemaker*
*Pall Mall Gazette*
*Racing Post*
*Racing Illustrated*
*The Awakener*
*The Observer*

*The Sphere*
*The Sporting Chronicle*
*The Sporting Life*
*The Sporting Times*
*The Sportsman*
*The Suffragette*
*The Times*
*The Winning Post*
*Vanity Fair*
*Votes for Women*
*West Sussex County Times*

## (b) Periodicals (Specific Reference)

*Baily's Magazine, MR C Bower Ismay*, Vol. CVIII No. 691, September 1917

*British Racehorse*, Vol. III No. 5, *Pretty Polly* (Hislop), 1951

*British Racehorse*, Vol. XVIII No. 4, *The Admiration Family at Eyrefield* (Burrell), 1961

*British Racehorse*, Vol. XXX No. 5, *Clarehaven* (Onslow), 1978

*British Racehorse*, Vol. XXXII No. 4, *Eyrefield Lodge* (McMillan), 1980

*Chaucer Review*, Vol. 42 No. 3, '"Faire Emelye": Medievalism and the Moral Courage of Emily Wilding Davison' (Collette), 2008

*The Clarion*, 'The Life of Emily Davison' (West), June 1913

*European Racehorse*, Vol. 8 No. 3, 'The Continuing Influence of Pretty Polly' (Tanner), 1988

*New Statesman*, 'Deeds not Words' (Atkinson), June 2005

*Pacemaker*, 'Eyrefield Lodge Stud' (Tanner), October 1988

*Pall Mall Magazine*, 'Spearmint in Private' (Moorhouse), 1906

*Social Research*, Vol. 75 No. 2, 'Emily Wilding Davison: secular martyr?' (Gullickson), 2008

*Sports Illustrated*, 'Death & Suffrage at Epsom' (Cottrell), August 1972

*Staffordshire Studies*, Vol. III, 'Tom Coulthwaite of Cannock Chase' (Godwin), 1993

*Thoroughbred of California*, 'The Reiff Brothers' (Burke), November 1948–March 1949

*Times Higher Education*, 'Pankhursts and Provocation' (Liddington), January 2003

*Women's History Review*, Vol. 4 No. 1, 'The Prison Experiences of the Suffragettes in Edwardian Britain' (Purvis), 1995

## (c) Books

Acton, *Silk and Spur* (Scribner's 1936)

Allison, *Memories of Men and Horses* (Grant Richards 1922)

Atkinson, *The Suffragettes in Pictures* (Sutton Publishing 1996)

Atkinson, *The Purple White & Green* (Museum of London 1992)

Atkinson, *Votes For Women* (Cambridge University Press 1988)

Browne, *History of the English Turf* (Virtue & Company 1931)

Childs, *Racing Reminiscences* (Hutchinson 1952)

Churchill, *My Early Years* (Odhams 1930)

Colmore, *The Life of Emily Wilding Davison* (The Women's Press 1913)

Cook, *A History of the English Turf* (Virtue & Company 1904)

Crawford, *The Women's Suffrage Movement: A Reference Guide* (UCL Press 1999)

Donoghue, *Just My Story* (Hutchinson 1923)

Galtrey, *Memoirs of a Racing Journalist* (Hutchinson 1934)

Gill, *Racecourses of Great Britain* (Barrie & Jenkins 1975)

Good, *Good Days* (Hutchinson 1941)

Good, *The Lure of the Turf* (Odhams 1957)

Griswold, *Race Horses and Racing* (Dutton's 1926)

Hyland, *The Irish Derby* (JA Allen 1980)

Jarvis, *They're Off* (Michael Joseph 1969)

John, *Holloway Jingles* (Glasgow WSPU 1912)

Johnson, *Eyrefield Stud* (Brindley & Sons, Undated)

Kaltenberger, *Big Game Hunting in East Africa* (Edward Arnold 1928)

Lambton, *Men and Horses I Have Known* (Thornton Butterworth 1924)

Lees-Milne, *The Enigmatic Edwardian* (Sidgewick & Jackson 1986)

Lenehan, *A Guid Cause: the Women's Suffrage Movement in Scotland* (Mercat Press 1995)

McKinstry, *Rosebery: Statesman in Turmoil* (John Murray 2005)

Marsh, *Trainer to Two Kings* (Cassell 1925)

Matarasso, *A Voyage Closed and Done* (Michael Russell Publishing 2005)

Mathieu, *The Druids Lodge Confederacy* (JA Allen 1990)

Mitchell, *The Fighting Pankhursts* (Jonathan Cape 1967)

Morley & Stanley, *Life and Death of Emily Wilding Davison* (Women's Press 1988)

Mortimer, *The History of the Derby Stakes* (Michael Joseph 1962)

Morton, *My Sixty Years of the Turf* (Hutchinson 1930)

Oldham, *The Ismay Line* (Journal of Commerce 1961)

Onslow, *The Heath and the Turf* (Arthur Barker 1971)

Pankhurst, Christabel, *Unshackled* (Hutchinson 1959)

Pankhurst, Emmeline, *My Own Story* (Women's Press 1914)

Pankhurst, Sylvia, *The Suffragette Movement* (Longmans, Green & Co 1931)

Pethick-Lawrence, *My Part In A Changing World* (Victor Gollancz 1938)

Parmer, *For Gold and Glory* (Carrick & Evans 1939)

Pease, *The History of the Northumberland Hussars* (Constable 1924)

Pease, *Edmund Loder: A Memoir* (John Murray 1923)

Plumptree, *The Fast Set* (Andre Deutsch 1985)

Porter, *John Porter of Kingsclere* (Grant Richards 1919)

Pugh, *The Pankhursts* (Allen Lane 2001)

Purvis, *Emmeline Pankhurst* (Routledge 2000)

Rhodes James, *Rosebery* (Weidenfeld & Nicolson 1963)

Richardson, *Laugh a Defiance* (Weidenfeld & Nicolson 1953)

Seth-Smith, *Derby 200* (Guinness Superlatives 1979)

Sievier, *The Autobiography* (Winning Post 1906)

Sloan, *Tod Sloan by Himself* (Grant Richards 1915)

Sleight, *One-way Ticket to Epsom* (Bridge Studios 1988)

Smither & Klaue, *Newsreels in Film Archives* (Flicks Books 1996)

Spurgin, *On Active Service with the Northumberland & Durham Yeomanry* (Walter Scott Publishing 1902)

Stewart, *History of the XII Royal Lancers* (Oxford 1950)

Sturgess, *A Northamptonshire Lad* (Northampton Libraries 1982)

Tanner, *Great Jockeys of the Flat* (Guinness 1991)

Tanner, *Pretty Polly: An Edwardian Heroine* (National Horseracing Museum 1987)

Tegner, *The Northumberland Hussars* (Frank Graham 1969)

Tyrell, *Running Racing* (Quiller Press 1997)

Welcome, *Infamous Occasions* (Michael Joseph 1980)

Welcome, *Irish Horse-racing* (Macmillan 1982)

Wilson, *How to Survive the Titanic* (Bloomsbury 2011)

Wilson, *Shadow of the Titanic* (Simon & Schuster 2011)

Wynn-Jones, *The Derby* (Croom Helm 1979)

American Racing Manual

Bloodstock Breeder's Review

Canadian Thoroughbred Stud Book

Racing Calendar

Ruff's Guide to the Turf

# Index